D0709132

The Future of Play Theory

SUNY Series, Children's Play in Society
Anthony D. Pellegrini, editor

The Future of Play Theory

A Multidisciplinary Inquiry into the Contributions of Brian Sutton-Smith

Edited by
Anthony D. Pellegrini

STATE UNIVERSITY OF NEW YORK PRESS

Published by
State University of New York Press, Albany

© 1995 State University of New York

All rights reserved

Printed in the United States of America

No part of this book may be used or reproduced in any manner whatsoever
without written permission. No part of this book may be stored in a retrieval system
or transmitted in any form or by any means including electronic, electrostatic,
magnetic tape, mechanical, photocopying, recording, or otherwise
without the prior permission in writing of the publisher.

For information, address State University of New York Press,
State University Plaza, Albany, N.Y., 12246

Production by Christine Lynch
Marketing by Nancy Farrell

Library of Congress Cataloging-in-Publication Data

The future of play theory : a multidisciplinary inquiry into the
    contributions of Brian Sutton-Smith / Anthony D. Pellegrini, editor.
        p.   cm. — (SUNY series, children's play in society)
    Includes bibliographical references.
    ISBN 0-7914-2641-6 (acid-free paper). — ISBN 0-7914-2642-4 (pbk.
  :   acid-free paper)
    1. Play.   2. Play—Psychological aspects.   3. Child psychology.
  I. Pellegrini, Anthony D.   II. Sutton-Smith, Brian.   III. Series.
  HQ782.F87   1995
  155.5'18—dc20   94-41396
                                                          CIP

10   9   8   7   6   5   4   3   2   1

CONTENTS

Part IV: Play As Self

INTRODUCTION

The present volume is to honor a colleague upon the occasion of his retirement from the University of Pennsylvania. Like most such volumes, this one brings together a group of distinguished scholars to comment on the work of a major thinker in the field. Brian Sutton-Smith is certainly a distinguished scholar; his distinction, however, covers a number of different fields, such as children's play and games, narrative language and thought, and sibling relationships. Additionally, he has crossed a number of disciplinary boundaries in his research, including anthropology, folklore, history, literary criticism, and psychology. This volume, like Brian's career, draws scholars from these various disciplines, literally from anthropology to zoology. He has had a major impact on all these fields. As an indicator of the diversity of his work, an appendix listing his research in play is included. (The efforts of Dr. F. F. McMahon in assembling these references is gratefully acknowledged.)

When I approached Brian on the subject of this volume celebrating his retirement he responded that such a volume "was an intellectual replica of the Golden Bough where an old man gets beheaded and his place taken by the young and new King." In true fashion, Brian prefers to remain alive. He wished this volume to be a genuinely interdisciplinary venture, like his career. Thus, I have gathered together a group of scholars to write about one aspect of Sutton-Smith's work: children's play. The volume is organized around four ways in which Sutton-Smith viewed play: Play as Progress, Play as Power, Play as Fantasy, and Play as Self. The concluding chapter will be a synthesis by Sutton-Smith.

The idea that scholars should take the perspective of the child when studying play is inherent in much of Sutton-Smith's writing. Perhaps the clearest examples of this perspective come from observing children's play in relation to power. This notion is very evident in his writings on children's play-fighting and play with "war toys." Sutton-Smith has insisted that play-fighting and play with toy guns, and the like, is just that, "play." Thus, if we want to understand the function of this behavior we must sweep away our biases and try to understand the phenomena for what it is. John W. Loy and Graham L. Hesketh's chapter addresses competitive play among the Plains

Indians of North America. In this chapter the psychological origins of the agon motive of this "composite culture" are explored. Drawing upon Barkow's (1975) biosocial theory of prestige and culture, Loy suggests that the use of competitive play enhances self-esteem in warrior societies.

A similar argument is developed in the chapters by Anthony D. Pellegrini and Jeffrey Goldstein. Pellegrini's chapter is on rough-and-tumble play (R & T) in childhood and adolescence. R & T as used by Pellegrini is similar to the notion of agon, as used by Loy, to the extent that players are exhibiting quasi-agonistic behaviors which serve some positive function in the development of young males. Goldstein looks at three different forms of quasi-agonistic play: R & T, play with war toys, and play with videogames having aggressive themes. While much less research has been conducted on the last two topics, as compared with the first, Goldstein suggests that some of the same anti-play biases, and anti-male-play biases especially, may be operating. He calls for a clear distinction between playful aggression and real aggression so that the outcomes of these sorts of play can be more clearly charted. Thus, the idea in each of these chapters is that these sorts of behavior may serve important societal functions and should not be confused with less functional aggressive behavior.

Biologists, of course, have made very important contributions to the study of play. For example, the theoretical work of Fagen (1981) has helped me, at least, to begin to understand this very complex phenomena. In part 1, Play As Progress, there are two biologically oriented chapters (Smith's and Fagen's) and one leisure studies–oriented chapter (Chick and Barnett's). All three examine the commonly held belief that play is adaptive and leads a species towards higher developmental status. Peter K. Smith's chapter, however, goes beyond the mere reporting of a research program to utilizing an autobiographical genre to trace the career of a play researcher interested in biology, play, and education. Smith's interests in the many aspects of play parallel those of Sutton-Smith in some ways; for example, both have been interested in both fantasy and rough play. Smith also examines the distinction between rough play and aggression. Like the other researchers, Smith finds a clear distinction between the two.

More interestingly, Smith, also like Sutton-Smith and Fagen, warns against the "play ethos," or what Sutton-Smith called the idealization of play. The warning pertains to the all-too-frequent assumption that play is all good to all players, be they chimps or children. Robert Fagen points out that play can have a darker side as well as serving some positive functions. For example, he notes (echoing Pellegrini's findings) that some sorts of play can be exploitive. Some forms of rough play can turn into bullying. Fagen goes on to suggest that scientists should begin to consider play from an aesthetic perspective. Of course this is consistent with Sutton-Smith's view of play as performance. Fagen goes on to warn, however, that aesthetics, like more traditional theories applied to play, have limitations: Aesthetics may explain human adults' social interaction but they probably don't explain the play-fighting of rats or chimps!

In their chapter on children's play and adult leisure, Gary Chick and Lynn A. Barnett explore the degree to which children's play leads to other forms of play, or leisure, in adulthood. Such issues are embedded in a larger theoretical discussion of socialization, culture, and the extent to which children, and their play, contribute to or copy culture.

Differentiating the child's perspective on play from that of the adult can also be applied to "functions" of play. Specifically, play researchers have often taken an "outsider" perspective on studying children's play. "Detached objectivity," many of these researchers argue, is necessary to study children scientifically. Sutton-Smith has questioned the ways in which children and their play are represented (Sutton-Smith & Kelly-Byrne, 1984). It has been suggested that the view that play is preparation for adulthood is a typically adult-centric interpretation of play. For example, such an interpretation would hold that fantasy play is best understood in terms of the ways in which it relates to future cognitive or emotional well-being. A child's interpretation of fantasy would hold that it may be antithetical to adult culture.

Four chapters are concerned with a specific sort of play: fantasy play. Greta G. Fein's chapter continues the theme that play has a "darker side" as she discusses results of clever experiments designed to explore what motivates children's play narratives. Like Sutton-Smith, she concludes that fantasy is sometimes troubling and chaotic.

Stephen Kline examines the role of toys and television advertising for toys on children's fantasy play. He embeds his discussion of toys in the larger play literature, particularly that work studying symbolic play and rough-and-tumble play. Kline reports interesting age-differences for the influence of television on play.

Jerome L. Singer also examines the relation between television viewing and fantasy but he embeds it in a larger life span perspective. In a provocative chapter, Singer suggests that fantasy play during childhood may influence daydreaming and pretending games during adulthood.

What are the origins of fantasy play in childhood that have such long-lasting effects? Probably the most frequently assumed source is the play of the mother-child dyad. Various theoretical orientations, such as attachment theory and psychoanalytical theory, assume that play with the mother provides the basis from which spring subsequent forms of play, and indeed of other social relationships. The chapter by Lisa M. Youngblade and Judy Dunn questions this assumption. Their data, collected in various large, long-term and naturalistic observations, suggest that the social fantasy of preschoolers with their siblings is *not* related to the play of the target child and his or her mother. Siblings seem to provide an important and different relationship context from which children's social skills develop. This important finding should remind us, as Sutton-Smith's earlier work on siblings did twenty-five years ago (Sutton-Smith & Rosenberg, 1970), to look beyond the mother-child dyad if we want to understand children's social development.

The final section addresses the notion of play as self. The chapter by Helen B. Schwartzman specifically addresses the ways in which children and their play have been represented in ethnographies. Extending her earlier and often-cited work on fantasy play, *Transformations* (Schwartzman, 1978), issues related to researcher/informant are addressed. Bernard Mergen's chapter is an historical examination of the play of children. His premise is that to understand children's play we must examine it in its everydayness. Consistent with Sutton-Smith's folklore and historical work, Mergen examines different sorts of evidence, such as television programs, autobiographies, and surveys to provide meaning to the concept of play in lives of American children throughout our history. In the final chapter, Brian Sutton-Smith reflects upon his work in play and upon the chapters in this volume.

In short, this is a provocative volume. It provides various perspectives, both theoretical and methodological, on children's play.

REFERENCES

Fagen, R. (1981). *Animal play behavior.* New York: Oxford.

Schwartzman, H. (1978). *Transformations: The anthropology of children's play.* New York: Plenum.

Sutton-Smith, B., & Rosenberg, B. (1970). *The siblings.* New York: Holt, Rinehart & Winston.

Sutton-Smith, B., & Kelly-Byrne, D. (1984). The idealization of play. In P. K. Smith (Ed.), *Play in animals and humans* (pp. 305–22). Oxford: Basil Blackwell.

Part I

PLAY AS PROGRESS

1

PETER K. SMITH

Play, Ethology, and Education: A Personal Account

Starting with my doctoral thesis, I have spent some twenty years with a strong research interest in children's play. In this chapter, I'll take the opportunity to recall my earlier thoughts and experiences as well as my more recent ones, and reflect on how our ideas and interests have changed over that period. In my own work in the area of children's play I have made use of various methodologies and perspectives. Sometimes I have contributed ideas of my own; more often, perhaps, I have developed someone else's idea more thoroughly, or succeeded in disproving it. Even more often, I have felt that Brian Sutton-Smith got there first. Whether it was a critical insight into play-tutoring studies, or the idealization of play, or the emphasis on rougher forms of play as well as the more adult-sanctioned object and fantasy play, Brian has been in early, providing challenging comments on what we are doing. Reading his work and mulling over his thoughts, as well as more recently knowing him as a person, have been some of the main pleasures of being a play researcher for so much of my career. I am therefore especially pleased to contribute to this volume, dedicated to him and to his achievements.

My interest in play, and any expertise I have in ethology, arose by accident. When studying my undergraduate course in psychology at Cambridge University in 1966–67, the English translation of Konrad Lorenz's book *Das sogenannte bose*, or *On Aggression*, had just been published. It's message— that human aggression had an instinctive force which needed some kind of outlet (maybe organized sports!)—was, I knew, controversial. Robert Hinde, who was lecturing in zoology in Cambridge at the time, had publicly criticized the shortcomings of Lorenz's arguments. Still, I was fascinated by the topic, and interested too in the work on ethology and animal behavior which Thorpe, Hinde, and others had been pursuing with such distinction at Cambridge. I found the ethological approach to learning, for example, much more interesting in its emphasis on real-life behavior, than the so-called behaviorist tradition and psychological learning theory of the time, then still a strong influence in Cambridge psychology.

I went to Sheffield University to carry out my doctoral thesis. At the time, the Sheffield Department had a policy, innovative for the United Kingdom

3

(though commonplace in North America), of allowing graduate students six to twelve months of general training before specializing. I enjoyed this, but I still felt I was interested in studying aggression, probably in humans. Kevin Connolly, who was my doctoral supervisor, had returned from the International Ethological conference in Stockholm in 1967; there, he had heard Niko Tinbergen give his talk "War and Peace in Animals and Man" (subsequently published in 1968), in which he advocated some application of ethological ideas to human behavior.

Kevin suggested I take this up and apply observational and ethological methods to human aggression. Being a child psychologist, he also suggested starting with children. This appealed to me, too; having spent a year teaching on the Voluntary Service Overseas scheme in Singapore, I found education and child development a naturally interesting area. I therefore got permission to visit day nurseries in Sheffield to carry out observational/ethological studies of children.

Day nurseries in Britain take children from around nine months to school age, nearly five years. They open longer hours than nursery schools or playgroups, and cater for children of working mothers, as well as giving priority to families with some social disadvantage. They are run by social services departments rather than education departments, and generally have a "free-play" philosophy rather than an "educational" one. They were an excellent introduction to observing a wide variety of child behavior.

Of course, I went with the intention of observing aggressive behavior. Well, I did see some aggressive behavior, and I faithfully recorded it. But, it wasn't very frequent. A real fight might be the "highlight" of the day, although snatching of toys and bickering were more common. Nevertheless, just recording aggressive behavior would have meant long periods of blank record sheets. Bearing in mind the need to get a Ph.D. in three years, I decided to maximize my input by recording generally what children did. And what children did, mostly, was play.

OBSERVATIONAL/ETHOLOGICAL STUDIES OF PLAY

I had two main sources of influence at this period. First was that of the ethologists. Desmond Morris (1967) had just edited a volume called *Primate Ethology*, which for a while was my most-thumbed sourcebook (I should add that this was a more straightforwardly "academic" book than some of Morris's later volumes). These and similar ethological works pointed out the importance of observing behavior in natural surroundings if you wanted to get a true picture of the range of behavior, and its function(s). The adaptive significance of behavior, how it functioned to promote an individual's survival and fitness, was a core interest of ethologists, as was its evolutionary history.

The part of this to which I and several other "human ethologists" of the period took most readily was that of observation in natural surroundings. This implied spending some time familiarizing oneself with the setting and the behavior in that setting; then, and only then, developing behavior categories to describe the range of behavior seen; and then looking at individual differences, behavior sequences, environmental influences, and so forth.

It may seem surprising now, when observational methods are an accepted part of the psychologist's repertoire (certainly in developmental psychology), but the "just watching" approach was radical at the time. Traditional psychologists went in with hypotheses, to do experiments. I still recall the skepticism of some colleagues—including other graduate students—when I explained I was watching children playing in day nurseries. When was I going to do serious stuff and test something out? I wasn't too worried about this, as I had already seen the trap for psychologists in getting into premature experimentation too quickly, as in the sterile "rat-work" of the Hullian tradition.

In fact, the value of just watching proved itself early, in what is probably the first "child ethology" article, the chapter by Nick Blurton Jones (1967) in Desmond Morris's volume. This was an account of observations he had made of nursery-school children, and in it Nick described the components of "rough-and-tumble play," similar to that described by Harlow in rhesus monkeys. Rough-and-tumble play, or play-fighting, looks like real fighting—it involves wrestling, pushing, rolling, grappling, chasing, and so on—but it is accompanied by laughter, smiling, and friendship. It is largely distinct from aggression. Later work, including my own, showed that it took up some 10 percent of time in many school playgrounds. Yet incredibly, this was the first scientific description of it in children, unless we go back to the work of Karl Groos (1901) at the turn of the century. A lot of prior writings on children's play had ignored it, or dismissed it as "horsing around," through a lack of disinterested prior observation of what children did.

I said that the ethological work was one source of influence. The other was the observational work in child development, carried out in North America in the 1930s. I discovered this fortuitously, so far as I remember, coming across Ruth Arrington's (1943) review in the *Psychological Bulletin* by accident. This led me to the observational works not only of Arrington but of Florence Goodenough, Dorothy Thompson, Mildred Parten, and many others, often based at the then newly founded clinics or laboratories of child study or child welfare, set up in the United States in the 1920s. These researchers were interested in describing what two-year-olds did, three-year-olds did, four-year-olds did, as basic knowledge for the new generation of kindergarten teachers and teacher trainers.

In doing so, they worked through most of the issues which still occupy observational researchers—what are you going to observe (not everything!);

how are you going to categorize it; what sampling methods will you use; how reliable are observers; does the presence of the observer change the behavior being observed? It is still of interest to read these pioneer works. One fascinating monograph by Arrington (1931) actually documents the evolution of a category scheme—you can see how she grappled with trying to embrace the range of children's behavior in a list of categories which went through several changes.

This earlier observational work was not generally known by child psychologists or ethologists—the passage of thirty years during which observational methods were scarcely used had almost cast these studies into limbo (a sobering thought as we write our own next article). However I did write a review of them with Kevin Connolly (Smith and Connolly, 1972) in the book *Ethological Studies of Child Behavior*, edited by Blurton Jones. Later, Gerhard Fassnacht wrote a much more thorough review and critique of these studies in his book *Theory and Practice of Observing Behavior* (1982).

OBSERVATIONS OF CHILDREN'S PLAY

I spent about six years watching preschool children playing. First this was for my Ph.D thesis, "Social and Play Behavior of Preschool Children" (1970). This was the work done in the day nurseries, where I categorized types of play, degrees of social behavior, and the typical age differences and sex differences found. I was also interested in the contrast between the more sedentary indoor play, often with objects on tables such as stickle-bricks, wooden blocks, jigsaws; and the more active outdoor play, including much rough-and-tumble playing, chasing, climbing, and using large apparatus. Indeed, when carrying out factor analyses of individual differences between children, based on behavioral observations, a differential preference for either play with objects or for active physical play emerged as a major factor second only to social maturity. Play preference seemed to be an important aspect of differences between children, but the physical environment also appeared important in facilitating or inhibiting certain kinds of play.

This led to the next three years work, after Kevin Connolly and I obtained support from the Social Science Research Council. (At the time, social science was thought of as a science. Since then, the government in the United Kingdom decided that much social science was not science, so the SSRC became the ESRC, or Economic and Social Research Council). I had observed how children played very differently in indoor and outdoor environments. Why was this? The question has some complexity, as outdoor environments not only have much more space, they also provide different toys—fewer small toys, more large apparatus, usually. What were the differential effects of space, and toys, on children's behavior? This seemed an attractive area of research. The ethological work had emphasized the strong influence of environment on social behavior, as in the writings of Crook

(1970). Recent studies of "crowding" in both animals and humans, for example, by Hutt and Vaizey (1966) and McGrew (1972) had specifically suggested strong effects. Also, there were practical implications for nursery design in finding out what resource considerations, in terms of space and toys, might be considered optimal.

Conceptually, the earlier studies on human crowding had been limited by only considering space as a factor. Since children play with toys and apparatus a great deal, these are obviously also very important "resources" which may be in plentiful or short supply. If, as in some previous studies, crowding was varied by doubling the number of children in the same space, then you were also doubling the number of children sharing the same toys. Which was more important?

To look at this, we decided to separately vary both space and toys relative to numbers of children. We were able to do this by starting up our own preschool playgroup and running it for three years. In the first year, we varied space, by having large curtain screens leaving one-third, two-thirds, or all of a large area for the children to play in, and by having either one, two, or three sets of toys available. Each toy set was identical so only the amount of toys, not the kind of toys, was varied. Each space condition was covaried with each toy condition, giving nine different environments, which were presented on different days according to a Latin square design. The children were used to such variation from the start of the playgroup, so novelty was not a confounding factor.

This study showed clearly that toy availability had a generally greater effect than space availability. With more toys, children broke up into smaller clusters to play with them. There was less aggression and less squabbling over popular items. There was also, however, less sharing of items. The main effect of space variation was simply on physical activity and not on social behavior. There was one proviso to this latter conclusion—if space became *very* cramped, then active and rough-and-tumble play fell off very sharply, and aggressive behavior did increase.

A subsidiary study looked at types of toys. We contrasted play when just table toys were provided with play when just large apparatus was provided. This provided dramatic contrasts (Smith, 1974). The children were rather surprised when only chairs, tables, climbing frames, and rocking boats were put out, but in fact quickly put these items to very imaginative uses—making "trains" out of a line of chairs, "dens" out of tables, turning chairs and tables upside-down to make spaceships, and so forth. A few children found this noisy and strange and stayed close to the playgroup staff, but most found this more "adventure playground" atmosphere very exciting and responded to it with unusual creativity.

In the second year of the project, we varied the size of the playgroup— the number of children attending on a given morning varied from around ten to around thirty. We provided resources (space, toys) commensurate to the numbers of children, so as to look at effects of size unconfounded by effects of crowding. We did not find much effect on free-play activities, but there were effects on friendships—smaller groups produced close friendship networks with more cross-sex play, though larger groups did give more scope for finding a really close friend. The results of all these projects were written up in *The Ecology of Preschool Behavior* (Smith and Connolly, 1980).

This book did I think succeed in providing, for a while, a reasonably definitive statement of how resource variation affected children's play. But looking back on it, I think it also demonstrates how one can combine observational methods with experimental rigor. Too often, *observation* and *experiment* are presented as opposites. They are not. *Observation* is a way of getting data—to be contrasted with interview, questionnaire, diary, recording device, and so forth. *Experiment* refers to the degree of control the researcher has over what goes on, which is a separate issue. Usually, it is true, observation—and especially "natural" observation—is done in low-control, nonexperimental conditions. But in so far as a playgroup is considered a "natural environment" for preschool children, we had succeeded in combining good control of the relevant variables (amounts of space and toys) with observational methodology.

PLAY AND EDUCATION

The third year of the SSRC-funded project with our playgroup was on a different topic, and a more "educational" one. I had earlier observed how day nurseries had a predominantly free-play regime; within limits of safety to others and care of property, children could largely do what they wished without instruction or interference from adults (who were usually trained as nursery nurses). In nursery schools, by contrast, the staff, many of whom were trained teachers, engaged in a great deal of organized activities with children; there was a lot of "play" but in a more instructional sense, with less of the spontaneous free play I had observed so much in the day nurseries. There were differing views about which philosophy was best for the child.

We decided to look at this "experimentally." We had been running two distinct groups of children in our playgroup, so as to provide an inbuilt literal replication of our findings (Lykken, 1968). Now, we arranged for one group to have a free-play, "day nursery"–type curriculum, while the other experienced a more structured, adult-organized, "nursery school" curriculum. These contrasting experiences continued for about eight months. Again, observations were made of the children's behavior.

The outcomes indicated positive and negative features to both approaches. The structured curriculum did bring about much more interaction with adults, naturally enough. It also resulted in greater increases in attention span in the children—something which increases anyway with age, but adult encouragement at task persistence may be a useful feature of a structured curriculum. On the other hand, the free-play curriculum allowed children to work out friendships and conflict resolution skills with age-mates more readily. In brief, the structured curriculum had some cognitive benefits, the free-play curriculum some social peer-related benefits. A mix of both is probably best, the mix perhaps varying with needs of different children from different home environments (Smith and Connolly, 1980, 1986).

This work prompted further interest in the educational significance of play. I had become interested in the fantasy and sociodramatic play which was often evident at these ages. Some of this was quite active and "rough-and-tumbly"—children chasing each other being spacemen, "Dr. Who and the Daleks" for example; other sociodramatic play was more sedentary, such as having pretend meals in the home corner. I had noticed that this kind of play was actually more frequent in our free-play curriculum group than in our structured curriculum group. But then, it could be said that this had been our own doing. We had more or less guided the latter playgroup into doing structured activities such as drawing and coloring, shape matching and picture lotto, making creative work—things which furthered conventional educational goals at this age but which rarely included fantasy or pretense. Thus, sociodramatic play had not been encouraged and little of it happened in our structured curriculum group. Our children (many from quite middle-class homes) had, however, engaged in quite a lot of such play spontaneously when they had the time and freedom to do so.

At this time I came across Sara Smilansky's (1968) book *The Effects of Sociodramatic Play on Disadvantaged Preschool Children*. Smilansky extolled the virtues of sociodramatic play in children's development, but was worried that "disadvantaged" children (by which she primarily referred to children of some families recently immigrated into Israel) showed little of such play. She argued that play tutoring—adults encouraging children to act out roles, and helping by providing props and ideas when necessary to keep things going—not only increased the amount of such play, but had useful if not essential developmental benefits: socially, cognitively, and linguistically.

Our playgroup staff had not done this kind of play tutoring at all. Should they have? Was the evidence for this effectiveness compelling? Several other researchers had gone further than Smilansky in seeking proof. Saltz, Dixon, and Johnson (1977) had compared groups of children (from socioeconomically disadvantaged backgrounds), one that had received extra play tutoring experience and one that had not. The play tutored children improved more, developmentally.

Being sometimes obsessional, I gathered together all of these studies which I could find. There were quite a number—about a dozen, generally in the United States. Their findings were certainly encouraging. In fact, different researchers had measured all sorts of developmental aspects of children—concentration span, sentence length, conservation, intelligence scores, creativity—indeed, whatever had been measured, play tutoring seemed to help! This seemed too good to be true. Perhaps it *was* too good to be true. On thinking about these studies, I realized that none had used anything like our structured curriculum group. None had employed adult intervention in a nonfantasy context. They had all contrasted play tutoring (encouraging fantasy, with extra adult intervention) with no-treatment control (no encouragement of fantasy, but also no extra adult intervention). But what about skills tutoring (no encouragement of fantasy, but extra adult intervention)? Would not this be an essential extra control condition if the benefits of play tutoring were to be ascribed to the fantasy play and not to the tutoring itself?

It did seem possible that tutoring itself—just the extra adult involvement—would help children, for example in their language development. Anyway, it was a hypothesis worth testing. I did an initial study with Susan Syddall in which we compared outcomes of a play scheme for two groups of children, one of which had fantasy play tutoring, the other skills tutoring. The outcomes showed little difference between the two groups (Smith and Syddall, 1978). Since the tutoring was common to the two groups, but not the fantasy, this study suggested that the tutoring might be the more important aspect.

This study had been on a small scale, and replication was clearly needed. With a grant from the SSRC, Mary Dalgleish, Guy Herzmark, and I carried out a similar design on a larger scale. We worked in two nursery schools located in socioeconomically disadvantaged areas of Sheffield. In each school, one class experienced extra play tutoring, while another very similar class experienced extra skills tutoring. Observations of the tutor confirmed that she interacted with the children to about the same extent in the two conditions, but confined encouragement of fantasy activities largely to the play tutoring condition.

We got the same results as before. Both groups improved on a variety of cognitive and linguistic measures, presumably due to getting older and to general experiences in the nursery, including tutoring experiences. But there were few (if any) differential effects—the fantasy play tutored children did not improve any more than the other children (Smith, Dalgleish, and Herzmark, 1981). This general finding has since been replicated by Brainerd (1982) and Christie and Johnsen (1985) in the United States. It does suggest that Smilansky was wrong to hypothesize a particular, unique function to fantasy and sociodramatic play (a position she still holds; see Smilansky and Shefatya, 1990); though pragmatically speaking, for nursery school teachers play tutoring can be enjoyable, and is clearly as effective as skills tutoring so far as cognitive and language development is concerned.

A SKEPTICAL VIEW OF THE FUNCTIONS OF PLAY

Thinking about the flawed design of some earlier play tutoring studies, and getting somewhat negative outcomes from my own attempts, was one factor which led me to be a bit more skeptical about the prevalent view that "play was essential for development." At this time—the 1970s—and indeed from at least the 1930s until the present day, the "play ethos" has been very influential in educational circles in Britain and North America, if not elsewhere. This has held that "play is a child's work" (Isaacs, 1929), and that "play is essential for survival"; it is well defined in a British Government report on children's play from 1973, which stated that "the realization that play is essential for development has slowly but surely permeated our educational system and cultural heritage" (Department of the Environment, 1973).

This was a prevailing view, and I accepted it without question through the 1970s. Some dissenting voices, however, were beginning to be heard. I remember attending a conference on the biology of play (published in Tizard and Harvey, 1974), which was held in Farnham, United Kingdom, in the summer of 1975. I had talked about individual differences in children's play styles. At that conference, Barbara Tizard had cast doubt on the curriculum value of free play, pointing out how very structured regimes such as in Chinese kindergartens could, despite some reservations, bring about startling achievements in some respects. Also, Corinne Hutt had started to advance her distinction between "ludic" and "epistemic" forms of play, together with the notion that ludic forms might not have significant cognitive functions in a developmental sense (see the much later book by Hutt, Tyler, Hutt, and Christopherson, 1989, for an account of this; Corinne Hutt's untimely death in 1979 prevented her developing it as fully as it deserved). This latter idea I found difficult to accept. I remember being skeptical, and advancing arguments to back up my belief that play was really valuable. This was also the belief of most others. I remember that Corinne got a somewhat unsympathetic hearing. Later, I was to change my views.

Of course, Corinne's views were not entirely new. To some extent her ludic/epistemic distinction echoed the assimilation/accommodation distinction of Piaget (1951); and as Brian Sutton-Smith had pointed out back in 1966, there is not much obvious cognitive benefit to play in Piaget's theory, if play is primarily assimilative (Sutton-Smith, 1966). If play means adapting the world to you, then you yourself don't need to change.

But was there evidence that play—real ludic, assimilative play; free play with objects; or fantasy play—was developmentally useful? Bruner's views

(1972) on the uses of immaturity and the development of early skilled action provided a theoretical framework which could support this position; free play allowed spontaneous combination and recombination of action schemes which could enhance creative use of objects and problem solving. And at the Farnham conference, Kathy Sylva had provided experimental backing for this. Adapting the paradigm in which Kohler's chimpanzee, after experience with sticks, used a stick to rake in a banana through a cage, she devised a problem-solving task for children; they had to clamp two long sticks together to make a tool long enough to reach and rake in a piece of chalk from the far end of a table.

Sylva argued from her results that free play was a useful experience for this. She compared the performance of children with different prior experiences. Some had free play with sticks and clamps, some had forms of training in counting and comparing the length of sticks. The finding that the free-play children did best appeared convincing, and I remember it reaching the national press in Britain as proof of the value of play.

Actually, some of Sylva's training-group conditions included clamping two sticks together, which made it all the more surprising that the free-play group did best. Susan Dutton and I tried an extension (literally) of her task. We arranged that to rake in a marble (which we thought might be more rewarding than chalk), the child first had to clamp two long sticks together, as in Sylva's task, and then (moving the marble further back) had to clamp *three* long sticks together. The training condition involved showing how two sticks could be joined, but not three. We thought this might give a clearer test of Bruner's hypothesis that play would assist innovative problem solving.

Our results bore this out. For the two-stick problem ("direct" problem solving), there was not much difference between the play and training groups; but for the three-stick problem ("innovative" problem solving), the play group were clearly superior. This study (Smith and Dutton, 1978) came to be cited along with Sylva (1977) in texts and articles arguing the value of play.

At this point I was happy. But then I read a chapter by Cheyne (1982). Cheyne argued that studies such as Sylva's were susceptible to experimenter effects. The same experimenter had both given the different play and training conditions, and then subsequently tested the children on the problem-solving task. Remembering "Clever Hans" and the literature on experimenter effects, Cheyne argued that the experimenter might unconsciously have been favoring the free-play children in some way, perhaps through nonverbal encouragement, more lenient scoring, and so forth. Also, he argued that Sylva had over-generously interpreted her results to favor the play hypothesis. Certainly, on looking back at Sylva's work in detail, including her dissertation where it is most fully reported (Sylva, 1974), the advantages claimed for the play-group children do not seem all that evident.

By contrast, the results from the Smith and Dutton (1979) study had seemed very clear. There was no question here of which way the results pointed. But could experimenter effects have been at work in this study? Yes, as Susan Dutton had seen the children through both the play/training conditions and the testing and scoring. This was worrying and I resolved to try to disprove Cheyne's hypothesis.

At that time, Tony Simon came to join me as a graduate student, and I persuaded him to take up this challenge. We decided to rerun the Smith and Dutton study, but ensuring that one experimenter did the play and training while another experimenter did the testing and scoring blind to the prior treatment condition. This was logistically a bit more difficult, but obviously essential given Cheyne's criticisms. I was confident we would still get the same result.

We did not; we found no difference between the play and training conditions. I well remember arguing with Tony Simon about this. I didn't believe it. Perhaps we hadn't run enough children? Perhaps the two groups were not well matched? Perhaps (a clever but desperate argument!) there was a "reverse experimenter effect" with the first experimenter favoring the training children in some way?

All these seemed unlikely explanations, but obviously we had to replicate our failure to replicate Smith and Dutton. We did this, twice more. Each time, we got the same result—no difference between play and training groups. We also, we think, pinned down the likely experimenter effect which had operated in the Smith and Dutton study; this was related to the willingness to give hints to children in the different conditions—an unwitting procedural effect which strongly affects the scoring. We had some trouble, at first, publishing our findings. Perhaps unfortunately, some journals are not so interested in "failures to replicate," and some referees (like me, earlier) were reluctant to believe it. But the studies were eventually published (Simon and Smith, 1983, 1985; Smith, Simon, and Emberton, 1985). I think they provide a nice example of how experimenter effects can be important—usually we don't guard against them until someone demonstrates their impact in that domain.

Other studies had also been done using paradigms similar to those of Sylva. For example, Dansky and Silverman (1973, 1975) had shown that playing with common household objects produced more imagined creative uses for them than training experiences with the objects. They had in fact taken the inspiration for these studies from one of Sutton-Smith's earlier papers linking play and creativity. Emboldened by Tony Simon's work, Susan Whitney and I tried to replicate the Dansky and Silverman results, but using blind experimental procedures. We failed to do so (Smith and Whitney, 1987). In another experimental variation, Golomb and Cornelius (1977) had claimed that a few short play sessions could bring about conservation skills in four-year-olds. Guthrie and Hudson (1979) had failed to replicate this. Altogether, a number of studies which had tried to link play experience to problem solving now seemed to be in disarray.

In thinking about this, Tony Simon and I concluded that the experimental situations employed were just not ecologically very valid ways of trying to demonstrate any functions of play. The experiments were usually short—about ten or fifteen minutes—whereas any benefits of play might be slow and cumulative; the experiments involved "asking" or "requiring" children to play, when supposedly we were interested in benefits of free play. The experiments were clearly susceptible to experimenter effects, so any apparent findings were not robust.

The play tutoring studies inspired by Smilansky did seem more ecologically valid—they lasted longer, often several months, and involved classroom curricula, but they had had their own problems with control groups. All in all, the experimental literature on play seemed plagued with difficulties; and looking back over some fifteen years, I felt that the preconceptions of many researchers (including, for a while, my own) had clearly influenced how they had designed experiments and how they had interpreted them. The play ethos had had a strong influence on research. I wrote up this argument in Smith (1988).

In doing so, I became very aware of Brian Sutton-Smith's views on the idealization of play. In a broader context still, Brian's work illustrated how views of children's play varied culturally and historically, how and why the toy industry had developed, how play and work had become separated, how children's play became "idealized" in a leisure- and consumer-oriented society (Sutton-Smith and Kelly-Byrne, 1984; Sutton-Smith, 1986). Also, Brian pointed out forcefully how play had many facets to it, and how really spontaneous play could show many features different from the idealized view. Some play could be rude, violent, anarchic. This accorded well with my thinking about how different rough-and-tumble play was from the more "educational" forms of play I had largely been looking at in the later 1970s.

BACK TO ETHOLOGY

The laboratory paradigm approach to studying the functions of play may seem a long way from the ethological approach, and in some ways it is, although ethologists have not been averse to experimentation and there have been ingenious experimental studies of animal play—for example by Dorothy Einon and her collaborators (e.g., Hole and Einon, 1984). In a target article for *Behavioral and Brain Sciences* (Smith, 1982), I tried to put together the animal and human literature on the functions of play, surveying observational, correlational, and experimental studies. In so far as "play" could be considered as a unitary behavioral phenomenon—in retrospect, maybe more of a mistake than I thought at the time—I argued that it could give safe practice for useful later skills in cases where such practice was either danger- ous for young animals (for example, fighting and predatory behavior) or unlikely to occur (for example, problem-solving skills with objects, in children). At the time I wrote this, the experimental work on children's play had not been thoroughly criticized.

Interestingly, as the critique of the experimental paradigm for looking at the functions of children's play emerged in the early 1980s, so also did a critique of work and assumptions on animal play. Martin and Caro (1985) provided a very well thought out and argued case that the benefits of animal play might have been considerably overestimated. They argued that the costs of such play were low, and that therefore the benefits could also be small. Also, such benefits—for example, practice in predatory skills—might be achievable by a variety of means, not just play experience. Again, the appar- ent failure of some experimental studies to come out with clearcut results added fuel to their arguments.

Martin and Caro clearly bring out the complexity of issues in considering developmental functions. Neither their critique of the animal work nor mine of the work on children's play (Smith, 1988) was intended to suggest that play has no function. I still find this implausible. But we were both arguing that many previous researchers in the area had gone too far in assuming many functions for play and in assuming that these functions were essential (the play ethos). This had even distorted the direction of research for a while. Rather than providing simple answers, one has to consider issues such as whether play has benefits which can also be provided by other kinds of experiences; whether some minimum level or "threshold value" of play is all that is needed; whether the value of playful experiences varies appreciably by culture and individual experience. I think these questions are still substan- tially unanswered.

PLAY-FIGHTING AND AGGRESSIVE PLAY

My own interests in the 1980s moved away from fantasy and sociodramatic play to rough-and-tumble play. I thought that perhaps we had been putting too much emphasis on supposed cognitive benefits of some forms of play which actually were very culturally determined. By contrast, play-fighting or rough-and-tumble play seemed to be a cultural universal, something in hu- man nature where it was useful to draw parallels with nonhuman primates and other mammal species in which play-fighting and play-chasing could also be observed.

In part, this work was a return to observational and ethological approaches. I first carried out a study with Annie Humphreys, supported by a grant from the Foundation for Child Development. We observed seven-, nine-, and eleven-year-olds in playtime breaks, and also obtained friendship and dominance data. Rough-and-tumble play took up about 10 percent of the time, and was characterized by being engaged in with friends and, at the older ages only, with children of similar dominance status (Humphreys and Smith, 1987).

Following this, Michael Boulton, a graduate student of mine in the 1980s, commenced long (forty-minute) observations of focal children through lunchtime play breaks, focusing on play-fighting and play-chasing and the forms they took, and doing sequential analyses of behavior (Boulton and Smith, 1989). His work provided very fine-grained data on the forms of play-fighting, and how it compared with real fighting (Boulton, 1991a, 1991b).

This work continued with colleagues in Italy (Costabile et al., 1991; Smith et al., 1992). We combined observational approaches with playback of videotapes of play fights and real fights, as well as sociometric interviews and structured interviews about play-fighting with children, to obtain further insight into questions such as why children play-fight, how often it is confused with real fighting, what cues are used to tell the difference, and which children make mistakes and why this happens. An interesting theoretical prediction stemming from Robert Fagen's masterful review of animal play (Fagen, 1981), is that confusion between real fighting and play-fighting might arise for either of two reasons: genuine errors (misinterpreting a play signal) or cheating (deliberately using the play convention to inflict hurt) (Smith, 1989).

It is still not certain how much these two possibilities apply to children's play-fighting, but progress is being made. Work by Tony Pellegrini (1988, 1991) has shown that peer-rejected children are more likely to escalate play-fighting to real fighting, and Michael Boulton and I found that sociometrically rejected and neglected children make more errors on the videotape test, being less able to distinguish play-fighting and real fighting accurately. This work brings together theoretical perspectives from ethology with sociometric studies and with information processing approaches to social skills (Dodge et al., 1986). Tony Pellegrini and I are currently taking this further, with Ersilia Menesini and Rebecca Smees, using videotape playback to both participants and nonparticipants in encounters to compare their judgments of intention in different episodes.

My own research interests are currently most concentrated on the area of school bullying. This is a topic of considerable public concern, and our research is helping to provide schools with useful knowledge about what to do and which interventions work (Olweus, 1993; Smith and Sharp, 1994). Perhaps, after a long detour in play research, I have got back to aggression again as I had planned twenty years earlier! But I have no regrets about the time spent in play research (anyway still continuing). As I hope this chapter has made clear, it provided salutary lessons about the importance of ecological validity, the dangers of experimenter effects, the scope for innovative procedures, the importance of crossing disciplinary boundaries, and the impact of the wider social context on how we produce theories and how we devise research projects.

REFERENCES

Arrington, R. (1931). *Interrelations in the behavior of young children.* New York: Teachers College, Columbia University.

Arrington, R. (1943). Time sampling in studies of social behavior: A critical review of techniques and results with research suggestions. *Psychological Bulletin, 40,* 81–124.

Blurton Jones, N. (1967). An ethological study of some aspects of social behavior of children in nursery school. In D. Morris (Ed.), *Primate ethology* 347–68. London: Weidenfeld and Nicolson.

————. (Ed.). (1972). *Ethological studies of children's behavior.* Cambridge: Cambridge University Press.

Boulton, M. J. (1991a). A comparison of structural and contextual features of middle school children's playful and aggressive fighting. *Ethology and Sociobiology, 12,* 119–45.

————. (1991b). Partner preferences in middle school children's playful fighting and chasing: A test of some competing functional hypotheses. *Ethology and Sociobiology, 12,* 177–93.

Boulton, M. J., & Smith, P. K. (1989). Issues in the study of children's rough-and-tumble play. In M. N. Bloch & A. D. Pellegrini (Eds.), *The ecological context of children's play* (pp. 57–83). Norwood, NJ: Ablex.

Brainerd, C. J. (1982). Effects of group and individualized dramatic play training on cognitive development. In D. J. Pepler & K. H. Rubin (Eds.), *The play of children: Current theory and research* (pp. 114–29). Basel: S. Karger.

Bruner, J. S. (1972). The nature and uses of immaturity. *American Psychologist, 27,* 687–708.

Cheyne, J. A. (1982). Object play and problem-solving: Methodological problems and conceptual promise. In D. J. Pepler & K. H. Rubin (Eds.), *The play of children: Current theory and research* (pp. 79–96). Basel: S. Karger.

Christie, J. F., & Johnsen, E. P. (1985). Questioning the results of play training research. *Educational Psychologist, 20,* 7–11.

Costabile, A., Smith, P. K., Matheson, L., Aston, J., Hunter, T., & Boulton, M. 1991). A cross-national comparison of how children distinguish serious and playful fighting. *Developmental Psychology, 27,* 881–87.

Crook, J. H. (1970). Social organization and the environment: Aspects of contemporary social ethology. *Animal Behavior, 18,* 197–209.

Dansky, J. L., & Silverman, I. D. (1973). Effects of play on associative fluency in preschool-aged children. *Developmental Psychology, 9,* 38–43.

————. (1975). Play: A general facilitator of associative fluency. *Developmental Psychology, 11,* 104.

Department of the Environment. (1973). *Children at play: Design bulletin 27.* London: HMSO.

Dodge, K. A., Pettit, G. S., McClaskey, C. L., & Brown, M. M. (1986). Social competence in children. *Monographs of the Society for Research in Child Development, 51,* no. 2.

Fagen, R. M. (1981). *Animal play behavior.* New York: Oxford University Press.

Fassnacht, G. (1982). *Theory and practice of observing behavior.* London: Academic Press.

Golomb, C., & Cornelius, C. B. (1977). Symbolic play and its cognitive significance. *Developmental Psychology, 13,* 246–52.

Groos, K. (1901). *The play of man.* London: W. Heinemann.

Guthrie, K., & Hudson, L. M. (1979). Training conservation through symbolic play: A second look. *Child Development, 50,* 1269–71.

Hole, G. J., & Einon, D. F. (1984). Play in rodents. In P. K. Smith (Ed.), *Play in animals and humans* (pp. 95–117). Oxford: Basil Blackwell.

Humphreys, A. P., & Smith, P. K. (1987). Rough-and-tumble, friendship and dominance in schoolchildren: Evidence for continuity and change with age. *Child Development, 58,* 201–12.

Hutt, C., & Vaizey, M. J. (1966). Differential effects of group density on social behavior. *Nature, 209,* 1371–72.

Hutt, S. J., Tyler, S., Hutt, C., & Christopherson, H. (1989). *Play, exploration and learning: A natural history of the preschool.* London: Routledge.

Isaacs, S. (1929). *The nursery years.* London: Routledge and Kegan Paul.

Lorenz, K. (1966). *On aggression.* London: Methuen.

Lykken, D. (1968). Statistical significance in psychological research. *Psychological Bulletin, 70,* 151–59.

Martin, P., & Caro, T. M. (1985). On the functions of play and its role in behavioral development. *Advances in the Study of Behavior, 15,* 59–103.

McGrew, W. C. (1972). *An ethological study of children's behavior.* London: Academic Press.

Morris, D. (Ed.). (1967). *Primate ethology.* London: Weidenfeld and Nicolson.

Olweus, D. (1993). *Bullying in schools: What we know and what we can do.* Oxford: Blackwell.

Pellegrini, A. D. (1988). Elementary school children's rough-and-tumble play and social competence. *Developmental Psychology, 24,* 802–06.

———. (1991). A longitudinal study of popular and rejected children's rough-and-tumble play. *Early Education and Development, 2,* 205–13.

Piaget, J. (1951). *Play, dreams and imitation in childhood.* London: Routledge and Kegan Paul.

Saltz, E., Dixon, D., & Johnson, J. (1977). Training disadvantaged preschoolers on various fantasy activities: Effects on cognitive functioning and impulse control. *Child Development, 48,* 367–380.

Simon, T., & Smith, P. K. (1983). The study of play and problem solving in preschool children: Have experimenter effects been responsible for previous results? *British Journal of Developmental Psychology, 1,* 289–97.

———. (1985). Play and problem-solving: A paradigm questioned. *Merrill-Palmer Quarterly, 31,* 265–277.

Smilansky, S. (1968). *The effects of sociodramatic play on disadvantaged preschool children.* New York: Wiley.

Smilansky, S., & Shefatya, L. (1990). *Facilitating play: A medium for promoting cognitive, socio-emotional and academic development in young children.* Gaithersburg, MD: Psychosocial & Educational Publications.

Smith, P. K. (1970). Social and play behavior of preschool children. Doctoral dissertation, University of Sheffield.

———. (1974). Social and fantasy play in young children. In B. Tizard & D. Harvey (Eds.), *Biology of Play,* 123–45. London: S.I.M.P./Heinemann.

———. (1982). Does play matter? Functional and evolutionary aspects of animal and human play. *Behavioral and Brain Sciences, 5,* 139–84.

———. (1988). Children's play and its role in early development: A reevaluation of the 'play ethos.' In A. D. Pellegrini (Ed.), *Psychological bases for early education* (pp. 207–26). Chichester: John Wiley & Sons.

———. (1989). The role of rough-and-tumble play in the development of social competence: Theoretical perspectives and empirical evidence. In B. H. Schneider,

G. Attili, J. Nadel, & R. P. Weissberg (Eds.), *Social competence in developmental perspective* (pp. 239–55). Dordrecht: Kluwer.

Smith, P. K., & Connolly, K. J. (1972). Patterns of play and social interaction in preschool children. In N. Blurton Jones (Ed.), *Ethological studies of children's behavior*, (pp. 65–95). Cambridge: Cambridge University Press.

———. (1980). *The ecology of preschool behavior.* Cambridge: Cambridge University Press.

———. (1986). Experimental studies of the preschool environment: The Sheffield project. In S. Kilmer (Ed.), *Advances in early education and day care* (vol. 4), (pp. 27–66). Greenwich, CT: JAI Press.

Smith, P. K., Dalgleish, M., & Herzmark, G. (1981). A comparison of the effects of fantasy play tutoring and skills tutoring in nursery classes. *International Journal of Behavioral Development, 4*, 421–41.

Smith, P. K., & Dutton, S. (1979). Play and training in direct and innovative problem solving. *Child Development, 50*, 830–36.

Smith, P. K., Hunter, T., Carvalho, A. M. A., & Costabile, A. (1992). Children's perceptions of playfighting, playchasing and real fighting: A cross-national interview study. *Social Development, 1*, 211–29.

Smith, P. K., & Sharp, S. (Eds.) (1994). *School bullying: Insights and perspectives.* London: Routledge.

Smith, P. K., Simon, T., & Emberton, R. (1985). Play, problem-solving and experimenter effects: A replication of Simon and Smith (1983). *British Journal of Developmental Psychology, 3*, 105–107.

Smith, P. K., & Syddall, S. (1978). Play and nonplay tutoring in preschool children: Is it play or tutoring which matters? *British Journal of Education Psychology, 48*, 315–25.

Smith, P. K., & Whitney, S. (1987). Play and associative fluency: Experimenter effects may be responsible for previous findings. *Developmental Psychology, 23*, 49–53.

Sutton-Smith, B. (1966). Piaget on play: A critique. *Psychological Review, 73*, 104–10.

———. (1986). *Toys as culture.* New York: Gardner Press.

Sutton-Smith, B., & Kelly-Byrne, D. (1984). The idealization of play. In P. K. Smith (Ed.), *Play in animals and humans* (pp. 305–21). Oxford: Basil Blackwell.

Sylva, K. (1974). The relationship between play and problem-solving in children 3–5 years old. Doctoral dissertation, Harvard University.

————. (1977). Play and learning. In B. Tizard & D. Harvey (Eds.), *Biology of Play* (pp. 59–73). London: S.I.M.P./Heinemann.

Tinbergen, N. (1968). On war and peace in animals and man. *Science, 160*, 1411–18.

Tizard, B., & Harvey, D. (Eds.). (1974). *Biology of Play*. London: S.I.M.P./Heinemann.

2

ROBERT FAGEN _____

Animal Play, Games of Angels, Biology, and Brian

This chapter on the biology of animal play has an unusual title, and I hope it encourages a few readers, otherwise uninterested in the topic, to proceed further with the text. The chapter reflects an intellectual debt to Brian Sutton-Smith. Brian's ideas have guided me and many other play scholars, preventing a fool's rush into egregious error on more than one occasion, and reminding us to laugh at ourselves (or else).

The chapter introduces some new biological ideas about evolution of behavior. Its intended audience includes students of play, generalists who follow scholarly ideas about play, and scientists interested in Brian Sutton-Smith's life and work. These inquiries define intellectual concerns spanning the human sciences, the performing and visual arts, and education. Biologists who share these concerns may also be interested in this updated, nontechnical, and nonmathematical version of ideas on play previously presented elsewhere (Fagen, 1981, 1984, 1987, 1992, 1993, 1994). Scholars and others who appreciate Brian Sutton-Smith's ideas, or who have recently become interested in his studies of play, should find this chapter useful. It will present a biological consensus on animal play, to the extent that one can be said to exist, as well as alternative approaches to play that are familiar from Sutton-Smith's work.

Seen edge-on, rather than from a center of mass defined by consensus among established practitioners and by current media treatments of the topic, the biological study of behavior looks like a very different discipline from the one known to most scientists and general science audiences. A radically different approach to the study of communication and social relations is now helping to reformulate the biology of behavior. This approach is based on recent reanalyses of Darwin's work that call for a fundamental role in evolutionary change for aesthetics and performance theory. In contrast, much of what is now known as sociobiology (whether presented in popular or in scientific language) and human evolutionary biology are based on an older interpretation of Darwinism that may now be losing favor with an increasing number of scholars active in the field. Reformulated on the ground of evolutionary aesthetics, an enlarged and amplified version of Darwinism incorporating a balanced view of sexual selection true to Darwin's own intentions is necessarily of great importance to anyone interested in the problem of human nature—to students of the human condition, to educators, and to students and practitioners of the performing and visual arts. This is a kind of biology that might very well interest scholars who find Brian Sutton-Smith's work interesting.

It pays, of course, to be reasonably sure that one approaches the leading edge of the discipline, rather than some other fringe. I intend to show that the ideas involved are indeed important and represent significant new biological discoveries, and that there is ample reason to suppose that these ideas will ultimately transform the entire field. My approach will be to present the biology of play as a case study by reviewing past and current approaches. I will review scientific findings on animal play in the light of newer advances in the field. Lately, these advances have attracted renewed attention to the study of animal play. I will define contrasting biological bases for these approaches to play and outline some new perspectives now beginning to develop.

PLAY

Play occurs in only a small minority of the Earth's million or more animal species. Animal play is easy to recognize. Specific movement qualities and signal patterns characterize the familiar play behavior of cats, dogs, and human children as well as play of other animals. Mammals and birds, and perhaps a few fishes and reptiles, are the only kinds of animals know to play.

Animal play forms vary. They include physical interactions between mothers and offspring or between actual or potential mates, chasing and wrestling among infants and juveniles, and spontaneous series of elaborate and varied body movements.

Play movements (Fagen, 1981) include "exaggerated gestures, jerky movements, grotesque play faces, and light fast movements" (Sutton-Smith, 1989) along with free-flowing but more weighted "galumphing" actions (Miller, 1973). Play signals include a relaxed, open-mouthed facial expression known in both mammals and birds (Fagen, 1981) and a variety of locomotor and rotational body movements, often performed off-center, off-balance, or located in a plane transverse to the longitudinal body axis (Fagen, 1981; Sade, 1973; Wilson & Kleiman, 1974).

Immediate consequences and ultimate significance of animal play in its many forms are matters of active research and occasional controversy. These matters will be discussed in detail in the appropriate sections of this paper. So far as is known, play seems to have several biological functions, many with direct social significance. One function may be to facilitate the ability to judge whether or not defensive actions are appropriate in given situations.

Another is to reduce social distance between individuals and to develop intimate social bonds that may approach what some humanists still term love. Play could foster these results in many ways. One aspect of play that seems particularly significant in this context is that the occurrence, amount, and qualities of play performances can indicate the player's current well-being and therefore future reproductive success. In nonhumans, the audience for these performances is small and intimate, but in humans the audience is far broader.

Animal play has recently been "hot" again, judging from the spate of popular articles (e.g., Angier, 1992; Brown, 1994; Ford, 1983; Sleeper, 1991; Wickelgren, 1993. In this latest repetition of a familiar pattern, play was rediscovered by scientists, reformulated for a broad audience of nonspecialists, and will in time be disregarded for a while by scientists and nonscientists alike. Such cycles of popularity beset many intrinsically interesting scholarly specialties, and they are probably of no more significance than changes in dress fashions, in musical taste, or in the art market. Nevertheless, it is once again open season on play. Nothing comparable has happened since the Bruner (1972) boomlet of twenty years ago. The current deluge of insistent telephone calls and faxes from writers, reporters, and media impresarios has turned more than a few heads, and might make even the most confirmed rationalist embrace conspiracy theories of intellectual history. Whoever and whatever calls the shots in this domain finally has it right. Or so play researchers, blinking in unaccustomed spotlights, might well believe.

For Brian Sutton-Smith, a scholar of a very different sort, the season on play has always been open. Without pausing for anything less important than an occasional tennis match, Sutton-Smith has examined play during a research career that now spans half a century. His open approach to play admits both new ideas and new students to the topic. His work is nothing if not authoritative. And yet its persistent playfulness saves us (and him) from that most mind-deadening of intellectual tactics, the appeal to ultimate authority.

Sutton-Smith has sought to present his ideas in a way that keeps them from becoming dogma. He has attempted to foster public and scholarly skepticism about any and all cozy intellectual consensuses on play. His intent is to ensure that scholarly ideas and their social consequences never limit children's empowerment as human beings and as players.

Some biologists could well profit from Sutton-Smith's example. It is important to make scientific information about the natural history of play available to scholars and to other readers outside biology. Such information needs to be presented in a way that can help responsible people use it wisely, and that should make irresponsible uses identifiable and very visible. Outside biology, there is real demand for current scientific information about animal play. Particular lines of argument in psychology call for evidence from animal studies. Periodically, the media approach scholars for information on animal play. Such information travels far. It ramifies invisibly through networks of immense complexity. It may reemerge many miles and many years from its source. It is important to question just where and how scientific information on animal play might fit into these larger projects. Specifying these relationships makes it easier to see why certain kinds of results on animal play are especially interesting and useful to scholars outside biology and to the media. We can also reach a better understanding of how findings on animal play can be misinterpreted and misused even with the best intentions (or otherwise). And we can understand how abstruse scholarly studies of animal play can have immense impacts on the world of ideas at large, sifting inevitably through the underlying strata of power, then of money, and even all the way down to ordinary individuals muddling through their lives.

I will present the natural history and science of animal play from perspectives currently in use by practitioners in the field. These perspectives—ethology, comparative psychology, and evolution ("Darwinism") have a variety of implications and connotations, about which scholars in the respective specialties named do not always agree.

After presenting this summary, I will describe animal play from a naturalist's perspective and will seek to summarize what scientists have made of this information. I will seek to characterize, where appropriate, what I understand to be the principal interests in and uses of information on animal play in disciplines outside biology, by the media, and by the public. Wherever possible, even at the cost of some speculation, I will take a set of general perspectives that Brian Sutton-Smith's work has made accessible and will examine the natural history of animal play in the light of these other, nonbiological perspectives. Indeed, animal play proves very amenable to such novel, interdisciplinary approaches.

Although the current surge of popular and scholarly interest in animal play shows little sign of abating, students of play should be aware of growing competition from a lofty source—the world of angels (e.g., Gibbs, 1993). Angels can intervene in human lives and are otherwise decorative and useful. They dance in small spaces, they inspire poets, and they make superb music. Like play, angels have long been a topic of scholarly speculation and popular interest, although scientists seem to disregard them. Indeed, the study of angels and the study of play, and the popular ramifications of these enterprises, seem to offer certain similarities. They are based at least in part on speculation, hope, and romanticism. Their scholarly and popular cultural histories interact strongly. Rahner (1972) explored the boundaries of play, humor, and spirituality (no doubt assisted by an angel or two). Theologian Rahner's goals were not unlike those of scientists: to "get down to the roots of things" (p. 29), albeit by different means. He proposes that mere seriousness will not do, and that "a spirit of fun, of irony and of humor often digs deeper and seems to get more easily—because more playfully—down to the truth" (p. 29). For more on play in relation to spirituality, cosmology, and other matters generally considered to be the province of angels, see Handelman (1992) and discussions of mother-young play, *ludus amoris*, evolutionary aesthetics, and certain aspects of medieval spirituality in Fagen (1992). On this matter, we will allow Charles Darwin the last word: "If all men were dead then monkeys make men.—Men make(s) angels—" (Barrett et al., 1987, p. 213).

CURRENT APPROACHES TO ANIMAL PLAY

Ethology

Ethology is the study of behavior from a comparative, phylogenetic perspective. It places heavy emphasis, as did Darwin, on close, careful, direct observation of ongoing behavior and on contrasts between selected species or groups of species. Ethologists also do experiments and concoct theories, but the great strength of ethology lies in its power to see a given kind of behavior in many ways as it naturally occurs, as well as in its use of the comparative method. Trained in anatomy, morphology, and medicine, ethologists find it convenient to erect behavioral classifications, thinking as comparative anatomists do about inherited structures when considering the classic problems of their field: the evolution, function, development, and motivation of animal behavior. The classical ethologists observed animals in their own households, in zoos, and in the wild. Their attitudes varied from idealistic objectivity to virtual participant-observation. It is a truism that ethologists love their animals. Unlike comparative psychologists or evolutionary biologists, ethologists have a professional habit of observing and thinking about their pet animals, both domestic and wild, and they tend to spend their lives in proximity to if not in close social contact with one or more individual animals. Ethologists continue a holistic tradition of Continental philosophy that comparative psychologists and evolutionists may find baffling and opaque. Ethology has never embraced high technology for its own sake, and even in these days of automatic data recording and portable video, ethologists often depend on longhand field notes. But other approaches are possible. Indeed, the movement notation methods used by Israeli ethologist Ilan Golani (e.g., Golani, 1992) and his students, and the application of musical and theatrical techniques to the study of behavior in the laboratory of Canadian ethologist John Fentress (e.g., Bolivar, Cohen, and Fentress, in press), suggest ethologists' continued willingness to be creative and innovative seers of the natural lives of animals.

Comparative Psychology

Comparative psychologists are not just psychologists who study nonhuman animals in addition to white rats. More correctly, comparative psychologists are psychologists who exploit the full diversity of animal behavior to research classic problems in their field, such as perception, cognition, and motivation. Comparative psychologists differ from ethologists because of their intellectual upbringing: they were trained in positivistic, reductionistic North American or British departments of psychology (and tend to work in psychology departments), they do experiments all the time, and they never believed in biological determinism or psychohydraulic models, which is probably all right. Professionally, though not necessarily as individuals, they do not form personal relationships with the animals they study. Comparative psychology, like ethology, is doing well these days. Awareness of these unique features of comparative psychology helps when one surveys the heterogeneous literature on animal play. It is not enough simply to say that comparative psychologists are sort of like ethologists but don't believe in genes or instincts or whatever it was that Lehrman didn't like about Lorenz's science forty years ago.

Darwinism

Darwin stated four truisms:

1. Individual organisms vary.

2. Variation can be heritable.

3. Individuals increase in number faster than do their resources.

4. Individuals that vary in one particular way may gain resources to survive and reproduce better than individuals that vary in some contrasting way.

These four principles enabled Darwin to explain and predict changes in the characteristics of biological populations in time and space, and ultimately to analyze the origin of species in nature. Darwin's key ideas were further developed (by Darwin himself and by others) to explain between-sex variation, and they ultimately encountered Mendelian genetics and mathematical models in a fertile context that proved, at least for a while, most effective in explaining animal and plant diversity.

Philosophical and historical bases of Darwin's thought are just as interesting as its empirical consequences. Using Darwin's unpublished notebooks as well as little-known scientific articles published during Darwin's lifetime, Michael Ghiselin (1974, 1982) discovered important aspects of Darwinism that had been previously overlooked. Darwin's theory of sexual selection, for example, seems to have been widely misinterpreted by generations of Darwin scholars and popularizers. Darwin's thought now appears to have been much more in keeping with the idea (which, as we have seen, we also encounter in current ethological methodology) that aesthetic considerations are essential for observing and explaining natural diversity. Darwin's ideas of the aesthetic impulse, like his ideas of inheritance, tended to be a bit vague, but they prefigured a potential revolution in biological thought that, perhaps, still awaits an appropriate counterpart of Mendelism. So far as is known, an aesthetic impulse of unknown origins appears necessary in order to explain much about male-female and parent-young relationships, animal communication, and cooperative behavior.

Certainly, animal play makes sense in this light. Biologists are actively debating the possible origins and implications of this view, often twisting themselves into philosophical and theoretical knots to avoid possible lapses into metaphysics, mysticism, and vitalism. But, as Ghiselin has shown, the mechanism is a straightforward consequence of Darwin's thought. Aesthetic preferences are primary and affect choices about resources (including habitat and food), mates, social companions and relationships, and movement in space and time in ways that do not always directly follow from simple considerations of eugenics or economics. But eugenic and economic considerations are, of course, the basis of the current-day biological sciences of behavior in relation to environment and phylogeny, including evolutionary ecology, behavioral ecology, and sociobiology. The implications of this finding could be enormous. As has long been argued by evolutionary biologists and others, large-scale shifts in the way scientists view life on earth have a way of influencing views of human nature, human behavior, and human society. Answers to questions of origins about the aesthetic impulse as proposed by Darwin may still lie beyond biology, at least for the present, but these answers seem linked to ways (perhaps nonadaptive) that complex brains of the vertebrate sort necessarily function.

Evolutionary biologists tend to be bullish on biodiversity, and some individuals may even, at times, be accused of hugging trees. But, like comparative psychologists, they have no professional tradition of bonding with individual animals. Although comparative psychology seems to reflect a traditional professional standard by which psychology as a whole finds intrinsic value in the human condition, evolutionary biologists refuse to allow such scruples to tie their hands and may at times express various degrees of misanthropy. It is becoming increasingly apparent how Darwin's principles are being misapplied to derive a regressive political platform based on genetically determined family values, and it is very clear that individuals with particular social and economic interests are finding such arguments extremely handy.

It is traditional in psychology and anthropology, though not in ethology or other areas of biology, for authors to reveal a bit about themselves by way of self-criticism. These areas of the human sciences have become relatively sophisticated about the degree to which individuals' backgrounds can shape their "objective" science, and a modicum of self-characterization is now expected in humanistic and interdisciplinary work. Sutton-Smith has been especially generous with his public, offering many amusing and insightful perspectives on himself and on his ideas (e.g., Sutton-Smith, 1993). Here as elsewhere, Brian is a hard act to follow.

I was trained as a biologist and applied mathematician, chiefly at Harvard, where I studied sociobiology (in those days, a sunnier and more cautious science as regards human nature, although I suppose the ultimate program was already well in place) while majoring in theoretical and mathematical biology. I have spent most of the past ten summers in the field studying the play of brown bears, most of the past five winters doing dance and choreography, continue to write about animal play, and live and work in Alaska.

NATURAL HISTORY OF ANIMAL PLAY

Without doing too great a disservice to the immense variety of play behavior and of animals in nature, we can provisionally erect five grades of animal play activities, arranged in order of ascending complexity. These are fuzzy categories. Many individuals of the species assigned to a particular grade will occasionally show play patterns belonging to a higher grade, and some (especially my cats and golden retriever) will often do so. Animals at any given grade will also freely perform play patterns known from all grades lower than their own. Moreover, training by humans, or simple experience with humans as play partners, can induce animals to play at higher grades of complexity than those known from the wild. Finally, play of many, perhaps most, species of mammals and birds remains almost entirely unknown. There are especially large blank spaces in our comparative map of play in bats, cetaceans, birds, marsupials, and most families of rodents—not to mention aardvarks!

Grade 1: One-sided or noninteractive, isolated brief single actions. This grade of play is best known from certain rodents in which it has been studied with particular care. These actions include play contacts that are not immediately answered by defense or counterattack, brief jerky movements, and single forms of movement performed repeatedly. They are not always immediately recognizable as play by an untrained observer and may merge with actions from other categories of behavior, especially in immature animals. This grade represents a heterogeneous collection of behaviors from which play seems to emerge in development and evolution.

Grade 2: Social noncontact play and solo play. Many hoofed mammals (ungulates), some rodents, a number of different kinds of birds, and other miscellaneous species exemplify this category. These species generally play by moving their bodies in or through space in varied ways involving both locomotor and rotational activity. Running, jumping, and combinations of many different movement patterns can occur. There is little or no contact play (not even forms of play in which contact is neither frequent nor prolonged) in these species.

Grade 3: Contact and noncontact social play. Grade 3 species can play socially using body contact (e.g., wrestling and sparring). They may even alternate contact and noncontact play forms during the same games or play bouts. Most primates and carnivores, many ungulates, some birds, many pinnipeds, a fairly large number of marsupials (though perhaps not the majority), and a fair number of species from virtually every other mammalian order represent this category. These animals exhibit a spectrum of friendly, lively social interactions ranging from noncontact chasing to sparring and wrestling. They also play on their own by moving their bodies and/ or by interacting with objects and the landscape. During this solo play, communicative patterns associated with social play sometimes occur, suggesting that the animals include both social and solo play forms under a single category of play. Each species has its own characteristic mix of contact and noncontact play, but the preferred balance point can also vary situationally to a great extent within each species. Noncontact social play (e.g., chasing) occurs both in Grade 2 and in Grade 3 species, but may be more elaborate or complex in Grade 3 species. For example, the paths in space followed during chases may be more intricate, with reversals of direction, reversals of role in which the chaser becomes the animals being chased, and sharp turns. Or, features of the landscape may be used in games primarily involving chasing (e.g., hide and seek, tag).

Grade 4: Complex social play. Social carnivores, large parrots, common ravens and perhaps a few other corvids, some nonhuman primates, and many other animal species from African and Indian elephants to certain whales, dolphins, and porpoises exemplify this level of complexity. These species play social games involving objects and features of the landscape. Adult social play occurs regularly outside the contexts of male relations or relations between parent and immature offspring.

Grade 5: Social play involving special intimacy or cognitive interaction. Common chimpanzees (*Pan troglodytes*), as well as their close relatives among the anthropoid apes, typify the highest grade of play. Here, tickling, playful constructions using objects, and reciprocal mother-young play involving maternal structuring or behavioral scaffolding of social interchange are all common.

WHAT ANIMAL PLAY MEANS BIOLOGICALLY

Movement qualities, unique communicative patterns, and the distinctive choreography of animal play allow us to recognize and characterize play in animals. A variety of behavioral signals, including facial expressions, bodily postures and movements, and sounds, some highly idiosyncratic, serve to initiate and maintain play and to communicate information about the immediate well-being of the players (Fagen, 1981, 1992). Throughout the history of ethology and comparative psychology, and at an accelerating pace during the last decade, scientists studied play's structure, development, motivation, and immediate biological consequences.

Structure

Play is episodic. A given game consists of rounds of activity separated by brief pauses. Behavior may vary between rounds, but each game often seems to have a particular theme. For example, a bout of social play may include episodes of chasing, wrestling, sparring, and playful competition for objects. In these little dramas, narrative and nonnarrative phases tend to alternate in a way that in itself represents a kind of narrative about one or more relationships. Higher-order structures of this type in play have largely gone unnoticed in a context of inquiry that was analytic and sought to characterize play in terms of sequences of molecular acts of different well-defined types.

If occurrences of play were independent over time, a search for higher-order structures would be futile. For this reason, it was initially necessary for students of play to demonstrate the empirical reality of "playtimes" in the lives of animals, during which one or more forms of play were especially likely to occur. Evidence on this question long remained qualitative and anecdotal (see the summary in Fagen, 1981, pp. 202–5). Recently, Judy Loeven (1994) statistically demonstrated higher-order temporal structure in timber wolf (*Canis lupus*) play. Her findings demonstrate the reality of playtimes in animals. Wolves, and presumably other animals, do not simply play for a while and then do something else instead. Their behavior includes play sessions during which they pause from their play activity, but remain in a play mood and resume playing after the pause. This pattern of activity might appear rhythmic to an observer because play durations have a distinct mode. Play does not simply terminate at a time independent of that at which it began. Moreover, play is more likely to resume than to terminate after a pause unless several play-pause cycles have already occurred.

Playtime in animals is real and has special significance. This finding opens up new modes of inquiry about animal play. It represents an important departure from previous lines of research that usefully differentiated play into distinct developmental categories but in the process tended to lose sight of the overall coherence and unity of play in the natural lives of animals. Given the reality of playtime, it becomes meaningful to characterize entire play sessions in terms of the forms of play that occur and to ask if all play sessions are basically the same from beginning to end except for pauses (at a given age, developmental stage, for an individual, etc.) or if different phases exist (e.g., Fagen, 1981, pp. 325–28). Might play sessions have temporal structure analogous to that of string quartets or symphonies, with individual movements that occur at predictable stages of the play session and that differ from one another in tempo, intensity, or other aspects of movement quality? Such patterned performances are widespread in human culture, and are by no means restricted to music. Folktales of many cultures have particular forms, as most readers of this paper will not be surprised to learn (we begin, in English, with "Once upon a time" and end, perhaps, with a moral; the formal structure of Russian folktales can be considerably more complex, with up to five distinct named parts—see, e.g., Afanas'ev, 1975.)

Evidence that play sessions are real makes questions about their temporal structure possible and indeed inevitable. And this line of inquiry further extends in directions that link play and games to story and myth. Here is a gateway to other spaces and times, to the universals in myth and fairytale optimistically proposed by such classical scholars as Joseph Campbell and Sir James Fraser, and even to Karl Jung's archetypes. To those familiar with narrative and performance in both human and nonhuman settings, it may prove useful to develop a unified theoretical framework for looking at games, stories, myths, and Jungian archetypes. As their putative biological precursor, structures in animal playtime would then represent a tractable model for the problem.

Development

Play exhibits some affinity with prenatal movements, but really comes into its own some time after birth—sooner in precocial species than altricial species. Play movements are a mix of generalized patterns from sexual and affiliative spheres of action, and may also include some other kinds of generalized action patterns. These additional forms of behavior can be referred to a general area of the repertoire from which also emerge specific patterns having affinities with aggressive (especially defensive aggression), predatory, and/or predator avoidance systems of behavioral control. These findings mean that play patterns may resemble aggression, predator defense, friendly contact, et cetera but are not their developmental precursors. In fact, it is quite common for (so-called) play-fighting and play-chasing to emerge as recognizable behaviors quite independently of the developmental course of aggressive behavior, of predation, or of predator defense.

Motivation

Play clearly has its own demonstrable motivation. It makes sense to say that an animal wants to play. Animals will perform complicated behaviors to get a chance to play. Some games or forms of play may be especially attractive to a particular individual in the particular situation where it finds itself, but play is itself a distinct motivational category and one form of play can readily substitute for another. For example, two squirrel monkeys can find ways of playing together that they will both accept, depending on who is larger, stronger, or more dominant (Biben, 1986, 1989). Domestic dogs and cats who want to play, but who know that it is dangerous to risk a misunderstanding or loss of control that might result in injury to a human partner, may start a game with an object and thus keep teeth or claws from contacting the human. Animals have play-signals that say they want to play in general or that express their play mood, and other signals for particular kinds of games.

Biological Consequences

Risk and Other Negative Consequences   Play is risky. Events likely to result in injury or death can occur in play, as demonstrated by a significant body of primary literature (Clarke & Glander, 1984; Fossey, 1983, pp. 62, 88; Goodall, 1986, pp. 98, 100; Harcourt, 1991; Stanford, 1991; Strum, 1984). Evidence from human children is even more comprehensive and points to the same conclusion (Fagen, 1993). A number of other miscellaneous, biologically significant consequences of animal play—time, energy, loss of prey—have also been demonstrated. In terms of the behavioral ecologist's economic metaphor, play has costly aspects that can decrease the chance of survival to reproduce.

Other Effects (Positive?) on the Player   Reasoning that play must make some difference in addition to reducing survival, or it would not have evolved, biologists have used their senses and their imaginations to propose many possible positive effects of play experience. This argument is not strictly orthodox, as there is evidence for all kinds of dysfunctional (or simply klutzy) behavior in animals. North American porcupines fall out of trees with some regularity (Wolkomir and Wolkomir, 1994). Brown bear cubs may occasionally follow strange mothers and nurse from them for several days (Walker, 1993). A number of theoretical mechanisms can ensure the persistence of such "nonadaptive" behaviors in evolutionary time, and there is no a priori reason to consider play exempt. However, the trend of current biological arguments, taking these factors into consideration, still seems to favor some adaptive significance for play. This is so even if we cannot yet say just what that significance is in all cases, and cannot assume that play has the same significance for survival and reproduction across different animal species (Fagen, 1993).

Case histories, ecological data, and one set of experiments offer the best evidence to date that animal play is biologically important in addition to being motivated and fun. Three major findings, each indicating a different kind of function for play, will now be reviewed.

1. Levels of play indicate yellow baboons' present well-being and future reproductive success.

Levels of play in early development directly reflect levels of nutrition, which in turn predict lifetime reproductive success. Fagen (1993) reviewed field data on yellow baboon nutrition and behavior collected by Stuart Altmann, and found that play directly indexed both current and prospective well-being in this carefully studied primate species. The best information available to one baboon about another's current nutritional level is the amount of time that the other baboon spends playing. Unsurprisingly, female baboons that enjoy better nutrition as juveniles also tend to reproduce more successfully as adults. These facts alone could explain the evolution of play in animals (Fagen, 1992).

2. Play helps rats learn when to act in self-defense.

An absence of play per se, under laboratory conditions in which other confounding factors such as social interaction and self-initiation of behavior can be ruled out, has measurable consequences in laboratory rats (Einon & Potegal, 1991; Potegal & Einon, 1989). Rats that play less are inept at judging when to feel threatened by a situation and at judging when a situation does not call for defensive actions. Defensive behavior of rats with little or no play experience is seldom appropriate to the situation. Either they act very defensive when nothing threatens them, or they fail to defend themselves in an appropriate manner against real threats. Paradoxically, they are emotionally thin-skinned, with a hair-trigger aggressive reaction against harmless stimuli that they seem to find intensely threatening, and they let themselves get pushed around and bullied or taken advantage of, or even hurt, as if they were totally oblivious to these real threats.

3. Adult play has the shape of love.

Play does not normally persist in adulthood, although many individual counterexamples exist (Fagen, 1981). Adult play in nature occurs most often in one of two contexts: a parent with is offspring, or two prospective or actual mates. These contexts for play both seem to indicate social bonding functions rather than development of specific motor skills or survival abilities. That evolution has acted to ensure persistence of play across the lifespan in precisely those social contexts involving the closest, most intimate, and potentially most emotionally positive kinds of dyadic relationships is important. It indicates that whatever play does for immature or adult animals, it seems to have "the shape of love," a phrase that Kirkland and Lawrence (1990) earlier used in a different context. Interestingly, Pellis's (1993) extensive observations of many different species and genera of muroid (mouse-like) rodents also suggest that *juvenile* rodent play may have an affiliative and/or sexual function, rather than serving merely as aggressive training. However, because of the difficulty of collecting appropriate data (and hopefully because of valid humane considerations), Pellis did not test the hypothesis that play develops skills that a muroid rodent might use to avoid and to defend against predators.

In contrast to the simple and carefully analyzed play of rodents, primate play can exhibit great complexity, and many aspects of primate play continue to defy all but the mot humanistically oriented analyses (Fagen, 1993). Though the problems of doing research on primate play are especially difficult, three recent studies of primate play all indicate the importance of social factors. Brown (1988) found that juvenile and adolescent lowland gorillas chose play partners who were like their future social partners. Female gorillas disperse from their natal groups and interact mainly with adult males in their new groups, whereas males remain in their natal groups as adults and interact with both males and females. Play preferences of gorillas who were not yet adults followed these patterns in several different groups observed in confinement. Males played with other males and with females, but females seldom played together.

Pellegrini (this volume) and Smith (this volume) both consider the significance of affiliative play for human children. Rough-and-tumble interaction is "a playful, affiliative category" for human children, but adolescents use rough-and-tumble play in ways that exhibit their social dominance (Pellegrini, this volume). Might a follow-up study on courtship play in human adolescents reveal a *second* functional shift, from play back to affiliation? Smith (this volume), like Pellegrini, has illuminated the subjective and multifactorial nature of human play, revealing the importance of early experience and judgments of intention in determining the shape and qualities of play and quasi-play interactions. In humans, as in rats, play (and threat?) may well be matters of subjective assessment and evaluation for the participants as well as for the observers. A strong (if indirect) line of argument links individual rats whose lack of play has affected their ability to evaluate threatening situations with individual human children whose early social experience is somehow negative and whose behavior in a play setting amounts to escalated self-defense.

Play and Individual Adaptation   Common chimpanzees offered idyllic images to field biologists until about 1975, when a female named Passion and her daughter Pom began killing other mothers' infants. Passion, a cold mother and a loner, seldom played with her infants and had to move frequently and range widely in order to find enough to eat (Goodall 1986, pp. 77, 283; Goodall, 1990, p. 39; Plooij, 1979). Interestingly, Pom was not very playful with her own infants (Goodall, 1990, p. 40). Lack of play probably could not have been the sole or direct cause of Passion's and Pom's killing of infants. Other possible factors included general, widespread social instability and violence, including intercommunity attacks beginning about 1974, that may have resulted at least in part from heavy artificial feeding with bananas by humans in the past (ca. 1965–1968) and subsequent reductions and changes in the abundance and distribution of bananas supplied (Goodall, 1986, pp. 242–43; Wrangham, 1974). Experimental modifications of banana provisioning methods continued after 1969 (Wrangham 1974).

Evidence from Gombe indicates that play is one of a complex of factors that vary together in nature. Relative absence of play frequently occurs together with harmful or pathological behavior. Just as in the case of play-related risks, evidence from human studies is more extensive than evidence from animal studies. Sutton-Smith (1993) reviews evidence for real benefits of human parent-child play. Werner (1989) identified playfulness as one of a complex of behavioral and situational factors that enabled children at risk to have relatively happy and productive lives.

All findings cited here, both animal and human, suggest that play relates to fundamental levels of individual adaptation. We lack evidence that specific motor skills and behavioral tactics and strategies are fostered by play. Play does seem to involve high-risk behaviors demanding superb physical skill. High-speed turns in domestic horses (Fagen & George, 1977) and young chimpanzees' wild leaps from one tree branch to another in play (Goodall, 1986) are clearly related to motor skills important for survival. Young animals of these species seldom if ever perform these actions outside of a play context, where they may affect strength and skill. But they may be even more important for self-confidence or in other global contexts analogous to that of the rats who had to learn to judge just when it was necessary to act in self-defense.

Walker and Byers (1991) indicated a possible genetic basis for locomotor play in house mice, and Byers (quoted in Angier, 1992) correlates maximal rates of play in ontogeny with known age-specific rates of muscle fiber development in young mammals, arguing for a genetically based, generalized physical-training effect of play. But this evidence for physical-training effects, like that of Fagen and George (1977), is indirect.

Following Harlow, animal studies consistently sought specific functional effects for play on later domain-specific competence as a predator, as a fighter, in copulation, or in experimentally arranged social contexts. These experiments are numerous, their history spans many decades, and they involve a variety of species and paradigms. But, as Caro (1988) convincingly argues, none of them has produced any evidence that play enhances specific biological functions by developing the competences necessary to execute the skilled actions called for by a particular functional need. Recall that young animals are often fully competent at fighting against each other. Precocial animals can find food and even escape predators when young. Social skills, whether they involve parenting or decisions about whether or not to behave defensively in a given situation, seem more germane. Cognitive factors, such as the ability to make decisions about whether or not to be defensive, seem to be involved in some way. (But is this an issue of "cognition" or one of "emotion"? Biologists are seldom required to draw such distinctions.)

Play As Performance   Biologists, even those interested in courtship displays or, more generally, in evolutionary aesthetics, seem unaware of the potential power of a performative approach to their science. Like other academics, they face the occupational hazard of mind-centeredness. In consequence, they look to animals for forerunners of human cognition, as if academia somehow belonged on the highest rung of primate phylogeny, and they view animal minds through a narrow window defined by the world of books, disciplines, and research. But none of these mental commitments is necessary, and they may ultimately be very limiting and even regressive. The head may be farther from the ground than any other part of the body, but that does not make it "higher" or the rest of the body "lower." One of the first lessons to be learned in any dance class is that when you move, "center" does not mean head. Today, the search for biological bases of mind has a much narrower scope than it did in Darwin's time. It seems to have degenerated into a sort of scavenger hunt through the literature of natural history, accompanied by scientific-seeming experiments, in which the goal is to demonstrate that animals have the kinds of intellectual skills that humans use to succeed in Western schools or in academic careers. The question of animal awareness, developed as an academic enterprise, has become too narrow to include love, grace, and inventiveness in movement, or playfulness itself. This narrowness represents the same kind of problem that we considered earlier when discussing the cyclic popularity of play, and it may even have the same origin.

Sutton-Smith (1993) correctly questions the emphasis on cognition, from Piaget to Bruner and beyond, that led students of human play up several blind alleys. He rejects narrowly cognitive paradigms and correctly suggests (Sutton-Smith, 1989) that performance, rhetoric, and metaphor might be productive concepts for play scholars. Fagen (1992, 1993, 1994) views animal play from the perspective of performance, including Western concert dance. If biologists are not yet rushing to Ballet I class, they might at least consider the basics of performance theory, as presented, for example, by Sutton-Smith (1989) and/or by Schechner (1969, 1985, 1988).

Idealization of Animal Play   Sutton-Smith and Kelly-Byrne (1984) cautioned against idealization of play. Animal play can be fun to watch and to do (Fagen, 1992). It need not be romanticized. One-sided bullying is frequent, as has been repeatedly noted. Play is, to some extent, an attitude (Fagen, 1993; Sutton-Smith & Kelly-Byrne, 1984). Social play takes on a character that is the product of both players' attitudes at the very least.

Sutton-Smith's cautions regarding romanticization stem from his ethical discomfort with ideas that might be used to limit children's freedom to play as they wish. Some sociobiologists, on the other hand, embraced a "dark side" view of play at one time. They hinted that play's true evolutionary significance may be to interfere with others' normal development in a way that is emotionally and biologically damaging in the short or long term (see the arguments reviewed in Fagen, 1981, p. 473–74).

Human behavior patterns that normally benefit individuals and that society values can also function in a damaging way. Why should play be exempt from this generalization? Normal parental behaviors can be used for pathological control; a relationship based on mutual attraction can become a vehicle for power; humor can serve aggressive and destructive ends; science, the arts, and the media can manipulate the preconscious mind and reinforce prejudice and bigotry. Were none of this the case, there would be no need for angels to walk the earth in human form.

Biologically, play may have helped some animals to survive and reproduce by means of effects that harm no one, whereas it helped other animals (perhaps a minority—statistics are irrelevant to this argument) survive and reproduce by being cruel, manipulative, and controlling. That's biology, and life too, as any nine-year-old knows. When play, love, beauty, humor, and ideas are seen as threatening, those threatened naturally seek to diminish them under the excuse that they are not intrinsically good and can even be harmful. Biologists like to distinguish between function of behavior in the sense of immediate, present-day consequences, and (adaptive) function in the sense of past history—those aspects of the behavior that caused it to evolve. Sometimes, just as in evolutionary morphology, information on the "design" of a behavior can be helpful in drawing such distinctions. Criteria for evaluating arguments and evidence in this area can be baffling, even to biologists, but the argument from design is valid (Caro, 1988) and seems to suggest that play evolved through a series of phases involving development of physical capacity and skill, development of close positive dyadic social relationships, assessment of well-being, and (although this last is not yet well understood) integrative aspects of individual personality in relation to the physical and social environment, still inadequately characterized as self-confidence, emotional resilience, and a sense of fun. Without these gifts, we are most certainly lost, as powers, potentialities, and dark alignments have always known quite well. Is it any surprise that such forces, whatever names we may give them, may seek to suppress play by more or less heavy-handed means, and may even work to manipulate popular conceptions of play, as Sutton-Smith (1993) has long argued in his discussions of relationships linking play, children, and those who exercise or seek to exercise power over others? No wonder it makes sense for the public to be well-informed about play, to be choosy and skeptical consumers of ideas and media presentations on play, and for play scholars to be as honest as possible about their own interests and biases (including possible beliefs in angels, real or metaphorical).

CONCLUSIONS

Studies of animal play offer evidence for biological bases of human playfulness. Play in both humans and nonhumans involves many of the same characteristic body movements and communicative signal patterns. Functional significance of animal play, so far as is known, involves three different aspects of social relationships: (1) play serves to indicate current well-being and future reproductive success; (2) play helps animals (rats) learn when to act in self-defense and when not to; (3) play is important in developing and maintaining close, emotionally positive dyadic social relationships in adulthood and between parents and offspring. Play may also be important in developing physical capacity and in producing a well-integrated personality, but specific mechanisms and direct empirical evidence for these functions are lacking. Play has negative aspects and should not be idealized or romanticized, but its best-demonstrated effects all seem to benefit the player(s) in ways that enhance individual and dyadic well-being in the present/or and in the future, at little or no cost to any larger social entity.

To do justice to the material reviewed to date, a final speculation seems necessary. Inevitably, as Sutton-Smith, Rahner, and many other scholars have argued, it will be found that an approach based on pure aesthetics is every bit as inadequate as an approach based on an economically grounded struggle for existence. Aesthetic impulses may explain complex social behavior of many higher vertebrates, but, as Peterson and Goodall (1993, pp. 45–46, 181, 338) note, they do not suffice to explain chimpanzee behavior. Nor, for that matter, does a reactionary retreat to the dark side, whether by sociobiologists or by choreographers and theatre directors who have (rightly) long since tired of impersonal abstractions, cardboard characters, and saccharine stories, offer any convincing new answers. I see a simple way out, however. (So did Aristotle.) There are several ways to tell a story about our origins and about the human condition. A performance can appeal aesthetically to its audience's sense of beauty; it can be effective through shock, fear, and horror; and it can make people laugh. Evolutionary aesthetics tends to tell stories about origins by examining biological bases of the aesthetic sense in humans and nonhumans. Earlier scientific stories about human nature tended to adopt a (theatrically, perfectly legitimate) tragic mode, the more-or-less inevitable consequence of preoccupation with genes, environments, or both. It would not surprise any student of Brian Sutton-Smith's work to hear me suggest that evolutionary biologists might also profit from adopting a comic approach to the key problems of their field. When was the last time anyone heard a funny story about human origins? Klutzes didn't just happen. They evolved. So did clowns.

Resolution of these issues is, at least initially, a task for theory. This consideration in no way implies a retreat from empirical evidence; after all, Darwin was a theoretical biologist (Ghiselin, 1969). New and interesting questions are the stuff of theoretical biology, which in turn inspires other biological fields. Such questions now include humor, laughter, and the "lighter side" of play. Play between parent and offspring, between mates, and between friends combines affection with humor in precisely the way that is necessary in order to embrace a biological view of human nature that lies beyond the working of a merely aesthetic impulse.

ACKNOWLEDGMENTS

I thank Judy Loeven, Tony Pellegrini, and Joanne Tanner for comments on this manuscript and for copies of unpublished material.

REFERENCES

Afanas'ev, A. (1975). *Russian fairy tales.* New York: Pantheon Books.

Angier, N. (1992, 20 Oct.). The purpose of playful frolics: Training for adulthood. *New York Times,* C1, C8.

Barrett, P. H., Gautrey, P. J., Herbert, S., Kohn, D., & Smith, S. (Eds.). (1987). *Charles Darwin's notebooks, 1836–1844.* Ithaca, NY: Cornell University Press.

Biben, M. (1986). Individual- and sex-related strategies of wrestling play in captive squirrel monkeys. *Ethology, 71,* 229–41.

––––––. (1989). Effects of social environment on play in squirrel monkeys: Resolving Harlequin's dilemma. *Ethology, 81,* 72–82.

Bolivar, V. J., Cohen, A. J., & Fentress, J. C. The effects of semantic and formal congruency of film and music on film interpretation. *Psychomusicology,* in press.

Brown, S. G. (1988). Play behavior in lowland gorillas: Age differences, sex differences, and possible functions. *Primates, 29,* 219–28.

Brown, S. L. (1994). Animals at play. *National Geographic, 180* (6), 2–35.

Bruner, J. S. (1972). Nature and uses of immaturity. *American Psychologist, 27*, 687–708.

Caro, T. M. (1988). Adaptive significance of play: are we getting closer? *Trends in Ecology and Evolution, 3*, 50–53.

Clarke, M. R., & Glander, K. E. (1984). Female reproductive success in a group of free-ranging howling monkeys (*Alouatta palliata*) in Costa Rica. In M. F. Small (Ed.), *Female primates: Studies by women primatologists* (pp. 111–26). New York: Alan R. Liss.

Einon, D., & Potegal, M. (1991). Enhanced defense in adult rats deprived of playfighting experience as juveniles. *Aggressive Behavior, 17*, 27–46.

Fagen, R. (1981). *Animal play behavior.* New York: Oxford University Press.

———. (1984). Play and behavioral flexibility. In P. K. Smith (Ed.), *Play in animals and humans* (pp. 159–73). Oxford: Blackwell.

———. (1987). Play, games, and innovation: Sociobiological findings and unanswered questions. In C. B. Crawford, M. F. Smith & D. L. Krebs (Eds.) *Sociobiology and psychology: Ideas, issues and applications* (pp. 253–68). Hillsdale, NJ: Erlbaum.

———. (1992). Play, fun, and communication of well-being. *Play and Culture, 5*, 40–58.

———. (1993). Primate juveniles and primate play. In M. E. Pereira & L. A. Fairbanks (Eds.), *Juvenile primates: Life history, development, and behavior* (pp. 182–96). New York: Oxford University Press.

———. (1994). Applause for Aurora: Sociobiological considerations on exploration and play. In H. Keller, K. Schneider & B. Henderson (Eds.), *Curiosity and exploration* (pp. 333–39). New York: Springer.

Fagen, R., & George, T. K. (1977). Play behavior and exercise in young ponies (*Equus caballus* L.). *Behavioral Ecology and Sociobiology, 2*, 267–69.

Ford, B. (1983). Learning to play, playing to learn. *National Wildlife, 21* (3), 12–15.

Fossey, D. (1983). *Gorillas in the mist.* Boston: Houghton Mifflin.

Ghiselin, M. T. (1969). *The triumph of the Darwinian method.* Berkeley: University of California Press.

———. (1974). *The economy of nature and the evolution of sex.* Berkeley: University of California Press.

———. (1982). On the evolution of play by means of artificial selection. *Behavioral and Brain Sciences, 5*, 165.

Gibbs, N. (1993). Angels among us. *Time, 142* (27), 56–65.

Golani, I. (1992). A mobility gradient in the organization of vertebrate movement (The perception of movement through symbolic language). *Behavioral and Brain Sciences, 15*, 249–308.

Goodall, J. (1986). *The chimpanzees of Gombe*. Cambridge, MA: The Belknap Press of Harvard University Press.

———. (1990). *Through a window: My thirty years with the chimpanzees of Gombe*. Boston: Houghton Mifflin.

Handelman, D. (1992). Passages to play: Paradox and process. *Play and Culture, 5*, 1–19.

Harcourt, R. (1991). Survivorship costs of play in the South American fur seal. *Animal Behavior, 42*, 509–11.

Kirkland, G., & Lawrence, G. (1990). *The shape of love*. New York: Doubleday.

Loeven, J. (1994). The ontogeny of social play in timber wolves, *Canis lupus*. Master's thesis, Dalhousie University.

Miller, S. (1973). Ends, means, and galumphing: Some leitmotifs of play. *American Anthropologist, 75*, 87–98.

Pellis, S. M. (1993). Sex and the evolution of play fighting: A review and model based on the behavior of muroid rodents. *Play Theory and Research, 1*, 55–75.

Peterson, D., & Goodall, J. (1993). *Visions of Caliban*. Boston: Houghton Mifflin.

Potegal, M., & Einon, D. (1989). Aggressive behaviors in adult rats deprived of playfighting experience as juveniles. *Developmental Psychobiology, 22*, 159–72.

Plooij, F. (1979). How wild chimpanzee babies trigger the onset of mother-infant play—and what the mother makes of it. In M. Bullowa (Ed.), *Before speech* (pp. 223–44). Cambridge: Cambridge University Press.

Rahner, H. (1972). *Man at play*. New York: Herder & Herder.

Sade, D. S. (1973). An ethogram for rhesus monkeys. I. Antithetical contrasts in posture and movement. *American Journal of Physical Anthropology, 38*, 537–42.

Schechner, R. (1969). *Public domain*. Indianapolis: Bobbs-Merrill.

———. (1985). *Between theater and anthropology*. Philadelphia: University of Pennsylvania Press.

———. (1988). *Performance theory* (rev. ed.). New York: Routledge.

Sleeper, B. 1991. Animals at play. *Animals, 124* (6), 18–23.

Stanford, C. B. (1991). The capped langur in Bangladesh: Behavioral ecology and reproductive tactics. *Contributions to Primatology, 26.* Farmington, CT: S. Karger.

Strum, S. C. (1984). Why males use infants. In D. M. Taub (Ed.), *Paternalism* (pp. 146–85). New York: Van Nostrand Reinhold.

Sutton-Smith, B. (1989). Introduction to play as performance, rhetoric and metaphor. *Play and Culture 2*, 189–92.

———. (1993). A memory of games and some games of memory. In *Life before story: The autobiographies of psychologists from a narrative perspective.* New York: Praeger.

Sutton-Smith, B., & Kelly-Byrne, D. (1984). The idealization of play. In P. K. Smith (Ed.), *Play in animals and humans* (pp. 305–22). Oxford: Blackwell.

Walker, C., & Byers, J. A. (1991). Heritability of locomotor play in house mice, *Mus domesticus. Animal Behavior, 42*, 891–98.

Walker, T. (1993). *River of bears.* Stillwater, MN: Voyageur Press.

Werner, E. (1989). High-risk children in young adulthood: A longitudinal study from birth to 32 years. *American Journal of Orthopsychiatry, 59*, 72–81.

Wickelgren, I. 1993. It's not just a game. *Current Science, 78* (10), 4–5.

Wilson, S., & Kleiman, D. (1974). Eliciting play: A comparative study. *American Zoologist, 14*, 341–70.

Wolkomir, R., & Wolkomir, J. (1994). Prying into the life of a prickly beast. *National Wildlife, 32*, 34–39.

Wrangham, R. W. (1974). Artificial feeding of chimpanzees and baboons in their natural habitat. *Animal Behavior, 22*, 83–93.

3

GARRY CHICK AND LYNN A. BARNETT _____

Children's Play and Adult Leisure

> Still some things seem reasonable. Namely that my early intensive and later successful game play provided a disposition to be interested in games.
>
> Brian Sutton-Smith (1993)

> Western science is built on the obsessive and hitherto successful search for atomic units, with which abstract laws and principles can be derived. Scientific knowledge is written in the vocabulary of atoms, subatomic particles, molecules, organisms, ecosystems, and many other units, including species. . . . Both theory and experimental analysis in science are predicated on the assumption—the trust, the faith—that complex systems can be cleaved into simpler systems. And so the search proceeds relentlessly for natural units until, like the true grail, they are found and all rejoice.
>
> E. O. Wilson (1992)

INTRODUCTION

The epigraphs above encapsulate the theme and goals of this paper. In the first, Sutton-Smith (1993) documents his socialization, through early game play, into a general, and life-long, interest in games. Thus, one theme of this paper will be to examine how children's play may be a vehicle of socialization for adult leisure. In the second, Wilson points out the success of systematic categorization and reductionism in much of Western science. What he does not point out, but alludes to ("hitherto"), is that this success—through the discovery of fundamental units of analysis—is breaking down in some areas. Further, this success has never occurred in social science to any degree similar to that in the physical and biological sciences. Given these two views, the overarching question to be addressed here is the following: How is children's play related to adult leisure and how can children's play be compared with adult leisure? Further, what are the units of analysis that may be used for such a comparison if, indeed, any such units are even plausible?

We will focus on the first part of the question through the perspective of socialization/enculturation. Is children's play socializing and enculturative and, if so, to what end? As for the second part of the question, what exactly is

45

it that is internalized through socialization or enculturation? Each of these questions will be dealt with in turn.

SOCIALIZATION AND ENCULTURATION

The terms *socialization* and *enculturation* suggest disciplinary roots, the former associated typically with psychology and sociology and the latter with anthropology. Socialization is probably the more commonly used and understood term but that may be because there are more psychologists and sociologists than anthropologists (although some anthropologists prefer the term socialization, as well [e.g., Ember and Ember, 1988, pp. 402–4]). Regardless, the concept is quite old, captured, for example, by the poetic claim that "as the twig is bent, the tree's inclined." A variety of theories suggest how socialization and enculturation[1] take place and how their subsequent effects are manifested, but in general both refer to the idea that individuals learn the patterns of behavior that are appropriate for the culture of which they are members. Socialization and enculturation most often refer to the cultural learning processes of children and it is probable that most cultural information assimilation takes place during one's early years. But this is not exclusively the case. Individual roles change with age and cultures change over time, though the rates of both may vary widely cross-culturally. Moreover, children, through their play, may be part of the culture creation process itself, a point that will be further discussed later in this paper. Some typical definitions of socialization and enculturation are given below.

Ember and Ember (1988) describe socialization as "the development, through the influence of parents and others, of patterns of behavior in children that conform to cultural expectations" (p. 402). Lenski and Lenski (1982), who are sociologists, describe socialization as "the process through which individuals become functional members of their society" (p. 31). A psychologist, Robert Hess (1970), described socialization as "the patterns of antecedent variables which shape behavior and tie it to the social system in which an individual lives" (p. 457). Enculturation, on the other hand, is defined by Harris (1975) as "a partially conscious and partially unconscious learning experience whereby the older generation invites, induces, and compels the younger generation to adopt traditional ways of thinking and behaving" (p. 145).

These definitions suggest that sociologists, psychologists, and anthropologists, whether they are discussing socialization or enculturation, are referring to pretty much the same thing. The crucial distinction to be made, suggested by Harris (1975), is not so much between socialization and enculturation but between *society* and *culture*. For him, a society is "a group of people who share a common habitat and who are dependent on each other for their survival and well-being" (p. 145). Culture, on the other hand, is described by Harris as "the total socially acquired life-way or life-style of a group of people" (p. 144). Thus, every individual has social relationships with the members of his or her family, but the nature of these relationships is cultural, that is, defined by cultural rules.

There are many definitions of culture but most reflect the idea that culture is composed of "information." In an early formulation of this kind of definition, Roberts (1964) referred to culture as a system of information and to any particular culture as an "information economy" wherein information is created, used, stored, and even lost. If we accept the idea that culture is information (how the information may be packaged or encoded is dealt with later in this paper) then it is probably wrong to think that it is shared only unidirectionally, that is, from parents to children, from the older to the younger, or in a general sense, from those who possess more of it to those who have less.

Cultural innovation may take place in play, a behavior pattern or context usually attributed to the young, leading to consequent information distribution. Kroeber (1948), for example, suggested that what he termed "human play impulses" are responsible for "all of the discoveries and innovations of pure science and fine art—those intellectual and aesthetic pursuits which are carried on without reference to technology or utility" (p. 165). He gave, as examples, the bicycle, the automobile, and, possibly, the bow and arrow. He also noted that the advanced New World cultures—the Mayans, Aztecs, and Incas—failed to develop a number of utilitarian inventions, including the wheel, even though excavations in 1944 near Tampico, Mexico, uncovered wheeled toys. The principle of the wheel was known and used in play. It never had any utilitarian function probably because of a lack of any suitable beast of burden.

Similarly, Huizinga (1955) emphasized the creative aspects of play as a medium for imagination and cultural transformation. In the words of Finkelstein (1987), "rather than reflecting culture, play precedes it" (p. 19). Moreover, even if children's play could not be implicated in the creation of culture (that is, new information), it is crystal clear to every parent that socialization/enculturation is an imperfect medium for information transmission. Children not only do not end up as carbon copies of parents, but, according to sociobiological theory, for example, they *should* not (Trivers, 1974). The imperfection of cultural transmission through socialization is also apparent at the cultural level. For as yet unknown reasons, some cultures, such as the Amish, are remarkably resistant to the assimilation and utilization of new information while others—American culture, if such a thing can be said to exist—apparently welcome it with open arms.

Thus, it should be kept in mind (though most of the studies to be reviewed below fail to reflect it) that play, whether among children or adults, may be a fertile ground for the creation of culture. This is despite the fact that the concepts of socialization and enculturation typically imply processes that serve to inculcate the young with the details of adult culture for the presumed benefit of all (Barash, 1977). The processes may not be quite so simple.

PLAY AS SOCIALIZING AND ENCULTURATING

The literature on play and development is extensive and will not be dealt with here except to note several recent reviews and compendia of papers that provide previews. These include Barnett (1990), Johnsen (1991), Varga (1991), Fisher (1992), Gottfried and Brown (1986), Moore (1986), Block and King (1987), and Salamone (1989). Fisher (1992), in the meta-analysis of forty-six studies conducted between 1974 and 1987 that dealt with the importance of play to childhood development, found substantial evidence from these studies that play contributes to improved performance outcomes in three more or less distinct areas. These were cognitive development, linguistic development, and affective-social development. In her review, Barnett (1990) presented evidence consonant with Fisher's conclusions.

The literature on the socializing and enculturative value of play is much less extensive than that on its developmental consequences. In his recent bibliography of post-Schwartzman (1978) anthropological studies dealing with play, Salamone (1989) categorized publications under various headings but neither socialization nor enculturation was among them.[2] Nevertheless, concern with the value of play as a force in enculturation is quite old. Groos's (1898, 1901) *practice theory*, while not precisely a theory of socialization or enculturation, nevertheless held that play serves to hone or rehearse skills that would be used in adult life by both animals and humans. The essence of this theory is presented in modern form by Smith (1982). Based on considerations of biological evolution and natural selection, Smith argues that the principal function of animal play is to afford indirect practice for activities that otherwise might be unlikely or unsafe if undertaken directly. For humans, the effects of cultural evolution must also be taken into account inasmuch as these effects have both altered the human environment and changed the basis for the selection of certain types if behavior. According to Schwartzman (1978), "play as practice or rehearsal for adult activities has since become one of the most commonly accepted explanations available in the literature" (p. 100).

Schwartzman provides a detailed review of functional studies that hold play to be socializing and enculturating. Among the authors she cites is George Herbert Mead (1932), who held that play permits children to imagine themselves in various social roles. Games afford children the opportunity to assume their own role but in relationship to all of the other players in the game. Thus, it may be necessary to suppress one's own identity for the sake of the team. When a child can accomplish this, he or she is well along in becoming a fundamental member of society. Schartzman also includes Malinowski among those who viewed play as a functional mechanism for enculturation. Because of the simplicity of this explanation for play, the functionalists in anthropology, who were in ascendance from the 1930s through the 1950s, tended to ignore or minimize play as a phenomenon in its own right. The socialization/enculturation function of play was so obvious, given that it was mere imitation of adult behavior, that there was little need to consider it in depth (Schartzman, 1978).

Fortes's (1970, orig. 1938) study of the Tallensi was one important departure from this perspective and he provided "one of the most significant and insightful investigations of children's play available in the ethnographic literature," as well as a critique of the metaphor of play as imitation that was in vogue at the time (Schwartzman, 1978). At about the same time, Raum (1940) furnished another early critique of the play as imitation metaphor. In his book *Chaga Childhood*, play among Chaga children is described not so much as an imitation of adult life than as a caricature or satire of adult society (Schwartzman, 1978).

More recent studies of the socializing/enculturative aspects of play include Eifermann's (1970) study of games among children in Israeli kibbutzim, Salter's (1974) study of aboriginal Australian games, Lancy's (1975, 1976) research on the relationships between children's play and adult life among the Kpelle, McDowell's 1976) paper on riddling and enculturation, and Martin's (1982) study of the role of traditional games and play in socialization among the Hanahan of Buka. Allison (1982) looked at sport and socialization while Harkness and Super (1986) studied play using the concept of the "developmental niche" among rural children in Kenya. The developmental niche is described as the physical and social settings in which children live, the culturally prescribed systems of child rearing, and the psychology of children's caretakers. Finally, Heine (1984) considered the enculturative aspects of play and games among the Tlingit of southeastern Alaska. In general, these studies reflect the "practice" theory of play. However, this perspective has been challenged by Schwartzman (1978), Sutton-Smith (1976), Sutton-Smith and Kelly-Byrne (1984), Sutton-Smith and Magee (1989), and others (e.g., Fortes [1938] and Raum [1940] as noted above), mostly for being simplistic and for failing to recognize that aspects of children's play are antithetical to adult culture.

A somewhat different approach to the problem of play and socialization is exemplified by the studies of games by Roberts, Sutton-Smith, and their colleagues that were conducted during the 1960s and 1970s (Roberts and Sutton-Smith, 1962; Roberts, Sutton-Smith, and Kendon, 1963; Sutton-Smith, Roberts, and Kozelka, 1963; Barry and Roberts, 1972; Roberts and Barry 1976). According to Sutton-Smith and Roberts (1981):

> In these studies, significant relationships were established between patterns of child rearing and distinctive types of games. In general, the more types of games present, the more severe the socialization process. Most illuminating is the paper of Roberts and Barry (1976) showing that cultures with games of strategy and skill present are more likely to require more industry, obedience, and responsibility from their children and yet be low in the inculcation of self-reliance, honesty, and trust. The authors conclude that "if games built character, that character may be less than ideal" (1976, p. 39). (p. 442).

Thus, socialization for industry, obedience, responsibility, self-reliance, honesty, and trust takes place during child rearing but also in game play that occurs during childhood. Further, the game options available to or selected by adults reflect these cultural emphases. Finally, the level of cultural emphasis on these character traits (of industry, obedience, etc.) has at least potentially adaptive significance for societies in their particular techno-economic situation. For example, in a recent study, Roberts and Cosper (1987) showed that the degree of hierarchy found in three blue-collar occupations and the degree of involvement by employees in games of strategy covaried positively. One interpretation of this relationship is that involvement in games of strategy (1) helps assuage conflicts engendered by the multiple levels in hierarchical organizations and (2) provides a learning situation wherein players could become more skilled in the exercise of strategy in their real-world circumstances.

An additional finding of this series of studies is that games are related to cultural complexity, that is, more complex societies have both more games and more complex games. Sutton-Smith and Roberts (1981) suggest that it is possible that individuals living in complex societies must spend more time and effort in assessing the motives of others, who may not be exactly forthright. They propose that parents, as members of hierarchical social or economic institutions in complex societies, convey their values (such as industry and obedience but also distrust and suspicion regarding honesty) to their children, as these are the values that they find relevant in their own lives. These values are then reflected in the games that parents teach to their children. Modern sports, such as football or basketball, provide nearly perfect examples of this, especially at higher levels of competition (i.e., high school, college, or professional). Coaches typically value hard work, obedience, and responsibility from their players. But players are often taught not to be self-reliant but to depend on the coaches for decision making. And they may be encouraged to be dishonest. While players may acknowledge the commission of a foul after being apprehended by officials, to turn oneself in for committing a foul is unthinkable in most sports.

CHILDREN'S PLAY AND ADULT LEISURE

A handful of studies published over the years have been based on the premise that the leisure activities in which individuals engage as either children or adolescents are likely to be engaged in as adults, as well. The results of these studies have generally been equivocal, and many of the studies themselves are subject to criticism for their methods. Only one study, to our knowledge, examines the relationships between the leisure of adults and the play of children—parents and their children, in this case. These two sets of studies will be reviewed briefly below.

Child Leisure—Adult Leisure Socialization

At first glance, it seems odd to refer to any of the activities of children as "leisure," but this appears to have been done in several studies for a couple of reasons. First, the focus of the studies was on adult behavior, and the samples of individuals studied (with one partial exception) were adult. The other reason is that it is difficult to translate between play and leisure, both of which are notoriously slippery concepts. As will be discussed below, this may be termed the "units of analysis problem" and is simply the idea that the direct comparison of what children do in their play and what adults do in their leisure is problematic, as there seems to be no common unit with which both can be measured.

In an early study of the relationship between child and adult leisure, Patrick (1945) found little correlation between the activities in which individuals engaged as adults and those of their childhoods. Sofranko and Nolan (1972) studied hunting and fishing activities of a sample of adults and found that their current level of participation was significantly related to their level of participation during their "youth" or "childhood."[3] Contrary to their expectations, neither area of residence as a youth nor source of introduction (i.e., parents, friends, etc.) of the activity were related to the level of adult participation. Yoesting and Burkhead (1973) looked at the impact of the level of participation in thirty-five outdoor recreation activities as a child on level of participation as an adult. They found that about 40 percent of the thirty-five activities were participated in during both childhood and adulthood but, similar to the findings of Sofranko and Nolan (1972), childhood residence had no effect on either the level of participation as an adult nor the types of activities engaged in as an adult. In a follow up study, Yoesting and Christensen (1978) found a positive relationship between the number of outdoor activities engaged in as a child and as an adult, but the kinds of activities pursued as a child were unrelated to the kinds of activities pursued as an adult.

Kelly (1974) found that about half of the 744 different leisure activities pursued by a sample of Oregon adults were begun as children and that family associations were instrumental in the learning of 63 percent of them. A follow-up study (Kelly, 1977) supported these results. McGuire, Dottavio, and O'Leary (1987), using data from the 1982–83 Nationwide Recreation Survey, divided individuals aged sixty-five or older into either "expanders" or "contractors" based on their reported patterns of leisure involvement. Expanders were operationalized as individuals who had added at least one new outdoor activity to their repertoire after their sixty-fifth birthday but had not quit doing any during the preceding year. Contractors were operationally defined as those who had not added any new outdoor activities after age sixty-five or who had ceased to participate in at least one activity in the year prior to the study. Individuals who did not fit these criteria were excluded from the study. Expanders were found to continually initiate new activities during their lives, though some 30 percent of the activities in which they first engaged prior to age sixty-five were initiated before their eighteenth birthday. Contractors, on the other hand, had initiated approximately 60 percent of the activities that they pursued at the time of the research prior to the age of eighteen. No sociodemographic variables were found to be related to either expander or contractor status.

Scott and Willits (1989) criticized earlier research on child leisure–adult leisure consistency on methodological grounds. First, the studies focused on adult participants, rather than nonparticipants, and doing so ignores the possibility that adult nonparticipants may have been involved in the various activities as children or adolescents. Further, it is possible that many, or even most, youthful participants fail to continue their involvement as adults. Second, all of the studies utilized data obtained from adult informants who were asked to recall their patterns of leisure participation as children or adults.[4] Selective recall, bias, or other distortion may render such information unreliable (cf. Bernard, Killworth, Kronenfeld, and Sailer, 1984). To circumvent these problems, Scott and Willits utilized longitudinal data from a 1984 follow-up study of individuals first surveyed as high-school sophomores in 1947. They found that greater involvement in specific types of activities as a high-school sophomore was related to more frequent participation in the same types of activities when informants were in their early fifties.

To summarize briefly, the authors of these studies made the relatively straightforward hypothesis that engagement in leisure activities, either as children or adolescents, would predispose individuals to continue to engage in the same activities as adults. To varying degrees this hypothesis was supported. However, only one of the studies actually used longitudinal data and none of them dealt with socialization or enculturation as processes but, rather, with the outcomes—that is, whether or not individuals pursued the same leisure activities as adults as they had as youths. As such, these studies offer hints about the consistency of engagement in certain expressive activities from youth to adulthood but tell us little about the socializing effects of play.

Child Play–Adult Leisure Socialization

In 1986 we published a paper (Barnett and Chick, 1986) that was a first effort to explain some of the antecedents of children's play behavior. We hypothesized that the play styles of children are significantly influenced by indirect messages, as opposed to direct instruction, that parents communicate from their own leisure behavior and their feelings about their leisure. Social (or cultural) learning is generally thought of as that which occurs in individuals through their interactions in the social environment (e.g., Bandura, 1986). We were interested in some aspects of the social environment's influences on children, but not in others. For instance, we were not concerned with direct instruction in play by parents. We were curious about how and the extent to which parents, through their own leisure, provide models for their children's play styles. Thus, we attempted to learn if children, through the observation of their parents' leisure and through the acquisition of information about the affective characteristics of leisure for their parents—however transmitted—are influenced in their styles of play.

The sample for the study included ninety-seven (forty-eight male, forty-nine female) preschool children who were enrolled in several day-care centers. They ranged in age from 34.4 months to 63 months. All were the natural children of both parents and both parents were present in the home since the birth of the children. Day-care teachers were asked to rate each child on a forty-eight–item playfulness questionnaire, modified from Leiberman's (1967) scale. Two teachers, who were familiar with the children, rated the play of each child on a five-point scale in terms of physical spontaneity, social spontaneity, cognitive spontaneity, manifest joy, and sense of humor.

Both the mothers and the fathers of the children were asked to complete a survey without consulting each other and to return them by mail separately. Each survey contained a leisure satisfaction scale, a leisure attitude scale, and a leisure activity participation scale. In addition, information was obtained on the age and occupation of both parents, household income, family size, number and age of male and female siblings of the day-care child, and birth order, age, and gender of the day-care child.

A premise of the study was that parents who enjoy and value their leisure would likely influence their children to similarly enjoy and value their play. Therefore, we correlated the measures of parents' leisure with the playfulness ratings of their children. All analyses were conducted separately for boys and girls and within gender for same- and opposite-sex parents. There were numerous statistically significant relationships between both the leisure characteristics of parents and the play styles of their children and family characteristics and children's play styles. On the other hand, we found no relationships between parents' leisure attitudes and the play styles of their children. In general, more relationships were found between parent's leisure and boys' play than was the case for girls, and the majority of relationships tended to be cross-sex typed. Certain types of play appeared to be more influenced by the leisure satisfaction of parents than by their leisure behavior, while the reverse was true for other play styles. Finally, family characteristics appeared to be as important for children's playfulness as the leisure satisfaction or behavior of their parents.

While many of the relationships that we found (see Barnett and Chick, 1986, for a summary) between playfulness and family characteristics are well grounded in previous research, the theoretical foundations for the relationships that emerged between parents' leisure and the playfulness of their children are more tenuous. Nevertheless, the study did provide good evidence that at least some aspects of the "expressive atmosphere" provided by parents through their own leisure appear to be transmitted to their children. Whether the play styles thus inculcated then result in similar or related leisure behavior, satisfactions, or attitudes when the children reach adulthood is an open question. Thus, this study tells us something about possible processes of play-leisure socialization, but nothing about outcomes. Finally, it also does not address the question of whether styles and/or the degree of playfulness among children influence the leisure of their parents. By their very nature, correlational studies are of little value in assessing directions of influence, and the assumption that cultural information flows solely, or even predominantly, from parents to children or from the old to the young is one perpetrated, of course, by adults.

Summary of Findings

Virtually all of the studies mentioned above are either purely descriptive in character or correlational. The correlational studies generally used play as the independent variable, while aspects of development—cognitive, linguistic, social, et. cetera—have been regarded as the dependent variable(s). In studies of play and enculturation, both may be regarded as dependent variables, possibly covarying with some other variables or variables. Considering the excerpt from Wilson quoted at the beginning of this paper, it is evident that the studies of play and development or of play and enculturation cited above do not conform to his ideal character of western science—they ignore the problem of atomic units of analysis. In developmental studies, for example, various kinds of instrumentals are used to record or measure play, and whatever units these instruments measure are simply correlated with the measurement units used to gauge development, typically from some other kind of scale (see Fisher, 1992, for examples).

In studies of play and enculturation, the units of analysis problem may even be more severe, and appearances can be deceiving. For example, if children in a society wherein hunting is important for subsistence play with toy bows and arrows while adults use real bows and arrows in the hunt, the play and the "real" activities may appear to be homologous and the enculturative effects of the play are seemingly obvious. The problem is that children in societies where bows and arrows are no longer used for subsistence level hunting many also play with toy bows and arrows. Here, the enculturative aspects of this variety of play are much less obvious (cf. Sutton-Smith and Roberts, 1981). In correlational studies this problem can be alleviated somewhat by avoiding direct comparison of what are presumably the same activities among both children and adults. Instead, measures of play styles of children may be compared with affective characteristics of leisure or actual leisure behavior of adults (e.g., Barnett and Chick, 1986). Nevertheless, we are still left with the old reminder, "correlation does not imply causation." As pointed out by Sutton-Smith and Roberts (1981) in regard to play and other cultural variables, "We may assume either that these variables truly antecede play and are necessary to it, or that these variables and play are implicated in some other pattern of variables that is not determined by this analysis" (p. 436).

The methodological criticisms noted by Scott and Willits (1989) with respect to the child leisure–adult leisure studies are also significant, though their own study appears to support the findings of earlier research. At least one other criticism can be leveled, as well. The meaning of activities may change for participants over time or may be different for individuals at different life stages. Chick and Roberts (1986) found that the basic natures of games change for players as they become more expert. For example, a beginning pool player almost always approaches the game as one of physical skill, sometimes with elements of luck.[5] With increasing expertise, the skill elements of the game become no less important but become less the focus of play as strategic elements come to the fore (Roberts and Chick, 1979; Chick and Roberts, 1986). Similarly, a neophyte may regard poker as primarily a game of chance, rather than strategy, a situation that a veteran player will quickly exploit. So the same game may have vastly different qualities for beginners as opposed to veterans and be pursued for different reasons. It is very likely that the same is true of the outdoor and other activities engaged in by the informants in the child leisure–adult leisure studies reviewed above. In fact, most leisure researchers would now be uncomfortable with operationalizing leisure simply by listing activities without referring to the meaning of those activities for participants. Activities as units of analysis are handy, but incomplete. Finally, the child leisure–adult leisure studies focused on later childhood and adolescence, beyond the age of six for the most part. Socialization and enculturation begin at birth and though they continue through the life span, a substantial portion of the cultural learning that individuals acquire occurs prior to late childhood or adolescence.

UNITS OF ANALYSIS

This brings us to the second part of the question posed in the introduction to this paper. Both the physical and the biological sciences are resplendent with hierarchically organized systems of relatively discrete units: such things as galaxies, stars, elements, molecules, and atoms in the former; and species, individual organisms, and genes in the latter. Unfortunately, the social and behavioral sciences lack such hierarchical order and deterministic comportment. Actually, in certain ways, the physical and biological worlds are messier than they first appear. Combining atoms into molecules typically results in substances with emergent properties utterly unlike those of the constituent elements. Water is a common example. Though a molecule of hydrogen and oxygen, it has physical properties completely different from either of its atomic parents. Further, when we try to study water in motion we discover yet more emergent properties, some of which may be inherently non-deterministic and unpredictable. The situation in an ecosystem of living and nonliving entities is even more complicated. Hence, it is not difficult to understand that the units of analysis problem has plagued the social and behavioral sciences or that our ability to predict human behavior except in the most general ways has been abysmal.

Nevertheless, any researcher who chooses to compare behaviors or to explain or predict behavior must at some point face the units of analysis problem. What is the content of socialization or enculturation and what are the units in which that content comes? The answer to the first part of the question, of course, is that culture is what is enculturated, but that is not much of an answer. The fact is that studies of socialization, enculturation, or cultural learning in some other guise have simply not dealt with the problem of what it is that is being enculturated. For example, a recent article on "cultural learning" by Tomasello, Kruger, and Ratner (1993) generated thirty-two peer commentaries and an author's response. But the issue of units of analysis was broached by only one of the commentary authors (Gabora, 1993) and not at all by the authors in their target article or their response. With this one exception, neither the authors of the target article nor of the commentaries specify what is actually learned in the process of cultural learning, except to indicate that it is "behavior and information" (Tomasello et al., 1993, p. 495).

Studies of socialization and enculturation have so far ignored the units by which cultural information is transmitted, so we must seek guidance elsewhere. Instead of asking what it is that is being passed from parents to children, from the older to the younger, among peers, or, in the most general sense, from one who has information to another who lacks it, we might ask instead what is it that changes when a culture variegates through processes such as invention and assimilation. How is cultural information that is passed along to others, either among individuals of the same generation or between succeeding generations, packaged or encoded?

The Units of Culture

Some thirty years ago Marvin Harris (1964) attempted to isolate the units of culture. He set out to identify "cultural things" with "the assumption that it is desirable to bestow upon them an epistemological status logically equivalent to the status of the entities which are the object of inquiry in the physical sciences" (p. 3). The name for the "smallest cultural unit" chosen by Harris was "actone," a term borrowed from psychologists Barker and Wright (1955). For Harris, an actone was "a label for very small or 'molecular' behavior bits," and consists "of a bit of body motion *and* an environmental effect produced by that motion" (p. 36). Further, neither the motion nor the effect can fall below an observer's visual or auditory threshold, and all observers must agree that an actone has occurred when, in fact, it has occurred. Harris then grouped actones into an hierarchical system that included episodes, episode chains, nodes, and nodal chains.

Harris's painstaking approach to the units of analysis problem had little impact in anthropology and now has been all but forgotten. But, as much as anything else, his effort reflects Harris's continuing efforts to keep anthropology scientific (with natural science as the model) in the face of what he perceives to be a rising tide of humanist, interpretivist, and symbolic perspectives in the field. Later work, in which Harris demarcated his cultural materialist agenda (e.g., Harris, 1979), has been much more enduring, though Harris himself appears to regard his efforts as a lonely battle against the exponents of antiscience whom he now perceives to be ascendant in anthropology. In his later work, however, Harris has not persisted in discussing the minimal units of culture.

Durham (1991) provides an excellent review of other units of culture that have been proposed "that are capable of replication and thus of sequential transformation" (p. 187). The most common unit that he found was "idea." This, he suggested, has several attractive features:

> ideas have conceptual reality, they are socially transmitted, and they can be organized and structured into full, coherent systems of thought. In addition,

provided they are successfully transmitted through time, ideas can acquire their own social history. (p. 188)

But, Durham concludes, "idea" is really too general and includes such unwanted components as strictly individual thoughts and undesirable connotations including ideals, essences, and patterns.

Another approach to the problem has taken place in the context of asking whether culture affords a second system of information inheritance that can be distinguished from the genes, the presumed unit of biological inheritance (Durham, 1991). While this disjunction of culture and the gene is often taken for granted, it has not gone undisputed. Flinn and Alexander (1982), for example, challenged the notion that culture and genes provide distinct units of inheritance or that the mechanisms by which these units are transmitted are distinct. They asserted that the units of cultural evolution are specific phenotypic properties of the organism, which they termed "traits" (Durham, 1991, p. 33). For them, a trait is never exclusively cultural or genetic. The transmission of traits depends on environmental influences, the genetic integrity of the organism, and the organism's history of genetic selection. So, for Flinn and Alexander, traits encompass both genes *and* culture. Cavalli-Sforza and Feldman (1981), on the other hand, do distinguish cultural transmission from genetic inheritance, referring to "cultural traits" (p. 7) as "traits that are learned by any process of nongenetic transmission, whether by imprinting, conditioning, observation, imitation, or as a result of direct teaching" (p. 73).

Lumsden and Wilson (1981) propose the basic unit of culture to be the "culturgen," which is defined as any member of "an array of transmissable behaviors, mentifacts, and artifacts" (p. 7) that may be in the possession of a particular population. "Mentifacts," they assert, are "mental constructs having little or no direct correspondence with reality" (p. 27). This part of their definition of the culturgen is offputting to Durham (1991), inasmuch as he prefers an ideational view of culture; to regard ideational phenomena as having little "correspondence with reality" is hardly palatable when they form the basis for one's concept of culture.

Other units that Durham (1991) found in the literature include " 'belief,' 'thought,' 'rule,' 'value,' 'principle,' 'premise,' 'postulate,' 'instruction,' and 'concept,' " (p. 188). These are rejected much on the same grounds as "idea." Durham then proposes a minimum set of properties for a useful "unit of culture." It will:

> (1) consist of information that actually or potentially guides behavior; (2) accommodate highly variable kinds, quantities, and ways of organizing information; and (3) demarcate bodies of information that are, in fact, differentially transmitted as coherent, functional units. (p. 188)

Durham (1991) regarded two cultural units to be capable of meeting the above conditions: the "symbol" and the "meme." A symbol, for Durham, is "any vehicle for the transmission of socially meaningful information" (p. 188). The meme was originally used by Dawkins (1976) and is held to be "the unit of information that is conveyed from one brain to another during cultural transmission" (Durham, 1991, p. 188). Of the two, Durham selected "meme" because "symbol" is used in everyday parlance, and thus has a priori connotations, and because there are some appropriate antecedent usages of "meme" or of similar terms, such as "mneme," "mnemotype," "mnemon," and "neme" (see Durham, 1991, for a review of these terms).

Durham takes the term *meme* "to represent actual units of socially transmitted information, regardless of their form, size, and internal organization" (p. 189). Further, he divides alternative forms of memes into two categories. The first of these, the "holomeme," is a more inclusive group that consists of all variants, including latent or unexpressed forms, of a given meme while the second, the "allomeme," refers to a "subset of holomemes that are actually used as guides to behavior by at least some members of a population in at least some circumstances" (p. 189). Durham provides several examples of allomemes, including different sects of religious thought that may coexist within a population, differing conceptions of how long a post partum sex taboo should be, and differing techniques for subsistence procurement. He notes that these examples imply varying information content in the allomemes.

Rambo (1991) lacks Durham's confidence in the concept of the meme. He indicates that the understanding of cultural evolution in terms of fundamental cultural units of selection

> is constrained by the lack of even the approximation of an adequate description of the nature of such a unit. The meme and its equivalents are still at best metaphorical suggestions. Much more work will be required to convert this idea into an empirically useful construct. Development of understanding of problems of variation, selection, and transmission is in large measure dependent of progress in defining the unit of selection. (p. 90)

Further, he states that:

> Formulation of a theoretically plausible, and empirically usable, characterization of a unit for storage and transmission of cultural information is, in my view, the major task that must be completed before further advance can occur in the study of cultural evolutionary processes. (p. 69)

So, according to Rambo, we currently lack a unit of cultural transmission, but in order to make any headway in the study of cultural evolution, we must have one. If he is correct, then his conclusion must be taken into account in looking at the information transmission that takes place during the processes of socialization and enculturation, as well.

Boyd and Richerson (1985), on the other hand, reject the notion that culture is somehow encoded as discrete "particles" (p. 37–38). They regard Dawkins's (1976) "meme" (and, thus, presumably Durham's [1991] use of the same term) and Lumsden and Wilson's "culturgen" as examples of the particulate view of cultural information.[6] They believe that it is possible to construct a "cogent, plausible theory of cultural evolution" (pp. 37–38) without the need to refer to particles of culture that can be transmitted to others through socialization and/or be altered by various cultural processes. Rather than proposing some abstract unit of culture, for them social learning involves the transmission of "stable behavioral dispositions" (p. 40).[7]

Other Approaches to the Units of Culture Problem

The search for and analysis of culture patterns has been part and parcel of anthropological research for many years. Kroeber (1948) referred to a particular type of culture pattern as the "systemic pattern" and defined it as

> a system or complex of cultural material that has proved its utility as a system and therefore tends to cohere and persist as a unit: it is modifiable superficially, but modifiable only with difficulty as to its underlying plan. . . . What distinguishes these systemic patterns of culture—of well-patterned systems, as they might also be called—is a specific interrelation of their component parts, a nexus that holds them together strongly, and tends to preserve the basic plan. (pp. 312–13)

Kroeber gave plow agriculture, monotheism, the alphabet, and the *kula* ring, a system of economic exchange among certain Melanesian groups, as examples of systemic patterns. To these examples, Roberts and Chick (1979) added games while Romney and Weller (1989) included patterns of kinship.

Roberts and Chick and their colleagues (Roberts and Chick, 1979; Roberts, Chick, Stephenson, and Hyde, 1981; Roberts, Golder, and Chick, 1980; Chick and Roberts, 1987) developed a technique that they termed "behavioral space analysis" to analyze aspects of systemic culture patterns. Each systemic pattern is accompanied by a "high concordance linguistic code," that is, an aggregation of linguistic tags or labels that refer to particular behaviors associated with the pattern. Moreover, the high concordance linguistic code is well known to individuals who are familiar with the pattern. Roberts and Chick provided procedures for eliciting the elements of linguistic codes from individuals familiar with cultural patterns and then representing them in hierarchical and spatial models that display the structure of the patterns.

In three of their studies (Roberts and Chick, 1979; Roberts, Golder, and Chick, 1980; Chick and Roberts, 1987) Roberts and Chick and their colleagues examined how patterns differed for individuals who had greater or lesser degrees of cultural competence in them. Experts had more sophisticated knowledge of the patterns (which happened to be playing eight-ball pool, piloting a P-3 antisubmarine patrol plane, and operating a metal lathe), as would be expected. But, in addition, it was found that cognitive and affective aspects of behaviors that were known to both experts and nonexperts differed depending on expertise. These results suggest that cultural knowledge (among peers, in these cases) can be studied using this technique. The units of analysis problem is approached hierarchically: total culture patterns are broken down into systemic patterns, which in turn are analyzed by means of their constituent high concordance linguistic codes.

Behavioral space analysis has most recently been used by Santos-Acuin and Pelto (1992) to analyze the daily activities of a sample of Filipino mothers. Several behaviors that involve either child care or, possibly, child socialization, such as "wash kids," "feed kids," "put kid(s) to sleep," "care for kids," and "play with kids" were examined. Santos-Acuin and Pelto found that the activities of the mothers could be roughly grouped into "housework" (which included, incidentally, "taking care of husband"), "child care," and "self-care." This particular utilization of behavioral space analysis does not involve either a systemic culture pattern or a high concordance linguistic code, as discussed above, but what Barsalou (1983) has termed an "ad hoc category," that is, a category of things or events that is not "natural," such as the category of "birds," but that is created for a particular goal or understanding, such as "things to take on a camping trip." Similarly, the activities or events that comprise socialization or enculturation probably do not constitute either a systemic pattern or a high concordance linguistic code but should be recognizable as part of an ad hoc category. Examination of the organization of activities and behaviors that are constitutive of socialization/enculturation, in general, and of play as part of socialization/enculturation, in particular, should thus be amendable to behavioral space analysis. Although the technique has been used to compare the cultural competence of experts and nonexperts that presumably result from socialization and enculturation, it is not clear at this time how it might be used to evaluate or compare the effects of socialization and enculturation across time.

CONCLUSION

Brian Sutton-Smith has often stated that the only thing that play prepares the child for is more play. In the context provided by the studies cited above, we may reasonably ask whether this is true only for the short term, that is, child's play leads only to more child's play, or whether it holds for the long term, as well. If the latter case is correct, as is implied by the quote from Sutton-Smith at the beginning of this paper, then we may infer that play is important in the socialization of adult leisure. Regrettably, the research reviewed above does not provide conclusive evidence for this inference.

The child leisure–adult leisure studies reviewed earlier are suspect on both conceptual and methodological grounds and, in any case, show that only about 50 percent of the leisure activities engaged in by adults were initiated in late childhood or adolescence. This means, of course, that about 50 percent were not. Further, since only activities in which the adult informants were involved at the time of the research were measured, the enculturative outcomes of the numerous activities common in children's play but rare in adult leisure (e.g., children's games, play with toys) were not subject to evaluation. Given these and the other objections to this line of research that were noted above, it is difficult to put much faith in direct comparisons of lists of activities presumably initiated in childhood and continued through adulthood. An alternative explanation for the findings of the child leisure–adult leisure studies is that general play styles are learned in childhood and that these are then manifested in adult leisure (cf. Barnett and Chick, 1986). Some of the activities enjoyed by adults may be the same as those engaged in earlier, while others may differ. But all, or most, may manifest aspects of the play styles acquired during childhood.

The correlational studies cited avoid the units of analysis problem by bypassing it; no assumption is made that children are inculcated with some sort of particulate units of culture (i.e., "play memes") that are later manifested in their behavior (i.e., "leisure memes"). Studies of this kind permit fallback to a position, such as that of Boyd and Richerson (1985), wherein particulate units are not regarded as essential to the study of the relationship between childhood play and adult leisure. The "stable behavioral dispositions" that they hold to be the content of enculturation appear to be similar to what were termed "themes" in older discussions of cultural transmission (e.g., Opler, 1945). Though the study of Barnett and Chick (1986) was not intended to deal with cultural themes, the relationships between kinds of playfulness among children and affective characteristics of the leisure of their parents could be thought of as thematic in nature. The series of cross-cultural studies by Roberts, Sutton-Smith, and their colleagues, cited earlier, were similar in that they were concerned with the inculcation of apparently important cultural themes, including achievement, obedience, responsibility, and honesty, and the kinds of games extant in cultures. Future research could be designed to explicitly examine themes common to the play of children and the leisure of their parents or of others in enculturating roles. At its best, such research would be longitudinal.

Though Durham (1991), Lumsden and Wilson (1981), Rambo (1991), and others are searching for fundamental units of culture that can be transmitted among individuals and are potentially modifiable over time, their quests have not produced any so far that clearly have empirical utility. The method of "behavioral space analysis," developed by Roberts and Chick (1979) produces systems of linguistically coded behavior packages that seem to meet Durham's minimal set of properties for a useful culture unit. That is, the high concordance linguistic codes that characterize systemic culture patterns (1) appear to guide behavior, (2) accommodate variable kinds of information, and (3) demarcate information that is transmitted as coherent and functional units (cf. Durham, 1991; Roberts and Chick, 1979). Moreover, these high concordance linguistic codes tend to remain stable if the patterns themselves do not change over time. On the other hand, if the patterns do change, so do the linguistic codes associated with them. Nevertheless, though comparisons of the cultural control of systemic patterns by individuals of different levels of skill are easily managed using the technique, there have been no attempts to date to generalize the methodology to studies of socialization nor to any comparisons that are conceptually longitudinal.

It is possible that behavioral space analysis could be refined so that it would be useful for the study of socialization and enculturation, generally, and for research on the relationship between the play of children and their subsequent leisure as adults. It is also possible that further refinement of some possible unit of cultural information, along the lines of the meme or the culturgen, may prove to be an empirically useful construct, rather than just an interesting metaphor. In fact, Dawkins's (1976) and Durham's (1991) meme, Boyd and Richerson's (1985) stable behavioral disposition, and Roberts and Chick's (1979) high concordance linguistic code seem to have a lot in common, and it may be that further consideration, including empirical operationalization, of these concepts will result in a consensus unit of cultural transmission. As of now, however, Wilson's (1992) "true grail" remains elusive.

If Sutton-Smith is correct in saying that play prepares the child for more play and, moreover, that early involvement in games leads to a later interest in games, as in his case, then it is remarkable that so little research effort has been directed at the child play–adult leisure relationship. If only through correlational techniques (e.g., Barnett and Chick, 1986), the initial means to begin such a program of study appear to be at hand. Such research would surely contribute to knowledge of the enculturative aspects of children's play and, more generally, to the understanding of the nature of play and of culture itself.

NOTES

1. Schwartzman (1978) points out that in practice it is difficult to distinguish socialization and enculturation. She, therefore, chose to use the term *socialization* to refer to both processes. However, the term *enculturation* appears to us to better capture the idea of cultural learning or the transmission of cultural information, while

socialization connotes the process by which individuals learn to interact appropriately with other members of their society. The difference, if there is one, is subtle and one that cannot always be made easily. Hence, we will use both terms interchangeably in this paper to refer to the processes by which cultural information is transmitted and received, thereby permitted the learning of culturally appropriate behavior.

2. Salamone did include such studies under the categories of "Ethnographies" and "Developmental Studies." Apparently there simply were not enough studies of the socializing/enculturative effects of lay to warrant a separate category.

3. Neither "youth" nor "childhood" were operationalized in the study and appear to be used interchangeably.

4. They were also asked to recall their behavior over the recent past. While this may not be quite so problematic as recall of the activities of one's childhood or youth, research on the reliability of recall data casts doubt on this information, as well (see Bernard, Killworth, Kronenfeld, and Sailer, 1984, for a review of research on the reliability of retrospective data).

5. Technically, pool has no element of luck or chance as defined by Roberts, Arth, and Bush (1959). That is, outcomes are not influenced by either a randomization device or by nonrational guesses. Many players, however, regard a "slop" shot, wherein a ball is pocketed by accident, as due to chance when, in fact, it is simply the result of unskillful play.

6. It is difficult to tell whether Dawkins (1976) actually thinks of memes as particulate. He indicates that memes may appear to be nonparticulate (pp. 209–10).

7. As with the use of the term *social learning* in the article by Tomasello et al. (1993) and the commentaries on it, we regard "social learning" as used here by Boyd and Richerson to be synonymous with the term *socialization*. Boyd and Richerson (1985) define social learning as "the nongenetic transfer of patterns of skill, thought, and feeling from individual to individual in a population or society" (p. 34).

REFERENCES

Allison, M. T. (1982). Sport, culture, and socialization. *International Review of Sport Sociology, 17*(4) 11–37.

Bandura, A. (1986). *Social foundations of thought and action.* Englewood Cliffs, NJ: Prentice Hall.

Barash, D. P. (1977). *Sociobiology and behavior.* New York: Elsevier.

Barker, R., & Wright, H. (1955). *Midwest and its children.* New York: Harper and Row.

Barnett, L. A. (1990). The developmental benefits of play. *Journal of Leisure Research, 22*, 138–53.

Barnett, L. A., & Chick, G. E. (1986). Chips off the ol' block: Parents' leisure and their children's play. *Journal of Leisure Research, 18*, 266–83.

Barry, H. C., III, & Roberts, J. M. (1972). Infant socialization and games of chance. *Ethology, 11*, 296–308.

Barsalou, L. W. (1983). Ad hoc categories. *Memory & Cognition, 11*, 211–27.

Bernard, H. R., Killworth, P. D., Kronenfeld, D., & Sailer, L. (1984). The problem of informant accuracy: The validity of retrospective data. *Annual Review of Anthropology, 13*, 495–517.

Block, J. H., & King, N. R. (1987). *School play: A source book*. New York: Teachers College Press.

Boyd, R., & Richerson, P. J. (1985). *Culture and the evolutionary process*. Chicago: University of Chicago Press.

Cavalli-Sforza, L. L., & Feldman, M. W. (1981). *Cultural transmission and evolution: A quantitative approach*. Princeton: Princeton University Press.

Chick, G. E., & Roberts, J. M. (1986). Strategy and competence: Perceived change in the determinants of game outcomes. In K. Blanchard, W. W. Anderson, G. E. Chick, & E. P. Johnsen (Eds.), *The many faces of play* (pp. 255–64). Champaign, IL: Human Kinetics Publishers.

Chick, G. E., & Roberts, J. M. (1987). Lathe craft: A study in "part" appreciation. *Human Organization, 46*, 305–17.

Dawkins, R. (1976). *The selfish gene*. New York: Oxford University Press.

Durham, W. H. (1991). *Coevolution: Genes, culture, and human diversity*. Stanford: Stanford University Press.

Eifermann, R. (1970). Cooperation and egalitarianism in kibbutz children's games. *Human Relations, 23*, 579–87.

Ember, C. R., & Ember, M. (1988). *Anthropology* (5th ed.). Englewood Cliffs, NJ: Prentice Hall.

Finkelstein, B. (1987). Historical perspectives on children's play in school. In J. H. Block & N. R. King (Eds.), *School play: A source book* (pp. 3–15). New York: Teachers College Press.

Fisher, E. P. (1992). The impact of play on development: A meta-analysis. *Play and Culture, 5*, 159–81.

Flinn, M. V., and Alexander, R. D. (1981). Culture theory: the developing synthesis from biology. *Human Ecology, 10*, 383–400.

Fortes, M. (1970, orig. 1938). Social and psychological aspects of education in Taleland. In J. Middleton (Ed.), *From child to adult*. Garden City, NY: Natural History Press, pp. 14–74.

Gabora, L. M. (1993). Cultural learning as the transmission mechanism in an evolutionary process. *Behavioral and Brain Sciences, 16*, 519.

Gottfried, A. W., & Brown, C. C. (1986). *Play interactions: The contribution of play materials and parental involvement to children's development*. Lexington, MA: Lexington Books.

Groos, K. (1898). *The play of animals*. London: Chapman and Hall.

———. (1901). *The play of man*. New York: Appleton.

Harkness, S., & Super, C. M. (1986). The cultural structuring of children's play in a rural African community. In K. Blanchard (Ed.), *The many faces of play* (pp. 96–103). Champaign, IL: Human Kinetics Publishers.

Harris, M. (1964). *The nature of cultural things*. New York: Random House.

———. (1975). *Culture, people, nature: An introduction to general anthropology*. New York: Thomas Y. Crowell.

———. (1979). *Cultural materialism: The struggle for a science of culture*. New York: Random House.

Heine, M. K. (1984). *The enculturative function of play behavior and games among the Tlingit Indians of southeast Alaska*. Master's thesis, University of Western Ontario.

Hess, R. (1970). Social class and ethnic influence upon socialization. In P. H. Mussen (Ed.), *Carmichael's manual of child psychology* (vol. 2). New York: Wiley.

Huizinga, J. (1955). *Homo ludens: A study of the play element in culture*. Boston: Beacon Press.

Johnsen, E. P. (1991). Searching for the social and cognitive outcomes of children's play: A selective second look. *Play and Culture, 4*, 201–13.

Kelly, J. R. (1974). Socialization toward leisure: A developmental approach. *Journal of Leisure Research, 6*, 181–93.

———. (1977). Leisure socialization: Replication and extension. *Journal of Leisure Research, 9*, 121–32.

Kroeber, A. L. (1948). *Anthropology: Culture patterns and processes*. New York: Harcourt, Brace & World.

Lancy, D. F. (1975). The role of games in the enculturation of children. Paper presented at the 74th Annual Meeting of the American Anthropological Association, San Francisco, CA, December 2–6.

————. (1976). The play behavior of Kpelle children during rapid cultural change. In D. F. Lancy & B. A. Tindall (Eds.), *The anthropological study of play: Problems and prospects* (pp. 72–79). West Point, NY: Leisure Press.

Leiberman, J. N. (1967). *Playfulness: Its relationship to imagination and creativity.* New York: Academic Press.

Lenski, G., & Lenski, J. (1982). *Human societies: An introduction to macrosociology* (5th ed.). New York: McGraw-Hill.

Lumsden, C., & Wilson, E. O. (1981). *Genes, mind, and culture.* Cambridge, MA: Harvard University Press.

Martin, N. T. (1982). Socialization through traditional play and games in the Hanahan society of Buka. In J. T. Parrington, T. Orlick, & J. H. Samela (Eds)., *Sport in perspective* (pp. 185–92). Ottawa: Sport in Perspective.

McDowell, J. (1976). Riddling and enculturation: A glance at the cerebral child. *Working Papers in Sociolinguistics, 36.*

McGuire, F. A., Dottavio, F. D., & O'Leary, J. T. (1987). The relationship of early life experiences to later life leisure involvement. *Leisure Sciences, 9*, 251–57.

Mead, G. H. (1932). *Mind, self, and society.* Chicago: University of Chicago Press.

Moore, R. (1986). *Children's domain: Play and place in child development.* Beckenham, Kent: Croom Helm.

Opler, M. E. (1945). Themes as dynamic forces in culture. *American Journal of Sociology, 51*, 198–206.

Patrick, C. (1945). Relation of childhood and adult leisure activities. *Journal of Social Psychology, 21*, 65–79.

Rambo, A. T. (1991). The study of cultural evolution. In A. T. Rambo & K. Gillogly (Eds.), *Profiles in cultural evolution: Papers from a conference in honor of Elman R. Service* (pp. 23–109). Ann Arbor: Anthropological Papers, Museum of Anthropology, University of Michigan.

Raum, O. (1940). *Chaga childhood.* London: Oxford University Press.

Roberts, J. M. (1964). The self-management of cultures. In W. H. Goodenough (Ed.), *Explorations in cultural anthropology* (pp. 433–54). New York: McGraw-Hill.

Roberts, J. M., Arth, M. J., & Bush, R. B. (1959). Games in culture. *American Anthropologist, 61*, 597–605.

Roberts, J. M., & Barry, H. C., III. (1976). Inculcated traits and game-type combinations. In T. T. Craig (Ed.), *The humanistic and mental health aspects of sports, exercise, and recreation* (pp. 5–11). Chicago: American Medical Association.

Roberts, J. M., & Chick, G. E. (1979). Butler County eight ball: A behavioral space analysis. In J. H. Goldstein (Ed.), *Sports, games, and play: Social and psychological viewpoints* (pp. 65–89). Hillsdale, NJ: Lawrence Erlbaum Associates.

Roberts, J. M., Chick, G. E., Stephenson, M., & Hyde, L. L. (1981). Inferred categories for tennis play: A limited semantic analysis. In A. T. Cheska (Ed.), *Play as context* (pp. 181–95). West Point, NY: Leisure Press.

Roberts, J. M., & Cosper, R. L. (1987). Variation in strategic involvement in games for three blue collar occupations. *Journal of Leisure Research, 19*, 131–48.

Roberts, J. M., Golder, T. V., & Chick, G. E. (1980). Judgment, oversight, and skill: A cultural analysis of P-3 pilot error. *Human Organization, 39*, 5–21.

Roberts, J. M., & Sutton-Smith, B. (1962). Child training and game involvement. *Ethology, 1*, 166–85.

Roberts, J. M., Sutton-Smith, B., & Kendon, A. (1963). Strategy in games and folk tales. *Journal of Social Psychology, 61*, 185–99.

Romney, A. K., & Weller, S. C. (1989). Systemic culture patterns and high concordance codes. In R. Bolton (Ed.), *The content of culture: Constants and variants* (pp. 363–81). New Haven, CT: HRAF Press.

Salamone, F. A. (1989). Anthropology and play: A bibliography. *Play and Culture, 2*, 158–81.

Salter, M. A. (1974). *Play: A medium of cultural stability.* Paper presented at the International Seminar on the History of Physical Education and Sport, Vienna, Austria, April 17–20.

Santos-Acuin, C. C., & Pelto, P. P. (1992). Exploration of mother's activities: A multidimensional scale. *Cultural Anthropology Methods Newsletter, 4*(2), 4–5, 10.

Schwartzman, H. B. (1978). *Transformations: The anthropology of children's play.* New York: Plenum Press.

Scott, D., & Willits, F. K. (1989). Adolescent and adult leisure patterns: A 37-year follow-up study. *Leisure Sciences, 11*, 323–35.

Smith, P. K. (1982). Does play matter? Functional and evolutionary aspects of animal and human play. *Behavioral and Brain Sciences, 5*, 139–84.

Sofranko, A. J., & Nolan, M. F. (1972). Early life experiences and adult sports participation. *Journal of Leisure Research, 4*, 6–18.

Sutton-Smith, B. (1976). *The dialectics of play.* Schorndoff, West Germany: Verlag-Hoffman.

———. (1993). A memory of games and some games of memory. In J. Lee (Ed.), *Life before story: The autobiographies of psychologists from a narrative perspective.* New York: Praeger.

Sutton-Smith, B., & Kelly-Byrne, D. (1984). The idealization of play. In P. K. Smith (Ed.), *Play in animals and humans* (pp. 305–22). London: Blackwell.

Sutton-Smith, B., & Magee, M. A. (1989). Reversible childhood *Play and Culture, 2*, 52–63.

Sutton-Smith, B., & Roberts, J. M. (1981). Play, games, and sports. In H. C. Triandis & A. Heron (Eds.), *Handbook of cross-cultural psychology: Developmental psychology*, (vol. 4) (pp. 425–71), Boston: Allyn and Bacon.

Sutton-Smith, B., Roberts, J. M., & Kozelka, R. M. (1963). Game involvement in adults. *Journal of Social Psychology, 60*, 15–30.

Tomasello, M., Kruger, A. C., & Ratner, H. H. (1993). Cultural learning. *Behavioral and Brain Sciences, 16*, 495–552.

Trivers, R. L. (1974). Parent-offspring conflict. *American Zoologist, 14*, 249–64.

Varga, D. (1991). The historical ordering of children's play as a developmental task. *Play and Culture, 4*, 322–33.

Wilson, E. O. (1992). *The diversity of life.* Cambridge, MA: The Belkap Press.

Yoesting, D. R., & Burkhead, D. L. (1973). Significance of childhood recreation experience on adult leisure behavior: An exploratory analysis. *Journal of Leisure Research, 5*, 25–36.

Yoesting, D. R., & Christensen, J. E. (1978). Reexamining the significance of childhood recreation patterns on adult leisure behavior. *Leisure Sciences, 1*, 219–29.

Part II

PLAY AS POWER

4

JOHN W. LOY AND GRAHAM L. HESKETH

Competitive Play on the Plains: An Analysis of Games and Warfare among Native American Warrior Societies, 1800–1850

PERSONAL PROLOGUE

In 1963, during my second year of doctoral study, I became keenly interested in the cross-cultural analysis of play and games as the foundation for an area of study now known as the sociology of sport. At first I was highly frustrated by the apparent lack of literature on the subject. However, I was as excited as a child on Christmas morning when I discovered four papers on a single afternoon written by Brian Sutton-Smith, John M. Roberts, and colleagues: "Games in Culture" (Roberts, Arth and Bush, 1959); "Child Training and Game Involvement" (Roberts and Sutton-Smith, 1962); "Strategy in Games and Folk Tales" (Roberts, Sutton-Smith, and Kendon, 1963); and "Game Involvement in Adults" (Sutton-Smith, Roberts, and Kozelka, 1963). These papers stimulated me to seek out all related publications by Brian and "Jack" Roberts, and I have continued to read their work for over a quarter of a century.

During my last year of doctoral work in 1967 I had the opportunity to meet Brian at an international workshop on the cross-cultural analysis of sport and games held at the University of Illinois, wherein he presented a paper coauthored with Jack entitled "The Cross-Cultural and Psychological Study of Games" (Sutton-Smith and Roberts, 1970). Having just earned my doctorate, I had the pleasure in 1968 of sharing a program with Brian at a symposium on the sociology of sport held at the University of Wisconsin where he addressed the topic of the two cultures of games (Sutton-Smith, 1969). And in 1969 I was a fellow participant at an international seminar for the sociology of sport in Macolin, Switzerland, where Brian discussed what he termed the "sporting balance" (Sutton-Smith, 1971).

Although I first met Brian in 1967, I did not meet his colleague Jack Roberts until 1975 when the three of us were participants at a national conference, "The Humanistic and Mental Health Aspects of Sports, Exercise and Recreation," held in Atlantic City. Brian gave a paper entitled "Current

73

Research and Theory on Play, Games and Sports" (Sutton-Smith, 1976); and Jack presented a paper entitled "Inculcated Traits and Game-Type Combinations: A Cross-Cultural View" (Roberts and Barry, 1976). I am greatly indebted to Brian for many personal and professional reasons, but I am perhaps most indebted to him for introducing me to Jack Roberts. This introduction led to my receiving an Andrew Mellon Postdoctoral Fellowship from the University of Pittsburgh in 1976, where I had the opportunity to interact with Jack Roberts on a daily basis for eight months, and where I became close friends with Garry Chick, who was then Jack's doctoral student in the Department of Anthropology.

Until Jack's death in 1990, I eagerly anticipated attending the annual meetings of the Association for the Anthropological Study of Play (TAASP) to have the chance of spending time with Brian, Jack, and Garry. As playful comrades in arms we shall forever be linked by the fact that each of us served a stint as president of TAASP. More important to note is the fact that Brian was a constant catalyst and a facilitator for activities and projects of mutual interest amongst the four of us. In short, Brian has greatly influenced my life and career in terms of the social correlates and consequences of collegiality over three decades.

In a more direct sense, I have specifically drawn upon Brian's work in the following ways. First, I incorporated many of his early concepts of play and games in my initial effort to describe the nature of sport (Loy, 1968). Second, I included his paper with John M. Roberts and Robert M. Kozelka on game involvement in adults in the first anthology in sport sociology (Loy and Kenyon, 1969). Third, I drew upon several of Brian's studies concerning ludic socialization in my chapter with Alan Ingham entitled "Play, Games and Sport in the Psychosociological Development of Children and Youth" (Loy and Ingham, 1973). Fouth, I developed a theory of sport spectatorship largely based on the conflict-enculturation hypothesis of Brian and Jack Roberts (Loy, 1981). Fifth, I have tried to work toward a sportive theory of play (Sutton-Smith, 1980) with reference to my particular interest in the agon motif (i.e., the pursuit of prestige through physical prowess) and Brian's seminal ideas about games as models of power (Sutton-Smith, 1989).

Because of my professional commitments to the sociology of sport per se, I have seldom had time to explore my initial interests in the cross-cultural analysis of play and games stimulated by my reading of Brian's early work. Fortunately, however, a few years ago I was lucky enough to convince Graham Hesketh, a graduate student from England, to examine the agon motif in the context of nineteenth-century Plains Indians societies for his master's thesis. This chapter in honor of Brian draws heavily from Graham's master's thesis and reflects I think that part of Brian's work showing the contesting, sportive, and status-seeking functions of play.

Last, but not least, I point out that Brian through the years has made constant reference to role reversals in the context of play and, thus, I believe it is symbolic that he began his professional career in New Zealand while I am completing my professional career in Aotearoa—"the land of the long white cloud."

J.W.L.

INTRODUCTION

The Agon Motif

The period from 1800 to 1850 has been called the "Golden Age" or "Climax Period" of Plains Indian Culture (see, for example, Hoebel, 1978; Morford and Clark, 1976). At first glance, it may appear somewhat misleading to speak of a single Plains Indian culture, in that, dependent upon choice of classification, twenty-seven to thirty-three tribes representative of six or seven language stocks resided in the Great Plains region of North America (see tables 4.1–4.3). However, all Plains tribes constituted warrior societies having an agon motif, and all were capable of communiating with one another, with varying degrees of success through a commonly shared sign language. Thus for present purposes we refer to the "composite culture" of thirty-three Plains Indian tribes during the first half of the nineteenth century, with special reference to the agon motif as a dominant theme of Plains Indian culture.

The essence of what we term the *agon motif* is captured in Huizinga's observation that:

> From the life of childhood right up to the highest achievement of civilization one of the strongest incentives to pefection, both individual and social, is the desire to be praised and honoured for one's excellence. In praising another each praises himself. We want the satisfaction of having done something well. Doing something well means doing it better than others. In order to excel one must prove one's excellence; in order to merit recognition, merit must be made manifest. Competition serves to give proof of superiority. (1955, p. 63)

While Huizinga demonstrated that many diverse forms of competition provide ways of showing superiority, he placed particular importance on agonal contests as proving grounds for making merit manifest. Paradigmatic examples of the agonistic themes and agonal contests described by Huizinga are most evident in archetypal warrior societies. Within these societies, "war activity offered the most prestigious avenue for displaying prowess but, since it was limited to contests with 'out-group members' or members of another tribe, athletic contests offered an acceptable substitute for displaying prowess between members of the same tribe or 'in-group' " (Morford and Clark, 1976, p. 164).

Table 4.1   Sample of Plains Indian Tribes

Arapaho	a b c d	Lipan Apache	
Arikara	b c	Mandan	b c d
Assiniboine	a b c	Missouri	b c
Bannock	b	Nez Percé	b d
Blackfoot	a b c d	Northern Shoshone	b
Cheyenne	a b c d	Omaha	b c d
Comanche	a b c d	Osage	b c d
Crow	a b c d	Oto	b c d
Flatheads	d	Pawnee	b c d
Gros Ventre	a b c d	Plains Cree	b c d
Hidatsa	b c	Plains Ojibwa	b c d
Iowa	b c d	Ponca	b c d
Jicarilla Apache		Sarsi	b c d
Kansa	b c d	—Dakota	a c d
Kiowa	a b c	Sioux—Teton Dakota	a b
Kiowa Apache	a b c	—Eastern Dakota	b
		Ute	b c d
		Witchita	b c d
		Wind River Shoshone	b c

Notes
a. Sample of typical Plains tribes from *The American Indian* (p. 218) by C. Wissler, 1922. New Haven: Oxford University Press.
b. Sample of Plains tribes from *North American Indians of the Plains* (p. 19) by C. Wissler, 1934. New York: Lancaster Press.
c. Sample of Plains tribes from *Indians of the Plains* (p. 4) by R. H. Lowie, 1954. New York: McGraw Hill.
d. Sample of Plains tribes documented by Human Relations Area Files (HRAF) at the University of Illinois.

We seek to show for our selected sample of Native North American warrior societies that (1) games and warfare were both forms of competitive play; (2) engagement in warfare was the primary avenue for the pursuit of prestige among adult men; (3) involvement in games and athletic activities was the primary avenue for the pursuit of prestige among young men, and the main means of becoming socialized for engagement in warfare; and, finally, (4) the pursuit of prestige through competition in agonal contests was the major strategy for maintaining self-esteem and striving for immortality in Plains Indian warrior societies.

Games and Warfare

Huizinga noted that "ever since words existed for fighting and playing, men have been wont to call war a game"; and contended that "indeed, all fighting

Table 4.2   Geographical Distribution of Plains Indian Tribes

Regional Groups	Specific Plains Indian Tribes	
The Northern Tribes	Assiniboine Blackfoot Crow Gros Ventre Sarsi	Plains-Cree Plains Ojibway (Plains Chippewa) Teton Dakota
The Southern Tribes	Arapaho Cheyenne Comanche Kiowa	Kiowa Apache Lipan Apache Jicarilla Apache
The Village or Eastern Tribes	Arikara Hidatsa Iowa Kansa Mandan Missouri Wichita	Omaha Osage Oto Pawnee Ponca Eastern Dakota
The Plateau of Western Tribes	Bannock Nez Percé Flatheads	Northern Shoshoni Ute Wind River Shoshoni

Note
From *North American Indians of the Plains* (p. 19) by C. Wissler, 1934, New York: Lancaster Press.

that is bound by rules bears the formal characteristics of play by that very limitation" (1955, p. 89). His statements are supported by the anthropological work of Chapple and Coon (1942) who summarize the linkage between games and warfare as follows:

1. Games constitute a category of play, distinguished by the fact that they take the form of competition between individuals or groups of individuals. . . . They . . . provide at all times a technique for increased interaction and serve as an outlet for this increase when needed. (p. 634)

2. A game canalizes potential conflict between opposing institutions by bringing about interaction at a high frequency but within the rhythmic order imposed by the techniques. (p. 635)

3. When the interaction rate in a game reaches a certain pitch of intensity the game becomes lethal, and when deaths come to be expected we are

Table 4.3   Distribution of Plains Tribes According to Language Stock

Language Stock	Plains Indian Trible Sample[a]	
Algonkian Family	Blackfoot (Piegan-Blood -Northern Blackfoot) Cheyenne Arapaho-Gros Ventre	Plains Cree Plains Ojibwa (Plains Chippewa)
Athabaskan Family	Sarsi	Kiowa Apache Jicarilla Apache Lipan Apache
Caddoan Family	Pawnee-Arikara	Wichita
Kiowan Family	Kiowa	
Siouan Family	Mandan Hidatsa Crow	Dakota-Assiniboin Iowa-Oto-Missouri Omaha-Ponca- Osage-Kansa
Shoshonnean or Uto-Azetecan Family	Northern Shoshone Wind River Shoshone -Comanche	Ute Bannock

Notes

From *Indians of the Plains* (p. 4), R. H. Lowie, 1954, New York: McGraw-Hill.
[a]Hyphenated tribes are those political groups speaking identical or vitually identical languages.

dealing with formalized warfare, which is merely an extension of the games configuration. Familiar examples are formal duels and the rules of chivalry. (p. 635)

Granted the assumption that warfare is an extension of gaming, it logically follows that game involvement can serve as a primary means of socialization for engagement in warfare. Various forms of play and games taken to symbolize hunting and/or warfare not only serve to prepare youth for warrior roles in terms of symbols, strategies, techniques, and technologies of combat, but also in terms of cognitive, mental, and psychological capacities.

Max Weber, for example, stressed the importance of "the game" in feudal ideology for European knights and Japanese samurai as follows:

Originating in an army of warriors for whom the battle between individuals was decisive, feudalism made skillful handling of weapons the object of military education; it had little use for mass discipline to perfect a collectively organized military effort. As a result the feudal style of life incorporated the game as an important means of training that inculcated useful abilities and qualities of character. The game was not a "pastime" but the natural medium in which the physical and psychological capacities of the human organism came alive and became supple. In this form of "training" the spontaneous drives of man found their outlet, irrespective of any division between "body" and "soul" and regardless of how conventionalized the games often became. The knightly strata of medieval Europe and Japan regarded the game as a serious and important aspect of life that had a special affinity with spontaneous artistic interests and helped bar the way to all forms of utilitarian rationality. (Bendix, 1962, p. 364)

In the following section we illustrate how both games and warfare represented "character contests" as well as "physical contests" for Plains Indian men, young and old. We also highlight how in the case of a particular form of warfare, namely, the raid, Plains Indians, like the knightly strata of medieval Europe, often removed considerations of utilitarian rationality in the course of agonal competition.

AGON ON THE PLAINS

Combat and Warfare

Valued Virtues   Athletic, hunting, and warfare activities represented "character contests" for young men and allowed them to display and confirm important moral attributes. A good description of the most valued virtues among Plains Indian warriors is contained in Elkin's (1940) commentary on the Arapaho value system:

> The qualities of personal behavior most prized by the Arapaho were bravery, good judgment, kindness and generosity. Fathers tried to imbue their sons with those qualities. From early manhood, they were judged by their possession of these virtues, and their status and prestige in society varied with the degree to which they demonstrated them. (p. 223)

Similarly, Hassrick (1964) noted for the Lakota Sioux:

> Bravery, Fortitude, Generosity, and Wisdom—these were the virtues which all men were expected to seek. While it was understood that no man could achieve excellence in all of these qualities it was believed that every man should endeavor to attain something of each. (p. 32)

He further observed that:

> Of the four great virtues, bravery was foremost for both men and women. To be considered full of courage, to have a strong heart, was an honor of extreme importance and worth great effort. Acclaim was accorded only to those who had proven themselves. (p. 32).

Other anthropologies have also emphasized that bravery was the central virtue of all Plains Indian tribes. Of the Crow Indians, Wildschut (1960) wrote: "Bravery was greatly admired ... and the warrior with many coups to his name acquired prestige not enjoyed by men of lesser fame" (p. 34). For the Dakota Sioux, Landes (1959) recorded: "Bravery under the circumstances defined as honorable, was ... a criterion of mature responsible maleness" (p. 46).

Associated with the virtue of courage or bravery was the moral quality of fortitude. To the Plains Indians, fortitude was expressed in terms of endurance and reserve; for example, the endurance of pain and physical discomfort, and the ability to show reserve during periods of emotional stress.

The valued virtues were not, of course, separate moral categories, but rather interdependent, as highlighted in the Plains Indian concern for generosity. The most successful warrior or hunter acquired the most items of value, but he was successful not for the number of buffalo he killed or the number of horses he had stolen, but for the amount he gave away.

However, in the final analysis, as Lowie (1935) has stated the case, "Social standing and chieftainship ... were dependent on military prowess; and that was the only road to distinction" (p. 215).

The Glorious Game of War   Evidence suggests that all Plains Indian tribes were, to greater or lesser degrees, involved in a wide range of warring activities. However, most anthropologists agree with Newcombe's (1950) assessment that Plains Indian "warfare was confined primarily to small war parties, raids, forays; that is, conflicts which were brief and usually indecisive" (p. 317). Moreover, most anthropologists agree as well that during the so-called golden Age of Plains Indian culture the horse raid was the most common military operation. Thus, it is highly likely that the descriptions of Plains Indian warfare by several anthropologists as a game or as a sporting contest for social prestige are with respect to the horse raid or similar small-scale military operations.

The following observations highlight the play elements and the ludic nature of small-scale Plains Indian warfare. Erodes (1972) describes Plains Indian warfare as follows:

> For the Plains Indian, the game of war was a glorious sport, and it played a very important role in his life. He did not make war as a white man did. His aim was not to kill or to conquer. The leader of a war party was disgraced if he lost as much as a single man, even if his raid was a success. Rather than risk the life of one of his own band, the leader would often let an enemy get away. (p. 47)

Lowie (1920) explained in a similar manner that "the Plains Indian fought ... above all because fighting was a game worth while because of the social recognition it brought when played according to the rules" (p. 356). He later added that "Plains Indian warfare . . . loomed as an exciting pastime played according to established rules, the danger lending zest to the game" (1940, pp. 221–22). From this perspective, Turney-High (1942) described an actual battle among the Assiniboine as "no more than a mildly dangerous game" (p. 103).

Benedict (1950), with reference to the Plains Indians in general and to the Crow tribe in paticular, observed that:

> Their war parties were ordinarily less than a dozen strong, and the individual acted alone in their simple engagements in such a way that stands at the other pole from the rigid discipline and subordination of modern warfare. Their war was a game in which each individual amassed coups. (p. 89)

The play element in Plains Indian warfare is also noted in accounts of Cheyenne warriors. Hobel (1978) held that:

> The fighting patterns of the Cheyenne established with virtuosities that go far beyond the needs of victory. Display of bravery tends to become an end in itself. Prestige drives override the more limited military requirements for defeat of the enemy. The show-off tends to supersede the mere soldier. War has been transformed into a great game in which scoring against the enemy often takes precedence over killing him. (pp. 76–77)

And Grinnell (1923) contended that:

> The Cheyenne men were all warriors. War was regarded as the noblest of pursuits, the only one for a man to follow; and from earliest youth boys were encouraged to excel in it. They were taught that no pleasure equalled the joy of battle; that success in war brought in its train the respect and admiration of men, women, and children in the tribe; and that the most worthy thing that any man could do was to be brave. It was pointed out that death in battle was not an evil and that such death besides being glorious, protected one from all the miseries which threaten later life and are inevitable to old age. (p. 405)

Although these accounts of Plains Indian warfare as a great game and glorious sport seem perhaps a bit idealistic, there is ample evidence in the graded scales of war honors that different tribes established that Plains Indian warfare was a game or a contest for prestige.

Deeds and Quests for Fame   In promoting the pursuit of prestige, the Plains Indians established elaborate lists of distinctive deeds that were graded according to the degree of difficulty. Six sets or systems of graded war honors are shown in table 4.4. Four of these systems are from the two largest language groups: the Blackfoot and the Cheyenne from the Algonkian family, and the Crow and Ponca from the Siouan family. The latter two sets of honor scales are from the smaller language famlies: the Wichita from the Caddoan family, and the Kiowa from the Kiowan family. A more complete list of war honors for a larger variety of tribes is given in table 4.5. However, this latter list is not based on rank order but merely illustrates the frequency with which deeds were standardized throughout all Plains Indian tribes.

The listings of war honors given in tables 4.4 and 4.5 illustrate that counting coup was often the most prized war honor. *To count coup*—a term handed down from the old French trappers and traders, meaning to strike a blow—consisted of touching with the hand, or with an object held in the hand, some portion of the body of an enemy. Grinnell (1923) described the coup in the Cheyenne tribe in these terms:

> To touch the enemy with something held in the hand, with the bare hand, or with any part of the body, was a proof of bravery—a feat which entitled the man or the boy who did it to the greatest credit.
>
> When an enemy was killed each of those nearest to him tried to be the first to reach him and touch him, usually by striking the body with something held in the hand—a gun, bow, whip, or stick. . . . The chief applause was won by the man who could first touch the fallen enemy. In Indian estimation the bravest act that could be performed was to count coup. (p. 30)

The Plains Indians honored the coup above all else not because of any direct result which accrued from the act itself, but because of the danger which has been successfully overcome in its achievement. To count coup was to court danger and to risk death.

Wallace and Hoebel (1952) explained the Comanche attitude toward the coup as follows:

> The Comanche, in conformity with the general Plains pattern, adhered to institutionalized procedure in giving social recognition of war honors: the practice of counting coup. This was an individual exploit, made in any contact with the enemy, after it had been socially and publicly recognized as worthy of distinction. In some respects it was a rough equivalent of an official citation after a modern engagement. (p. 246)

Coups, then, were deliberate acts performed before witnesses.

As demonstrations of bravery and physical prowess, some tribes recognized more than one coup struck on the same victim by different pesons. For example, the Assiniboine and Arapaho recognized four coups counted on a single enemy, whereas the Crow and Sioux only recognized the first coup on the first enemy slain in battle: "Recognition of plural coups on the same victim was, of course, an efficient way of providing enough coups to meet the cultural demands of the society" (Wallace & Hoebel, 1952, p. 24).

Table 4.4 Examples of Graded War Honor Scales Within Selected Tribes

Algonkian family	
Blackfoor (Piegan)[a]	Cheyenne[b]
1. Capture of an enemy gun	1. Counting first coup
2. Capture of an enemy lance	second coup
3. Capture of an enemy bow	third coup
4. Taking the enemy's life	fourth coup
5. Cutting a tethered horse from tepee	2. Capture of a shield
6. Leading a war party	3. Capture of a gun
7. Acting as a scout	4. Capture of a scalp
8. Capture of a shield	
9. Capture of a war bonnet	
10. Capture of a medicine pipe	
11. Driving off loose horses	

Siouan Family	
Ponca[c]	Ponca[d]
1. Count coup on an unwounded enemy	1. Saving a comrade
2. Count coup on a wounded enemy	2. Counting first coup
	second coup
3. Count coup on a dead enemy	3. Being wounded seriously
4. To kill an enemy	4. Horse stealing
5. To capture enemy horses	5. Most honors on war path
	Brave to kill a foe but this act was not considered on the scale
	Scalping was also recognized.

Siouan famly	Caddoan family
Crow[e]	Witchita[f]
1. Being first to count coup	1. Counting first coup
2. Snatching away a bow or a gun in hand-to-hand combat	2. Killing a foe
3. Theft of a picketed horse in a hostile campe	3. Scalping
4. Planning the raid	4. Scouting

Table 4.4 Examples of Graded War Honor Scales Within Selected Tribes *continued*

Kiowan family
Kiowa[g]

1. Counting the first coup
2. Charging the enemy while one's party was in retreat
3. Rescuing a comrade while one's party was in retreat before a charging enemy.
4. Charging the leading man of the enemy alone was comparable to suicide.

   Lesser credit came from:
5. Killing an enemy
6. Counting second coup
7. Getting wounded during battle in hand-to-hand combat
8. Fighting on foot
9. Counting third and fourth coups
10. Serving as a topadikí
11. Stealing horses

Notes
a. From Blackfoot Social Life (p. 40) by C. Wissler, 1911, *Anthropological Papers of the American Museum of Natural History, 1.*
b. From *The Cheyenne Indians: Their History and Ways of Life, 1,* (p. 36) by G. B. Grinnell, 1923, New Haven: Yale University Press.
c. From *The Omaha Tribe* (p. 439) by A. C. Fletcher & F. LaFleshe, 1911, Washington, D.C.: Bureau of American Ethnology Annual Report 27.
d. From Kansa Organizations (p. 794) by A. Skinner, 1915, *Anthropological Papers of the American Museum of Natural History, 11.*
e. From *The Crow Indians* (p. 216) by R. H. Lowie, 1935, New York: Farrar & Rinehart.
f. From the War Complex of the Plains Indians (p. 426) by M. Smith, 1938, *Proceedings of the American Philosophical Society, 78,* 425–65.
g. From *Law and Status Among the Kiowa Indians* (p-. 61) by J. Richardson, 1940. Monographs of the American Ethnological Society, *1,* New York: J. J. Augustin.

The reason that the first coup was often considered the most meritorious war honor is explained by Kennedy (1961):

> Sometimes an enemy feigned death and drew an ambitious warrior within range of his weapon with fatal results. For that reason, to count the first coup a person risked his life more than the one who shot from a distance.

Thus, a brave man did not carry a weapon that would do harm at a distance: to carry a lance was more creditable than a bow and arrow; a hatchet or war club more creditable than a lance; and, above all, the bravest deed was to go

Table 4.5 The Plains Indian Systems of War Honors

Language Group → Plains Tribes	Algonkian Family						Siouan Family										Caddoon Family			b		c		d
War Honors	Blackfoot	Cheyenne	Arapaho	Gros Ventre	Cree	Ojibwa	Mandan	Hidatsa	Crow	Sioux	Assiniboine	Iowa	Omaha	Ponca	Osage	Kansa	Arikara	Wichita	Pawnee	Sarsi	Apache	Comanche	Shoshone	Kiowa
To count first coup	×	×	×	×			×		×	×	×	×	×	×	×			×	×			×	×	×
To count second coup		×	×				×		×		×	×	×	×	×							×		×
To count third coup		×	×				×		×		×													×
To count fourth coup			×						×		×													×
Coup score dovetails into war honor scale		×							×		×													×
To scalp an enemy	×	×	×	×	×	×	×	×	×	×	×	×	×	×	×	×	×	×	×	×	×	×	×	×
To kill an enemy	×	×	×	×	×	×	×	×	×	×	×	×	×	×	×	×	×	×	×	×	×	×	×	×
To capture enemy horses	×	×	×	×			×	×	×	×	×			×		×						×	×	×
To capture enemy weapons	×	×		×					×	×	×													
To lead victorious war party	×	×	×	×	×	×	×	×	×	×		×	×	×	×	×	×	×	×	×	×	×	×	×
To be wounded in battle				×					×	×	×													×
To be first to scout enemy										×								×						
To charge the enemy while in retreat	×	×		×					×	×												×	×	×

Notes

The data in this table was compiled mainly from The War Complex of the Plains Indians (pp. 425–65) by M. W. Smith, 1938. *Proceedings of the American Philosophical Society,* 78.

a. The Sarsi and Apache tribes belong to the Athabaskan Family.
b. The Comanche and Shoshone belong to the Shoshonean or Uto-Aztecan Family.
c. The Kiowa belong to the Kiowan Family.

into a fight armed with nothing more than a whip or a long stick—often called a "coup stick."

A man's reputation depended upon the number of coups he could accumulate; his coup counter was his virtue. The most notable deed that a man could achieve was to be first to touch or strike a living, unhurt man and to leave him alive.

Chivalrous Contests   The preceding accounts of valued personal qualities, the ludic elements of warfare, and the graded scales of war honors attest that Plains Indians engaged in agonal war for reasons of personal honor and public prestige. Table 4.6 summarizes the main differences between agonal and nonagonal forms of war. Most of the primary features of agonal warfare illustrated in table 4.6 have been highlighted in our discussion to date. A notable exception, however, is the distinctive feature that agonal forms of warfare are governed by norms of fair play. Thus, in concluding our discussion of agon on the plains we want to show how Plains Indian warfare represented chivalrous contests between warriors of equal peer status.

The Plains Indian literature provides many fascinating accounts of fair play on the battlefield. But given spatial limitations, the following account must suffice to show the ethics of Plains Indians warfare. The following account is of an inner-tribal duel between a Cheyenne chief and the Mandan Chief Mah-to-toh-pa, narrated by Catlin (1857) after his visit to a Mandan village:

> At another time, a party of about one hundred and fifty Cheyenne warriors made an assault upon the Mandan village at an early hour one morning, drove off a considerable number of horses, and took one scalp. Man-to-toh-pa took the lead of a party of fifty warriors, all he could at that time muster, and went in pursuit of the enemy. About noon of the second day they came in sight of the Cheyennes. The Mandans seeing their enemy much more numerous than they had expected, were generally disposed to turn back and return without attacking them.
>
> They started to go back, when Mah-to-toh-pa galloped out in front upon the prairie and plunged his lance into the ground. The blade was driven into the earth to its hilt. He made another circuit around, and in that circuit tore from his breast his reddened sash, which he hung upon his lance's handle as a flag, calling out to the Mandans: "What! Have we come to this? We have dogged our enemy two days, and now when we have found them, are we to turn about and go back like cowards? Mah-to-toh-pa's lance, which is red with the blood of brave men, has led you to the sight of your enemy, and you have followed it. It now stands firm in the ground, where the earth will drink the blood of Mah-to-toh-pa! You may all go back, and Mah-to-toh-pa will fight them alone!"
>
> During this maneuver the Cheyennes, who had discovered the Mandans behind them, had turned about and were gradually approaching, in order to

Table 4.6

	Agonal War	Nonagonal War
Objective/ Goal of War	Quest for pesonal honor and prestige	Destruction or subjugation of enemy
	Acquisition of booty and spoils	Acquisition of territory
Combatants	Individualistic warriors	Amy of soldiers
	Collective agreement or individual commitment to obligations	Command and duty through military hierarchy
	Bound by honor code to limit impact	No limit—total war— no apparent code
	Individual identity displayed	Identity and rank not displayed
Means/Modes of conducting war	Dependence on personal skill	Dependence on military arsenal
	Individualistic combat	Massed formations
	Individualized weapons, swords, lance	Mechanized weaponry, fire power
	Maximize risk to self	Minimize risk to self
	Fighting intensely personal, close quarters or hand to hand	Fighting impersonal and at distance or long range
Aftermath	Impermanent impact	Usually a permanent or long lasting impact
	Limited kill	Multiple and indescriminate killing
	Ransom settlement possible under oath	Prisoners of war and occupation forces
	Death anticipated and ritually prepared for	Death not contemplated occurs as result of bad luck
	Trophy and celebration dances, games and deed embellishment	After battle anticlimax

Note
From W. R. Morford (personal communication November 14, 1993).

give them battle. The chief of the Cheyenne war-party seeing and understanding the difficulty, and admiring the gallant conduct of Mah-to-toh-pa, galloped his horse forward within hailing distance, in front of the Mandans, and called out to know "who he was who had struck down his lance and defied the whole enemy alone?"

"I am Mah-to-toh-pa, second in command of the brave and valiant Mandans."

"I have heard often of Mah-to-toh-pa. He is a great warrior. Dares Mah-to-toh-pa to come forward and fight his battle with me alone, and our warriors will look on?"

"Is he a chief who speaks to Mah-to-toh-pa?"

"My scalps you see hanging on my horse's bits, and here is my lance with ermine skins and the war-eagle"s tail!"

"You have said enough."

The Cheyenne chief made a circuit or two at full gallop on a beautiful white horse, then struck his own lance into the ground, and left it standing by the side of the lance of Mah-to-toh-pa, both of which were waving together their little red flags—tokens of blood and defiance. The two parties then drew nearer, on a beautiful prairie, and the two full-plumed chiefs, at full speed, drove furiously upon each other, both firing their guns at the same moment. They passed each other and wheeled, when Mah-to-toh-pa drew off his powderhorn, and by holding it up, showed his adversary that the bullet had shattered it to pieces and destroyed his ammunition. He then threw it way, and his gun also, drew his bow from his quiver, and an arrow, with his shield upon his left arm. The Cheyenne instantly did the same. His horn was thrown, and his gun was thrown into the air, his shield was balanced on his arm, his bow drawn. Quick as lightning, they were both on the wing for a deadly combat.

Like two soaring eagles in the open air, they made their circuits around, and the twangs of their sinewy bows were heard, and the war-hoop, as they dashed by each other, parrying off the whizzing arrows with their shields. Some lodged in their legs and others in their arms, but both protected their bodies with their bucklers of bull's hide. Many were the shafts that fled from their murderous bows.

At length the horse of Mah-to-toh-pa fell to the ground with an arrow in his heart. His rider sprang upon his feet prepared to renew the combat. The Cheyenne, seeing his adversary dismounted, sprang from his horse too, and presenting the face of his shield towards his enemy, invited him to come on. A few more arrows were exchanged, then the Cheyenne, having discharged all his arrows, held up his empty quiver, and dashing it furiously to the ground, with his bow and his shield, drew and brandished his naked knife!

"Yes!" said Mah-to-toh-pa, as he also threw his shield and quiver to the earth and grasped for his knife. But his belt was empty. He had left it at home? His bow was in his hand, with which he parried the Cheyenne's thrust and knocked him to the ground. A desperate struggle now ensued for the knife. The blade was several times drawn through the right hand of Mah-to-toh-pa, inflicting the most frightful wounds, and he was severely wounded in several parts of his body. At length he succeeded in wrestling the knife from the Cheyenne's hand, and plunged it into his heart.

Mah-to-toh-pa held up, and claimed in deadly silence, the knife and scalp of the noble Cheyenne chief. (pp. 184–86)

This account reported by Catlin is best understood in terms of the Plains Indian concern for individual and tribal honor.

During the Golden Age of Plains Indian Culture, horse raiding was recognized as the most common military event. The heroic raid on an enemy camp enhanced the prestige of the raiding group and augmented their tribal honor. Defeat and hesitation to take reprisal eradicated tribal honor and brought shame. The duel between Mah-to-toh-pa and the Cheyenne chief was instigated by this exchange. What was honor for the Cheyenne was shame for the Mandan. The purpose of Mah-to-toh-pa's attempt to retrieve the stolen horses was to vindicate tribal honor.

The reluctance of the Mandan warriors to attack the larger force of Cheyenne warriors was a declaration of defeat and shame. Mah-to-toh-pa, the Mandan chief and leader of the revenge party, was in a precarious situation. For him to turn back and admit defeat was to shoulder most of the shame and, by the rules of the contest system, to decrease his status ranking in the prestige hierarchy. By charging his warriors with cowardice and then electing to face the enemy alone Mah-to-toh-pa immediately vindicated his own honor and further shamed his warriors.

As successful raiders the Cheyenne would receive great prestige by returning to camp with a scalp and enemy horse without the loss of a single man. But, Mah-to-toh-pa's challenge could not be ignored; to have done so would have been a prestige decrement to their initial success.

When the Cheyenne chief requested to know who Mah-to-toh-pa was, the concern was not for his name but for his status. To have fought a warrior who was not an equal would have jeopardized the reputation of the Cheyenne chief had he lost. This, too, was Mah-to-toh-pa's concern. According to the rules of the game no prestige was gained in a victory against an inferior person. Satisfied with the Cheyenne's war record, Mah-to-toh-pa accepted the challenge as an equal.

Armed with a gun each the two mounted warriors fought according to an accepted code of honor. As soon as the powder horn of his adversary was shattered, the Cheyenne chief discarded his own gun and fought on equal terms with a bow and arrow. To have shot Mah-to-toh-pa from a distance knowing that his powder horn had shattered was a violation of the code of honor and would have brought shame to the Cheyenne chief. The same respect was given the Cheyenne chief when Mah-to-toh-pa lay down his quiver and arrows to resume the contest in hand-to-hand combat. With the advantage of a knife against a bow without arrows the contest was eventually determined by the superior physical prowess of Mah-to-toh-pa. In victory the Mandan Chief vindicated his own honor and restored the honor of his tribe despite the loss of a number of horses. In defeat, the Cheyenne Chief was not disgraced. He fought courageously and in abiding by the code of honor he died at the hands of the better man. The tribal code also prevented the larger Cheyenne party from annihilating Mah-to-toh-pa and his smaller band of warriors in retaliation for the loss of their chief.

In summary, there is good evidence to confirm that horse raiding among the Plains Indians represented a form of agonal warfare based on the pursuit of prestige, having ludic elements, and characterized by norms of fair play. But as Smith (1938) has summarized "agon on the plains":

> Plains warfare is classically typified as a great game. The prestige of the warrior depended upon his war honors and these were his counters in the game of war; yet, to insist upon such terminology is to attribute a playfulness to Plains warfare which was entirely lacking. The competition for war honors might hve been a game among warriors, but the only game played by a warrior and his enemy was the gamble of life and death. (p. 432)

Thus, as illustrated in the duel between the Mandan and the Cheyenne chiefs, agon on the plains was often a "battle to death" for pure prestige.

Games and Athletic Activities

Granted that engagement in warfare was the primary avenue for the pursuit of prestige among Plains Indian warriors, it is not surprising that the predominant athletic games and physical contests among boys and young men were directly related to their preparation to become warriors. The following accounts of equestrian and martial activities among Plains Indian youth illustrate the pattern socialization for warrior roles.

Physical Prowess and Equestrian Culture   The dominating characteristics of the "typical" nineteenth-century Plains Indian culture, according to Wissler (1922), were the use of the horse, the buffalo, the tipi, the soldier band, and the Sun Dance. It was with the introduction of the horse that one witnessed the most profound changes in the lives of the Plains Indian. More than producing a means of transport, the horse influenced the entire social, economic, and political milieu of Plains culture.

With the horse, the Plains Indian achieved greater mobility, mastered the buffalo, had an exchangeable asset that made him a greater trader, and was transformed from an impotent infantryman into a fierce cavalryman, a dangerous warrior, and an insatiable raider. As a beast of burden and a means of personal transportation, the horse had a fundamental value to all Plains

Indians. It enabled the hunter to provide plenty of food, clothing, and shelter for his dependents, and enabled the warrior to take more plunder and achieve greater honor by increasing the range of his military activities.

Riding was one of the first things a Plains Indian boy learned. Wallace and Hoebel (1952) described the training of the Comanche child in the following terms:

> He started riding in a pack on his mother's back long before he could walk. Next he was strapped to her saddle on a gentle mare. By the time he was four or five he was off on a pony of his own. Both boys and girls were taught to ride with or without a saddle. (p. 48)

In addition to the mastery of riding, Plains Indian boys learned to develop other skills of horsemanship, as illustrated by Tixier's (1968) description of the play patterns of the Kangas of the Osage tribe:

> These hardy children could be no more than five or six years old, and yet they were riding bareback on yearlings.
>
> . . . The Osage learn to ride from earliest infancy: they become surprisingly expert. They are able to hide themselves behind their horses at full gallop. At war, they escape the arrows of their enemies by concealing themselves so adroitly behind the flanks of their beasts that they show only one foot. At play, they gallop bare-back with bridles hanging loose, and lean so far over that one would think they were going to lose their balance. They shoot their arrows with surprising accuracy from this awkward position. It is seldom that they fall down, and when they do they never lose their horses, for, besides the Spanish bridle, which is released in the fall of the rider, the animals have around their necks a long horsehair tether, which ends in a huge knot; the coils, which unroll easily, are passed around the riders belt. When falling, the savage grasps the tether, lets it slip in his hand until the knot is at the end. The horse can go far enough not to hurt his master, who soon stops him with a slip knot around the horse's neck. (pp. 167–68)

With these skills a Plains Indian boy learned to pick up objects from the ground while his mount was travelling at full speed. At first, small, light objects were selected, but as a boy grew older and more proficient, heavier and more bulky ones were chosen. A boy eventually learned to pick up from the ground a man's body and swing it across his horse—for to rescue a fallen comrade in battle was the highest obligation of the Plains Indian warrior.

In the Comanche tribe, however, Wallace and Hoebel (1952) described a two-man rescue:

> Rushing neck by neck on either side of the prostrate person, both riders stooped at the same instant and swung the body in front of one of the riders. This stunt was practiced over and over on all lands of ground until riders and ponies could do it without a hitch. (p. 48)

In their games, the Plains Indians learned to discharge arrows with speed and accuracy, skills that translated to the hunt and war complex. Tixier (1968) observed a contest of this nature in the Osage tribe.

> Our provisioning being completed, the Osage organized a contest of a new kind, the prize for which was announced by the warriors.
>
> A curved branch was struck into the ground. From is top hung a trap supporting a narrow piece of meat six inches long. Men on horseback were supposed to shoot at this un-steady target with arrows. Dried branches placed twenty paces from the goal were to keep shooters at a distance. A hundred men took part in the contest, all on horseback, riding bareback, armed with a bow and two arrows. They formed a line two hundred paces from the branch. At a signal the warriors left at a gallop and passing in front of the target, one after the other, they dropped their bridles, leaned so low that it looked as they were going to fall, and shot their arrows while turning around. Their horses followed one another so very closely that frequently they came into contact.
>
> When all the marksmen had passed, judges recovered the arrows, which (to avoid disputes) bore distinctive marks. All were stuck around the target within a circle of two feet in circumference. The piece of meat was so lacerated that it was necessary to change it. No arrow had remained affixed to it and for this reason no prize was given in this first turn. The shooters had to run several times before all the prizes were given. As soon as the contestants had received their arrows from the hands of the judges, they went back to the line, then set out again at a gallop. These men, almost naked, riding bareback, leaned forward to take their aim, contracting their muscles while straightening on their chargers, and then shot while turning back. The target, which was struck repeatedly, was constantly swinging, and several times an arrow ran through it while it oscilated. This game was fascinating to watch. (pp. 253–54)

Horses were distinguished by the Plains Indian according to their value as buffalo runners or as horses specifically used in war. They were trained according to their need, either for speed over short distances or for speed and endurance over longer distances. For the Sioux, Hassrick (1964) explained that:

> The most valuable pony was the gelding race horse. The horse that could outrun all others was an indispensable asset. So highly prized was such an animal that its owner kept it under the closest guard, even picketing it at the tipi door. Some ponies became famous throughout the plains. Warriors took special note of such animals and actually made expeditions in the hope of capturing this or that renowed one. Race horses were given special care and threatment and used only when actually needed. Thus a man would ride a saddle horse in the war party and lead his race horse until the attack was made. (p. 162)

Consequently, horse races were a popular event among the majority of Plains tribes. These races were generally intratribal, although among allied tribes intertribal events were organized. Ewers (1955) informed us that:

> Although the Blackfoot participated in both intratribal and intertribal horse races in buffalo days, those races best remembered, and probably most common, were the ones between two societies of the same tribe. Generally men of the same society did not race against each other, even though several men of a society might own fast horses. (p. 228)

Similarly, Flannery and Cooper (1946) mentioned that horse races were usually between the two soldier police societies, the Stars and Wolves, or between the Gros Ventre and other tribes such as the Piegan.

Dodge (1883) described three methods of horse racing in the Comanche tribe:

> One method of racing is to start from a line and rush full speed at a tree, the one who first touches it being the winner. Another is to rush at a heavy pole placed horizontally about six feet from the ground, resting on forks firmly set. If the rider stops his horse an instant too soon he fails of touching the pole, if an instant too late, the horse passes under the pole, leaving the rider dangling to it or thrown to the ground.
>
> A third method is to fasten to the ground, two strips of buffalo hide from six to ten feet apart. The starting point is some two hundred yards from these strips, and the game is to run at full speed, jump the horse between the strips, turn him in his tracks, and return to the starting point. The horse which fails to get beyond the first strip, with all four of his feet, or which gets a single foot beyond the second strip, is beaten, even though he makes the best time. (p. 340)

The chase as the primary method of bison hunting necessitated that the Plains Indians had fast horses. In this, the greatest chance of success lay with the man mounted on the fastest horse. The bison hunt was therefore "a collective rather than a truly coopeative one because once the chase started, each man was on his own and had the right of disposal over whatever game he killed" (Flannery, 1953, p. 59). This was common practice in the communal hunt of many Plains Indian tribes.

The horse to the Plains Indian was an object of veneration and had a pervasive influence on the lives of all the selected tribes. If the Plains Indians were individualists par excellence, the horse served to accentuate that individualism.

Physical Prowess and Martial Culture   Throughout his early years the Plains Indian boy was instructed and groomed in the principle activities of life-hunting, and warfare. In fact, everything in his schooling was designed to prepare him for the exigencies of survival in life ahead. Listening, observing, imitating, participating in games of skill and fortitude, practicing the technique of running, shooting, riding, trailing, and hunting, all equipped him for the proud role of a warrior. Inherent in this role was the mastery of certain fundamental fighting skills that were a necessary prerequisite for the warrior ideal. Such skills were often formally taught by close relatives and informally practiced in the play activities of the young boys. In general, fighting skills were learned in individual games that required skill, endurance, daring, and the ability to withstand pain. Using examples from selected Plains Indian tribes in general, and from the Crow tribe in particular, the following section illustrates the child-training practices used to educate the aspirant warriors of the Plains Indians.

On the plains the lives and livelihood of the Plains Indians turned on their skill with the bow and arrow. Young boys were taught to use these weapons from a very early age. The father or grandfather usually instructed the boys in mastering the art of shooting the bow and arrow, although the precarious nature of survival on the Plains sometimes placed this responsibility on an uncle or elder brother. Plenty-Coups told Linderman (1962) of the time when his father gave him a bow and four arrows:

> The bow was light and small, the arrows blunt and short. But my pride in possessing them was great, since in spite of its smallness the bow was like my father's. It was made of cedar and was neatly backed with sinew to make it strong.
>
> . . . We always straightened our arrows with a bone straightener or with our teeth, before using them. First we shot for distance. No particular care was given to accuracy until the required distance was reached. Then we were taught to shoot for precision. This requires even more work than shooting for distance. My grandfather would place a buffalo chip for me as a target, then I could put an arrow through its center three times out of five shots, he would roll the chip for me to shoot at. This was an exciting game, shooting at a rolling buffalo chip. Sometimes our teachers would try a shot themselves.
>
> There never was any argument as to whose arrow finally pinned the chip to the ground, because all arrow shafts were marked. Each boy knew his own arrows, and those of other boys as well. Even the men of the tribe knew each other's arrows by their marks.
>
> The marking of arrows was not only individual, but tribal. The Crows call the Cheyennes The-Striped-Feathered-Arrows, because of the barred feathers of the wild turkey used in their arrow shafts.
>
> . . . Speed in shooting was very necessary, since both in war and hunting a man must be quick to send a second arrow after his first. We were taught to hold one, and sometimes more arrows in the left hand with the bow. They were held points down, feathers up, so that when the right hand reached and drew them, the left would not be wounded by their sharp heads. Sometimes men carried an extra arrow in their mouths. This was quicker

than pulling them from a quiver over the shoulder, but was a method used only in fighting or dangerous situations. (pp. 14–16)

After receiving instruction in the use of the bow and arrows, the boys spent much time in practice. Throughout all Plains tribes for which games have been recorded, those requiring skill in the use of the bow and arrow were manifold, being variations on similar themes based on moving or stationary targets. As pointed out by Plenty-Coups, they were all tests of skill in accuracy, speed, and distance. Moreover, these games were always a matter of individual rivalry; the reward for the winner counted in terms of the value of the stakes waged, usually the arrows that were discharged in the contest.

A common bow and arrow game among Plains Indian boys was described by Flannery (1953) for the Gros Ventre tribe:

A favorite sport among boys involved skill in shooting arrows. One game was to plant a marked arrow as a target. Then two boys would shoot two arrows and the one whose arrows came closest to the marker would take the arrows of his opponents. Sometimes they would see who could shoot the greatest distance. (p. 186)

A variation was described by Lowie (1935) for the Crow tribe:

In early spring the youngsters would say, "Let us shoot at a grass target." They then gathered up pupua grass, making a bundle about a foot long and thicker at one end, and tied it together with sinew or, if away from camp, with willow bark. This target was laid down on a hillside, possibly 40 feet away. The players divided into sides and wagered their arrows. Each side shot off four or five arrows, and whoever came closest to the target took all the opponents' arrows. As a sequel they threw the wisp into the air and tried to hit it. (p. 36)

Another common Plains Indian arrow-shooting contest which placed a premium on speed in fitting and discharging arrows was observed by Domenech (1860) in the Comanche tribe:

The players generally take each about ten arrows, which they held with their bows in the left hand; he whose turn it is advanced in front of the judges, and lances his first arrow upwards as high as possible, for he must send off all the others before it comes down. The victory belongs to him who has the most arrows in the air together; and he who can make them all fly at once is a hero, is praised and admired by every one, nay, considered as a supernatural being. (p. 198)

Domenech illustrated the exclusive nature of the achery contests in that "only the strongest and ablest young men of the tribe are allowed to peform in them. There every man plays for himself; there is no camp; the prize and honor belong to only one" (p. 198).

In addition to mastering the bow and arrow through contrived life situations in miniature, the Plains Indian boys were educated into a rough-and-tumble world of games requiring endurance, strength, and fortitude in preparation for the warrior lifestyle. Again, contests were always a matter of keenly fought competition and rivalry. Hassrick (1964) explained that in the Sioux tribe "team games for boys were of a rough-and-ready nature designed to offer excitement and fun as well as to encourage toughness and physical endurance" (p. 128). Some of these games have been described by Hassrick as follows:

> The Swing-Kicking Game took first place as a rugged conditioner, and there was no pretense at horseplay. Here two rows of boys faced each other, each holding his robe over his left arm. The game was begun only after the formality of the stock question, "Shall we grab them by the hair and knee them in the face until they bleed?" Then using their robes as a shield, they all kicked at their opponents, endeavoring to upset them. There seems to have been no rules, for the boys attacked whoever was closest, often two boys jumping one. Kicking from behind the knees was a good way of throwing an opponent, and once down he was grabbed at the temples with both hands and kneed in the face.
>
> Once released, the bloody victims would fight on, kicking and kneeing and bleeding until they could fight no longer. The game was over when one side retreated or someone yelled "Let us stop." As Iron Shell explained, "Some boys got badly hurt, but afterwards we would talk and laugh about it. Very seldom did any fellow get angry."
>
> The Buffalo-Hunt Game made no claim to gentleness but required dexterity as well as fortitude. "Here a boy was chosen who was brave and could stand a lot of collisions." He was supplied with a five-foot stick, to which was attached a large cactus leaf from which the center had been cut to represent the buffalo's heart. As the "buffalo" walked about holding his green, prickly heart before him, the hunters tried to pierce the heart with their bows and arrows.
>
> If the hunters missed he chased them a little with the cactus, but if an arrow went through the heart, he chased the hunter until he poked him with the cactus, and off to stick another. The place to strike was on the buttocks; some boys grunted, but others hollered.
>
> Throw at Each Other with Mud was a slightly more gentle spring pastime where teams of boys attacked with mud balls which they threw from the tips of short springy sticks. Each boy carried several sticks and an arsenal of mud as he advanced. "It cedrtainly hurt when you got hit, so you must duck and throw as you attack." Sometimes live coals were embedded in the mud balls to add zest to the game. (pp. 123–30)

Throw at Each Other with Mud was a favorite game among a number of Plains Indian tribes being described by Howard (1965) for the Ponca, Kennedy (1961) for the Assiniboine, and Lowie (1935) for the Crow.

The use of sham battles in the education of the novitiate warrior were a common feature of boyhood activity as well as an integral part of the entire training scheme. Among the Sioux boys, according to Hassrick (1964):

> The sadistic competition in war games showed the most marked form of aggressive outlet. The games were designed to simulate war and develop warrior-like stamina and toughness, thereby acquainting boys with the rigors of adult activity. The fights were with the imaginary enemies, not fellow playmates, and the phantasy served to make aggression extra- rather than intra-societal. (p. 291)

In the Cheyenne tribe, Hoebel's (1978) account illustrated how both boys and girls were caught up in the complex of war through play:

> War is also played with faithful mimicry of the real thing, including the dismantling of the "camp" by the girls, who flee to safety with their "children" and belongings while their "men" try to stave off the enemy. In play associated with the children's camps (which, incidentally, they call "large play" in contrast to small girls' and boys' play with dolls and toy bows and arrows which is called "small play"), they even put on Sun Dances. Some of the boys may pierce themselves with cactus thorns and dry chunks of wood, calling them buffalo skulls. (p. 99)

Catlin (1857) described how the youths of the Mandan tribe were educated in open field combat. He wrote:

> The sham-fight and sham scalp-dance of the Mandan boys is a part of their regular exercise and constitutes a material branch of their education. During the pleasant mornings of the summer, the little boys between the age of seven and fifteen are called out, to the number of several hundred, and divided into two companies, each of which is headed by some experienced warrior, who leads them, in the character of a teacher.
>
> They are led out into the prairie at sunrise. Their bodies are naked, and each one has a little bow in his left hand, and a number of arrows made of large spears of grass, which are harmless in their effects. Each one also has a little belt or girdle around his waist, in which he carries a knife made of a piece of wood and equally harmless. On the tops of their heads are slightly attached small tufts of grass, which answer as scalps, and in these costumes they follow the dictates of their experienced leaders, who lead them through the judicious evolutions of Indian warfare—of feints—of retreats—of attacks—and at last to a general fight. Many maneuvers are gone through, and eventually they are brought up face to face, within fifteen or twenty feet of each other, with their leaders at their head stimulating them on. Their bows are bent upon each other and their missiles flying while they dodge and fend them off.
>
> If anyone is struck with an arrow on any vital pat of his body, he is obliged to fall, and his adversary rushes up to him, places his foot upon him,

and snatching from his belt his wooden knife, grasps hold of his victim's scalp-lock of grass, and making a feint at it with his wooden knife, twitches it off and puts it into his belt, then enters again into the ranks of battle.

This training generally lasts an hour or more in the morning, is performed on an empty stomach, and affords them a rigid and wholesome exercise while they are instructed in the important science of war. Some five or six miles of ground are run over during those evolutions, giving suppleness to their limbs and strength to their muscles. After this exciting exhibition is ended, they all return to their village, where the chiefs and braves pay profound attention to their vaunting, and applaud them for their artifice and valor. Those who have taken scalps then step forward, brandishing them and making their boasts as they enter into the scalp-dance (in which they are also instructed by their leaders or teachers) jumping and yelling, brandishing their scalps, and receiving their sanguinary deeds to the great astonishment of their tender-aged sweethearts, who are gazing with wonder upon them. (pp. 131–32)

This account again demonstrates some of the common features of a form of Plains warfare. It illustrates the magnitude of the exercise, the various parameters and patterns of participation (including some of the skills and strategies used) and the outcome of the performance.

In summary, the entire play scheme for the Plains Indian became a basic pathway over which the young boy made a smooth transition to adulthood. This entailed formal training in, and mastery of, fighting skills. The aspiring warrior, throughout the training period, was taught to be self-reliant. In addition, games such as the sham battles, the swing-kicking, the buffalo hunt, the mud-throwing games, the many games of marksmanship and tests of strength, endurance, and fortitude were obviously appropriate to instilling the qualities necessary for good warriorship.

SUMMARY AND CONCLUSIONS

The Celebration of Heroes

In our brief analysis of games and warfare we have highlighted how the agon motif was most characteristic of Plains Indian culture from 1800 to 1850. Plains Indian warrior societies during this period represent agonal social systems, as their chief sociocultural characteristics are a spirit of rivalry expressed in a variety of agonal contests ranging from athletic games to chivalrous warfare, and an extreme emphasis on self-assertion, personal prowess, and the quest for individual fame, glory, and honor.

These agonal contests represent ritualized contests (1) between peers, (2) played according to a specific set of rules, (3) emphasizing the display and demonstration of physical prowess, (4) restricted to time and place, (5) having limited objectives, (6) providing tests of moral character and social worth,

(7) governed by prestige processes, and (8) offering a means of determining social rank, rewarding excellence, and according honor.

To nourish their desire for recognition the Plains Indians created various methods for publicizing deeds to as wide a public as possible. One major means was various forms of "victory celebration," including victory dances, singing songs to honor returning heroes, and naming ceremonies wherein a boy could abandon the name given to him at birth and select a more worthy name after performing a praiseworthy deed. Another major means was using various heraldic devices to display visible marks of achievement. An example of a set of heraldic devices is the war insignia of selected tribes (see table 6.7).

As Goode (1978) has noted, the importance of such symbolic awards is that they (1) sift and evaluate the participants and furnish information about how each individual ranks in a given area of achievement, (2) indicate that one's talents are worthy of respect, (3) provide proof that one has achieved a certain level of performance, (4) greatly influence the future careers of the individuals who receive them, (5) are public announcements that attract a far wider audience than just the winners, (6) give prestige to achievements that seem so outstanding that not honoring them is to deny some supposed values of society, (7) give prestige primarily to activities that do not play off very well materially, and last, but not least, (8) enhance the social identity of both individuals and groups (pp. 156–71).

Prestige, Culture and Self-Esteem

The agon motif is most marked within aristocratic warrior societies during what historians have labelled the "Heroic" or "Golden Age" of selected cultures. Thus it is not surprising that the agon motif was most characteristic of Plains Indian societies during what has been termed the "Golden Age" or "Climax Period" of Plains Indian culture from 1800–1850.

We suggest that the overriding cultural theme of the "composite culture" of the Plains Indians during the Climax Period was not unlike that of the Hellenic World described by Gouldner (1965), namely; "the active quest for fame through competitive achievement" (p. 45). We further suggest that the "ideal" Plains Indian warrior is very similar to the archetypal aristocratic warrior of ancient Greece depicted in Homer's epics. As Ossowska (1972) observed:

> Homer's warriors are constantly preoccupied with distinguishing themselves. Each book of the *Illiad* constitutes a story of the deeds proving someone's excellence (*aristeia*) which must be duly appreciated by others. The warriors are fascinated by what F. Znaniecki called "reflected ego." That is, the opinion (*time*) they enjoyed among their equals. (pp. 125–26)

Table 4.7 Examples of War Insignia within Selected Tribes

Crow[a]	
Achievements	Marks
Counting first coup or capturing an enemy gun	Entitled to wear a war shirt. A first coup entitled a warrior to a coyote tail at the heel of one of his moccasins if the deed was performed twice. Eagle feathers were attached to a coup stick if a coup had been struck on several occasions.
Leading a war party (pipe-holder)	A scalp could be tied to a horse's bridle
Cutting loose a picketed horse	A knotted and cut rope tied to a horse's neck. The number of horses captured was represented by strips of white clay under the horse's eyes or on its flank.
Recovering from a battle wound	Gave the right to paint the wound with a black circle and red stripes radiating from it.
Scalping an enemy	A scalp tied to a coup stick.
Knocking down a mounted enemy or an enemy on foot	A hand painted on a horse in white clay.
Mandan[b]	
Counting coup	Entitled to wear a wolf's tail at the heel of their moccasin.
First to count coup or kill an enemy	Entitled to paint a spiral line about his arm, with another winding in the opposite direction with three cross stripes.
Counting coup on or killing a second enemy	Entitled to paint left legging reddish brown.
Killing an enemy in equal fight before another enemy was killed	Wear a wolf's tail around each foot.
Counting coup a third time	Entitled to paint two lengthwise stripes with three cross stripes on each arm. This was the most honorable coup and no other distinctive marks were used, except that an additional eagle feather might be worked in the hair for each additional coup.
To be shot at six times	Wear six wooden sticks in the hair.

Table 4.7   Examples of War Insignia within Selected Tribes
continued

Ponca[c]	
Saving a comrade	For this a warrior was entitled to carry a little boy behind him on his horse, when he rode in a sham battle or parade.
Counting coup—especially between opposing lines	The right to wear a vertical eagle feather fastened to the scalp lock for first coup. A slanting eagle feather for second coup. Two feathers cut short for third coup. A split feather for fourth coup.
Wounded severely	Gave the right to paint the wound red and to wear a red feather.
Horse stealing	The right to wear a white shirt or blanket with horse tracks marked on it, or to carry a rope, unravelled at the end, or both.
Most on warpath	The war-bonnet was one of the badges of such a man provided he had done many deeds. So were the roach and eagle feather bustle.
To kill a foe (this act was considered brave but did not rank with the five deeds above or taking a scalp)	Gave the right to carry a gun or bow while dancing.

Notes

a. From Crow Indian medicine bundles (pp. 37–38) by W. Wildschut, 1960. *Contributions from the Museum of the American Indian Heye Foundation, 17.*

b. From *Illustrations of the manners, customs, and conditions of the North American Indians: With letters and notes written during eight years of travel and adventure among the wildest and most remarkable tribes now existing* (pp. 148–49) by G. Catlin, 1857. London: Henry G. Bohn.

c. From Kansa organizations (p. 794) by A. Skinner, 1915. *Anthropological Papers of the American Museum of Natural History, 11.*

Similarly, Donlan (1981) has written:

> We may sum up the Homeric aristocratic ideal by saying that worth or excellence, *arete*, was conceived of in the physical sphere almost exclusively, most specifically, in terms of prowess as a warrior. The aim of the high status warrior was public recognition of his ability. The Homeric proto-aristocrat endlessly competed with his fellows for prestige (*kydos, time*)

with the goal of being recognized as "best" (*aristos*); his greatest fear was failure and its accompanying humiliation. (p. 23)

Like the Homeric warrior, the Plains Indian warrior sought to be first among equals. The spirit of rivalry was highly institutionalized in Plains Indian societies. For example, among the Gros Ventre, rivalries were encouraged through enemy-friend relationships. Two warriors close in rank would form an enemy-friendship and each would try to outdo the other by all kinds of action and speech in competitive play. Ambitious warriors selected enemy-friends with care so as to assure worthy opponents. The blood brotherhood relationship was a similar, though less hostile, rivalry found in many Plains Indian tribes. In addition, to individual rivalries, intratribal warrior societies competed with each other for first rank. For example, the Foxes and Lumpwood societies of the Crow tribe were such keen rivals that they competed in annual coup-counting and wife-stealing competitions.

Although the competition between elite warriors was the most pronounced, hunters, scouts, orators, quillers, weapon makers, dancers, singers, tanners, tipi makers, herders, et cetera all competed with their peers. Competition was particularly pronounced in the activities of young men aspiring to become warriors. In all cases, the rewards for outstanding achievements in various forms of "playful" competition were increased reputation, accord of honor, and superior status. As Huizinga (1955) observed, "virtue, honour, nobility and glory fall at the outset within the field of competition, which is that of play" (p. 64).

REFERENCES

Barkow, J. H. (1975). Prestige and culture: A biosocial interpretation. *Current Anthropology, 16*(4): 553–72.

Bendix, R. (1962). *Max Weber: An intellectual portrait.* New York: Anchor Books.

Benedict, R. (1950). *Patterns of culture.* New York: Mentor Books.

Catlin, G. (1857). *Illustrations of the manners customs and conditions of the North American Indians: With letters and notes written during eight years of travel and adventure among the wildest and most remarkable tribes now existing.* London: Henry G. Bohn.

Chapple, E. D., & Coon, S. (1942). *Principles of anthropology.* New York: Henry Holt.

Dodge, R. I. (1883). *Our wild Indians: Thirty-three years' personal experience among the red men of the great west.* Hartford, CT: A. D. Worthington.

Domenech, A. M. (1860). *The great deserts of North America* (vol. 2). London: Green, Longman, Longman & Roberts.

Donlan, W. (1981). *The aristocratic ideal in ancient Greece*. Lawrence, KS: Coronado Press.

Elkin, H. (1940). The northern Arapaho of Wyoming. In R. Linton (Ed.), *Acculturation in seven American Indian tribes* (pp. 207–55). New York: Appleton-Century.

Erodes, R. (1972). *The sun dance people*. New York: Alfred A. Knopf.

Ewers, J. C. (1955). *The horse in Blackfoot Indian culture*. Smithsonian Institution of American Ethnology, Bulletin 159. Washington D. C.: U. S. Government Printing Office.

Flannery, R. (1953). *The Gros Ventres of Montana. Part 1. Social Life*. Washington, D. C.: Catholic University of America Press.

Flannery, R., & Cooper, J. M. (1946). Social mechanisms in Gros Ventres gambling. *Southwestern Journal of Anthropology* (vol. 2). Albuquerque: University of New Mexico Press.

Fletcher, A. C., & Lafleshe, F. (1911). *The Omaha tribe*. (Report No. 27). Washington, D. C.: Bureau of American Ethnology.

Goode, W. J. (1978) *The celebration of heroes: Prestige as a control system*. Berkeley: University of California Press.

Gouldner, A. W. (1965). *Enter Plato*. New York: Basic Books.

Grinnell, G. B. (1923). *The Cheyenne Indians: Their history and ways of life* (vol. 2). New Haven: Yale University Press.

Hassrick, R. B. (1964). *The Sioux: Life and customs of a warrior society*. Norman: University of Oklahoma Press.

Hoebel, E. A. (1978). *The Cheyennes*. New York: Holt, Rinehart and Winston.

Howard, J. H. (1965). *The Ponca Tribe*. (Report 195). Washington, D.C.: Bureau of American Ethnology.

Huizinga, J. (1955). *Homo ludens: A study of the play element in culture*. Boston: Beacon Press.

Kennedy, M. S. (1961). *The Assiniboines*. Norman. University of Oklahoma Press.

Landes, R. (1959). Dakota warfare. *Southwestern Journal of Anthropology, 15*, 43–52.

LeVine, R. A., & Campbell, D. T. (1912). *Ethnocentricism: Theories of conflict, ethnic attitudes, and group behavior*. New York: Wiley.

Linderman, F. B. (1962). *Plenty-coups: Chief of the Crows*. Lincoln: University of Nebraska Press.

Lowie, R. H. (1920). *Primitive society*. New York: Boni and Liverright.

————. (1935). *The Crow Indians*. New York: Farrar and Rinehart.

————. (1940). *An introduction to cultural anthropology*. New York: Farrar and Rinehart.

————. (1954). *Indians of the plains*. New York: McGraw-Hill.

Loy, J. W. (1968). The nature of sport: A definitional effort. *Quest, 10*, 1–15.

————. (1981). An emerging theory of sport spectatorship: Implications for the Olympic games." In J. Segrave & D. Chu (Eds.), *Olympism* (pp. 262–94). Champaign, IL: Human Kinetics.

Loy, J. W., & Ingham, A. G. (1973). Play, games and sport in the psychological development of children and youth. In G. L. Rarick (Ed.), *Physical Activity: Human Growth and Development* (pp. 257–302). New York: Academic Press.

Loy, J. W., & Kenyon, G. S. (Eds.). (1969). *Sport, culture and society: A reader for the sociology of sport*. New York: Macmillan.

Morford, W. R., & Clark, S. J. (1976). The Agon Motif. *Exercise and Sport Sciences Reviews, 4*, 163–93.

Newcombe, W. W. (1950). A re-examination of the causes of plains warfare. *American Anthropologist, 52*, 317–30.

Ossowska, M. (1972). *Social determinants of moral ideas*. London: Routledge and Kegan Paul.

Richardson, J. (1940). Law and status among the Kiowa Indians. *Monographs of the American Ethnological Society, 1*, New York: J. J. Augustin.

Roberts, J. M., Arth, M. J., & Bush, R. R. (1959). Games in culture. *American Anthropologist, 61*, 597–605.

Roberts, J. M. & Barry, H., III. (1976). Inculcated traits and game-type combinations. In T. T. Craig (Ed.), *The humanistic and mental health aspects of sports, exercise and recreation* (pp. 5–11). Chiago: American Medical Association.

Roberts, J. M. & Sutton-Smith, B. (1962). Child training and game involvement. *Ethnology, 1*, 166–85.

Roberts, J. M., Sutton-Smith, B., & Kendon, A. (1963). Strategy in games and folk tales. *Journal of Social Psychology, 61*, 185–99.

Skinner, A. (1915). Kansa Organizations. *Anthropological Papers of the American Museum of Natural History, 11*, 1–210.

Smith, M. W. (1938). The war complex of the Plains Indians. *Proceedings of the American Philosophical Society, 78*, 425–65.

Sutton-Smith, B. (1969). The two cultures of games. In G. S. Kenyon (Ed.), *Aspects of contemporary sport sociology* (pp. 135–47). Chicago: Athletic Institute.

———. (1971). The sporting balance. In R. Albonico & K. Pfister-Binz (Eds.), *Sociology of Sport* (pp. 105–12). Basel: Birkhauser Verlag.

———. (1976). Current research and theory on play, games and sport. T. T. Craig (Ed.), *The humanistic and mental health aspects of sports, exercise and recreation* (pp. 1–4). Chicago: American Medical Association.

———. (1980). A sportive theory of play. In H. B. Schwartzman (Ed.), *Play and Culture* (pp. 10–18). West Point, NY: Leisure Press.

———. (1989). Games as models of power. In R. bolton (Ed.), *The content of culture: constants and variants—Studies in honor of John M. Roberts* (pp. 3–18). New Haven, CT: HRAF Press.

Sutton-Smith, B. & Roberts, J. M. (1970). The cross-cultural and psychological study of games. In G. Luschen (Ed.), *The cross-cultural analysis of sport and games* (pp. 100–08). Campaign, IL: Stipes Publishing Company.

Sutton-Smith, B., Roberts, J. M., & Kozelka, R. M. (1963). Game involvement in adults. *Journal of social psychology, 69*, 15–30.

Tixier, V. (1968). *Tixier's travels on the Osage prairies*. Norman: University of Oklahoma Press.

Turney-High, H. H. (1942). *The practice of primitive war* (vol. 1). The University of Montana Publications in the Social Sciences, No. 2.

Wallace, R., and Hoebel, E. A. (1952). *The Comanches: Lords of the south plains*. Norman: University of Oklahoma Press.

Wildschut, W. (1960). Crow Indian medicine bundles. *Conributions from the Museum of the American Indian Heye Foundation, 17*, 1–178.

Wissler, C. (1911). Blackfoot social life. *Anthropological Papers of the American Museum of Natural History, 7*, 1–64.

———. (1922). *The American Indian*. New York: Oxford University Press.

———. (1934). *North American Indians of the plains*. New York: Lancaster Press.

5

A. D. PELLEGRINI ⎯⎯⎯⎯⎯⎯⎯⎯⎯⎯⎯⎯⎯⎯⎯⎯⎯⎯⎯

Boys' Rough-and-Tumble Play and Social Competence: Contemporaneous and Longitudinal Relations

Brian Sutton-Smith has made important contributions to our understanding of many aspects of children's lives. The one that I focus on in this chapter is children's play. Sutton-Smith's (1967) contribution to our further understanding of this aspect of child development has been demonstrated at a number of levels. At the level of theory, his critique of Piaget's theory of play and development (Sutton-smith, 1966) has helped us better understand the interactions among play, imitation, and cognitive development. At more specific levels, his theorizing (Sutton-Smith, 1967) stimulated empirical study of the relations between play and creativity (Dansky and Silverman, 1973, 1975). More recently, he has helped us to better understand the role of rough play, from the child's point of view (Sutton-Smith, 1990).

The first time I met Sutton-Smith we were on a panel together to discuss play in Billings, Montana. At that time I was just beginning my work in the area of rough play and presented some preliminary cross-sectional data on rough play and aggression and the ways in which they were viewed by children and teachers. Brian's comments on my talk that day, and his subsequent feedback, have been important sources of insight for my work. An important aspect of the feed back has always been to try to understand the phenomenon from different perspectives. In the case of rough play it is very important to consider it from the child's point of view. Frequently, rough play has been considered a form of aggression, not play, by researchers. Children clearly know the difference, as Sutton-Smith (1993) has shown. In this chapter, I will look at a topic that integrates many of these aspects of Sutton-Smith's work: the role of rough play in children's development.

In recent years developmental psychologists have begun to examine a relatively neglected dimension of elementary-school–age children's play

---

Work on this project was partially supported with grants from the H. F. Guggenheim Foundation and from the National Institutes of Health/Fogarty Center.

behavior: rough-and-tumble play (R & T). As developmentalists have begun to study R & T, they, unlike ethological students of the topic, have often considered it a form of aggressive, not affiliative behavior. More recent ethologically oriented work has defined R & T as a set of affiliative behaviors which include the exhibition of positive affect (e.g., play face), vigorous movements (e.g., running), and reciprocal role taking (e.g., alternating between victim and victimizer in play fights). R & T is more frequently observed in males than in females. Further, the R & T of elementary-school boys, not girls, is related to aspects of social competence, such as peer affiliation and social problem-solving flexibility (Humphreys and Smith, 1987; Pellegrini, 1989). Specific design features of R & T, such as reciprocal social interaction, level of vigor, and symmetrical peer groupings, have been theoretically implicated in serving beneficial consequences in boys' developing social competence (Fagen, 1981, this volume; Pellegrini, 1988).

Studies examining beneficial consequences of play generally (Martin and Caro, 1985), and R & T specifically (Smith, 1989), have not, however, addressed the problem of equifinality, which suggests that organisms in open systems can reach specific outcomes via different routes (Sackett, Sameroff, Cairns, and Suomi, 1981). Further, studies of play have not empirically demonstrated relations between specific, theoretically relevant dimensions of R & T and dimensions of social competence. It may be, for example, that boys utilize forms of social interaction in addition to or instead of R & T in becoming socially competent. There are forms of social interaction, such as cooperative social games, comfort contact, and conversation, which, like R & T, also occur in symmetrical groups and involve reciprocal role taking.

The difference between R & T and these other behaviors is that the former is more flexible and vigorous. R & T, like other forms of play, is flexible because children generate novel behavioral patterns and strategies through subroutinization (Fagen, 1984; Smith, 1982; Sutton-Smith, 1967). The flexibility dimension of play generally, and of R & T specifically, has been nominated as an important contributor to children's cognitive and social competence status (e.g., Bruner, 1972). To my knowledge, however, research has not documented the empirical relations between flexibility dimensions of play and specific outcomes measures.

In short, the flexibility aspect of play has been theoretically proffered, but not empirically verified, as an important contributor to children's development. Further, it seems particularly important to "unpack" a molar category like R & T into component parts. The need for such unpacking seems particularly important for R & T because it is a controversial category to the extent that it may be considered a dimension of aggression or a dimension of prosocial play; specific subcomponents of R & T relate to prosocial outcomes while others relate to aggressive outcomes. For example, in a study of adolescent boys' R & T, physically rough dimensions of R & T, like tackle, related to aggression and dominance, while locomotive aspects of R & T, like chase, related to some boys' social competence (Pellegrini, 1988). Choice of specific dimensions of R & T to examine should be based on similarity between the design features of the play behavior and the outcome measure.

In the first study presented in this chapter, the relation between the flexibility dimension of R & T and flexibility in social problem-solving will be examined. Flexibility was defined here as the variety of different R & T behavioral components generated by a child. For example, if a child's R & T repertoire was composed of wrestle, hit-at, and pounce, he would receive a variety score of three. While there may be other, more desirable, measures of behavioral flexibility, such as the number of different roles take in R & T, behavioral variety seems to be a reasonable starting point to test this heretofore untested relation between flexibility in play and flexibility in social competence.

Children's R & T is also different from the other forms of reciprocal social interaction, as mentioned above, to the extent that it contains a physically vigorous element. This vigor element may make it particularly attractive to boys, not girls, and explain social affiliation patterns among boys (Maccoby, 1986). Boys may choose to play with each other because they are attracted to rough forms of play, like R & T. If this is the case, the vigorous dimension of R & T should be an important contributor to one aspect of their social competence: affiliation and popularity with peers. The contributions made by specific aspects of R & T (i.e., flexibility and vigor) to two aspects of social competence (i.e., social problem-solving flexibility and social preference by peers, respectively) will be examined in the first study presented.

The first objective of the first study was to examine the extent to which R & T was related to social problem solving and social affiliation. To address the problem of equifinality, the variance in the criterion measures due to games-with-rules and other forms of reciprocal social interaction will be statistically removed. R & T should account for a significant portion of the variance in social problem solving because of its flexibility dimension. This hypothesis is based on the assumption that children either learn or practice flexible social problem strategies in R & T.

R & T should also relate to one aspect of social affiliation—popularity—because R & T for most preadolecents is a friendly and cooperative venture with peers of similar sociometric and dominance status (Humphreys and Smith, 1987; see Pellegrini, 1994, for the case of R & T in adolescence). The specific dimension of R & T that should relate to popularity is the level of vigor in R & T. Vigorous play has been implicated in another aspect of social affiliation, gender segregation (Maccoby, 1986). It may be that boys prefer to play with others who also engage in forms of R & T and this is important to their peer popularity. As in the above analysis, contributions of R & T vigor to popularity will be determined after the variance due to other forms of reciprocal social interaction are controlled.

The equifinality problem will also be addressed in this study by examining relations among children's temperament, social competence, and aspects of R & T. Children's temperament is related to the equifinality issue to the extent that the flexibility and vigor features of R & T are also considered aspects of children's temperament. Consequently, the social competence benefits associated with R & T and specific playgroup composition may be due to temperament, not R & T; indeed, R & T may be an expression of this temperament.

The second objective of the first study was to determine the relation between two aspects of temperament—activity level and flexibility—and aspects of R & T. Next, the relations between R & T and measures of affiliation and social problem-solving was determined. Activity was chosen because it is related to aspects of R & T, vigorous play, and locomotion (Eaton and Enns, 1986; Routh, Schroeder, and O'Trama, 1979). Flexibility, or the willingness/ ability to change traditional roles and behaviors, was chosen because it is a common component in many definitions of play generally (e.g., Bruner, 1972), R & T specifically (Fagen, 1984), and social problem-solving flexibility. Relations between temperament and R & T should provide insight into the extent to which boys' R & T, and consequently any benefits associated with R & T, are being driven by temperament.

The third objective was to compare the social composition of boys' R & T groups with group composition during other forms of social interaction. Group composition is important to examine because it has been proffered as a contributor to children's prosocial and antisocial behavioral development generally (Maccoby, 1986), and, more specifically, for the benefits of R & T (Humphreys and Smith, 1987). Group size and dominance symmetry/asymmetry of playmates are particularly important group composition factors to consider. Group size is important to the extent that different size groups offer different opportunities to model prosocial and antisocial behaviors associated with different participants (Ladd, 1983; Maccoby, 1986). That children engage in R & T with children of similar status (Humphreys and Smith, 1987) and that these children are also prosocial (Coie and Dodge, 1984) may be a reason for the observed relations between R & T and social competence.

Dominance status of children, and the behaviors associated with establishing and maintaining dominance, also have important implications for social competence because they affect playmate choice and, correspondingly, group composition (Maccoby, 1986). Such a hypothesis is consistent with Fagen's (1981, 1984) seminal work on animal play and social-skills training, which posits that play will have beneficial social-skills training consequences if animals play in symmetrical, not asymmetrical, groups. In groups which are symmetrical in terms of dominance, or toughness, children will be equally matched, thus minimizing the possibility of one child exploiting the play bout for his aggressive and/or dominance exhibition ends. Symmetrical groups further allow children to learn and/or practice enacting numerous roles in which they take both superordinate (e.g., pinning a child in a play-fight) and subordinate roles (e.g., being pinned). These opportunities should lead to flexibility in other dimensions of social competence, such as flexible social problem-solving. Interaction in evenly matched groups should also relate to social affiliation in that R & T in symmetrical groups is often sustained and turns into cooperative social games; for example, R & T for popular children leads into social games-with-rules (Pellegrini, 1988).

In the first study, relations between specific dimensions of R & T and aspects of social competence will be presented. By controlling alternate routes to social competence—that is, the equifinality issue—a closer understanding of the functional role of R & T can be established. In the second study presented, the longitudinal relations, with a one-year lag, between aspects of R & T and social competence will be presented. Longitudinal relations are necessary to understand functional and developmental relation. The antecedent-consequence relations inherent in longitudinal designs are necessary to understand the causal mechanisms behind a specific function. Further, development must be studied longitudinally to the extent that we are trying chart the unfolding of a phenomenon across time. In both studies an effort was made to identify specific dimensions of R & T that related to measures of social competence. Examination of the role of specific design features of R & T also improves our understanding of the function of R & T.

STUDY 1:
CONTEMPORANEOUS RELATIONS
DURING CHILDHOOD METHOD

Subjects

The thirty-seven boys (M = 11.2-years-of-age) who participated in this study were selected from the total population of fifth-grade students in a public elementary school in a small city in the southeastern United States. These boys were a subsample of a larger, ongoing study at this school. Participation was determined by the boys' return of a parental consent form.

Procedures

Focal boys were observed for three-minute periods on their school playground during recess from September through June. Recess periods had durations ranging from twenty to twenty-five minutes. Between 120 and 150 children were on the playground for each period. Weather permitting, all children were required to go out, unless they had a medical excuse. There were three to five women (i.e., paraprofessional school personnel) supervising the recess periods. The playground had three distinct components: a blacktop area (approximately 10 × 100 yards); a contemporary playscape, which consisted of a climbing structure built with railroad ties and located in a pine forest; and a grass (100 × 20 yards) area that separated the blacktop from the playscape. There were no specific areas available for children to play basketball or baseball. Children were free to play in any of these three areas.

Children were observed, by two observers, according to focal child sampling rules and continuous recording rules (Martin and Bateson, 1986). More specifically, focal boys were observed, in counterbalanced order, continuously, for three-minute periods at least once per week for twenty weeks across the school year. Twenty observations per subject were used in data analyses. Focal children's behavior and the number and names of playmates were recorded by observers, who whispered information into the microphones of portable audiorecorders. The observers stayed close enough to the children so as to hear children's language and determine their facial expressions. Observers tried to remain unobtrusive by avoiding eye contact and not initiating interaction with the children. Initial pilot observations were conducted for two months so that children would habituate to the observers and so that the observers could identify the focal children and their peers.

Identification of focal children and their playmates was accomplished by the observers spending time with the children in the cafeteria for twenty to thirty minutes preceding recess. At this time, during which children were eating lunch, the observers noted the clothing worn by the children scheduled to be observed that day, as well as other identifying features. This information was placed on a card next to a picture of the focal children. These cards were placed in the order in which children were to be observed. Observer presence in the cafeteria also made them more familiar, and probably less obtrusive, to the children.

Behavioral Categories

The behaviors recorded were based on previous observations of the R & T of elementary-school children (i.e., Humphreys and Smith, 1984, 1987; Pellegrini, 1988). As noted above, focal children's behavior was recorded continuously for three minutes into an audiorecorder. The specific behaviors recorded follow.

R & T was defined along three dimensions. First, it was composed of the following *behaviors*: tease, hit and kick at, chase, poke, pounce, sneak-up, carry child, pile on, playfight, hold, and push. Second, R & T was defined according to *affect*: by the occurrence of a playface or wide smile (Blurton Jones, 1972). Third, R & T was defined according to *roles*; that is, children had to engage in alternating, reciprocal roles. In order to be coded R & T, a behavior had to meet all three criteria. R & T was scored along three dimensions: relative frequency, vigor, and flexibility.

Relative Frequency of R & T was the frequency of R & T bouts divided by the total other coded behavior.

Vigor of each R & T bout was coded, following Maccoby and Jacklin (1987), along a seven-point continuum with 1 for low and 7 for high; this scale was then collapsed into a 1–3 level measure.

Flexibility of all R & T behavior was coded on a 1–10 scale across all twenty observations. That is, a score of 1 was given if a boy exhibited 1:10 R & T behaviors, 2, if he exhibited 2:10, et cetra.

Games-with-rules, following Humphreys and Smith (1987), were social games with a priori rules which involved reciprocal roles (e.g., tag, clap/singing games, follow the leader, hop scotch, ball/catch games, and hide and seek).

Other forms of reciprocal social interaction included talking to a peer, comfort contact (e.g., patting on back), and swinging/pushing. In each case, each participant had to exhibit each dimension of the behavior in order for it to be considered reciprocal.

Group composition had two dimensions: *number* of children observed in the focal child's immediate group and *dominance/toughness composition*. In each case only interactions initiated by the focal child were recorded so as to minimize sampling bias (Humphreys and Smith, 1987). The number measure was simply the sum total of children in the focal child's group at the beginning of the sampling interval. The composition of the group was examined in terms of toughness symmetry and asymmetry. Focal boys' toughness status was compared to each of the children in his playgroup. The specific dominance/toughness measure used and the procedure for determining group symmetry and asymmetry are defined below.

Reliability was established by observers conducting fifty focal samples. The reliability for these fifty sessions was .72 (*kappa*).

Measures

All measures were administered by experimenters other than those doing the behavioral observations. Consequently, observers were not aware of children's sociometric, dominance, social problem, and temperament status.

Social problem-solving (SPS) status was determined using an adaptation of Spivak and Shure's (1979) Interpersonal Cognitive Problem Solving procedure. An experimenter presented individual children with five separate pictures of a child trying to get a toy from another child and five pictures of a child trying to avoid being reprimanded by an adult. Each child is asked to generate as many solutions to each problem as possible. All responses were recorded on a concealed audiorecorder. Experimenters followed scripts for each picture and used three prompts before changing pictures. Unlike the procedures recommended by Spivak and Shure, children's scores on this measure were the total number of *different positive* and *different negative responses* generated. That is, responses were differentiated as positive (such as trading, waiting for one's turn, and offering to pay for damage) or negative (such as lying, stealing, and hitting).

Dominance/toughness rank was determined as part of the sociometry procedure outlined above. Children were asked to identify the child in their class they thought was the "toughest" (Sluckin and Smith, 1977). This picture was taken out of the array by the experimenter, who then asked, "Now who is the toughest?" This procedure was repeated until no choices were made after three prompts. A child's score was his mean class rank. Group symmetry/asymmetry was determined by comparing the focal child's rank with those of each of his interactants, in pair-wise comparisons. The extent to which these pairings differed from chance was tested with Wilcoxon tests for correlated samples. Symmetrical groups were those where the ranks of the focal children and members of their groups did not differ from chance.

Popularity was determined following procedures outlined by Coie and Dodge (Coie, Dodge, and Coppetelli, 1982; Coie & Dodge, 1983). In this procedure, individual children were seated at a table before individual photos of his/her classmates. Each child was asked, first, to point to and name all of the children pictured. Next, they were asked to nominate the three peers they "like most" and the three peers they "like least". Boy's popularity score was a social preference score of likes-most minus likes-least nominations.

Temperament was assessed with the Dimensions of Temperament Survey (DOTS-R Child; Windle and Lerner, 1985). Children's teachers completed the whole instrument for each child in the spring of the year so as to maximize their knowledge of the children. Only two of the total nine dimensions were used in the analyses: General Activity and Flexibility. The instrument has factorial and predictive validity, as well as high internal consistency (Windle and Lerner, 1986; Windle et al. 1986). High scores on each factor indicate high levels of activity and behavioral flexibility, respectively.

STUDY 1: RESULTS/DISCUSSION

The first objective of the study was to determine the extent to which specific aspects of R & T (vigor and behavioral flexibility), independent of the other forms of reciprocal interaction, related to boys' popularity and social problem-solving flexibility, respectively. In this objective, regression analyses were used for each of the two criterion variables: number of "likes-most minus likes-least" nominations given by classmates and variety of positive and negative problem solutions generated. In order to minimize the number of predictor variables, games-with-rules and other forms of reciprocal interac-

Table 5.1   R & T group

Variable	Order entered	B value	R²	p
Popularity				
Reciprocal	1	.04	.07	.03
R & T/RF	2	− .87	.14	.08
R & T/Vigour	3	.09	.15	.59
Negative solutions				
Reciprocal	1	.98	.09	.31
R & T/RF	2	− .61	.09	.56
R & T/Flex	3	1.39	.32	.001
Positive solutions				
Reciprocal	1	3.67	.05	.32
R & T/RF	2	− 3.11	.05	.31
R & T/Flex	3	3.30	.22	.006

tion were aggregated into one variable and entered first into each of the three regression equations. Next, the relative frequency of R & T was entered into each equation. R & T vigor was then added to the model predicting popularity, while R & T flexibility was entered into each of the equations for social problem-solving. This analysis strategy helped determine the extent that variation in the criterion variables were due to relative frequency of R & T or specific dimensions of R & T, after variance due to other forms of reciprocal interaction was controlled. The results from each of these hierarchic regression analyses are displayed in table 5.1

For popularity, neither R & T/vigor nor reciprocal interaction added significant variance to the equation predicting popularity; relative frequency of R & T did account for significant variance (with a negative B-value) beyond that predicted by reciprocal social interaction. The regression equations were similar for both positive and negative social problem solutions. R & T/variety added significant variance to each measure while relative frequency of R & T did not account for a significant portion of the variance in these measures.

The second objective of the study was to examine the relations among two dimensions of children's temperament (activity and flexibility) and two dimensions of social competence (social problem-solving and popularity) and behavioral measures of R & T. The Pearson product moment correlations, which are displayed in table 5.2, revealed that activity and flexibility were significantly intercorrelated and both were significantly and positively related to popularity; no other temperament correlations were significant.

Table 5.2

	1	2	3	4	5	6	7	8
R & T/variety (1)	.45**	.64**	.25	.28	−.22	−.13	.18	
R & T flexibility (2)		.21	−.02	.24	.16	.34*	.54**	
R & T vigour (3)			.48**	.47**	.04	−.03	.18	
Activity (4)				.55**	.10	.04	−.02	
Flexibility (5)					.11	.04	.09	
Popularity (6)						.44**	.29	
Positive solutions (7)							.29	
Negative solutions (8)								

$^*p < .05; ^{**}p < .01.$

The third objective of this study was to compare the group composition of boys when they were engaged in three forms of reciprocal social interaction: R & T, social games-with-rules, and other forms of reciprocal social interaction. This was accomplished by examining the group size of each form of interaction and by comparing, within each of the three forms of interaction, the extent to which the group compositions were symmetrical in terms of dominance status.

In examining the group size of each social grouping for the three forms of interaction, a one way analysis of variance (ANOVA), with an independent variable at three levels (i.e., R & T, games-with-rules, and other forms of social interaction) was calculated with a dependent measure of mean group size. The ANOVA revealed no significant differences among R & T ($M = 3.16$), games-with-rules ($M = 3.6$), or other forms of reciprocal social interactions ($M = 4.0$) groupings.

To determine the extent to which the group compositions were symmetrical within each of the three forms of social interaction, the probability of the focal child's classroom mean dominance status differing from each playmate's dominance status was compared, in pair-wise fashion, to chance using the Sign Test. Specifically, within each of the three forms of social interaction, the ratio of symmetrical to asymmetrical groupings for each subject was calculated. Analyses indicated that the group compositions for each type of interaction were symmetrical beyond chance level: R & T, 24:34 were positive $p < .05$; games-with-rules, 36:50 were positive, $p < .05$; other forms of reciprocal interaction, 53:57 were positive, $p < .001$.

The first objective of this study was to examine the specific aspects of R & T which might be responsible for the associations reported in the literature between R & T and popularity and social problem-solving flexibility (Humphreys and Smith, 1987; Pellegrini, 1988). The specific approach used in this study followed a design-feature argument whereby specific behavioral and structural dimensions of R & T and outcome measures are compared (Fagen, this volume; Hinde, 1982). Design-feature arguments are sometimes used to suggest functional relations between sets of variables; similar features may serve similar functions. Regarding social affiliation, Maccoby (1986; Maccoby and Jacklin, 1987) has argued that one important reason for boys' gender segregation is their preference for vigorous play generally, and R & T specifically. Such play, because it is physically vigorous, may result in affiliation with other boys who also enjoy vigorous play. It should follow that boys' levels of vigor in R & T should be associated with popularity. The data did not bear out this claim. The reason for vigor not having its predicted correspondence with affiliation may have been due to the fact that most boys do not enjoy extremely vigorous play because it is too arousing; e.g., extremely vigorous play often involves risk taking (Maccoby, 1986). Moderately arousing R & T may have more affiliative appeal to more boys than extremely arousing play.

R & T flexibility was related to variety of positive and negative problem solutions. That flexibility was related to both outcome measures may have been due to the fact that it is a general indicator of children's behavioral repertoires. Children with varied behavioral repertoires should be more socially competent than those with less varied repertoires. The reason for the specific relation between R & T flexibility and social problem-solving flexibility is straightforward enough: R & T flexibility and variety of prosocial problem solutions are both examples of flexibility. One of the longstanding hypothesized, but untested, benefits of play relate to behavioral flexibility (e.g., Bruner, 1972; Fagen, 1984; Sutton-Smith, 1968). In play, it is argued, children become flexible through recombination and subroutinization of known behaviors. These flexible strategies are then generalized to other areas. Unfortunately, the data in this study do not permit such a directional hypothesis.

There are two rival hypotheses for these results. The first is that boys' social problem-solving flexibility is a dimension of their temperament and this temperament is responsible for the behavioral flexibility exhibited in R & T. The lack of a significant correlation between R & T flexibility and flexibility as a temperament construct, however, does not support this argument. The modest relation between behavioral and temperamental flexibility suggests that minimum variance is shared. This relation may reflect the fact that flexibility from one context to another is variable and not driven by temperament. While the temperament data are discussed below, certainly further research is necessary in this area.

The second rival hypothesis for the objective results is that frequency of engagement in R & T confounds R & T flexibility and that frequency of

R & T, not flexibility, contributes to affiliation and social problem-solving. This rival hypothesis is minimized by the nonsignificant contributions made by the relative frequency of R & T to the regression equations. Thus, it seems that the specific behavioral flexibility exhibited by children with a varied R & T repertoire is important in social problem-solving flexibility. Longitudinal designs are necessary to adequately address the ontogeny of this relation.

The second objective of this study was to examine associations among aspects of temperament (i.e., activity and flexibility), aspects of R & T, and psychometric measures. Of the six correlations calculated among the three measures of R & T and the two measures of temperament, only one, R & T vigor and temperament activity, was significantly correlated. Further, the two measures of temperament were not significantly related to popularity or to social problem-solving flexibility. This general lack of association between temperament and R & T is consistent with another study (Billman and McDevitt, 1980). In that study, of preschool children, only one of the six measures of R & T were related to activity, as measured by Thomas and Chess (1977).

There are a number of possible explanations for the lack of correspondence between temperament and behavioral and psychometric measures in the present study. First, it may be that a different measure of temperament would yield different results. The measure used, however, does have high psychometric qualities, including predictive and construct validity (Windle and Lerner, 1986). Indeed, the psychometric qualities of this instrument are further supported by the significant correlation ($r = .55$) between the two aspects of temperament in the present study, as in Windle et al. (1986).

Another possible explanation for the lack of association among these measures might be explained in terms of different contextual demands of teacher-student relations in the classroom and peer relations outside the classroom. For example, specific behaviors are demanded in a classroom but very different behaviors are demanded for interacting with peers on the playground. In the present study the temperament instrument was completed by teachers whose point of reference was the classroom while the behavioral measures were compiled in a peer interaction context, outside of the classroom, and the social problem-solving measure involved responses by children to hypothetical, non-classroom problems. The differing demand characteristics of each setting may be responsible for the lack of relations. Such differential contextual demands have been clearly documented by Lerner and colleagues (Lenerz et al., 1986), who reported significant differences between children's and parents' perceptions of contexts but there were insufficient cases of teachers' perceptions to warrant meaningful comparison. Future research should address differences among children's, parents', and teachers' perceptions of different contexts, as well as the relation between these variables and children's behavior.

The third objective of this study was to examine the composition of R & T groups, in terms of size and dominance symmetry, and determine the extent to which R & T differed on these characteristics from other forms of reciprocal social interaction. The results, generally, suggest that boys' R & T groups do not differ significantly from social games and other forms of reciprocal interaction; group size was about 3.5. This size is consistent with the mean reported by Ladd (1983) for popular, rejected, and average elementary school boys (3.6). Further, R & T groups, like the other forms of social interaction examined, were symmetrical in terms of boys' dominance status. In short, boys' R & T group composition was similar to other forms of social interaction on the playground.

The similarity in group size and composition, across social groupings, suggests that size and composition, *per se*, are not responsible for differential associations of R & T, compared to the other forms of interaction, with affiliation and social problem-solving measures. Consequently, in all social groupings boys had access to a similar number of behavioral models from whom they could learn/practice social skills necessary for affiliation and social problem solving. Obviously, the type of children composing these groups is an important consideration in such a social skills learning argument. That boys interacted with boys of similar toughness status suggests that they have opportunities to interact with similar children. Further, they had opportunities to learn/practice social problem solving problem strategies in a context that supports experimentation; children can try-out new strategies with equal dominance status peers with minimal threat that they will be exploited or dominated. This finding is consistent with the extant literature which suggests that children of similar dominance status tend to engage in R & T with each other (Humphreys & Smith, 1987). The reason for this, as noted above, is probably due to the fact that boys want to interact with others of similar toughness status so as to minimize the possibility of cooperative interaction moving into aggression.

That boy's groups are often typified by dominance-related behaviors (Maccoby and Jacklin, 1987; Savin-Williams, 1979) seemingly necessitate symmetrical groups to minimize the likelihood of these dominance-related behaviors moving into aggression. This is particularly likely to happen when children are engaged in forms of ambiguous social interaction, like R & T, and when rejected children are involved (Dodge and Frame, 1982; Pellegrini, 1988). Future research should examine the extent to which the R & T-to-aggressive transition is deliberate (as in the case of proactive aggressive children [Coie and Dodge, 1986], who may consciously exploit the playful tenor of R & T for their own ends [e.g., Fagan, 1981; Smith, 1989]) or due to information-processing deficits (more typical of reactive aggressive children [e.g., Coie and Dodge, 1986; Dodge and Frame, 1982]).

STUDY 2: LONGITUDINAL RELATIONS

In this study the longitudinal relations between R & T and social competence were examined. The one-year lag between the data collection points allows us to begin to make functional and developmental statements. Functional relations can also be established by design-feature arguments (Hinde, 1982). That is, when antecedent and consequence behaviors share similar behavioral and/or structural features, one may assume that the former and the latter are in a functional relation. In Study 2, specific design features of R & T and social affiliation will be examined. As in Study 1, the relations among R & T, social affiliation, and dominance/toughness were examined in Study 2. Other dimensions of social affiliation were also examined in Study 2: popularity and participation in cooperative games-with-rules. Previous contemporaneous research has shown that elementary school children's R & T changes to cooperative games-with-rules at a rate greater than chance; for example, chase turns in tag (Pellegrini, 1988). The behavioral (e.g., chasing) and structural (e.g., alternating roles) similarities between R & T and games may have been responsible for these proximal relations. Further, as the frequency of children's R & T decreases across the elementary school period, the frequency of games-with-rules increases (Rubin, Fein, and Vandenberg, 1983). Given these proximal and distal relations, one would except R & T at Year 1 to predict cooperative games-with-rules in Year 2.

R & T may also serve an affiliative function by predicting popularity. Guided by Study 1 results, a predictive relation between R & T and popularity is expected. Besides being correlated with popularity, R & T typically occurs among children who are friends (Humphreys and Smith, 1987; Pellegrini, 1989). R & T may provide children with opportunities to practice and learn skills, such as reciprocal role-taking, and strategies necessary for establishing and maintaining friendships. On the other hand, a literature exists suggesting that R & T is used by children to establish dominance relationships with peers (Fagen, 1981, this volume; Humphreys and Smith, 1987; Pellegrini, 1994). While the results of Study 1 did not support this contention, the idea is an interesting one and one worth pursuing because nonhuman primate and some child-development research posits that R & T may be used to exhibit dominance over peers so as to extract future benefits (Fagen, 1981; Humphreys and Smith, 1987; Neill, 1976).

In short, Study 2 examined the social affiliative function served by R & T in a longitudinal context. The dimensions of affiliation examined included:

engagement in cooperative games-with-rules, peer nominated popularity, and peer nominated dominance.

Method

Seventy two children, with a mean age of 7.5 years, participated in Study 2. They were from the same population as the participants in Study 1. They were enrolled in grades K, 2, and 4 during Year 1 and, correspondingly, in grades 1, 3 and, 5 during Year 2.

The observation and peer nomination (i.e., popularity and dominance status) procedures, too, were similar to those outlined for Study 1. Children's R & T and games-with-rules (e.g., tag, follow the leader, and catch) were observed.

STUDY 2: RESULTS/DISCUSSION

The first analysis involved predicting Year 2 games-with-rules from Year 1 components of R & T; no order was specified in the regression model. Two components of R & T (hit-at and pounce/pile-on) predicted games ($R2 = .19$, $p < .03$).

Next, Year 2 popularity was predicted by components of Year 1 R & T; because popularity is stable across the elementary-school years (Bernt and Hoyle, 1985), Year 1 popularity was entered into the regression equation first. Besides Year 1 popularity ($R2 = .23$, $p < .001$), sneak-up was the only other significant predictor ($R2 = .27$, $p < .01$). Regarding dominance, the extent to which Year 1 R & T predicted Year 2 toughness status was examined by first controlling Year 1 toughness status and then entering dimensions of R & T; no significant relations were detected.

The games-with-rules analysis replicates earlier sequential analysis suggesting that R & T leads to games (Pellegrini, 1988). The similarity of design features in the two behaviors is probably responsible for the relation. The R & T behaviors predicting games (hit-at and pounce/pile-on) are similar to behaviors in the game of tag. Hit-at, for example, is similar to behaviors used to tag a peer. Pounce/pile-on behaviors typically occurred in the context of an object being thrown and the receiver being tackled, not unlike football. These data suggest that R & T becomes transformed into cooperative games during the elementary-school period. Such a transformation helps account for the decline in R & T and increase in games during this period.

Next, the relation between R & T and popularity was examined; sneak-up was the only significant R & T component to predict popularity. Sneak-up may have been used as a group-entry strategy. Indeed, this behavior was the only R & T component that could have served as a group-entry strategy alone. Children may have used this as a strategy because they were confident that it would not elicit an aggressive response from their playmates, who are typically friends. Choice of friend as R & T playmates minimizes the possibility of wrongfully attributing aggressive intent to R & T initiations. Such initiations, in turn, result in subsequent interaction and affiliation.

Lastly, the relations between R & T and dominance were examined; the two were not related at any of the three grade levels. Children did not use R & T to exhibit dominance, probably, because it was done, as shown in Study 1, with friends and peers of similar dominance status. Further, dominance, in the form of toughness or aggression, does not seem to be an important part of affiliation.

GENERAL DISCUSSION

In the two studies reported here, an attempt was made to identify aspects of R & T which may serve a social-competence function in childhood. Two groups of children were studied: a younger group (7.5 years) in the longitudinal study and an older group (11.2 years) in the contemporaneous study. The approach taken was to unpack the molar category R & T into relevant design features. This approach yielded very different results for the two groups of children. For the younger group in the longitudinal study, dimensions of R & T were positively related to engagement in cooperative games-with-rules and popularity, not dominance. For the older group, R & T was negatively related to popularity, but also not related to dominance. An explanation for these results can be found in the nonhuman primate literature, where it has been shown that the rough play of subadults often results in aggressive exploitation (Fagen, 1981); aggression, in turn, is negatively related to popularity. Some biologists, like Fagen, suggest that early adolescence is a period of changing dominance relationships and players engaging in R & T may exploit the playful of tenor R & T so as to exhibit dominance over a weaker peer. In this way they can publicly establish or maintain dominance. Our measures of R & T, in both studies, were not, however, related to dominance, either in terms of peer-nominated dominance status or in terms of symmetry of playgroups. Work with adolescent boys, however, does suggest a "darker side" of play (Fagen, this volume). R & T is used to establish dominance relationships; particularly, it is often used by tough boys to victimize weaker boys (Pellegrini, 1994).

The differences in the two studies reported in this chapter may have been due to methods employed or age of the sample. Regarding methods, dominance was measured in the studies reported here by peer nominations of toughness. While this method is correlated with behavioral measures of dominance (Savin-Williams, 1979), categorizing children's dominance in terms of behavioral and relationship measures may yield different results. Behaviorally, more microlevel analyses might be insightful; for example, what is the probability of playful R & T moving into R & T where dominance is exhibited? From a relationship perspective, it is important to relate these specific behaviors to the peer context in which they are generated. While toughness symmetry in R & T groups is a starting point, it would also be interesting to look at the extent to which "bullies" initiate R & T and "victims" are the targets. As noted above, adolescent bullies often use R & T as an entree to victimizing weaker boys.

Regarding the different ages of the samples in the two studies, boys in Study 1 were older than those in Study 2 and their R & T was negatively but *not* significantly related to popularity. It may be that at this point of early adolescence boys are just beginning to use R & T to exhibit dominance; thus, the weak but negative relations between R & T and popularity. As boys get older, and still engage in R & T, the relation with dominance becomes stronger. Other work, with other boys (i.e., 13 years) supports this contention (Pellegrini, 1994). Thus, R & T seems to be positively related to dimensions of affiliation during the preschool and elementary-school periods; it may be related to dominance in adolescence (see Humphreys and Smith, 1984, for a review).

It also seems important to identify theoretically relevant design features of R & T as predictors of social competence. With the older sample, only the flexibility dimension of R & T, not the relative frequency of R & T, related to social problem-solving flexibility. With the younger sample, only specific dimensions of R & T related to games and popularity. These results suggest that R & T is not a unitary construct: different components seem to have different developmental trajectories. Again, this conclusion is supported when the R & T of adolescent boys is examined: physically rough R & T relates to dominance while other aspects, like chase, relate to social problem-solving (Pellegrini, 1994).

In conclusion, R & T is an interesting topic of study for a developmentalist to the extent that its functions seem to change from the early childhood period to adolescence. For children it is a playful, affiliative category, while for adolescents it is used as a way in which to exhibit dominance.

REFERENCES

Bernt, T., & Hoyle, S. (1985). Stability and change in childhood and adolescent friendships. *Developmental Psychology, 21*, 1002–15.

Billman, J., & McDevitt, S. (1980). Convergence of parent and observer ratings of temperament with observations of peer interaction in nursery school. *Child Development, 51*, 395–400.

Blurton Jones, N. (1972). Categories of child interaction. In N. Blurton Jones (Ed.), *Ethological studies of child behavior* (pp. 97–129). London: Cambridge University Press.

Bruner, J. (1972). The nature and uses of immaturity. *American Psychologist, 27*, 687–708.

Coie, J., & Dodge, K. (1983). Continuities and changes in children's social status: A five-year longitudinal study. *Merrill-Palmer Quarterly, 29,* 261–82.

—————. (1986). Hostile and instrumentally aggressive children: A social information processing perspective. Paper presented at the Annual Meeting of the American Psychological Association, Washington, D.C.

Coie, J., & Dodge, K., & Coppotelli, H. (1982). Dimensions and types of social status: A cross-age perspective. *Developmental Psychology, 18,* 557–70.

Dansky, J., & Silverman, I. (1973). Effects of play on associative fluency. *Developmental Psychology, 9,* 38–43.

—————. (1975). Play: A general facilitator of associative fluency. *Developmental Psychology, 11,* 104.

Dodge, K., & Frame, C. (1982). Social cognitive biases and deficits in aggressive boys. *Child Development, 53,* 620–35.

Eaton, W., & Enns, L. (1986). Sex differences in human motor activity. *Psychological Bulletin, 100,* 19–28.

Fagen, R. (1981). *Animal play behavior.* New York: Oxford University Press.

—————. (1984). Play and behavioral flexibility. In P. K. Smith (Ed.), *Play in animals and humans* (pp. 159–74). London: Basil Blackwell.

Hinde, R. (1982). *Ethology.* London: Fontana.

Humphreys, A., & Smith, P. K. (1984). Rough-and-tumble in preschool and playground. In P. K. Smith (Ed.), *Play in animals and humans* (pp. 241–70). London: Blackwell.

—————. (1987). Rough-and-tumble play, friendship and dominance in school children: Evidence for continuity and change with age. *Child Development, 58,* 201–212.

Ladd, G. (1983). Social networks of popular, average, and rejected children in school settings. *Merrill-Palmer Quarterly, 29,* 283–307.

Lenerz, K., Kincher, J., Lerner, J., & Lerner, R. (1986). Contextual demands for early adolescent behavioral style. *Journal of Early Adolescence, 6,* 279–91.

Maccoby, E. (1986). Social groupings in childhood: Their relationship to prosocial and antisocial behavior in boys and girls. In D. Olweus, J. Block, & M. Radye-Yarrow (Eds.), *Development of antisocial and prosocial behavior: Research, theory, and issues* (pp. 263–80). New York: Academic.

Maccoby, E., & Jacklin, C. (1987). Gender segregation in childhood. In H. Reese (Ed.), *Advances in child development* (vol. 20) (pp. 239–87). New York: Academic.

Martin, P., & Bateson, P. (1986). *Measuring behavior.* London: Cambridge University Press.

Martin, P., & Caro, T. (1985). On the functions of play and its role in behavioral development. In J. Rosenblatt, C. Beer, M. C. Bushel, & P. Slater (Eds.), *Advances in the study of behavior* (vol. 15) (pp. 59–103). New York: Academic.

Pellegrini, A. D. (1988). Elementary school children's rough-and-tumble play and social competence. *Developmental Psychology, 24,* 802–06.

————. (1989). Elementary school children's rough-and-tumble play. *Early Childhood Research Quarterly, 4,* 245–60.

————. (1994). The rough-and-tumble play of adolescent boys of differing sociometric status. *International Journal of Behavioral Development, 17,* 525–40.

Routh, D., Schoeden, C., & O'Trama, L. (1979). Development of activity levels in children. *Developmental Psychology, 10,* 163–68.

Rubin, K., Fein, G., & Vandenberg, B. (1983). Play. In E. M. Hetherington (Ed.), *Handbook of child psychology* (vol. 4) (pp. 693–779). New York: Wiley.

Sackett, G., Sameroff, A., Cairns, R., & Suomi, S. (1981). Continuity in behavioral development: Theoretical and empirical issues. In K. Immelmann, G. Barrow, L. Petrinovich, and M. Main (Eds.), *Behavioral Development* (pp. 23–57). New York: Cambridge University Press.

Savin-Williams, R. (1979). Dominance hierarchies in groups of early adolescence. *Child Development, 50,* 142–51.

Sluckin, A., & Smith, P. K. (1977). Two approaches to the concept of dominance in preschool children. *Child Development, 48,* 917–23.

Smith, P. K. (1982). Does play matter? Functional and evolutionary aspects of animal and human play. *The Behavioral and Brain Sciences, 5,* 139–84.

————. (1989). The role of rough-and-tumble play in the development of social competence: Theoretical perspectives and empirical evidence. In B. Schneider, G. Attili, J. Nadel, & R. Weissberg (Eds.), *Social competence in developmental perspectives* (pp. 239–55). Hingham, MA: Kluwer Academic Publishers Group.

Spivak, G., & Shure, M. (1979). *Social adjustment of young children.* San Francisco: Jossey-Bass.

Sutton-Smith, B. (1966). Piaget on play: A critique. *Psychological Review, 73,* 104–110.

————. (1967). The role of play in cognitive development. *Young Children, 22,* 364–69.

————. (1968). Novel responses to toys. *Merrill-Palmer Quarterly, 14,* 151–58.

————. (1990). School playground as festival. *Children's Environment Quarterly, 7,* 3–7.

Thomas, A., & Chess, S. (1977). *Temperament and development.* New York: Brunner/ Mazel.

Windle, M., Hooker, K., Lerner, K., East, P., Lerner, J., & Lerner, R. (1986). Temperament, perceived competence, and depression in early and late adolescence. *Developmental Psychology, 22,* 384–92.

Windle, M., & Lerner, R. (1985). *Revised Dimensions of Temperament Survey—Child (Self).* Rochester, NY: Autnov.

————. (1986). Reassessing the Dimensions of Temperamental Individuality Across the Life Span: The Revised Dimensions of Temperament Survey (DOTS-R). *Journal of Adolescent Research, 1,* 213–20.

6

JEFFREY GOLDSTEIN

Aggressive Toy Play

INTRODUCTION

This chapter considers play with aggressive toys and video games. There are perhaps two dozen studies of aggressive toys and games and an equal number of scholarly essays on the subject. These have considered only a limited number of aspects of war play, using a narrow range of theories and focusing on a few public issues surrounding war toys and war play. Although involving fewer publications to date, the debate about video games mirrors that of war toys (Provenzo, 1991; Sacher, 1993).

An attempt is made in this chapter to broaden the discussion by introducing further theoretical perspectives and raising additional issues that also may enlighten us about the nature, purposes, and effects of such play. The chapter begins with an overview of data on war play and war toys. Theories and methods used in the study of war play are reviewed, and these are followed by additional perspectives that might be applied fruitfully to the subject of war play. The purpose here is not to examine critically the findings of this research. In fact, they are presented here somewhat uncritically, because our interest is not so much with their findings as with the limited range of questions that have been asked and approaches taken. For reviews of this literature see Goldstein (1992), Smith (1994), and Sutton-Smith (1988).

AGGRESSIVE PLAY

Aggressive play includes mock fighting, rough-and-tumble play, and/or fantasy aggression. When imaginary battles are waged or war toys used, we refer to war play. Aggressive toys and war toys are those that children use in play-fighting and fantasy aggression, including but not limited to toys that resemble weapons. Lego bricks formed into a gun or a stick used as a mock weapon are considered aggressive toys in this context.[1] To flesh out this discussion, we also refer to violent video games, those with fighting, shooting, or war-like themes. These are considered together because all involve images or themes of violence and aggression, and because, in studying them, researchers have used the same group of theories and methods.

Who Plays Aggressive Games?

Nearly every study on the subject reports that boys far more than girls engage in war games and aggressive play. Studies reporting sex differences in aggressive play have been conducted in India, Italy, Germany, Japan, Mexico, the Philippines, the United Kingdom, and the United States, in addition to cross-cultural analyses of archival data (see Humphreys and Smith, 1984; Jukes, 1991; Pellegrini, this volume, Roopnarine et al., 1992; Suito and Reifel, 1992).

In her interviews with ten-year-old German children, Wegener-Spöhring (1989) found that 76 percent of the boys owned toy guns, compared with 29 percent of the girls. Costabile et al. (1992) report that 57 percent of English children and 36 percent of Italian children age 2–6 years are reported by their parents to engage in war play. Fewer than 10 percent of those reported to play war games are girls. Although neither the Wegener-Spöhring nor Costabile et al. studies is based on a representative sample, the results are consistent with other findings that war play and rough-and-tumble play are overwhelmingly the prerogative of boys. Neither the age of the child (from two to six years) nor social class was a major influence in war play in the research of Costabile et al.

Based on reports by parents in Italy and England, war play begins at about two years of age. For those children who engage in it, war play occurs only about once a week on average. Most war play is social, involving at least two children and often groups of players.

It is not just young boys who engage in war play, but men as well. The decades since the Vietnam war have seen the development and growth of mock–war games, like paintball, designed for men (Gibson, 1992). Men in military fatigues spend a day or longer in mock battle with an "enemy," who is stalked and captured or shot with paint pellets or a laser gun. During the 1991 war in the Persian Gulf, sales of replica weapons, priced far beyond the means of most children, were reported to be brisk (*The Economist*, 23 Feb. 1991; *The Wall Street Journal*, 31 Jan. 1991).

Sex Differences in Aggressive Play

By age two, and sometimes evident as early as one year of age, boys and girls tend to play differently and prefer different, usually "gender-appropriate,"[2] playthings (Caldera, Huston, and O'Brien, 1989; Fein et al., 1985; Goldstein, 1992). Although both girls and boys show a preference for sex-typed toys, girls are less rigid in this regard, showing greater willingness to play with "boys' toys" than boys are to play with "girls' toys" (Almqvist, 1989; Eisenberg et al., 1985). Sex-stereotyped play increases with age, reflecting social influences, mainly parental and peer modeling (Moller, Hymel, and Rubin, 1992;

Rheingold and Cook, 1975; Zammuner, 1987). These sex differences were noted in research as early as 1933 by Parten.

Children are more readily accepted by their peers when they play with "sex-appropriate" toys. When children choose toys considered appropriate for their sex, playmates of the same sex approach them (Berndt and Heller, 1986; Eisenberg, Tryon, and Cameron, 1984; Moller, Hymel, and Rubin, 1992). Indeed, among the reasons for making these toy choices may be the desire for peer approval, the wish to avoid negative reactions from peers, and the desire to engage in further interactions with peers of the same sex (Shell and Eisenberg, 1990). Furthermore, teachers tend to leave children alone if they are playing with sex-stereotyped toys (Fagot, 1984).

Whether a toy is perceived as appropriate for a boy or a girl is determined partly by the child's same-sex peers. Four- and five-year-olds viewed a toy as a "boys' toy" if they previously observed mainly boys playing with the toy, and as a "girls' toy" if girls were seen playing with the toy (Shell and Eisenberg, 1990).

Video games, particularly those involving shooting and war-like themes, are far more appealing to boys than to girls. Kubey and Larson (1990) report that 80 percent of videogame play among children nine to fifteen years of age is by boys. Relative to boys, girls reported far less affect and arousal while playing video games. When an aggressive fantasy theme is added to a video game, boys like the game more, and girls less, than the same game without an aggressive theme (Malone, 1981).

Cooper, Hall, and Huff (1990) studied fifty-two boys and girls in grades 6 through 8 (age eleven to fourteen years) who used mathematics programs with themes that appeal mainly to boys (shooting or propelling objects through fantasy space, graphic feedback, action, aggression) or appeal mainly to girls (absence of aggression/shooting, verbal feedback, cooperative). The programs were used either in isolation or in a computer room with other students nearby. In the latter, social setting, girls reported experiencing greater stress using "masculine programs" and boys reported greater stress using "feminine programs." These effects were obtained only when the subjects' schoolmates were present, suggesting the importance of potential peer disapproval.

Effects on Aggression

If we take at face value the approximately two dozen studies of war toys, plus the equal number of studies of video games with violent themes, it appears that they increase the frequency and duration of *aggressive play*, but whether they influence *aggressive behavior* (that is, the intention to injure others) is not as certain (Sacher, 1993; Smith, 1994; Sutton-Smith, 1988).

Findings from studies of war toys are diverse, if sparse. War toys have been found to

Table 6.1   Effects of War Toys on Aggressive Play and Aggressive Behavior

	Girls	Boys
Aggressive Play	?	++
Aggressive Behavior:		
Short-term	0	+
Long-term	0/?	?

++ = highly reliable finding
 + = moderately consistent finding
 0 = no reliable evidence
 ? = inconsistent or insufficient data

- enhance aggression (Sanson and Di Muccio, 1993; Turner and Gold-smith, 1976; Watson and Peng, 1992),
- reduce aggression (Bonte and Musgrove, 1943; Gribbin, 1979),
- have no bearing on aggression (Sutton-Smith, Gerstmyer, and Meckley, 1988; Wegener-Spöhring, 1989).

Few studies report that war toys affect the behavior of girls. (See table 6.1.)

In the better-designed studies, aggressive toys appear to give rise to an *immediate increase in aggressive behavior*. This effect does not generalize to other physical settings, for example from playroom to classroom (Turner and Goldsmith, 1976; Wolff, 1976). Aggression returns to baseline once the aggressive toys are withdrawn, or shortly after the video game has been put aside (Turner and Goldsmith, 1976).

Attitudes Toward War Play

Children and adults tend to view aggressive play differently, with children making a sharper distinction between playful and real aggression (Fry, 1990; Pellegrini, 1988; Smith and Boulton, 1990; Wegener-Spöhring, 1989; Sutton-Smith, Gerstmyer, and Meckley, 1988).

Males and females differ in how they interpret an episode of rough play. According to studies by Connor (1989), females are more likely to interpret rough play as "aggression," while men are more likely to see it as "play." Women who, as children, had engaged in aggressive play were more apt to interpret the episodes as play than as aggression. Likewise, parents with firsthand experience of video games have more favorable attitudes toward them than do adults with no experience (Sneed and Runco, 1992).

How might these biases influence judgments of children's play? I have heard many teachers, mostly women, comment on the outdoor play of their elementary-school students during recess. The boys are often seen chasing, fleeing, running chaotically, making noise, pretending to shoot one another, while small groups of girls can be seen talking quietly. The boys' behavior is interpreted by teachers as more aggressive than that of the girls. However, it is possible in such a situation that the girls are behaving more aggressively than the boys. If aggression is defined as the attempt to harm another, then the boys engaged in typical rough-and-tumble or war play are cognizant of the fantasy frame within which such play is specifically *not* aggression. Indeed, the most aggressive boys, who do not play within this implicitly agreed upon framework, do not participate as often in aggressive play (Willner, 1991). The girls in this instance may be talking about a classmate in such a way as to cause her embarrassment or psychological injury, for example, excluding her from the conversation (Lagerspetz, Bjorkqvist, and Peltonen, 1988). If this behavior is deliberate, then on this playground, despite outward appearances, it is the girls and not the boys who are aggressive.

Judgments of aggressive play, including war play and use of video games with violent themes, elicit two major reactions from adults (see Smith, 1994). Opponents of such play, such as Carlsson-Paige and Levin (1987) and Miedzian (1991), argue that war play impoverishes the child's imagination, fosters imitative violence, perpetuates war, and is unseemly. Proponents of this sort of play argue that it is a natural, even inevitable aspect of boys' play. They point out that the young males of all primate species engage in play-fighting. Furthermore, this sort of play heightens imagination and role-taking and affords the child an opportunity to come to terms with war, violence, and death. [These ideas underlie play therapy (Singer, 1994).] Finally, proponents argue that war play reflects adult behavior and values.

There are behavioral, cognitive, aesthetic, and ethical components of war play, aggressive toys, and video games with violent themes. Children's play, and some toys and video games, may be unaesthetic, violating all sorts of social norms. According to at least one author (Smith, 1994), toy manufacturers have a moral obligation to draw the line at offensive items, even if harmful effects are unproven. We do not want to argue this point, but only indicate that attitudes about war play are, and apparently always have been, ambivalent (Beresin, 1989; Twitchell, 1989).

Part of the ambivalence about video games arises from a kind of "technophobia," anxiety about complex technology. Contemporary toys incorporate modern technology to an unprecedented extent. And no toys have

Table 6.2   Predominant Theories Used in the Study of War Play

to 1960	PSYCHOANALYTIC THEORY. Catharsis. Play therapy. E.g., Lowenfeld 1935; Feshbach, 1956; Mallick & McCandless, 1966.
1960s to early 1980s	LEARNING and SOCIAL LEARNING THEORIES. Modeling, Imitation. Frustration-Aggression Cue Theory. E.g., Lovaas, 1961; Turner & Goldsmith, 1976; Slife & Rychlak, 1982.
1980s to date	ETHOLOGY and SOCIOBIOLOGY E.g., Boulton, 1991a, 1991b; Fry, 1990; Pellegrini, 1989; Smith, 1982.
1980s to date	SOCIAL CONSTRUCTION. ROLE THEORY. E.g., Connor, 1989; Sutton-Smith, Gerstmyer & Meckley, 1988; Jukes & Goldstein, 1993.

ever been as complex as today's video games. So it is not surprising that video games generate controversy.

THEORIES AND METHODS IN THE STUDY OF AGGRESSIVE PLAY

The study of aggressive play, war toys, and video games with violent themes has been limited to a few areas of concern (mainly their effects on aggressive behavior) and restricted to a limited number of theoretical approaches. Predictably, the theories used to guide research on aggressive play have been those in vogue at the time the research was conducted (table 6.2).

The same may be said of research on video games. Considering video games to be like television programs, most researchers use social learning theory to study imitation of pro- and antisocial behavior following play with video games containing pro- or antisocial themes (e.g., Chambers and Ascione, 1987; Cooper and Mackie, 1986; Graybill, Strawniak, Hunter, O'Leary, 1987; Silvern and Williamson, 1987).

Notably absent from the study of war play and video games are Piagetian and other social-cognitive developmental theories, and a variety of symbolic interactionist views (Fine, 1983). This may be attributed partly to the fact that the research focused on the effects that aggressive play has on aggressive behavior, and not on other possible effects, such as cognitive and social skills, self-presentation, and social identity. (These are discussed further in the final section of the chapter).

A brief review of the most common approaches to the study of war play demonstrates the rather limited range of theories and methods utilized to date.

Biological/Ethological Approaches

Perhaps the oldest views of the functions of play are biological and physiological notions of energy control and regulation. In 1860 Herbert Spencer wrote that the purpose of play is to deplete "surplus energy" (which people apparently possessed in those days). The influence of this idea is still found in the use of recess in elementary schools to allow children to "blow off steam" after sitting through their lessons (Pellegrini, 1989a).

Observational studies of rough-and-tumble play use methods and concepts from ethology and sociobiology (e.g., Boulton, 1991a, 1991b; Costabile et al., 1991; Pellegrini, 1989b). Because these have not been systematically used in the study of war toys or video games, they are not discussed here. But they are promising and are considered again below in the final section of the chapter.

The philosopher Karl Groos (1898) saw the play of animals and children as preparation for adult life. Play activities vary from species to species but, according to Parker (1984), are always fragments of longer functional adult activities, like fighting, fleeing an enemy, or hunting. This is known as the *practice hypothesis.*

Transhistorical and cross-cultural studies of rough-and-tumble play support the view that play is practice for adult activities (e.g., Fry, 1990). In both ancient and modern cultures, social norms are reflected in the games considered appropriate for children (Keefer, Goldstein, and Kasiarz, 1983; Lever, 1978; Roberts and Sutton-Smith, 1962; Twitchell, 1989). Humphreys and Smith (1984) conclude that "the most likely original function of human rough-and-tumble play, in an evolutionary sense, is as practice for fighting and hunting skills. This is the only hypothesis which has so far provided a convincing explanation of the forms of the activity and the appreciable sex differences" (p. 262).

Traditionally sex-typed play has other biological underpinnings. In a broad way, the differential activity levels of boys and girls may have something to do with their preference for toys that easily lend themselves to active play. Activity level tends to be higher in boys (Eaton and Enns, 1986; Maccoby and Jacklin, 1974). As a result, they may prefer activities and toys that facilitate highly active forms of play (Jukes and Goldstein, 1993).

More concretely, several studies show a hormonal influence on play styles and toy preferences. Meyer-Bahlburg, Feldman, Cohen, and Ehrhardt (1988) have documented a relationship between prenatal exposure to the synthetic female hormone progestogen and a reduction in rough-and-tumble play in both sexes. Toy preferences have also been related to prenatal exposure to hormones. Both boys and girls exposed prenatally and in early postnatal months to high levels of androgen showed greater preference for traditionally boys' toys at ages three to eight years (Berenbaum and Hines, 1992).

Recent biological views of play emphasize not energy but physiological arousal, hedonic arousal, metabolic energy, and thermoregulation (Apter, 1992; Barber, 1991; Burghardt, 1984).

Psychoanalytic Views

Psychoanalytic notions of play have been used primarily as a basis for play therapy (Lowenfeld, 1935; Singer, 1994) and, in studies of aggressive play, as the source of ideas about aggression catharsis. For example, in what is probably the first experiment on toy guns, Feshbach (1956) derived hypotheses from psychoanalytic theory about the role of fantasy in regulating aggression. With the appearance of rich behavioral and cognitive theories in the 1960s, psychoanalytic views tended to fall into disuse in the study of play, although they still underlie much of play therapy.

Social Learning Theories

Social learning theory is widely used to explain the development of sex-typed toy preferences and sex-role stereotypes. Many studies find that parents purchase sex-stereotyped toys for their children, particularly if the parents themselves hold traditional sex-role attitudes (Eckerman and Stein, 1990; O'Brien and Huston, 1985; Rheingold and Cook, 1975; Zammuner, 1987). Children who choose traditional sex-typed toys are more likely to have parents who hold traditional attitudes about sex roles (Repetti, 1984).

Social learning of play styles is not restricted to personal influence, but also involves mass media effects, such as the portrayal of boys and girls in toy packaging and advertising (Schwartz and Markham, 1985).

Adults pass their own sex-role attitudes on to children along with the toys they give to them. As parental attitudes about sex roles change, they are reflected in toy purchases for their children. Singer and Singer (1990) observed that girls are increasingly likely to play with traditionally boys' toys and parents are increasingly willing to purchase such toys for them.

The vast majority of studies of aggressive play use social learning theory to predict that exposure to toy weapons will result in a disinhibition of aggression or the enactment of aggressive scripts learned from previous exposure to aggressive models (e.g., Slife and Rychlak, 1982).

One variant of social learning is Huesmann's cognitive script model (1988), used in recent research on toy guns by Lovaas (1961) and Jukes (1991). Sanson and DiMuccio (1993) interpret war toys as cues that activate scripts of aggressive behavior stored in memory. These scripts are thought to come from television cartoons and toy advertising (Carlsson-Paige and Levin, 1990; Miedzian, 1991).

Studies of video games rely upon social learning theory to predict that exposure to games with violent themes will result in learning and imitation of aggression. These studies are based in theory and design upon the far more numerous studies of television violence (e.g., Schutte, Malouff, Post-Gordon, and Rodasta, 1988; Chambers and Ascione, 1987).

Is television violence research relevant to video games? "It would appear that heavy video game viewing [sic], like television viewing, will have a negative effect upon children, since video games offer models of violence and opportunities for practicing aggressive techniques vicariously," writes McMeen (1985). "Because television research so clearly demonstrates a relationship between this intense engagement and subsequent aggression when the program content is violent, investigations of the effects of video game playing usually have predicted a similar relationship" (Funk 1992, p. 53).

The video game–television comparison may be inappropriate. There are similarities, of course: In both cases, children witness repeated acts of stylized violence on a two-dimensional screen. However, there are important differences between playing video games and watching television. Among other things, there are differences in content and in the social setting in which these media are used. Furthermore, television viewing is, relative to video game play, a passive activity, while video game playing is more active, with choices, responses, and controls in the hands of the players. Video game players are participants in an interactive system that allows them to regulate the pace and character of the game. This, in turn, gives them increased control over their own emotional states during play (Zillmann, 1987). Video games often involve cooperation among players, while television viewing does not. Furthermore, the fantasy characters of video games often seek to avoid violence. (See table 6.3.)

Frustration-Aggression and Arousal Theories

In what is regarded by many as the most convincing research on the aggression-instigating effects of toy weapons, Turner and Goldsmith (1976) rely on Berkowitz's variation of social learning theory. Much as in cognitive script theory, toy weapons are said to act as cues that elicit aggressive behavior among frustrated or angry children.

Table 6.3   Some Differences between Television Violence and Video Games with Violent Themes

Television	Video Games
Real and fictional violence	Fictional violence only
Realistic looking violence	Stylized, symbolic aggression
More passive	More active
Little control over images on the screen	Great control over images on the screen
No control of pacing, timing	Control over timing of action
Little or no interaction with others during viewing	Frequent interaction with others during play

Methods in the Study of Aggressive Play

Widely differing definitions and measures have been used to study aggressive play. Researchers frequently fail to distinguish between play-fighting, physical aggression, and verbal aggression (see Smith, 1994). According to Sutton-Smith (1988), the greatest problem in many of these studies is the failure to distinguish between real and playful aggression and between verbal and physical aggression (problems that still plague much research on war toys [e.g., Potts, Huston, and Wright, 1986; Sanson and DiMuccio, 1993]).

Researchers often impose play on children, which may make the task into something which, to the children, is not play (Salamone and Salamone, 1991). Pellegrini (1989b) found that even the same type of play, rough-and-tumble, may be playful and prosocial or aggressive and antisocial depending, in this instance, on the child's sociometric standing.

Only a limited number of dependent variables has been measured in the study of aggressive toy play, namely, physical and verbal aggression, aggressive play, and, less often, preference for war toys. Arousal, novelty, activity level, cognitive and social skills, and reasons for engaging in war play have not been explored systematically.

Not only are a very few (ill-defined) dependent measures used in these studies, but they fail to consider adequately alternative explanations and dependent measures. For example, in studies where aggression is the dependent variable, a measure of arousal/activity level would help eliminate alternative explanations that the behavior is simply one of heightened activity rather than behavior with specifically aggressive intent.

There appear to be systematic differences in the results and conclusions of aggressive play research depending upon the method used. Researchers who observe play from a distance tend to reach different conclusions about aggressive play than those who interact with the children—for example, through the use of verbal questionnaires or interviews (e.g., Connor, 1989; Wegener-Spöhring, 1989). Remote observers are more apt to interpret play-fighting as real aggression, and to conclude that such play contributes to, or actually is, aggression (e.g., Mendoza, 1972; Turner and Goldsmith, 1976). When children are interviewed, researchers are more apt to distinguish play-fighting from actual fighting, (e.g., Bonte and Musgrove, 1943; Sutton-Smith et al., 1988), as are the children themselves. These different interpretations arising from method are similar to the anthropologists' distinction between *etic* and *emic* perspectives (Triandis, 1972). The emic perspective is an attempt to capture the essence or idiosyncratic reality of a culture. Etic constructs are attempts to communicate this information to those outside the culture.

Most war-play and videogame research is short-term and does not occur in the natural settings where children play. In addition, play is imposed on the children and not freely undertaken, dependent measures combine aggressive play with verbal and physical aggressive behavior, and observers are frequently aware of the study's hypotheses. There are few longitudinal studies or observations of children's spontaneous war play, or of how children use and talk about their play (cf., Kubey and Larson, 1990).

Despite the consistency in findings of sex differences in aggressive play, it is worth noting that whether children are perceived to be playing or acting aggressively is a judgment that depends upon, among other things, the observer's age, sex, and prior experience with such behavior (Goldstein, 1992).

If the study of aggressive play and war toys has been limited in theory and method, what additional prospects are there for understanding further the appeal and consequences of such play? In the following section we consider some possibilities.

FURTHER APPROACHES TO THE STUDY OF WAR TOYS AND PLAY

Even if play is a sort of practice for a vague and indeterminate future, what motivates it in the present? Among the possibilities suggested here are that play is a means of exploring the environment, a mechanism for self-regulation (of physiology, arousal, emotion), and a means of establishing social identity. We consider approaches from three interrelated levels of analysis: physiological/biological, psychological, and social.

Physiological/Biological Approaches

There are recent versions of play theory based on self-regulation of physiological states. Beginning with Berlyne's (1960) theory suggesting that arousal produced by features of games and toys—by their novelty, complexity, and unpredictability—contributes to satisfying increases and decreases in arousal, Apter (1992) expands this view in his examination of dangerous sports.

One characteristic of rough-and-tumble play, war play, and other forms of potentially dangerous or frightening entertainment is that they occur within a framework of safety and comfort. Children want to hear the frightening parts of their favorite stories only in the safety of a parent's arms. Based on the views of Berlyne and Apter, the oscillation between fear and safety, tension and repose, may itself be pleasant.

Psychological Approaches

Traditional psychological approaches to aggressive play tend to focus on learning, particularly of aggression, and far less often on cognitive and social-psychological aspects of such play. There are many little-explored facets of play that may be informative. Below we consider one cognitive consequence of intense play, an altered sense of reality.

One attraction of fantasy play, indeed of any repetitive activity, may be the production of a displaced sense of time and place, referred to variously as "deindividuation" (Zimbardo, 1969) and "flow" (Csikszentmihalyi, 1990).

As Turkle (1984) notes: "When you play a video game you enter into the world of the programmers who made it. You have to do more than identify with a character on the screen. You must act for it. Identification through action has a special kind of hold. Like playing a sport, it puts people into a highly focused, and highly charged state of mind. For many people, what is being pursued in the video game is not just a score, but an altered state" (p. 83). Like other repetitive physical activities, play offers the promising possibility of entering a novel, appealing state of involvement and intensity. This helps explain the attraction of dangerous sports, like skydiving, and why businessmen sometimes spend their weekends shooting paint pellets at one another (Murphy and White, 1978).

Social Approaches

Self Regulation   Berlyne proposed that play occurs because it provides the players with satisfying levels of stimulation. This can be seen as a form of self-regulation of arousal states.

In play, children explore not only their physical environment, but their emotional, social, and cultural environments also.[3] According to Zillmann (1987), entertainment, including play, is a means for achieving emotional and physiological self-regulation.

Children in war zones often play war games, not only in imitation of the adult behavior around them but also as a means of coping with anxiety, fear, and loss (Bonte and Musgrove, 1943; Jukes and Goldstein, 1993).

Leisure activities enable the participant to experience a level of stimulation, arousal, and affect most appropriate or comfortable at the moment. A game may be chosen because it produces relaxation or excitement, encourages activity or passivity, solitude or sociality. This is the cognitive and social counterpart to the view of play as a form of thermoregulation. It suggests that aggressive play is substantially influenced by the current situation and by transient emotional and physiological states. This view is supported by data from Jukes and Goldstein (1933), who found that induced cognitive, emotional, and arousal states significantly influence preference for aggressive toys.

Social Identity   The public choices people make, like the clothing they wear and the music they listen to, and also their style of play and choice of playthings, are used to define themselves to others. Children appear to use sex-typed toy play as a way to identify with a positive reference group (same-sex peers), to distinguish themselves from a negative reference group (such as parents or children of the opposite sex), and to elicit predictable reactions from others (such as approval or disapproval from teachers or parents).

Children may try out roles to get a "feel" for them, imagine having control and power that they lack in nonplay settings, and engage in social comparison with real and imaginary companions in an attempt to answer questions about themselves and others (see Brown, 1990).

In short, children may engage in particular forms of play for a host of reasons, ranging from the wish to experience a temporary alteration of "consciousness," to a desire for particular emotional and physiological states, to the use of play as a form of social communication. These and other positions can be seen in table 6.4, where they are applied to play with one type of object, war toys.

Methods

We do not know much about the social ecology of war play, that is, where and how it develops spontaneously and what course it follows through to its conclusion. There are few data on the forms of war play in school and home. Who initiates this type of play? When, with whom, and where? How long does it last, and how is it terminated? What are the dynamics and scripts for this play? The ethological work of Smith, Boulton, and Pellegrini, and the sensitive observations of children at play by Sutton-Smith and his colleagues, come closest to the kind of research I have in mind.

Of all the approaches used to date, ethological studies tend to use the broadest and perhaps most interesting range of dependent measures. The social relationships among players, the kinds of behaviors exhibited during play (such as facial expressions), the duration of play, and the social consequences of play have been studied by Humphreys and Smith (1984), Smith

Table 6.4   Twenty-five Reasons for Play with War Toys

Biological/Physiological
1. To achieve a pleasing level of arousal/stimulation/excitement.
2. To expend energy, engage in intense physical activity.
3. Hormonal influences.

Psychological
4. To achieve a desired emotional state.
5. Priming/cognitive salience of aggression.
6. To try to understand violence, war, death.
7. To feel in control of aggression.
8. To allay anxiety about violence, war, guns.
9. To engage in fantasy/imaginative play.
10. To experience an "altered state of consciousness"/"flow."
11. To practice strategic planning, problem solving.
12. To set goals and determine effective means for accomplishing them. To gain a sense of mastery.

Social
13. To belong to a positive reference group.
14. To experience intimacy.
15. Direct modeling by peers or family.
16. Indirect modeling: influences of media, marketing.
17. Rewards and encouragement for such play.
18. Salience within a culture of war, fighting.
19. Learn to control and resolve conflict and aggression.
20. To wield power; to affect others.
21. To exclude oneself from a (negative reference) group (e.g. parents, girls, boys who disapprove of these games).
22. To elicit a predictable reaction from parents/teachers.
23. To sample a variety of adult roles.
24. To role play.
25. To reflect cultural values, themes (if a culture values dominance, aggression, and assertion, this will appear in children's play and recreation).

and Boulton (1990), Pellegrini (1989b), and Sutton-Smith, Gerstmyer, and Meckley (1988). These have not been applied to the study of war toys or video games.

Among the dependent variables rarely or never studied in war play are its effects on imagination, militarist attitudes, attitudes toward violence and weapons, and the ability to cope with violence and death, such as the loss of a relative or a pet. What are the long-term effects, if any, of such play on militarism, aggression, role taking, problem solving, self-concept? There are few studies of adult rough-and-tumble or war play (see Gergen, 1991).

So far the only individual difference variable consistently studied is sex. Pellegrini (1989b) and Willner (1991) show the importance of the child's relationships with his or her playmates in understanding aggressive play. Smith (1994) has urged that more attention be paid to individual differences.

Summary and Conclusion

By way of summary, let us take one example of aggressive play—play with war toys—and apply these admittedly inchoate ideas to it. Some of the possible reasons a boy might play with a toy gun are listed in table 6.4.

We can see that many needs may be satisfied in war play, most of them having little or nothing to do with aggression per se. Among them we have suggested curiosity; exploration; coping; anxiety and fear reduction; self-regulation of cognitive, emotional, and physiological states; and social identity. All social play occurs simultaneously at different levels of explanation and activity. To date, few of these possibilities have been considered.

NOTES

1. Some competitive games modeled on war, such as chess and go, are not included in this discussion, for the sake of convention.

2. The terms *sex-typed* and *gender-appropriate* here designate play styles and toys that are used predominantly by, or marketed primarily to, boys or girls. In fact, these activities and toys lie on a continuum between "for girls only" and "for boys only."

3. Hutt (1979) distinguishes between exploratory behavior and play, based in part on the duration of the activity.

REFERENCES

Almqvist, B. (1989). Age and gender differences in children's Christmas requests. *Play and Culture, 2*, 2–19.

Apter, M. (1992). *The dangerous edge.* New York: Free Press/Macmillan.

Barber, N. (1991). Play and energy regulation in mammals. *Quarterly Review of Biology, 66*, 129–47.

Berenbaum, S. A., & Hines, M. (1992). Early androgens are related to childhood sex-typed toy preferences. *Psychological Science, 3*, 203–06.

Beresin, A. R. (1989). Toy war games and the illusion of two-sided rhetoric. *Play and Culture, 2*, 218–24.

Berlyne, D. E. (1960). *Conflict, arousal, and curiosity.* New York: McGraw-Hill.

Berndt, T. J., & Heller, K. A. (1986). Gender stereotypes and social influence; A developmental study. *Journal of Personality and Social Psychology, 50,* 889–98.

Bonte, E. P., & Musgrove, M. (1943). Influences of war as evidenced in children's play. *Child Development, 14,* 179–200.

Boulton, M. J. (1991a). A comparison of structural and contextual features of middle school children's playful and aggressive fighting. *Ethology and Sociobiology, 12,* 119–45.

———. (1991b). Partner preferences in middle school children's playful fighting and chasing. *Ethology and Sociobiology, 12,* 177–93.

Brown, K. D. (1990). Modelling for war? Toy soldiers in late Victorian and Edwardian Britain. *Journal of Social History, 24,* 237–48.

Burghardt, G. M. (1984). On the origins of play. In P. K. Smith (ed.), *Play in animals and humans.* Oxford: Basil Blackwell.

Caldera, Y., Huston, A., & O'Brien, M. (1989). Social interactions and actions and play patterns of parents and toddlers with feminine, masculine and neutral toys. *Child Development, 60,* 70–76.

Carlsson-Paige, N., & Levin, D. E. (1987). *The war play dilemma.* New York: Teachers College Press.

———. (1990). *Who's calling the shots?* Philadelphia: New Society.

Carvalho, A. M. A., Smith, P. K., Hunter, T., & Costabile, A. (1990). Playground activities for boys and girls: Developmental and cultural trends in children's perceptions of gender differences. *Play and Culture, 3,* 343–47.

Chambers, J. H., & Ascione, F. R. (1987). The effects of prosocial and aggressive video games on children's donating and helping. *Journal of Genetic Psychology, 148,* 499–505.

Connor, K. (1989). Aggression: Is it in the eye of the beholder? *Play and Culture, 2,* 213–17.

Cooper, J., Hall, J., & Huff, C. (1990). Situational stress as a consequence of sex-stereotyped software. *Personality and Social Psychology Bulletin, 16,* 419–29.

Cooper, J., & Mackie, D. (1986). Video games and aggression in children. *Journal of Applied Social Psychology, 16,* 726–44.

Costabile, A., Genta, M. L., Zucchini, E., Smith, P. K., & Harker, R. (1992). Attitudes of parents to war play in young children. *Early Education and Development, 3,* 356–69.

Costabile, A., Smith, P. K., Matheson, L., Aston, J., Hunter, T., & Boulton, M. (1991). Cross-national comparison of how children distinguish serious and playful fighting. *Developmental Psychology, 27*, 881–87.

Csikszentmihalyi, M. (1990). *Flow: The psychology of optimal experience.* New York: Harper.

Eaton, W. O., & Enns, L. R. (1986). Sex differences in human motor activity level. *Psychological Bulletin, 100*, 19–28.

Eckerman, C. O., & Stein, M. R. (1990). How imitation begets imitation and toddlers' generation of games. *Developmental Psychology, 26*, 370–78.

Eisenberg, N., Tryon, K., & Cameron, E. (1984). The relation of preschoolers' peer interaction to their sex-typed toy choices. *Child Development, 55*, 1044–50.

Fagen, R. (1984). Play and behavioral flexibility. In P. K. Smith (Ed.), *Play in animals and humans.* Oxford: Basil Blackwell.

Fagot, B. I. (1984). Teacher and peer reactions to boys' and girls' play styles. *Sex Roles, 11*, 691–702.

Fein, G., Johnson, D., Kosson, N., Stork, L., & Wasserman, L. (1985). Sex stereotypes and preferences in the toy choices of 20-month-old boys and girls. *Developmental Psychology, 11*, 527–28.

Feshbach, S. (1956). The catharsis hypothesis and some consequences of interaction with aggressive and neutral play objects. *Journal of Personality, 24*, 449–62.

Fine, G. A. (1983). *Shared fantasy: Role-playing games as social worlds.* Chicago: University of Chicago Press.

Fry, D. P. (1987). Differences between playfighting and serious fighting among Zapotec children. *Ethology and Sociobiology, 8*, 285–306.

———. (1990). Play aggression among Zapotec children: Implications for the practice hypothesis. *Aggressive Behavior, 16*, 321–40.

Funk, J. B. (1992). Video games: Benign or malignant? *Developmental and Behavioral Pediatrics, 13*, 53–54.

Gergen, M. (1990). Beyond the evil empire: Horseplay and aggression. *Aggressive Behavior, 16*, 381–98.

Gibson, J. W. (1993). *Warrior dreams.* New York: Macmillan.

Goldstein, J. H. (1992). Sex differences in aggressive play and toy preference. In K. Bjorkqvist & P. Niemela (Eds.), *Of mice and women: Aspects of female aggression.* (pp. 65–76). San Diego: Academic Press.

Graybill, D., Strawniak, M., Hunter, T., & O'Leary, M. (1987). Effects of playing vs. observing violent vs. non-violent video games on children's aggression. *Psychology: A Quarterly Journal of Human Behavior, 24*, 1–8.

Gribbin, M. (1979). Granny knows best. *New Scientist*, Nov. 1, 350–51.

Groos, K. (1898). *The play of animals*. New York: Appleton.

Huesmann, L. R. (1988). An information processing model for the development of aggression. *Aggressive Behavior, 14*, 13–24.

Humphreys, A. P., & Smith, P. K. (1984). Rough-and-tumble in preschool and playground. In P. K. Smith (Ed.), *Play in animals and humans* (pp. 241–66). Oxford: Basil Blackwell.

Hutt, C. (1979). Exploration and play. In B. Sutton-Smith (Ed.), *Play and learning*. New York: Gardner.

Jukes, J. (1991). Children and aggressive toys: Empirical studies of toy preference. Doctoral dissertation, University College London.

Jukes, J., & Goldstein, J. H. (1993). Preference for aggressive toys. *International Play Journal, 1*, 81-91.

Keefer, R., Goldstein, J. H., & Kasiarz, D. (1983). Olympic Games participation and warfare. In J. Goldstein (Ed.), *Sports violence* (pp. 183–94). New York: Springer-Verlag.

Kubey, R., & Larson, R. (1990). The use and experience of the new video media among children and young adolescents. *Communication Research, 17*, 107–30.

Lagerspetz, K. M. J., Bjorkqvist, K., & Peltonen, T. (1988). Is indirect aggression typical of females? Gender differences in aggressiveness in 11- to 12-year-old children. *Aggressive Behavior, 14*, 403–14.

Lever, J. (1978). Sex differences in the complexity of children's play and games. *American Sociological Review, 43*, 471–83.

Lovaas, O. I. (1961). Effect of exposure to symbolic aggression on aggressive behavior. *Child Development, 32*, 37–44.

Lowenfeld, M. (1935). *Play in childhood*. London: MacKeith.

Maccoby, E. E., & Jacklin, C. N. (1974). *The psychology of sex differences*. Stanford CA: Stanford University Press.

Mallick, S. K., & McCandless, B. R. (1966). A study of catharsis of aggression. *Journal of Personality and Social Psychology, 4*, 591–96.

Malone, T. (1981). Toward a theory of intrinsically motivating instruction. *Cognitive Science, 4*, 333–69.

McMeen, G. R. (1985). Video game violence in computer software/courseware. *Educational Technology, 25* (12), 21–22.

Mendoza, A. (1972). Effects of exposure to toys conducive to violence. *Dissertation Abstracts International, 33*, 2769–70.

Meyer-Bahlburg, H. F. L., Feldman, J. F., Cohen, P., & Ehrhardt, A. A. (1988). Perinatal factors in the development of gender-related play behavior: Sex hormones versus pregnancy complications. *Psychiatry, 51*, 260–71.

Miedzian, M. (1991). *Boys will be boys.* New York: Doubleday.

Moller, L. C., Hymel, S., & Rubin, K. H. (1992). Sex typing in play and popularity in middle childhood. *Sex Roles, 26*, 331–53.

Murphy, M., & White, R. (1978). *The psychic side of sports.* Reading, MA: Addison-Wesley.

O'Brien, M., & Huston, A. (1985). Development of sex-typed behavior in toddlers. *Developmental Psychology, 21*, 866–71.

Parker, S. T. (1984). Playing for keeps: An evolutionary perspective on human games. In P. K. Smith (Ed.), *Play in animals and humans* (pp. 271–93). Oxford: Basil Blackwell.

Parten, M. (1933). Social play among preschool children. *Journal of Abnormal and Social Psychology, 28*, 136–47.

Pellegrini, A. D. (1988). Elementary-school children's rough-and-tumble play and social competence. *Developmental Psychology, 24*, 802–06.

———. (1989a). What about recess, really? *Play and Culture, 2*, 354–56.

———. (1989b). Categorizing children's rough-and-tumble play. *Play and Culture, 2*, 48–51.

Potts, R., Huston, A. C., & Wright, J. C. (1986). The effects of television form and violent content on boys' attention and social behavior. *Journal of Experimental Child Psychology, 41*, 1–17.

Provenzo, E. F. (1991). *Video kids: Making sense of Nintendo.* Cambridge: Harvard University Press.

Repetti, R. L. (1984). Determinants of children's sex stereotyping: Parental sex-role traits and television viewing. *Personality and Social Psychology Bulletin, 10*, 457–68.

Rheingold, H., & Cook, K. V. (1975). The contents of boys' and girls' rooms as an index of parents' behavior. *Child Development, 46*, 459–63.

Roberts, J. M., & Sutton-Smith, B. (1962). Child training and game involvement. *Ethnology, 1*, 166–85.

Roopnarine, J. L., Ahmeduzzaman, M., Hossain, Z., & Reigraf, N. B. (1992). Parent-infant rough play: Its cultural specificity. *Early Education and Development, 3*, 298–311.

Sacher, W. (1993). Jugendgefährdung durch Video- und Computerspiele? [Video and Computer games: A threat to the young?] *Zeitschrift für Pädagogik, 39*, 313–33.

Salamone, F. A., & Salamone, V. A. (1991). Children's games in Nigeria redux: A consideration of the "uses" of play. *Play and Culture, 4*, 129–38.

Sanson, A., & DiMuccio, C. (1993). The influence of aggressive and neutral cartoons and toys on the behavior of preschool children. *Australian Psychologist, 28*, 93–99.

Schutte, N. S., Malouff, J. M., Post-Gordon, J. C., & Rodasta, A. L. (1988). Effects of playing video games on children's aggressive and other behaviors. *Journal of Applied Social Psychology, 18*, 454–60.

Schwartz, L. A., & Markham, W. T. (1985). Sex stereotyping in children's toy advertisements. *Sex Roles, 12*, 157–70.

Shell, R., & Eisenberg, N. (1990). The role of peers' gender in children's naturally occurring interest in toys. *International Journal of Behavioral Development, 13*, 373–88.

Silvern, S. B., & Williamson, P. A. (1987). The effects of video game play on young children's aggression, fantasy, and prosocial behavior. *Journal of Applied Developmental Psychology, 8*, 453–62.

Silverman, S. B., & Williamson, P. A. (1987). The effects of video game play on young children's aggression, fantasy, and prosocial behavior. *Journal of Applied Developmental Psychology, 8*, 453–62.

Singer, D. G. (1994). Play as healing. In J. Goldstein (Ed.), *Toys, play, and child development* (pp. 147–65). New York: Cambridge University Press.

Singer, D. G., & Singer, J. L. (1990). *The house of make-believe: Play and the developing imagination.* Cambridge: Harvard University Press.

Slife, B. D., & Rychlak, J. F. (1982). Role of affective assessment in modeling aggressive behavior. *Journal of Personality and Social Psychology, 43*, 861–68.

Smith, P. K. (1982). Does play matter? Functional and evolutionary aspects of animal and human play. *Behavioral and Brain Sciences, 5*, 139–58.

———. (1994). The war play debate. In J. Goldstein (Ed.), *Toys, play and child development.* New York: Cambridge University Press.

Smith, P. K., & Boulton, M. (1990). Rough-and-tumble play, aggression and dominance: Perception and behaviour in children's encounters. *Human Development, 33*, 271–82.

Smith, P. K., Hunter, T., Carvalho, A. M. A., & Costabile, A. (1992). Children's perceptions of playfighting, play-chasing and real fighting: A cross-national interview study. *Social Development, 1*, 211–29.

Sneed, C., & Runco, M. A. (1992). The beliefs adults and children hold about television and video games. *Journal of Psychology, 126*, 273–84.

Suito, N., & Reifel, S. (1992, May). Gender differences in Japanese and American sociodramatic play. Paper presented at the International Council for Child's Play, Paris.

Sutton-Smith, B. (1988). War toys and childhood aggression. *Play and Culture, 1*, 57–69.

Sutton-Smith, B., Gerstmyer, J., & Meckley, A. (1988). Play-fighting as folkplay amongst preschool children. *Western Folklore, 47*, 161–76.

Triandis, H. C. (1972). *The analysis of subjective culture.* New York: Wiley.

Turkle, S. (1984). *The second self.* New York: Simon & Schuster.

Turner, C. W., & Goldsmith, D. (1976). Effects of toy guns and airplanes on children's antisocial free play behavior. *Journal of Experimental Child Psychology, 21*, 301–15.

Twitchell, J. (1989). *Preposterous violence.* Oxford: Oxford University Press.

Watson, M. W., & Peng, Y. (1992). The relation between toy gun play and children's aggressive behavior. *Early Education and Development, 3*, 370–89.

Wegener-Spöhring, G. (1989). War toys and aggressive games. *Play and Culture, 2*, 35–47.

Willner, A. H. (1991). Behavioral deficiencies of aggressive 8–9-year-old boys: An observational study. *Aggressive Behavior, 17*, 135–54.

Wolff, C. (1976). The effect of aggressive toys on aggressive behavior in children. Unpublished doctoral dissertation. University of Montana.

Zammuner, V. L. (1987). Children's sex-role stereotypes: a cross-cultural analysis. In P. Shaver & C. Hendrick (Eds.), *Review of Personality and Social Psychology* (vol. 7). Newbury Park, CA: Sage.

Zillmann, D. (1987). Mood management: Using entertainment to full advantage. In L. Donohew, H. Sypher & T. Higgins (Eds.), *Communication, social cognition, and affect* (pp 147–71). Hillsdale, NJ: Erlbaum.

Zimbardo, P. G. (1969). The human choice: Individuation, reason, and order versus deindividuation, impulse, and chaos. In D. Levine (Ed.), *Nebraska symposium on motivation* (pp. 237–307). Lincoln: University of Nebraska Press.

Part III

PLAY AS FANTASY

7

GRETA G. FEIN

Toys and Stories

I first came across Brian Sutton-Smith's work in the late 1960s as I was gathering material for a chapter on play to appear in *Day Care in Context* (Fein and Clarke-Stewart, 1973). It was then that I found his provocative study of children's novel responses to toys (Sutton-Smith, 1968). Here at last were ideas that went beyond the behaviorist-psychoanalytic or quasi-clinical interpretive paradigm that formed the bulk of the play literature of that era. Here at last was someone who could translate neat ideas into interesting settings into systematic observations of children's behavior. I wrote asking him for any other papers. With wonderful but typical generosity, he sent me an entire prepublication copy of *Child's Play* (Herron and Sutton-Smith, 1971). What a gold mine! It permitted me to think about play in a far richer and less apologetic way than ever before. I met the man himself a couple of years later when he came to Yale University to give a colloquium.

From then on, I was on his mailing list, and, a couple of years later, began to receive copies of his work on children's storytelling, often before they were published. This work, put together with the rest, tells a wonderful story of intellectual growth and curiosity. True, we differ on many issues. I find Gadamer and Heidegger as obscure as LISREL. Brian's uncanny ability to see connections is quite independent of the research style or worldview of a particular period. In the 1970s, Brian generated studies of children's narrative competence that have turned out to be classics in the field (Magee and Sutton-Smith, 1983; Sutton-Smith, 1975; Sutton-Smith, Botvin, and Mahoney, 1976; Botvin and Sutton-Smith, 1977). It is through this work that we first meet the idea that expressive forms have their own distinctive structure. A measure of the power of his contribution may be that it takes the rest of us so long to catch up. In my view, Sutton-Smith is one of the most original and gifted scholars in our field. At any rate, the idea that expressive forms share some common features has belatedly led me and my students to studies of children's narrative competence. It is this work that provides the topic of this chapter.

Narrative competence is the ability to comprehend and produce decontextualized information. One expression of this competence is the ability to produce and comprehend stories, to understand story events and characters' actions as temporally sequenced and causally motivated (Pellegrini, 1985). Productive narrative competence refers specifically to the ability to tell an original story that contains an appropriate setting with characters who react to a central problem through a sequence of goal-directed behaviors and related events which move to a plausible conclusion (Galda, 1984). Most researchers agree that these elements constitute the central structural features of a well-formed story (Botvin and Sutton-Smith, 1977; Mandler, 1984; Shapiro and Hudson, 1991). In one of the earliest analyses of children's stories, Sutton-Smith and his colleagues described different structural models that capture the idea that a good story poses a problem—a threat or lack—which is responded to and nullified or overcome (Botvin and Sutton-Smith, 1977; Sutton-Smith, Botvin, and Mahoney, 1976).

In addition to a grammatical structure, children's narratives draw upon a knowledge base. This knowledge base is housed in schema, particular types of mental structures, used to represent generic concepts in memory (Hudson and Shapiro, 1991). Mandler (1984) distinguishes between *event schema* and *story schema.* An event schema describes generalized knowledge about an event sequence such as morning at nursery school. Event schema yield *chronicles* or personal narratives. In contrast, a story schema is a mental structure which contains sets of expectations about how a story will proceed. The child's developing story schema forms a basis for the telling of original *tales.* Although the child acquires event schema as well as story schema, early stories are more like chronicles than tales. These chronicles may resemble scripts or personal narratives, but they lack the core structural components described by Sutton-Smith (1975), that is, a particular problem to which a character reacts, attempts to resolve, and arrives at a resolution that eliminates or transforms the problem. In fact, the work of Sutton-Smith and colleagues suggests that the crucial structural component of stories is not a dispassionate, generalized grammar but, rather, meat-and-potato universal themes that capture deeply held human concerns.

Longitudinal studies of children's productive narrative competence find that young children are unable to construct narratives that satisfy the requirements of story well-formedness (Applebee, 1978; Botvin and Sutton-Smith, 1977). Many of their stories fall short of encompassing a problem, goal, and resolution (Applebee, 1978; Morrow, 1986). The stories of children less than three years of age are more like primitive chronicles in which order can be changed without bringing about a change of meaning (Botvin and Sutton-Smith, 1977).

This first component of story schema children represent is setting, which includes temporal orientation, spatial orientation, and character identification. The main character is identified at two years of age, with related characters appearing at three years. Action sequences are the most typical form used by four-year-olds, who can recall sequences more easily than they can create them (Trabasso, Stein, and Johnson, 1981). Some four- and five-year-olds create well-formed stories with a goal or purpose. These stories indicate the storyteller has grasped the concept of causal relationships (i.e., antecedents and consequences). Even though four-year-olds still tell chronicles, these are beginning to include information about problems and problem-solutions, as well as affective themes (many of which are negative); in addition, they seem to appreciate what the characters involved in the action know, think, and feel (Ames, 1966; Applebee, 1978; Botvin and Sutton-Smith, 1977; Feldman, Bruner, Renderer, and Spitzer, 1990). Although children's stories improve after four years of age, their stories continue to lack information about the setting, initiating actions, and goals (Leondar, 1977; Pradl, 1979). These elements tend to be present by the age of six (Applebee, 1978; Botvin and Sutton-Smith, 1977). Initiating events and consequences appear in children's original stories at about seven or eight years of age (Sutton-Smith, Botvin, and Mahoney, 1976). However, these developmental limitations may be dependent in part on how and when stories are elicited (Morrow, 1986; Sutton-Smith, 1975).

The years from four to five seem to be a period of transition during which story performance is exceptionally sensitive to training or context, especially when opportunities for story enactment are provided. Low-income children exposed to several months of thematic-fantasy and dramatic-play training show striking improvements in their ability to order unfamiliar picture sequences and tell coherent stories about these sequences (Saltz, Dixon, and Johnson, 1977). This conclusion is consistent with other studies demonstrating that picture-sequence support improves storytelling when the story has been previously enacted or told (Pellegrini, 1985; Pratt and McKenzie-Keating, 1985). However, an opportunity simply to preview the pictured sequences does not enhance story quality (Shapiro and Hudson, 1991). Thus, story enactment experiences make a unique contribution to children's grasp of narrative forms.

Young children also tell more complete, more cohesive, and more elaborate stories when immediate environmental supports are provided. Pictured event sequences support storytelling, especially when children have been alerted to the problem element. Guttman and Frederiksen (1985) compared three story production conditions. In one, the children retold a story illustrated by sequenced pictures; in another, only the pictures were available, and in the third, the same characters were illustrated in a single picture. The most supportive condition combined retelling and picture sequences; the poorest support came from the static single picture, largely because young children tend to label and list pictured objects. A critical element in this effect may be the illustration of emotionally arousing problem events, specifically, the presence of a plot unit similar to the lack–lack liquidated, villainy–villainy nullified dyads described by Botvin and Sutton-Smith (1977). A pictured cookie-baking sequence is better recalled when the cookies burn than when they do not (Shapiro and Hudson, 1991). Put another way, a familiar, temporally ordered canonical script is easier to tell about when it is interrupted by an unexpected, disruptive, frustrating event that promises to thwart the central characters' goals.

However, these conclusions must be tempered by problems inherent in the picture elicitation methodology. When given pictures, young children may label and list picture elements—a response often encouraged during mother-child bookreading but one that interferes with story production (Guttman and Frederiksen, 1985). Successful picture-sequence interventions may simply pull children away from a response tendency that interferes with story production rather than provide direct support for storytelling. Thus, whether problem information can itself be used by four-year olds in their storytelling is still an unsettled matter.

When stories are solicited with familiar topics (Can you tell me a make-believe story about Halloween?), preschoolers include few story elements, with fewer than 25 percent adding a problem element (Hudson and Shapiro, 1985). However, some story stems (the doctor's office) yielded more story elements than others. Stein (1988) observed a similar content effect. Stories about Alice at the seashore were scriptlike chronicles, whereas those about a big grey fox who lived in a cave were tales with plot units such as villainy–villainy nullified. Conceivably, some themes lend themselves better than others to the dramatic imbalances that transform a chronicle into a tale. Lucariello (1990) used a story comprehension procedure to investigate kindergartners' understanding of story sequences that either preserve the scriptlike character of ordinary events or violate these sequences. In the breach stories, an ordinary, familiar event sequence (a birthday party) was modified by unusual events (child throws water on the candles). Children who heard breach stories added two to four times more thematically relevant information in their accounts of story events. Even though children's appreciation of ordinary, canonical events may be necessary for story comprehension and production, it is clearly not enough. The missing link in narrative development may reside in children's ability to decontextualize structural imbalances, conflicting states, or more generally problematic, troubling events. This link requires children to represent these as decontextualized elements, a competency which is emerging but not consolidated in four-year-olds. Although stem methods in story research are useful, they provide children only with linguistically encoded information and no opportunity to enact story components. Story-stem elicitation methods may also underestimate children's structural knowledge.

REPLICA PLAY AND STORY PROPS

Studies of young children's replica play suggest that props may also support storytelling in the preschool years. Several researchers have noted the similarity between the language children use in symbolic play and in other decontextualized language activities (Pellegrini, 1985; Rubin and Wolf, 1979). Since symbolic play is an early developing narrative form, it may prepare the way for other forms, such as storytelling. The link between play and storytelling may be especially strong in replica play because in constructing replica play texts the child assumes the role of an outside narrator. The child participates in two ways: as actor giving voice to story events and as stage manager–director providing justifications and explanations for these events (Rubin and Wolf, 1979). Replica play can be viewed as a naturally evolving play form which uses narrative structures that may not function in the absence of replica objects, especially animate figures. Wolf, Rygh, and Altshuler (1984) reported that their four-year-olds were able to ascribe speech, action, sensations, perceptions, psychological states, emotions, and obligations to replica figures in the course of playing out imaginary sequential events. Thus, replica play figures alone might support storytelling without the adult-crafted themes found in picture sequences and story stems. Put another way, the knowledge base that feeds good stories is characterological, not episodic. It is about actors and their expected roles, rather than events and their sequencing.

Wright (1992) evaluated the hypothesis that replica figures would enhance the structural quality of stories told by four- and five-year-olds. One group was given props (figures of a girl, a boy, a baby, a robot, and a dinosaur) and the other was not. As expected, children in the prop condition told structurally more sophisticated stories than those in the no-prop condition. However, a character-based enhancement of story quality can come about in different ways. First, the figures might simply prime the storytelling process by providing story characters; if so, replica figures function primarily as triggers, simply getting the children started. If this explanation is correct, the composition of the prop set should have little effect on story structure or theme. Sets with different figures will yield the same results.

A second possibility is that the figures serve to remind children of a story theme; if so, the figures function more like script markers than triggers. Script markers simply identify what the story will be about—a birthday party, a trip, or some other familiar event. If this explanation is correct, sets with thematically different figures should have little impact on structure, but a strong effect on theme. Stories will better fit a script model rather than a story model; they are more likely to be chronicles than tales (Hudson and Shapiro, 1991).

A third possibility is that the figures evoke Proppian problem types, as analyzed by Botvin and Sutton-Smith (1977). Replica figures representing ordinary family characters should yield stories about familiar events that are more like chronicles than tales. These scriptlike narratives will lack the nuclear dyads through which tales provide motivations and resolutions. However, when figures associated with problem states are included, children's stories should show structural advances through the addition of nuclear dyads and themes appropriate to the figures. More specifically, children's knowledge of ordinary events may be important in their daily conduct; but, for storytelling or other narrative processes, it is disruptions or breaches of the ordinary that make events memorable and tellable (Bruner, 1990; Lucariello, 1990).

In order to examine these possibilities, my students and I created two sets of replica props. One set was designed to elicit stories about family life and ordinary, routine events. The canonical set contained six figures: an adult male, adult female, boy, girl, baby, and dog. Another set was designed to elicit more sophisticated, problem stories by presenting at least one character incompatible with the others. The problem or breach set contained the first four figures, but an alligator and a nine-inch piece of wool thread were substituted for the baby and the dog.

A STUDY OF TOYS AND STORIES

Participants were 26 four-year old middle class children (13 boys) who attended child-care centers located near a major city on the East Coast. Two original stories were elicited on separate days, three or four days apart. On one day, the canonical family set was provided; on the other day, the breach (alligator) set was provided. Elicitation conditions were counterbalanced. In each condition the child was asked to tell a story about anything he/she wishes, using any or all of the figures. Our data set thus included fifty-two stories, half from boys and half from girls.

Texts were coded in four ways. We assessed length, genre (chronicle vs. tale), structure, and nuclear dyad. Length was measured by the number of propositions (i.e., independent clauses including a subject and predicate). For genre, we distinguished between chronicles and tales. A *chronicle* was defined as a sequence of events or descriptions that might or might not be tied together by a common theme but lacked a problem element. A *tale* was defined as a narrative for which there was at least one dyadic structure such as lack–lack liquidated or villainy–villainy nullified.

To assess structural complexity, we expanded the Proppian model described by Botvin and Sutton-Smith (1977) to better accommodate the diverse stories we collected. This expansion led to a 7-tier scale used to rate each story told. Levels 0–3 contain no dyadic plot units, whereas levels 4–7 contained at last one.

Level 0: Lists   Stories at this level were single events, lists of characters or attributes; for example, "This (touching adult male) is the daddy, this is the mommy, this is the baby. . . . "

Level 1: Arbitrary event sequences   These stories consisted of multiple events that were not connected by temporal or causal relations; for example, "The little baby was crying. And the dog was looking at him. And the Daddy was there. . . . And then the girl was sleeping. And the other one wanted to rest."

Level 2: Thematic sequences   These stories contain multiple events connected by a shared theme; for example, "Hi (speaking for the girl to the boy). What is your name? My name is Lisa. Wanna be my friend? This is my dog. This is my baby. This is my sister. Bye, bye."

Level 3: Problematic state/no reaction   A problem appears but there is no attempt to resolve it and thus a dyadic pair never occurs; for example, "I like to tell about the little crocodile. He (alligator) moves to eat him (adult male). And he eats the foots up. And he goes to the next one. . . . And then he goes to him. And then he eats his leg." In this story there is villainy but no effort to nullify it.

Level 4: Dyadic structure frames story   A problem-resolution dyad occurs but events that mediate between problem and resolution are omitted. This level is the same as level 2 in the Botvin and Sutton-Smith (1977) model; for example, "There's a monster (adult male). And he's coming in the woods. And he's going to get the baby (moving baby). He's dead (male figure falls down)." Stories at this level need not have a successful outcome; someone might have fought the monster but the monster escaped.

Level 5: Dyadic chaining   At this level, dyadic units are repeated with only slight variation. The net effect is a round in which a problem occurs and is alleviated, only to recur in some form. This structure seems to provide a transition between levels 4 and 6 on the original scale; for example, "Once upon a time there was a man. And he climbed a mountain. Then 'whooo' crash (figure falls). And then he fell to the bottom rock. He said, 'I must of hit my head harder than I thought,' He jumps up 'augh' onto the top mountain. And then he falls again. And he breaks his bone that time. Then his son comes along. 'La,la,la,la,la,la, . . . Augh, oooh.' And then he breaks his leg bone that time. And then his older sister comes along. . . . " The story continues though other characters (younger sister, older sister) all of whom fall down the mountain. The story ends without any of the characters achieving success, although each character makes an effort to climb the mountain.

Level 6: Dyad with intermediate secondary elements   This is level 3 in the original model. One of the characters faces a problem and two or more events intervene to facilitate a problem solution; for example, "The baby was sitting on the pet alligator. The alligator started eating the baby. And the mom said, 'No, no.' And smacks him on the butt. Then the alligator starts nipping at the mom's arm. Then at her legs and neck. And then her dress so the daddy could see her underwear. Then the daddy came and said, 'No,' to the alligator. And said, 'We are going to cook you.' The mommy stabbed him. And pulled all the skin off. And then put him in the oven. And cooked him . . . "

Level 7: A cycled level 6   This level is similar to level 5 in the original model. Actually, the above example was coded at level 7 because more happened: "And when she did he was alive! And the mommy called, 'Hey! Dinner is ready.' And so they all walked. And the sister picked up the baby. And took her to the kitchen. And said, 'Here, mommy.' And she said, 'Here's your porridge now. You better sit down at the table while I get that wrapper on.' So, she wrapped him around that thing (the red wool) and put him right up for dinner. And she tighted it up. And tied it in a bow and knot. And just wrapped it around like that (wraps wool around alligator). And when she did, the daddy picked it up and put it outside. And that's the end."

Stories coded at level 3 or above were also coded for the themes of lack–lack liquidated and villainy–villainy nullified. All but one story fit into these two categories.

PROPS DO MAKE A DIFFERENCE

Chronicles and Tales   The analysis for chronicles and tales yielded the striking results shown in table 7.1. We used chi square procedures to evaluate these differences. With canonical props, only 31 percent of the children told tales, but with problem props, 62 percent did so ($p < .001$). Note also the striking differences between boys and girls. Regardless of prop type, girls told more tales than did boys ($p < .01$); yet tale telling improved for both groups with the breach set.

Story Structure   Scores for story structure are also shown in table 7.1. Again, chi square analyses indicate a significant effect for props. With canonical props, 18 children (70 percent) scored at the lowest level; this group is reduced by half to 9 (35 percent) with the breach set ($p < .05$). With the canonical set, only 2 boys scored better than level 3; with breach props, 9 boys did so. The effect of props differed for girls, who were more likely to be at levels 4–5 with canonical toys. With problem props, more girls reached levels 6–7.

Themes   We also show theme data in table 7.1. Girls' stories with canonical toys were likely to be lack–lack liquidated stories (5 out of 6). Characters get lost and want to go home, babies go from house to house looking for a family. Lack themes became fewer with breach toys (3 out of 8), but all together, girls told more lack–lack liquidated stories than did boys (57 percent vs 9 percent). Although story theme changed with the props, 4

Table 7.1   Canonical and Breach Props: Story Genre, Level, Theme, and Length

| | Canonical | | Breach | |
	Girls	Boys	Girls	Boys
No. Tales	6	2	10	6
Story structure				
Levels 0–3	7	11	4	4
Levels 4–5	5	2	4	8
Levels 6–7	1	0	4	1
Theme				
Lack	5	0	3	1
Villainy	1	1	5	8
Other	0	1	0	0
Length (no. propositions)				
Median	25	24	19	12
No. Children above 20	9	8	5	3

Note
Data are the number of children who tell tales, whose stories are at each level, and whose stories reveal themes of a particular type.

children told lack–lack liquidated stories about the alligator. In these stories, the alligator is cast as a pet who is walked home on a leash, whose jaws provide a quiet home for a lady, or who might be a friendly though unpredictable baby dragon. Nevertheless, the theme of villainy increased substantially with breach toys, from 2 to 13 instances.

Propositions In order to describe the length of the stories, they were scored for the number of propositions. These scores were highly skewed, with scores ranging from 2 to over 100. Because mean scores may be deceptive, we calculated the proportion of scores above the approximate median of 20. These data are striking (table 7.1). For both boys and girls, stories told with the breach set were shorter than those told with the canonical set. With canonical toys, 17 children told stories containing more than 20 propositions; with the breach set, only 8 did so, a drop of more than 50 percent ($p < .01$). Changes for individual children yield the same pattern: 16 children told shorter stories, 6 children told longer stories, and 4 children showed no change when they use the breach set.

CERTAINTIES AND CAUTIONS

Earlier, I presented three ways of thinking about the effect of replica props on four-year-old's stories. If young children simply have trouble getting started, props serve merely as triggers with little effect on theme or level. The resulting stories might be longer, or require less prompting, but otherwise their quality and content are unaffected. Clearly the findings above are incompatible with this view. The breach set affected story type, level, length, and theme.

A second possibility was that props are script markers. If so, props affect story content (i.e., the script that is rendered) but not its structural level. With one exception, the findings do not conform to this view. The comparisons yielded strong effects for both structure and theme. Breach stories were structurally more complex, and the presence of a toy alligator provoked more stories about villainy–villainy nullified. However, as script theory would expect, stories about the cannonical set contained more propositions than stories about the breach set. Children had more to say about familiar characters, but in this case, the extent of the knowledge base had little bearing upon the narrative quality of the story (Hudson and Shapiro, 1991).

These results are more compatible with the view that narrative thought is organized around vivid, unexpected, or disturbing events; departures from the commonplace and orderly (Fein, 1989). As Sutton-Smith (1986) never stops reminding us, it is the dark, chaotic, and passionate side of human consciousness that fires imaginative thought. Obviously children must have some sort of a knowledge base to tell a story. What, exactly does this base essentially consist of? For the four-year olds in our study, the essential knowledge base was of *characters* and their situations, rather than scriptlike action sequences. Some characters such as the baby or the alligator were more likely than others to evoke Proppian problems and the conflicts associated with them (Botvin and Sutton-Smith, 1977). The baby is helpless, the alligator is hostile. These *psychological* attributes of key figures are expressed through appropriate actions. Thus, props facilitate storytelling when they tap children's affective knowledge (Fein, 1987; 1989). Not only do children produce better stories with some props than others, it is clearly the *meaning* of the figures that affect story content and structure; the issue for children's original stories is *who*, rather than *where* or *what*. Information about setting, specific events, or outcomes—whether in story stems or pictures—are not needed.

Depending on which figures were used, even the canonical set could yield a good story. Lack–lack liquidated stories told with these props often featured lost or abandoned children and various efforts to alleviate their situation as in the following poignant tale:

> Once upon a time there was a little baby
> that didn't have a mom or dad.
> And they . . . and then the little boy was walking along
> And saw the baby.
> And then the little baby loved him.
> And then they walked home,

And then a mother came,
And then saw the little baby
And they loved it, and they loved it,
And then they got a little puppy,
And then they got a father,
And then a babysitter,
And that's the story.
And the family decided if they wanted to keep the baby
Or give him to someone else.
And they decided to give it to someone else.
They decided to give it to Lisa.
And the mother knocked at the door
And said, "Here's a little baby
That we don't want it any more.
Can you take care of he?"
And she said, "Yes."
And then we walked,
And the baby walked in,
And then Lisa went inside to have some breakfast,
And then . . . had a nap,
And then the mother went home,
And said "Goodnight,"
And that was the end of the story.
And the Lisa decided not to take it. . . .

The story continues through one more cycle, in which events such as knocking on the door, asking "Can you take care of this baby?" going inside, and taking a nap are repeated, ending finally with the baby again abandoned by people who "decided not to take it."

In this and other stories, canonical events may serve a metanarrative function more than a content function. They add rhythm to the tale. More important, these events may be fillers (breakfast, a nap) that add suspense rather than substance to the tale. Do you think that these mundane life activities signal an end to the baby's abandonment? Oh, but these signals are misleading. It is always the actors who drive the tale: the helpless baby battered by an unpredictable world. In this sense, "canonicality" refers to the typical human condition in which babies are cared for and "breach" refers to the aberrant and alarming condition in which babies are abandoned. Children's knowledge of ordinary events may be important in their daily conduct, but for storytelling or other narrative processes, it is their emotional meaning that makes events memorable and tellable (Bruner, 1990; Sutton-Smith, 1986).

Villainy–villainy nullified stories occurred most often with the breach set. In many instances, the alligator precipitated a reconfiguring of the family figures into victims or defenders, additional evidence that four-year-olds grasp the essential elements of story schema but may not always use these elements to organize story material. Although the alligator was most often fear-producing, his behavior was not always aggressive and at times he was befriended rather than fought. Although we did not formally assess pronoun gender, the alligator was *always* male and the baby was either "it" or female, even though the actual figures were gender neutral. Here again we have striking evidence that children acquire at a very early age story-character prototypes that, when evoked, create the dramatic tensions that mark structurally sophisticated stories.

Most surely, Sutton-Smith's insight of almost twenty years ago is essentially correct (Sutton-Smith, 1975). The quality of children's stories depends on numerous factors, one of which is the condition under which the stories were told. The data presented here support this view. The structural level of four-year old's stories is not fixed, but rather a dynamic potential that can become realized with the appropriate supports. Vygotsky's notion of a "zone of proximal development" expresses this notion and encourages those interested in children's narrative competence to identify conditions that support it. Perhaps, regular experiences in supportive settings will lead children to become more deliberate and calculating in their use of story elements and less dependent upon props or other supports.

REFERENCES

Ames, L. B. (1966). Children's stories. *Genetic Psychology Monographs, 73*, 337–96.

Applebee, A. N. (1978). *The child's concept of story*. Chicago: University of Chicago Press.

Botvin, G. J., & Sutton-Smith, B. (1977). The development of structural complexity in children's fantasy narratives. *Developmental Psychology, 13*, 377–88.

Bruner, J. (1990). *Acts of meaning*. Cambridge: Harvard University Press.

Fein, G. G. (1987). Pretend play: Creativity and consciousness. In D. Gorlitz & J. F. Wohlwill, (Eds.). *Curiosity, imagination, and play: On the development of spontaneous cognition and motivational processes* (pp. 281–304). Hillsdale, NJ: Lawrence Erlbaum.

———. (1989). Mind, meaning, and affect: Proposals for a theory of pretense. *Developmental Review, 9*, 345–63.

Fein, G. G., & Clarke-Stewart, A. K. (1973). *Day care in context*. New York: Wiley.

Feldman, C. F., Bruner, J., Renderer, B., & Spitzer, S. (1990). Narrative comprehension. In B. K. Britton & A. D. Pelligrini (Eds.), *Narrative thought and narrative language* (pp. 1–78). Hillsdale, NJ: Lawrence Erlbaum.

Galda, L. (1984). Narrative competence: Play, storytelling, and story comprehension. In R. O. Freedle (Ed.) *New directions for child development: Children's planning strategies* (vol. 18). San Francisco: Jossey Bass.

Guttman, M., & Frederiksen, C. H. (1985). Preschool children's narratives: Linking story comprehension, production and play discourse. In L. Galda & A. Pellegrini (Eds.), *Play, language and stories: The development of children's literate behavior* (pp. 99–128). Norwood, NJ: Ablex.

Herron, R. F., & Sutton-Smith, B. (1971). *Child's play.* New York: Wiley.

Hudson, J., & Shapiro, L. R. (1991). From knowing to telling: Children's scripts, stories, and personal narratives. In A. McCabe & C. Peterson (Eds.), *Developing narrative structure* (pp. 89–134). Hillsdale, NJ: Lawrence Erlbaum.

Leondar, B. (1977). Hatching plots: Genesis of storymaking. In D. Perkins & B. Leondar (Eds.), *The arts and cognition* (pp. 172–91). Baltimore: Johns Hopkins University Press.

Lucariello, J. (1990). Cononicality and consciousness in child narrative. In B. K. Britton & A. D. Pellegrini (Eds.), *Narrative thought and narrative language* (pp. 131–40). Hillsdale, NJ: Lawrence Erlbaum.

Magee, M. A. & Sutton-Smith, B. (1983). The art of storytelling: How do children learn it? *Young Children, 38,* 4–12.

Mandler, J. M. (1984). *Stories, scripts and scenes: Aspects of schema theory.* Hillsdale, NJ: Lawrence Erlbaum.

Morrow, L. M. (1986). Effects of structural guidance in story retelling on children's dictation of original stories. *Journal of Reading Behavior 18,* 135–52.

Pellegrini, A. D. (1985). Relations between preschool children's symbolic play and literate behavior. In L. Galda and A. Pellegrini (Eds.), *Play, language and stories: The development of children's literate behavior* (pp. 79–97). Norwood, NJ: Ablex.

Pradl, G. M. (1979). Learning how to begin and end a story. *Language Arts, 56,* 21–25.

Pratt, M. W., & MacKenzie-Keating, S. (1985). Organizing stories: Effects of task difficulty on referential cohesion in narrative. *Developmental Psychology, 21,* 350–56.

Rubin, S., & Wolf, D. (1979). The development of maybe: The evolution of social roles into narrative roles. In E. Winner & H. Gardner (Eds.), *New directions for child development, No. 6, Fact, fiction & fantasy in childhood* (pp. 15–28). San Francisco: Jossey-Bass.

Saltz, E., Dixon, D., & Johnson, J. (1977). Training disadvantaged preschoolers on various fantasy activities: Effects on cognitive functioning and impulse control. *Child Development, 48,* 367–80.

Shapiro, L. R., & Hudson, J. A. (1991). Tell me a make-believe story: Coherence and cohesion in young children's picture elicited narratives. *Developmental Psychol-*

ogy, 27, 960–74.

Stein, N. L. (1988). The development of children's storytelling skills. In M. B. Franklin & S. Barten (Eds.), *Child language: A book of readings* (pp. 282–97). New York: Oxford University Press.

Sutton-Smith, B. (1968). Novel responses to toys. *Merrill-Palmer Quarterly, 14*, 151–58.

———. (1975). The importance of the storytaker: An investigation of the imaginative life. *The Urban Review, 8*, 82–95.

———. (1979). Presentation and representation in children's fictional narrative. In E. Winner & H. Gardner (Eds.), *Fact, fiction, and fantasy in childhood: New directions for child development* (pp. 53–65). San Francisco: Jossey Bass.

———. (1986). The spirit of play. In G. G. Fein & M. Rivkin (Eds.), *The young child at play: Reviews of research (vol. 4)* (pp. 3–16). Washington, D.C.: National Association for the Education of Young Children.

Sutton-Smith, B., Botvin, G., & Mahoney, D. (1976). Developmental structures in fantasy narratives. *Human Development, 19*, 1–20.

Trabasso, T., Stein, N. L., & Johnson, L. R. (1981). Children's knowledge of events: A causal analysis of story structure. In G. Bower (Ed.), *Learning and motivation* (vol. 15) (pp. 237–82). San Diego: Academic Press.

Wolf, D. P., Rygh, J., & Altshuler, J. (1984). Agency and experience: Actions and states in play narratives. In I. Bretherton (Ed.), *Symbolic play* (pp. 195–217). New York: Academic Press.

Wright, J. L. (1992). Correlates of young children's narrative competence: Maternal behaviors and home literacy experiences. Doctoral dissertation, University of Maryland, College Park.

8

STEPHEN KLINE _____

The Promotion and Marketing of Toys: Time to Rethink the Paradox?

"Culture arises in the form of play," wrote Johan Huizinga (1955, p. 26), who celebrated the transcendent creative spirit "which accomplishes itself outside and above the necessities and seriousness of everyday life." Good theories are not only transcendent, Brian Sutton-Smith reminds us, but also often arise out of playfulness expressed as a process of "paradoxical communication." And so it is not surprising that in his wide ranging theorizing about toys and culture, Sutton-Smith (1986) poses at least one paradox for us to play with: On one hand, Sutton-Smith the anthropologist asserts, toys are symbols which are communicating explicit meanings to children through play. On the other hand, Sutton-Smith the psychologist asserts, toys are the tools which children use to achieve autonomous imaginative expression and socioemotional growth.

Sutton-Smith's anthropological self is a keen observer of the many ways that toys acquire an increasingly important socializing role in modern families, becoming the signs of love, the preoccupations of solitariness, the technologies of rationality, and emblems of gender identity—and more generally the primary "possessions with which children can learn the materialistic culture habits of late twentieth century, American civilization" (1986, p. 6). He goes on to make a very convincing case that our attitudes to play are changing in large part because of the growth of "toy barns and toy cities," toy advertising and promotional programs have consolidated the marketplace as an "enormous institution for the control of play" (p. 169). But he does not conclude therefore that we should encourage educational play among children, or develop strategies to buffer children from the pressures of the toy marketers.

This is because, in spite of his acute observations of the social forces exerted on children's play, Sutton-Smith (the psychologist) remains a leading exponent of "free play" (and, ironically, an antagonist to the many educators who would promote only sanctioned play forms) because he maintains quite a fundamental belief in the transcendent spirit of creative players. He argues that ultimately "the plans of the playful imagination dominate the objects or the toys not the other way around" (1986, p. 204). Reminding us that toys do

165

not make the imagination their victim he urges parents and teachers to refrain from control, selection, guidance and training of play, because "domestication" can diminish playfulness. Sutton-Smith continues, therefore, to be one of the most radical exponents of what Peter Smith (1988) called the "play ethos"—the psychological belief in the maturational benefits of all forms of symbolic play.

THE PSYCHOLOGICAL PROMOTION OF PLAY

The advocacy of maturational benefits of play is a tradition which dates back over three centuries. The English philosopher John Locke devised a set of alphabet blocks based on his view that children could improve their learning by playing with toys. But he held a more guarded view of play, warning parents not to buy too many toys because overabundance teaches the child "never to be satisfied with what it hath" (1773, p. 343). Locke recommended that children learn best with toys they make for themselves from natural materials. Similarly valuing play but mistrusting toys, Fredrick Froebels was also a strong advocate of natural play, but his conception of the "kindergarten" as a play space or *spielraum* was defined situationally as a place buffered from the demands of rote learning and harshness rather than through use of particular objects. A similar view was adopted by Rudolph Steiner for his Waldorf schools, although he felt that children's natural urges to make toys could be valued as long as they expressed "the divine in nature" (Aeppli, 1986, p. 22) through self-made objects constructed of natural materials.

By way of contrast, Varga (1991) notes the persistent faith that twentieth-century educators have maintained in designed toys and play equipment. Although definitions of "good" or beneficial play have changed significantly during this century, she points out how the scientific observation of "stage appropriate" play contributed to the formation of the classroom activity centres and the formulation of new guidelines in the early schooling curriculum. She also remarks on the broad shift in the perceived value of play from socioemotional to cognitive benefits. Contrasting the earlier writers' distinction between "good playthings" and their opposite, she criticizes educators' current theories that simply conclude that any play which is "child-initiated, child-directed, and teacher-supported" is good.

Throughout this century, the perceived importance of "free play" has been used to justify toys, games, and sports in the schools. Turn-of-the-century educators who extolled the virtues of play and games as safe rehearsal in which coordination and motor skills could develop helped to create the playgrounds which no school or park is without. The release of excess energy and skills acquired in playing with blocks, tool sets, and playground equipment were also given as reason to incorporate playthings into the classroom environment. Maria Montessori, who recognized the role that tactile and perceptual learning has in laying the foundation of children's reasoning and numeracy, also designed a set of standard learning "toys" that children progress through on their own, which have become integral to the Montessori curriculum. In the 1930s, Susan Isaacs's introduction of role play centers as a spur to socioemotional learning had a profound influence on British educators and parents alike.

Much of the recent support of free play has been inspired by Piaget's structuralist model, which defined it primarily as successive stages of child-generated cognitive assimilation (practice, symbolic, games with rules). Applying this developmental model, researchers have produced an impressive array of studies that demonstrate how various play processes help children develop their creativity and consolidate their behavioral and cognitive schemata. Not surprisingly, studies of developmentally benign or even harmful play are noticeably absent from this literature. Since child-initiated pretending is viewed as the epitome of complex symbolic play, it is this kind of play which is most enthusiastically encouraged and supported in today's preschool. From the 1950s, Piaget's ideas about the role of perception and object manipulation had a major impact on schools' experimentation with nursery play centers (sand play, water play) which might promote the consolidation of particular cognitive development tasks. Early educators, often vociferous in their advocacy of free play, paradoxically propose a global play curriculum (Swinarski, 1991) based on educational toys, choosing ones with assumed universal benefits. It is the paradoxical notions of socialization and freedom associated with toys that need further elaboration.

RETHINKING THE PLAY ETHOS

The educators' and psychologists' optimistic view of the cognitive benefits of free play has largely been justified by studies undertaken in schools on a rather narrow selection of play activities (blocks, lego, family role play). Although school toys can inspire enthusiasm, fun, and engagement, research has demonstrated that the kind of play activity and the support it gets from adults in the environment are important factors in children's benefiting from play (Sylva, Roy, and Cants, 1984). The same seems to be true of imaginative play at home (Singer, this volume). Noting other limitations in the play research, Peter Smith (1988) remarks that "results linking dramatic play opportunities to gains in these competence domains are not so forceful as they appeared to be" (p. 221). Fisher (1992) similarly points out in his analysis of over forty studies that confused definitions, poor research designs, and publisher biases to positive results enormously weaken the case that all forms of symbolic play are equally beneficial.

Noting the educational demand characteristics of the classroom, researchers have also questioned whether substantial benefits are derived from the play activities undertaken on the playground, such as rough-and-tumble play, which can appear to be more concerned with social dominance and peer-preference formation than conceptual elaboration and creativity (Humphreys and Smith, 1987; Pellegrini, this volume). Similarly, those who study children's play with toys at home point out that although children spend enormous time playing with them, the activities and articulations often appear less extraordinary, less flexible, and questionably beneficial to cognitive structuration (Giddings and Halverson, 1981). Children tend to play with favorite playthings ritualistically. Indeed, the toys they have at home also tend to be gender-stereotypic toys that seem to encourage only specific play forms (doll play, action toys) in same-sex groups (Downs, 1983; Paley, 1984). In their study of children's play at home, Davie et al. (1984) observe what to them also appears to be less complex play:

> A great deal of the fantasy play observed was highly repetitive and stereotyped. The same play was performed repeatedly by individual children on different occasions and also different children would engage in very similar fantasization. This was particularly true of representational fantasy play, where the boys spend long periods parking and reparking toy cars and the girls arranging and rearranging domestic replica objects. (p. 113)

One wonders, then, if teachers were advocating a global play curriculum based on the kinds of toys children play with at home (like Barbie, Street Fighter II, and G.I. Joe) would the proposal not appear somewhat troubling? If rather than creativity and maturation, modern toys encourage children to develop more entrenched sex-role stereotypes, more imitation and aggressive play interactions, and more derivative fantasies, would we not rethink our purchases and more closely monitor children's play? The matter can only be decided if we look more closely at what toys children have at home and what they do with them.

CRITIQUES OF "FREE" TOY PLAY

Sutton-Smith's ultimate faith in the transcendent play spirit has therefore been questioned by both psychological and anthropological researchers largely because of the practical implications of continuing to hold this point of view. This critical perspective is most often found among sociological researchers who are more concerned with play as social communication—the way "a society expresses its interpretation of life and the world" (Huizinga, 1955, p. 46) and hence reinforces that interpretation in its children. Anthropologists have paid particular attention to the specific social content of toys and games, seeing them as objects and rules which express and reinforce a society's fundamental perceptions and values. As Schwartzman (1979) illustrates, this theoretical interest in toys as socialization ultimately privileged the communication of play over its imaginativeness and transformative potential. Because of their heightened interest in the social-emotional relations of play, anthropologists began to note the subtle variations of language, social interaction, and rules expressed in children's play even among closely connected groups. Clearly the player as well as the toy was culture bound.

This view of toys within a socialization process also inspired research into the implications of sex-stereotyped dolls, war toys and the impact of television toys on play. For example, the often observed gender differences in toy choices and play styles have led many researchers to question those assumed social and cognitive benefits of pretend-play gender-stereotypic toys (Liss, 1983). If toys were neutral or irrelevant to play, why did gender preferences develop so early and so deeply (Furby and Wilke, 1982), and on the other hand why did boys' and girls' play behavior differ when they played with the same toy (Liss, 1981; Schau et al., 1980)? Researchers noticed that by five years of age, children mostly want gender-stereotypical toys, although their parents often reinforce gender biases by assuming their children only want toys which are stereotypical (Schau et al., 1980; Caldera, Huston, and O'Brien, 1989). These emerging toy preferences appear to consolidate children's sex-role attitudes, not only in terms of toys but in their play with other children (Karpoe and Olney, 1983). As children age, they also prefer to play in same-sex groups, and apply their concept of the gender appropriateness of a toy in choosing playmates (Eisenberg, Tryon, and Cameron, 1984). Each sex responds differently to invitations to play and play models depending on the gender characteristics of both the toy and the playmate.

Viewing toy play in its social context, then, made it no longer possible to think of the toy simply as an object (devoid of meaning) being manipulated and transformed by children's imaginations, nor of the player as existing outside of their culture. Toys were chosen for play because they were social symbols making specific reference to attitudes and practices which come with our modern way of life. Even the imaginative transformations of play presume interpretation. In symbolic toy play children not only perform the cognitive transformation of the object (Jackowitz and Watson, 1980) but "decode" the meaning of both their toys and their play contexts in order to do so. Interpretation of these embedded messages is not fixed or closed but simply "cued" by known and perceived aspects of the toy (Potts, Huston, and Wright, 1986). Some meanings ascribed to the play will be derivative representations (child uses a baby doll to play mummy); in other cases it may be transformative (child uses the doll's hair as a broom); but in either case the child must use her stock of social knowledge to engage the toy and play.

Researchers observed that girls' doll play can be a dense social occasion characterized more by interaction and multifaceted speech acts than by object manipulation, mastery, and action (Liss, 1983). The social communication in play revealed the need for a different way of observing play interactions and a different theory that could account for the layered communication which seems to take place. Play communication can quickly vary through divergent references and multiple modalities, from rule defining to simple manipulation to arguing to talking to singing to storytelling, in a dizzying sequence of multilayered social dramatic enactments. It was difficult enough to observe and note what was going on, let alone provide a simple account of the benefits of such imaginary play episodes *where acts of interpretation and acts of imagination were blended seamlessly.*

The recent controversy over war toys in the schools help us bring into focus the implications of these theoretical questions concerning what is expressed in toy play. Critics of war play argue for bans on war toys (and related television programs) because they see these toys as symbols of militarism privileging a highly repetitive and imitative play form in boys which teaches that the use of force is a solution to all kinds of conflict. These critics are alarmed by the ritualization and lack of complexity of children's play with war toys, and believe that in play children are imitating and modeling militaristic attitudes (Carlson-Paige and Levine, 1987).

On the other side, defenders argue that the evidence for such effects is limited (Beresin, 1989). Sutton-Smith's (1988) review finds the design of most war play studies faulty and the results better explained by factors such as diminished social inhibition and modeling. He also argues that the social play activities children undertake with war toys bear similarities to folkplay— "age-old play habits of chase and escape, attack and defense, and acceptance and rejection between good and bad characters which have dominated the play of people throughout history" (p. 175). On close observation, war play appears rather nonviolent, consisting of a ritualized symbolic conflict with little physical contact (Sutton-Smith, Gerstmyer, and Meckley, 1988). The transitions from playfighting to real fighting in the classroom most often arise in struggles for the possession of toys and not out of mistaking a toy's violent design for reality.

Playfighting, Sutton-Smith and his colleagues argue, is preferred by boys because it allows them to explore some universal themes of struggles for dominance, friendship, toughness, and goodness within highly stylized patterns of interpersonal conflict including attack and defense, chase, escape, and capture (Sutton-Smith et al., 1988). Since these patterns are also found outside of the realm of play, they cannot be causally linked to the toy. Worrying about teachers' interference in play, Sutton-Smith (1986) maintains that play remains self-structuring and transformative rather than imitative because, as he says, "the expression in play relies much more on the communication of internal states than upon the appreciation of external representations" (p. 139). He goes on to add that, like a symbolic rough-and-tumble play, there may even be significant social and emotional benefits to war toys which stimulate these boys to learn about hierarchical social relations and emotional control in this very safe way.

Unfortunately, the knowledge that these combative behaviors are traditional does little to alleviate the worries of those parents who believe that letting children play with war toys merely encourages them to rehearse and consolidate aggressive behaviors and role constructs. Nor does it placate teachers when they see their classrooms disrupted by children threatening their fellows with Ninja Turtle maneuvers and Batman vocalizations as shown on television. To these critics it is impossible to cast aside the socialization which also takes place in toy play simply because it is sometimes imaginative. This is because, however creative the war play, the child must engage his or her stored culturally specific knowledge of weapons, characters, war tactics, military hierarchies, and imperative modes of speech. Where does that knowledge come from?

To resolve these controversies, therefore, we need to understand not only the activity exhibited by children with their toys, but the contexts of their play (including the factors in their environment) that influence and get expressed through play. Toys are complex symbolic goods that bring many different meanings to the play situation. To understand play, therefore, we must account for what children do with the toy's symbolic content. Research on the sociolinguistics of play for example, reveals the "densely layered" social communication which takes place, engaging thought, feelings and social interaction among players (Garvey, 1976). Play often is expressed in multileveled conversations as players interpret the toys or rules; organize, structure, and sequence their social behaviors; and define the boundaries to acts of pretending. Even classroom play with benign toys has features in common with improvisational theatre, including ordinary conversation, role-specific expressions, carefully sequenced perspective shifts, and even a directorial and announcer's voicing (Magee, 1989). It is the multiple processes of interpretation in symbolic play which leads researchers to their possibility for promoting social skills (Liss, 1981), language acquisition (Mathews and Mathews, 1982), and literacy (Galda and Pellegrini, 1985).

But communication is not only happening between the players. Since toys are symbolic objects designed with references to the social world in which they were built, knowledge and values have been conveyed to the child by the toymaker, through the packaging, through the advertising of the toy, and now in televised cartoons which feature it. This enormous promotional apparatus for defining and promoting children's understanding of the specific toy seems to tip the balance between imagination and interpretation in play. If war play appears imitative and repetitious it is largely because we see children employing a very narrow portion of their knowledge (characters and their actions) in their play—precisely that knowledge which has been communicated to them through the toy's design and promotion.

THE PROMOTION OF TOYS IN AMERICA

We often forget that throughout history, children have happily played *without* toys and manufactured playthings. Indeed, at the beginning of this century, manufactured toys were rather scarce and largely found in wealthier families. Yet from the beginning of the twentieth century, the oft-repeated idea that toys encouraged children's learning and development has helped make toys the sine qua non of home play as well—the primary tools of a child's growth and socialization. In this respect, the play ethos helped to make what had been considered idle pursuits and indulgences a legitimate activity for children.

America's emerging fascination with childhood and childrearing has permeated much of the popular writing and culture of this century (de Mause, 1974). And from the turn of the century, merchants and manufacturers, like teachers, began to think about serving children's special needs. It is notable, therefore, that by 1903 the fledgling American Toy Manufacturers Association had already begun to associate educators' theories of play's benefits with toys in pamphlets they issued. Meanwhile, merchants began to rearrange their shops, making children the "pivotal point" of promotions designed to increase business (Leach, 1993). Department stores and other children's merchandisers began to feature toy festivals, window displays, and children's goods sections at Christmas time, consolidating the idea that toys were the essential tools of innocence. Santa always arrived with a bagful of toys to make Christmas a "children's" festival. Domestic toy manufacturers were few, however, so until World War I the toys, like Saint Nick, were largely German craft imports.

Clearly the market for toys was being supported by a growing desire among American parents to meet children's socioemotional needs. One of the first and most original American toy designs was the Teddy Bear. Made by the Ideal Toy Company, who licensed Teddy Roosevelt's name for this prototype soft and cuddly toy, the Teddy Bear gave rise to a host of generic plush toys by capturing and reflecting the changing mood engulfing childhood. Teddy was less an object for manipulation than a persona kids could "feel" about and love. Rather than discipline and hard work, American parents learned to encourage the sentimental, sensual, and simple attachments of young children to their soft toys as an acceptable form of socialization.

Growing industrialization and the end of the war meant that cheaper, mass-produced playthings were coming in range of the average family. A small domestic toy and games industry strove to meet the growing demand for children's goods in the middle-class families, schools, youth clubs, and sports organizations. In the advertising of the modernist period, a picture of homelife often included a family scene with children's toys. Toys were fitting symbols of modern life—as leisure objects they referred to the rewards of hard work; as household goods they reflected the optimism of family life; and as children's things they invoked the delight of innocent pleasure (Marchand, 1985). The growth in the toy industries was built on a growing social acceptance of toys as the domestic necessities of the modern family—an idea constantly promoted by the industry.

The growing demand for lively and entertaining playthings was well understood by new toy manufacturers like Fisher-Price, who got an early start in the mass production of wooden pull toys. Their founders announced in their promotional material a commitment to five principles of good toymaking—intrinsic play value, ingenuity, strong construction, good value for money, and action—stating their belief that "a successful toy for the modern selective buyer . . . must be in demand for birthdays, parties and weekend trips, and meet the daily need for good cheer and recreation, for amusement and education" (Murray and Fox, 1987, p. 3). During the 1960s Fisher-Price set up its nursery research center and, based on their observations of early play, increasingly specialized in infant and preschool manipulation toys. Niche marketing helped them to become a world leader in preschool toys, which most contemporary parents will buy to meet those twin objectives of keeping their children happy while maintaining the normal developmental pace of their child (Kline, 1993).

Yet the post–World War II baby-boom years saw a growing emphasis on the "free" play of children and consequently the entertainment value of toys. Encouraged by writers like Dr. Spock, who proclaimed "that each child is an individual and should be allowed to be so" (p. 64), parents began to believe that it was important to let children meet their own needs by giving them what they wanted or even the money to buy toys for themselves. And of all the values that could be conveyed to children through toys, the Canadian Toy Manufacturers Association pamphlet (speaking, it seems, to parents on behalf of children) stressed fun: "Scientific advances, technological changes, social attitudes and customs, personal values and moral convictions can all be found reflected in the playthings we offer to our children. But perhaps most important of all, the true purpose of a toy or game is to entertain" (Canadian Toy Manufacturers, 1985). The pleasure and enjoyment of the child became the sign of a good toy. And though children had a poor memory for brand names and product attributes, if they really wanted a toy they were capable of putting lots of pressure on their parents (McNeal, 1987).

In the postwar period, toy merchants also learned to use television to let children know what kinds of fun they desired. In 1955 the toy maker Marx, with $50 million in toy sales, spent $312 on advertising. Today toy advertisers are children's marketing leaders, spending approximately $1 billion annually. This is why, as Stern and Schoenhaus (1990) note, "Mattel's decision to advertise toys to children on national television fifty-two weeks a year so revolutionized the industry that it is not an exaggeration to divide the history of the American toy business into two eras, before and after television" (p. 56)

The advantage of television advertising was that through it the toy company could directly communicate the fun, excitement, and peer context of play (Atkin and Held, 1977; Doolittle and Pepper, 1975). Since peer pressure and modeling could have an important influence on both toy preferences and playmates (Goldberg and Gorn, 1979), television promotions almost always included images of happy (and carefully chosen) actors playing with the toys. Television advertising proved a powerful instrument for promoting a sense of who plays with what toys—particularly the age and gender of the player (Ruble, Balaban, and Cooper, 1981). Mattel was one of the first toy makers to explore this potential of television promotions, discovering with their burp gun and mouseguitar promos on the enormously popular Mickey Mouse Club that television exposure could generate tremendous excitement and recognition among kids about a new toy "as seen on television." As Cy Schneider, the advertiser of these toys, stated, toy makers "began to see toys as *concepts* that could be depicted or demonstrated in television commercials" (1987, p. 169). The new category of "promotional toys" were likely to be the ones that were depicted as peer fun, which could benefit from directly advertising to children.

Barbie was the first doll to be heavily marketed with television advertising, which established her "backstory" as a fashion model, portraying her as a personality rather than a doll. Barbie was based on Mattel's research that indicated that what girls really wanted was not another baby doll but a doll that could help them to fantasize themselves as teenagers. They designed and promoted her as a model because their early research indicated young girls' interest in teen lifestyles and "fashion play." The success of Barbie not only revealed to marketers the potential of "personality" toys but pointed to a different conception of doll play—one in which meaning, subjective involvements, and private fantasies were paramount. And if a doll was a character, then symbolic play was a form of theatre in which the doll or truck was the stimulus to fantasy. Personality toy marketers were beginning to understand that they were in the entertainment business, even if their toy was a model spaceship.

Television is important in children's lives. Children not only watch it a lot, but also seemed to play at television, responding to the characters and situations it presented in a manner not unlike a game—to structure their imaginative exchanges as play (Reid and Fraser, 1980. Noting in their study the potential impact of television on imaginative activities of the child, Singer and Singer (1981) did not find that heavy viewing of television diminished imaginativeness. But they did discover that television's themes, characters, and their actions did permeate children's play, especially among the heavier viewers who had few alternatives and little family intervention. Television seemed to have an effect on the content of children's fantasies. Although concerned by this apparent link between play fantasy and television, Singer (this volume) remains optimistic that programs with prosocial themes and parental encouragement can help to ensure socioemotional learning.

Yet the growing connection between fantasy and television led the toymakers to increasingly use television's successes as their interpretive key to understanding children's culture. Market research revealed the tremendous appeal that familiar television heroes and animated characters had for children, and the importance that television was playing in laying the symbolic foundations of their lives (McCollum-Spielman, 1982). Television characters were the most familiar and most widely linked persona, so why not use them in promoting toys in a more direct and explicit way?

Yet it was a tricky business picking a winning personality toy, since children's passion for these faddish toys might quickly pass. To stabilize this situation, the toymakers also expanded their research efforts by attempting to measure a toys "play value"—a tautological concept, as they found the most useful measure of play values was a toy's success in the market, its attractiveness (children voluntarily choose it in tests), and the length of time children would play with it in free play (fascination). A good toy was any toy children would play with. Indeed, research and past successes held important lessons for toymakers concerned with the very subtle design factors that made children want a toy—and research showed that children wanted toys specific to their gender. Because developing and bringing promotional toys to market was costing more, the marketers wanted to be sure that the investment would pay, so they increasingly concentrated their resources behind a few well-researched toy lines, and stopped promoting thousands of others. These factors also favored a formulaic approach to marketing new toys. The success of *Star Wars*, for example, produced a panoply of futuristic action toys (Pearse, 1991). Even Lego designed futuristic themes into mini-bricks and began to advertise to children.

With deregulation of television in the United States in 1982, the toy marketers embarked on a massive new strategy for promoting their toys by using children's interest in television characters to sell toys. During the 1980s the toy merchants also became the leading advertisers on children's television, spending over $350 million in the expanding cycle of intense promotion. This new approach to "total marketing" utilized the animated series or film as an extended commercial to detail the backstory and create peer excitement around a new line of licensed personae. How this changed the toy's concept is seen in the Dyno-riders. Originally conceived as museum quality replicas of real dinosaurs, they were given good and bad humanoid riders who were in mental telepathy with them by the marketing and promotion agency because these motifs were deemed necessary to bring them to life (Stern and Schoenhaus, 1990).

Moreover, because of well-known age and sex preferences for characters and play values, all promotional toys were carefully positioned with scripted appeal for known market segments, becoming gender and age inflected in terms of the play they depict (Kline and Pentacost, 1990). Hasbro, for example, launched the twin action figures He-man and She-ra simultaneously to try to win share in both markets. Carebears on the other hand, had a familiar ambisexual anthropomorphism for the preschool market. American commercial television has since become saturated with promotional animation called "30-minute commercials" because the fictions are so obviously fashioned with promotional intentions (Eaton and Dominick, 1991; Englehardt, 1986). Because they must appeal to a narrow market segment, they are carefully scripted with the themes and motifs known to appeal to the niche play markets defined by gender and age (Kline, 1993). As one study found, younger children don't seem to understand the difference between the cartoon commercials and the programs, leading these researchers to believe the FCC's adjacency requirement is ineffective. As Wilson and Weiss (1992) go on to note, almost 25 percent of their sample believed the cartoons are commercials, which the authors argue arises from a general confusion "stemming from the fact that the cartoons featured toys as characters" (p. 386).

This confusion does not stop children from translating their interest in television into an enthusiasm about the toys. Four years after deregulation, toy sales had tripled while licensed character toys became the best sellers, rising to about 65 percent of the toy and game market. Toys and games are now the most desired gifts of young children. An American family annually spends about $423 on toys and games in the belief that they are at worst benign entertainments. Although industry sales statistics do not tell us much about what children do with their toys, they do indicate the preferences and attitudes that children and parents have formed about suitable playthings. Of the $17 million spent on toys and games in the United States in 1992, for example, educational toys accounted for less than five percent of sales. The predominant share of the spending went to the purchase of promotional toys— those cuddly creatures, fashion dolls, and action figures which are heavily advertised or featured in films and animations. A parallel promotional market is found in the video games sector, with $5.2 billion gross sales in the United States alone (Battelle and Johnston, 1993).

A Canadian study comparing letters to Santa during the autumn of 1987 found that television promotions profoundly influence childrens' desire for particular types of toys. Children in cabled regions which received American promotional cartoons (they were not allowed in Canada or Europe at the time) were twice as likely to ask for promotional toys for Christmas. At 53 percent, the proportion of cabled kids who requested at least one promotional toy might appear moderate. Yet because girls in this study appeared less fascinated with these programs (mostly targeted at boys), the saturation is quite considerable. The study noted that even though children without cable were little exposed to promotional television, they often had heard about these characters from friends and relatives and had seen them in the shops. Twenty-five percent requested these toys from Santa, but their preferences included more traditional playthings (skates, sleds) and non-toy presents than their cabled cousins (Kline, 1993).

The question of the impact of intensive promotional toy marketing on children's television and preferred heroes began to be asked around the world as cable and satellites brought these American promotional series and toys to other countries (Kline and Smith, 1993). A Canadian study found that especially among boys aged two to nine, the promotional shows were judged the most attractive, including Batman and Ninja Turtles. Girls in this age range tended to watch educational programs and sitcoms more than the boys, but also reported liking Little Mermaid, My Ponies, and Care Bears (VanderBurgh and Knoepfli, 1992). Clearly, the excitement and interest created by a popular television program translates into shared interest in a particular symbolic universe and its characters. The possibilities of play with these toys is premised upon a shared fascination, and an appropriate stock of knowledge which is part of the negotiation and interaction within that character play universe. In a peer context where children talk about and ultimately want to play with the most popular toys, they often chose these promotional toys.

With this communicational dynamic in mind, I undertook to study the links among television, character and toy preferences, and play, interviewing 143 six- to nine-year-old Canadian children about their use of television and toys. We also asked these children to draw pictures of themselves playing at home, submitting these play drawings to a detailed analysis. From this study it became clear that television and play jointly dominate children's home lives, as 75 percent of the children mention doing one or the other first thing after school (figure 8.1). Strongly gendered preferences in programs (figure 8.2) and toys (figure 8.3) were noted, and the number of favorite programs, characters, and toys which were promotional were highly correlated. Although not all children who follow a promotional series have that toy, most children who owned and favored a particular toy were likely to watch or to have watched the series (figure 8.4).

The drawings of themselves at play also revealed the extent to which social dramatic toys dominate the children's conception of play. Under 7

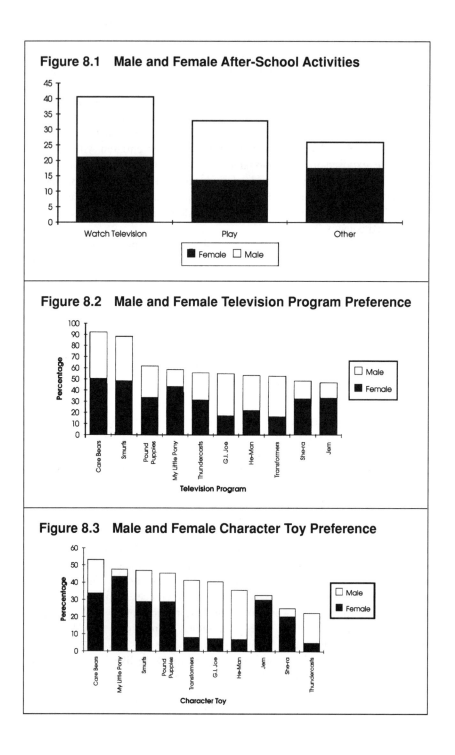

Figure 8.1   Male and Female After-School Activities

Figure 8.2   Male and Female Television Program Preference

Figure 8.3   Male and Female Character Toy Preference

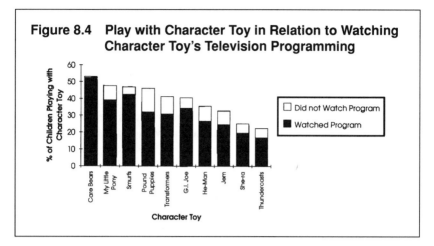

Figure 8.4   Play with Character Toy in Relation to Watching Character Toy's Television Programming

percent of the play drawings did not include some kind of toy (broadly defined), and almost 68 percent of the drawings showed children playing with toys of "identity." The children volunteered the license name in their description of over half of these toys. Rare among these pictures were play with construction and educational toys, and a small proportion did illustrate themselves playing with television or sound media.

Pointing out that there are no published studies of the impact of promotional toy advertising, Patricia Greenfield and her colleagues (1990) wondered whether these ready-made story lines provided on television may prevent children from using their imaginations creatively in play. Their study compared children's stories about Smurf and Troll toys after viewing either the Smurf program or a neutral play activity. Their control was designed to see if the audiovisual medium or the direct link to the narrative would cue more imitative or transformative references in the play story. Results indicated that for younger children, transformative stories were fueled by the link between toy and television, whereas for older children the television-toy stories were more derivative. The combination of cartoon and toys created the lowest proportion of creative imagination in the stories, but the authors conclude it is the television program, and not the toy, which diminishes creative play.

Similarly, in a Norwegian study of nursery children in households exposed (for the first time) to commercial television, Bjornebeck (1992) found the commercialized children to have formed a stronger interest in promotional toys, to place greater demands for these toys on their parents, and to have a more gender-stereotypical way of playing with them than those that weren't able to see these commercials and programs. In terms of imaginativeness, she states: "The creative drawing process and characteristics of gameplaying seem, however, to differ only in that inspiration for both is drawn from a narrower range of sources" (p. 18). In Holland, where these cartoons are shown on cable, children revealed a similar interest in television toys based on their liking of specific characters, themes, and traits (Stephenson, 1993). Fighting and shooting and gender appropriateness seemed in this study to be major reasons why children liked both the programs and the toys. When asked which programs they imitated in their play, *Teenage Hero Turtles* (in Europe) was tops.

Children like to use toys to convene social occasions in which their meaningful cultural objects can be discussed, arranged, and manipulated. Yet the majority of the play drawings described above were of solitary play. Other children were indicated in 32 percent while parents rarely were shown (4 percent); but mostly these play drawings indicated isolated fantasy play (64 percent)—a child immersed in the simulacrum "social world" of the toy. Comparing identity and traditional toys, for the sociality of play, these drawings indicated the extent to which toys are a "parasocial" communication event. Character toys and soft toys were four times as likely to be played with alone, whereas dolls and playground equipment were generally likely to be used in social play. Modern promotional toys, when coupled with television, seem to encourage children to play fantasy games which bear little thematic relationship to their lives (Funkhouser and Shaw, 1990; Cohen, 1974) and to do so in isolation. This seems to contrast with play in schools, where dramatic fantasy play (although relatively rare) is the most interactive type of play (Johnson and Ershler, 1981). This observation of the disconnected nature of action-hero fantasy is also important to counter those who have argued that "superhero" play has maturational benefits for the child because it allows them to experience mastery and learn new social skills (Kostelnik, Whiren, and Stein, 1986).

Many of the play scenes were imitative in the sense that children interpret the toy's symbolism in its most conventional sense (G.I. Joe is a soldier seeking revenge). Yet we also noted that in some cases children drew elaborate and quite creative play scenes including ironical, whimsical, and creative ideas (Jem dates Ken at McDonalds to get revenge on Barbie). In the play drawings, 18 percent made direct reference to the television programs in order to explain the game structure. Many more had program elements (characters, vehicles, etc.) (45 percent) which were being adapted in their play. Often these references were in the form of more abstract rules, situations, and experiences which players understand as the imaginary content of their toys. (e.g., Barbie fell over putting on tight pants, G.I. Joe wins because he is stronger). Yet the vast majority were the common forms

Sutton-Smith calls "folk play" (battle, tag, chase-and-rescue, dressing dolls, etc.). The key difference seems to be that this folkplay is often impregnated with the symbolism established by the television promotions (outfitting Barbie for a rock concert).

Occasionally, the implied rules and player subjectivity are articulated ("I'm pretending I am He-Man"), indicating enactive identity-taking (21 percent), and at other times narratives give temporal structure to the play ("Metlar is waiting to trap them"), which leads some researchers to wonder whether the children don't borrow the "play scripts" directly from television. Reference to wholesale thematic borrowing was made in 14 percent of the drawings, but in the stated games and episodic stagings, there was a strong sense of television narrative structures being used to "frame" play in subtle ways as stagings within known universes of discourse (25 percent). Combined, role taking and interactive pretending play occurred in 76 percent of the drawings, reflected the degree to which social drama has become a central factor of home play.

CONCLUSION

The postwar expansion of television marketing has helped to bring toys increasingly into focus as the royal road to play. Yet, as this essay has tried to show, toys do not arrive "unbidden" in children's lives. Ironically, during the last century, while psychologists urged play's autonomy, the toymakers were learning how to design and sell play characters as a novel form of fantasy entertainment. The modern promotional toy is carefully designed, tested, and marketed not only with a specific age group and gender in mind but with a strong view to a toy's social dramatic potential. Unburdened by the play ethos, the toy makers have come to see toys as a communication media through which children can represent and sometimes exchange their ideas, attitudes, and values. This study has shown that far from being devoid of meaning, modern promotional toys are discussed by children as their preferred point of access into a simulacrum universe, with links to television.

The growing world trade in toys (Playthings, 1991) reminds us that there already is global toy curriculum. Following a pattern laid down for Barbie, Ninja Turtles, Batman, and Mario have all become international supertoys by being heavily promoted by this marketing approach, which aligns toys and television at the poles of children's imagination. Although the consequences of character marketing remains unclear, this study has suggested that the intensified symbolism of television toys may shift the balance between transformative and interpretive processes of play. For this reason, any discussion of play and its benefits is going to have to account for the increasing influence of toy marketing on children's play.

REFERENCES

Atkin, C., & Heald, G. (1977). The content of children's toy and food commercials. *Journal of Communication, 27*, 107–14.

Barnett, L. A. (1991). Characterizing playfulness: Correlates with individual attributes and personality traits. *Play and Culture, 4*, 371–93.

Batelle, J., & Johnston, B. (1993, December). Seizing the next level: Sega's plans for world domination. *Wired*, 73–74, 128–31.

Beresin, A. R. (1989). Toy war games and the illusion of two-sided rhetoric. *Play and Culture, 2*.

Bjornebekk, R. T. (1992, August). Commercialization of children's television—the market forces' invasion of children's everyday lives? Paper presented in the IAMCR Scientific Conference, Brazil.

Brown, L. (1988). Fiction for children: Does the medium matter? *Journal of Aesthetic Education, 22*, 35–44.

Caldera Y., Huston, M., Aletha, C., & O'Brien, M. (1989). Social interaction and play patterns of parents and toddlers with feminine, masculine, and neutral toys. *Child Development, 60*, 70–76.

Canadian Toy Manufacturers. (1985). *Annual report*. Toronto, Ontario.

Carllson-Paige, N., & Levin, D. E. (1987). *The war play dilemma: Children's needs and society's future*. New York: Teachers College Press.

———. (1989). Young children and war play. *Early Childhood Research Quarterly, 4*, 393–402.

Cohen, D. H. (1974). Is television a pied piper? *Young Children, 30*, 2–3.

Davie, C. E., Hutt, S. J., Vincent, E., & Mason, M. (1984). *The young child at home*. Windsor, United Kingdom: NRER-Nelson.

DeMause, L. (1974). *The history of childhood*. New York: Harper Torchbooks.

Doolittle, J., & Pepper, R. (1975). Children's TV ad content: 1974. *Journal of Broadcasting, 19*(2), 131–42.

Downs, A. C. (1983). Letters to Santa Claus: Elementary school-age children's sex-typed toy preferences in a natural setting. *Sex Roles, 9*(2), 159–63.

Eaton, C. B., & Dominick, J. R. (1991). Product-related programming and children's TV: A content analysis. *Journalism Quarterly, 68*, 67–75.

Eisenberg, N., Tryon, K., & Cameron, E. (1984). Relation of preschoolers' peer interaction to their sex-typed toy choices. *Child Development, 55*, 1044–50.

Engelhardt, T. (1986). The Strawberry Shortcake strategy. In T. Gitlin (Ed.), *Watching Television* New York: Pantheon.

Exports boost profits for U. S. toymakers (1991, January). Editorial in *Playthings*, 36.

Fisher, E. P. (1992). The impact of play development: A meta-analysis. *Play and Culture, 5*, 159–81.

Funkhouser, G. R., & Shaw, E. F. (1990). How synthetic experience shapes social reality. *Journal of Communication, 40*, 75–87.

Furby, L., & Wilke, M. (1982). Some characteristics of infants' preferred toys. *Journal of Genetic Psychology, 140*, 207–19.

Galda, L. & Pellegrini, A. D. (Eds.). (1985). *Play language and stories: The development of children's literate behavior.* Georgia: University of Georgia Press.

Garvey, C. (1976). Some properties of social play. In J. S. Bruner, A. Jolly, & K. Sylva (Eds.), *Play: Its role in development and evolution* (pp. 570–83). Harmondsworth: Penguin.

Giddings, M., & Halverson, C. F. (1981, January). Young children's use of toys in home environment. *Family Relations, 30*, 69–74.

Goldberg, M., & Gorn, J. (1979). Television's impact on preferences for non-white playmates: Canadian Sesame Street inserts. *Journal of Broadcasting, 23*(1), 27–32.

Greenfield, P., Yut, E., Chung, M., Land, D., Kreider, H., Pantoja, M., & Horsley, K. (1990). The program-length commercial: A study of the effects of television/toy tie-ins on imaginative play. *Psychology and Marketing, 7*, 237–55.

Humphreys, A. P., & Smith, P. K. (1987). Rough and tumble, friendship, and dominance in schoolchildren: Evidence for continuity and change with age. *Child Development, 58*, 201–12.

Huizinga, J. (1955). *Homo ludens: A study of the play element in culture.* Boston: Beacon.

International market seen as key to industry growth. (1991, January). Editorial in *Playthings*, 13–14.

Jackowitz, E., & Ershler, J. (1981). Developmental trends in preschool play as a function of classroom program and child gender. *Child Development, 52*, 995–1004.

Karpoe, K. P., & Olney, R. L. (1983). The effect of boys' and girls' toys on sex-typed play in preadolescents. *Sex Roles, 9*, 507–18.

Kline, S. (1988). Limits of the imagination: Children's play in the age of marketing. In I. Angus & S. Jhally (Eds.), *Cultural politics in America* (pp. 291–316). London: Routledge and Kegan Paul.

————. (1993). *Out of the garden: Children's toys and television in the age of marketing*. London: Verso.

Kline, S., & Pentecost, D. (1990). The characterization of play: Marketing children's toys. *Play and Culture, 3*, 235–54.

Knight, J. (1984). Television: Plague or play partner? *International Association for the Child's Right to Play, 8* (7), pp. 5–6.

Kostelnik, M. J., Whiren, A. P., & Stein, L. C. (1986, May). Living with He-Man: Managing superhero fantasy play. *Young Children*, 3–9.

Leach, W. (1993). Child-world in the promised land. In J. Gilbert, A. Gilman, D. M. Scott, & J. W. Scott (Eds.), *The mythmaking frame of mind* (pp. 209–37). Belmont, CA: Wadsworth.

Liss, M. B. (1981). Patterns of toy play: An analysis of sex differences. *Sex Roles, 7*, 1143–50.

————. (1983). Learning gender-related skills through play. In M. B. Liss (Ed.), *Social and cognitive skills: Sex roles and children's play* (pp. 147–65). New York: Academic Press.

Locke, J. (1773). *Some thoughts concerning education* (14th ed.). London: J. Whiston. (Reprint).

Magee, M. A. (1989). Social play as performance. *Play and Culture, 2*.

Marchand, R. (1985). *Advertising the American dream: Making way for modernity, 1920–1940*. Berkeley: University of California Press.

Matthews W., & Matthews, R. (1982). Eliminating operational definitions: A paradigm case approach to the study of fantasy play. In D. J. Pepler & K. H. Rubin (Eds.), *The play of children*. New York: Basel.

McCollum-Spielman Topline Report. (1986). "Star Power 2: Understanding Kids and their Stars." *Topline, 4*(2), 1985.

McNeal, J. (1987). *Children as consumers*. Austin: University of Texas, Bureau of Business Research.

Murray, J. J., & Fox, B. R. (1987). *A historical, rarity, value guide: Fisher-Price 1931–1963*. Alabama: Books Americana.

Paley, V. G. (1984). *Boys and girls: Superheroes in the doll corner*. Chicago: University of Chicago Press.

Pearse, B. (1991, April). Action figures continue to figure in the action. *Playthings*.

Potts, R., Huston, A. C., & Wright, J. C. (1986). The effects of television form and violent content on boys' attention and social behavior. *Journal of Experimental Child Psychology*, 1–17.

Reid, L. N., & Frazer, C. (1980). Television at play. *Journal of Communication, 30*(4), 66–73.

Ruble, D. N., Balaban, T., & Cooper, J. (1981). Gender constancy and the effects of sex-typed televised toy commercials. *Child Development, 52*, 667–73.

Schau, C. G., Kahn, L., Diepold, J. H., & Cherry, F. (1980). The relationships of parental expectations and preschool children's verbal sex typing to their sex-typed toy play behavior. *Child Development, 51*, 266–70.

Schneider, C. (1987). *Children's television: The art, the business, and how it works.* Chicago: NTC Business Books.

Singer, J. L., & Singer, D. G. (1981). *Television, imagination, and aggression: A study of preschoolers.* Hillsdale, NJ: L. Erlbaum Assoc.

Smith, P. K. (1988). Children's play and its role in early development: A re-evaluation of the "play ethos." In A. D. Pellegrini (Ed.), *Psychological bases for early education* (pp. 207–25). New York: John Wiley and Sons.

Sydney, L. S., & Schoenhaus, T. (1990). *Toyland: The high-stakes game of the toy industry.* Chicago: Contemporary Books.

Stevenson, R. (1993). Children and television. Manuscript. University of Nijmigen.

Sutton-Smith, B. (1986). *Toys as culture.* New York: Gardner.

———. (1988). War toys and childhood aggression. *Play and Culture, 1*, 57–69.

Sutton-Smith, B., Gerstmyer, J., & Meckley, A. (1988). Playfighting as folkplay amongst preschool children. *Western Folklore, 47*, 171–76.

Schwartzmann, H. B. (1979). *Transformations: The anthropology of children's play.* New York: Plenum.

Swiniarski, L. B. (1991). Toys: Universals for teaching global education. *Childhood Education, 67*, 161–63.

Sylva, K., Roy, C., & Cants, M. (1984). The role of play in the problem-solving of children 3–5 years old. In J. S. Bruner, A. Jolly, & K. Sylva (Eds.), *Play: Its role in development and evolution* (pp. 244–57). Harmondsworth: Penguin.

VanderBurgh, C., & Knoepfli, H. (1993). *Batman would only live in the United States.* Toronto: Ryerson.

Varga, D. (1991). The historical ordering of children's play as a developmental task. *Play and Culture, 4*, #4, 322–33.

Wilson, B. J., & Weiss, A. J. (1992, Fall). Developmental differences in children's reactions to toy advertisements linked to a toy-based cartoon. *Journal of Broadcasting and Electronic Media.*

9

JEROME L. SINGER

Imaginative Play in Childhood: Precursor of Subjunctive Thought, Daydreaming, and Adult Pretending Games

In keeping with the tradition of audacity and playfulness which Brian Sutton-Smith has brought to his scholarly writings and public presentations, I should like to begin this chapter with a bold assertion that I hope may foster in the reader imaginative and creative speculation about the adaptive function of children's make-believe games. I will be proposing the hypothesis that early make-believe play, when suitably nurtured by a family and by other individuals or settings in which the child participates, may serve as the beginning for the emergence of a major dimension of human experience. This dimension can be termed the realm of the "possible," the ability of the growing child and, later, the effective adult to engage in subjective thought process, considering through private narratives alternative actions and life situations that may be both telic (functionally motivated) and paratelic (playful) in Apter's (1989) sense. My general approach involves an effort to integrate observations in research on children's play into the broader framework of basic theory and research in general psychology on cognition, emotion, motivation, personality, and social processes.

A PERSONAL NOTE

In an autobiographical statement, Sutton-Smith (1993) has produced a piece that is at one and the same time charming, self-revelatory, and theoretically provocative. Reading this delightful essay led me to realize that, although I had been acquainted with Sutton-Smith for almost thirty years, (and I had even gleaned some sense of his childhood from reading his books of New Zealand boys' life such as *Smitty Does A Bunk* [Sutton-Smith, 1961]) we shared much more in common than one might suspect from surface impressions. True, I had grown up in the Brooklyn and Bronx sections of New York City and he in far off Wellington, New Zealand, but we both participated in many of the same kinds of boys' street activities, athletic interests, and, particularly, opportunities in early childhood to engage in imaginative play. What emerges from his account is how much of his theorizing about the role

187

of power and competition in children's and adolescent's play stemmed from his own experience as a second son (in keeping with Alfred Adler's [1968] theories). Sutton-Smith's scholarly research on birth order obviously also reflects this experience.

As a firstborn son, and for seven years an only child, my own early experiences differ somewhat and my own theoretical leanings may therefore focus less on the power/competitive features of imaginative play and more on their relationship to mastery and confidence rather than competition.

On the whole, however, I perceive more similarities than differences in our backgrounds along the lines which might have sensitized us both to the significance of play as a dimension of human experience. If I were to characterize the overall thrust of differences between Sutton-Smith and myself in the way we have described play situations or tried to theorize about the functions of play in the developmental process it would be along the lines of his greater emphasis on the potential oppositional or rambunctious nature of play in contrast to my own focus on the more generally adaptive, perhaps even "nicer" features of children's play, a position I share with my wife and collaborator in much of this research, Dorothy Singer. Sutton-Smith although recognizing that encouragement of parents playing with their children is desirable (Sutton-Smith and Sutton-Smith, 1974) has tended to be more skeptical of the benefits for children of play training experiences, something which my wife and I have felt can be very valuable for most children (Singer and Singer, 1990). Can it be that there again his exposure to an older brother who may often have bedeviled him, teased him, or outplayed him has alerted him more to the demonic aspects of play while my perhaps less pressured early years left me free to explore the more positive features of play? I shall return to some of these issues later in this chapter as I lay out some of the dimensions of my view of imaginative play. Suffice it to say that at the very least I have set forth some of my personal childhood-based assumptions in much the same way as Sutton-Smith has although, since this is not a personal memoir, with much less detail. Even if I think that I'm right and Sutton-Smith is wrong on a number of points along the way (and as I write this I see the twinkle in his eyes and his impish grin before me), one cannot ignore the suggestiveness of the positions he has taken. The kind of forthright assertiveness he has shown in his work on play is what makes for serious scientific interchange and progress.

PLAY IN THE CONTEXT OF PSYCHOLOGY'S COGNITIVE-AFFECTIVE REVOLUTION

During almost the first sixty years of the twentieth century, psychology, influenced jointly by psychoanalysis and behaviorism, was dominated by an emphasis on various combinations of stimulus-response reductionism and presumably by biologically based drive energy motivational systems of the type fostered by Sigmund Freud in the last thirty years of his life. In this period, play was often perceived by the very few who even took notice of the phenomenon as largely an effort by children to come to grips with early conflicts about psychosexual impulses. Children's efforts to compromise these sensual needs with parental strictures were reflected in symbolic games that almost invariably were reduced by psychoanalytic theorists to sexual origins. The independent research of Kurt Lewin (1935), Lev Vygotsky (1966), and Jean Piaget (1962), all involving meticulous empirical investigation of actual children's behavior rather than the adult retrospective memories on which so many clinicians relied, were gradually influential in generating a major cognitive revolution that emerged in the early 1960s. This paradigm shift was also brought about through the neurophysiological studies which called into question the Freudian and behavioristic emphasis on peripheral drives such as hunger, thirst, and sex as primary human motivators. Studies of the brain and its arousal patterns as well as of the sleep cycle heightened an awareness of how much thinking goes on during the period when organisms are in reduced stimulus states of one kind or another. The emergence of the computer and the new investigative area of artificial intelligence also heightened a sensitivity to the great role played on daily human experience by information processing. One of the key factors in all of this was also the awareness that such information processing involved preparatory thought, what Miller, Galanter, and Pribram (1960) called "plans," and what, more recently, has become the standard usage in psychology, the theory of "schemas" and "scripts." Such expectancies are part of a sequential process in accumulating and retaining information from the environment that goes beyond the narrow focus of the earlier stimulus-response approaches (Bower, 1972; Singer, 1984; Tomkins, 1962).

Cognition and Emotion

The emphasis on the key role of information processing, curiosity, and expectancies as part of the way individuals maneuver themselves through their physical and social environments continues to be a dominant feature of modern experimental psychology and behavioral science in general. At the same time, the considerable and growing influence of theorists and researchers such as Ekman, Friesen, and Ellsworth (1982), Kreitler and Kreitler (1976), Izard, (1991), George Mandler (1984), Tomkins (1962), and many others has focused increasing attention on the close links between the cognitive system of the organism and human emotionality. This linkage can be addressed in relation to children by noting that we now regard human beings from their birth on as information-seeking creatures, curious and exploratory, striving to organize and to integrate novelty and complexity but also attempting to anticipate and match prior learning with new material. When they can integrate novelty and complexity with such preestablished schemas, they feel comfortable and, indeed, show the smile that (as Hanus Papousek's infant studies have shown) yield the smile that represents control over novelty and the assimilation of new events into prior concepts and scripts about the sequences of behavior (Papousek, Papousek, and Harris, 1987).

The "smile of predictive pleasure" described by Papousek and other observers such as Izard (1991) in their research on early childhood behavior is also comparable to the research on familiarity and positive emotions such as smiling and laughing reported in the research of Robert Zajonc (1980). The empirical studies and the extensive theoretical analyses of Tomkins point to the fact that while cognition and emotion may indeed be structurally differentiable in the body with respect to how they are activated and motorically expressed, they remain closely linked together in ultimate human response.

Within this framework I am proposing to set the nature of children's play as one major way in which the young child can deal with complexity and novelty of its environment and can be motivated emotionally (following Tompkins, 1962):

1. To reexperience or to reconstruct events, interactions or thoughts that evoke the positive emotions of *interest-excitement* or *joy* (smiling and laughter)

2. To avoid in action or thought those situations that have evoked the specific emotions of *anger, fear-terror, sadness-distress* (weeping) or the complex of *shame-humiliation-guilt*

3. To express our emotions as fully as possible

4. To control emotional expression where our social experiences suggest it is necessary

Making Sense of One's World

In this sense, early imaginative play of children can be understood as an effort of the growing organism to deal with the large objects and people around it by, first of all, trying to match such stimulus complexes with preestablished schematic structures or, failing this, by gradually reducing negative affects produced by extremely novel content through reshaping such material to manageable sizes that can be explored and manipulated by the child. This notion of "miniaturization" was expounded in a brilliant if not well known essay by Tomkins (1970) using analogies with computers and with other information models. This miniaturization concept clearly bears some relation to Piaget's "assimilation and accommodation" but it is dealt with by Tomkins in a fashion that bears a closer resemblance to our current understandings from artificial-intelligence research. I am proposing that a key feature of make-believe play, observable as early as eighteen months in the child (Fein, 1980) involves an effort to enhance positive affect and to reduce negative affect by seeking to cut down the large things around it to manageable proportions, as can be done through the use of dolls, blocks, soft toys, and other manipulable objects that can be assigned meanings roughly matching the real objects of its environment. In the course of now attempting, in Piaget's phrase, to assimilate this material to established schemas, the child also experiences the positive emotions of joy as he or she repetitively links earlier material with novelty in a controlled fashion. The child also has the opportunities to express emotions, including the negative ones of fear, sadness, or anger, through the vicarious experiences of these miniaturized objects.

Make-believe play thus becomes a critical way in which children learn to make sense of their world: the nursery, the family, the neighborhood, television (a new but omnipresent feature of the child's environment), and the ever-broadening social and physical settings that growing individuals must encounter.

Attachment and Autonomy

But beyond this cognitive requirement for the assignment of meanings and formation of structures (with the emotional implications just suggested), children also must confront a dialectic tension in their general motivation which reflects a critical polarity that persists throughout the life span (Bonanno and Singer, 1990; Singer, 1988). This tension is between, on the one hand, the need to feel attached or affiliated with others, for example parents, siblings, and other caregivers, and later friends or social groups; and, on the other hand, the need to preserve some sense of individuality and autonomy, some sense of privacy, personal competence, and individualized skill development. This fundamental human struggle—somehow to achieve a balance between attachment and the concomitant sense of community with others, and at the same time to sustain a sense of personal autonomy and power—has increasingly been emphasized by major personality theorists. Perhaps best described by David Bakan (1966), it can also be found in the writings of clinicians such as Andras Angyal (1965), Carl Jung (1971), and Otto Rank (1945). More recent efforts to elaborate the important implications both for clinical psychopathology (Blatt, 1990) and for personality and health psychology more generally (Singer and Bonanno, 1990) have also been extended to characterizing the developmental cycle described originally by Erikson (1962) and elaborated by Franz and White (1985) and Singer (1988).

To summarize this position briefly, in contrast with earlier motivational theories such as Freud's emphasis on polarities such as sex and aggression or Jung's on masculinity and femininity ("animus" vs. "anima"), this position proposes that all human beings are motivated, first of all, to make sense of their world and to assign meanings (the cognitive), and then, within that structure, to sustain some reasonable balance between the need for attachment and affiliation with others and also the desire to experience a personal sense of autonomy, individuality, and competence or power. In effect, I am proposing that the need to resolve the dilemmas of novelty and complexity, to sustain a sense of familiarity, and at the same time to enhance exploratory possibilities determines the *structural* features of the child's make-believe play efforts. The *content* of such play often shows the child's efforts both to demonstrate individual autonomy and mastery over specific content drawn from the family or the physical and social milieu, and, at the same time, to express the child's needs for belongingness and affiliation.

From this perspective it is not the question of some play being more masculine and other play being more feminine as reflections of an inherent male-female dichotomy in each child. Rather we need to go beyond this traditional and somewhat male-chauvinistic view to the recognition that both boys and girls as well as men and women are perennially confronted with some efforts to balance affiliation with autonomy. Our societies have often assigned and fostered greater emphasis on attachment and affiliation to women and autonomy and power to men. These gender attributions tend chiefly to sustain a long-established social position rather than to recognize that both men and women yearn for closeness and tenderness or opportunities of nurturance while at the same time seeking to feel independent and powerful.

In children's make-believe play one can again and again observe examples of shifts back and forth among both boys and girls from efforts to form linkages and attachments in their play objects towards assertions of personal power (sometimes through the sheer manipulation of the play objects or through the actual dialogue that before age six they speak out loud). In the follow excerpt drawn from the protocols of the late Rosalind Gould (1972, pp. 22–24) we can notice how ongoing make-believe play in a small group of four-year-olds exemplifies, on the one hand, the effort of these youngsters to come to grips with, organize, and miniaturize many aspects of adult talk about the sexes as well as stories and television images, and, at the same time, to work out in their own way their struggles with balancing attachment needs and autonomy or power needs. In the very act of play they are beginning to formulate some sense of individual identities and showing a kind of looking ahead to *what they might be*, that is, using the subjunctive conditionalities that are expressing a first anticipation of identity and selfhood. Note also that, once they are caught up in their play situation (a situation thoroughly under their control that they have entered what the British psychologist Alan Leslie [1987] has called the "metarepresentational" mode), they are relatively impervious to the attempts by a "real" girl, Oliva, to work her way into their ongoing game.

Chris: I hate women!

Teacher: Why do you say that, Chris?

Chris: Because when ya' marry them ya' hafta get your blood tested.

Teacher: What else do you think about women, Chris?

Chris: I think they're kookie! I think I'm gonna marry a princess . . . because they're better—they're prettier.

Jim: Yeah, because they have jewels and gold—and they have crowns.

Olivia: (comes over to the boys): What are your doing?

Jim and Chris: We're digging and looking for a princess.

Olivia: Well, I have a bride dress at home.

Chris: Aw, who cares about that.

Jim: Yeah, Ya' need a princess suit. (To teacher): Don't tell her we're gonna marry a princess.

Chris: Princesses have to wear their princess suits all the time or they'll be stripped of their beauty.

Olivia: (to teacher): What means "stripped of their beauty"?

Chris: Aw, go away! We hafta keep diggin'.

Teacher: Digging for what?

Chris: Digging for a princess, of course.

Jim: Yeah, ya' don't find them in New York. We're digging our way to find one

Chris: Well, ya' just don't marry one like the regular way. Ya' hafta save one first. Princesses fall in love with princes. Did ya' ever eat a princess?

Jim: NO! (They dig for awhile silently.) I dream about army things.

Chris: Well, I dream about that I'm a lieutenant with a lovely princess.

Olivia: Boys! Boys! I just found a real live earring from a princess. (She hands them a piece of crumpled paper.)

Jim and Chris: Get out of here! (They chase her away.)

Chris: (running around the hole he has dug): Romance! (Running full circle again.) Princesses! (Running full circle a third time.) Jewels! Let's get digging for those princesses!

Jim: No, we don't really want them. We hafta wait till we're grown up for that.

Chris: Yeah, till we're twenty-one!

Jim: Yeah

Chris: And then we can buy a real drill and shovel and a pick.

Jim: And a whole car and one of those things that go rrr-rrr.

Teacher: You mean a pneumatic drill?

Jim: Yeah.

Chris: But I wanna dig for princesses.

Jim: No!

Chris: Oh shucks. Josh, do you wanna marry a princess?

Josh: Sure I do.

Olivia: Do you know where you could get a real princess?

Josh: Sure I do.

Olivia: Do you know where you could get a real princess? In Ireland or England or something.

Chris: Yeah, then we could find one and . . . we could see the Beatles while we're there!

Jim: I love the Beatles. Yeah! Yeah! Yeah!

Chris: (running back from the group of girls in another part of the yard): I just went up to the princess' house and guess what—they scared me away.

Imaginative Play as a Critical Feature of Development

This vignette of "digging for a princess" demonstrates how imaginative play may provide the children with an opportunity for integrating scripts, identifying possible selves (Markus and Nurius, 1986), formulating their ideas about gender identities, and even beginning to develop schemas about self-as-child versus self-as-grown-up identities. I would like to propose then, within the framework established above, that children who do not regularly engage in make-believe play are significantly disadvantaged by the lack of opportunities to try our different roles, to try out possible selves, and to form scripts about real or potential human experiences as the boys Chris and Jim in the above vignette seem to do. I believe that children who have had less opportunity, encouragement, and, as the research of Leslie (1987) suggests in the case of autistic children, less constitutional predisposition toward regular make-believe play may be missing out on an important phase of becoming fully human. They may be missing out on important ways in which human beings can develop complex self-schemas and begin to organize their environment into the event sequences which we call scripts (Schank and Ableson, 1977), as well as learn how to express and to control emotionality. I believe that unless children have regular opportunities to incorporate into their repertory of skill this ability to miniaturize the complex world, they will be increasingly likely either to express impulses directly in overt aggressive or hasty behavior or to be regularly overwhelmed by anxiety and distress as they confront the inevitable incongruities and novelties of each new environmental encounter (Singer and Singer, 1990).

In the following sections, I will examine briefly some of the factors that determine the likelihood that children will use imaginative play adaptively, and I will also relate make-believe play on the one hand to individual differences and on the other to later adult tendencies to engage in imaginativeness, daydreaming, and various types of planning. I will also consider overt play behaviors of a make-believe type that persist in adults. For example, we will look at some kinds of pretend such as Masonic rituals, organizations forever refighting the Civil War in period costumes, and groups that create (with much dressing-up) alternative identities of the type found in the Society for Creative Anachronism.

Before moving ahead, let me briefly address a critical concern expressed by Sutton-Smith (1986) and again by Sutton-Smith and Kelley-Byrne (1984). Sutton-Smith has tried to be sure that play researchers do not overlook the often culturally biased interpretation of play as adaptive and valuable. He also points to the frequent violence that may arise from certain types of games or the other perhaps more sordid features of human experience that emerge in the course of forms of play, more specifically rule-based play such as gambling. I do not wish to minimize the reality of considerable cultural differences and also the likelihood that certain types of rule games may, on the one hand, foster self-defeating behaviors (gambling) or, on the other hand, may play into particular kinds of subtle cultural propaganda. *Monopoly*, after all, is a board game that trains one for a capitalist society. I am emphasizing, through the notion of a broadly inherent cognition, the central role of symbolism as a fundamental human skill. It is hard to believe that some form of such make-believe activity and practice of symbolic play would not be useful in most societies, although it might take forms that look very different on the surface.

Much of the more violent and dangerous features of play described by Sutton-Smith and Kelley Byrne call for the types of play more characteristic of older children or adolescents or even young adults. There seems little question that children between nine and twelve, in our society, having passed through a period of relative "innocence" and having more or less "bought hook, line, and sinker" their parent's or teacher's or religious group's positive assertions, are now capable because of the *internalization* of pretending and fantasy play to imagine alternative possibilities that hitherto were either unthinkable or frightening. Where parents seemed ideal and perfect they can now recognize flaws. Where the outside world was relatively confined and manageable through simple make-believe, they now confront genuine tragedy or potentially dangerous settings. No wonder that the nine- to twelve-year-olds begin to delight in trying out, under their control, new conditional approaches, enjoying the satire of *Mad* magazine or the fad, some years ago, of outrageous scenes depicted on playing cards, the *Garbage Pail Kids*. Where children up to about seven or eight are terrified by monster films or horror stories, the older age group begins to seek out such experiences. They are prepared to explore the incongruities and destructions of established schemas created by such films or stories while at the same time having the capacity to view them within a *pretend* framework. They thus find them increasingly manageable.

I will return again to this issue, but I want to express my concurrence with Sutton-Smith's suggestion that a significant role of play is to help us establish frameworks for dealing with the many difficulties and stressors of our inherently tragic life. What I am arguing is that we have to put such a conception into a developmental or age-specific framework, that is, to take into account what children can handle at different phases of their growing capacities. The more "perverse" or sinister facets of play reflect the efforts of middle-childhood and adolescence to come to grips with frightening events. Sutton-Smith (1986) has presented an example of how his own play with his children yields frameworks. He pretended with them to be a monster or ghoul simply by changing his expression. The children acted frightened at first but, knowing after all that this is their father, could quickly assimilate this incongruity with a recognition and integration of this material into a preestablished schema: "This is a game." Similarly, when they berated their father, he extremely exaggerated his reactions by pretending to cry or to be bumbling and foolish, behavior that he ordinarily does not display in daily life. As a result, he was helping the children increasingly to establish frames for reality and make-believe, what I would argue are schemas or scripts for establishing the differences between telic (clearly goal-directed or reality-oriented situations) and paratelic (clearly play or fantasy circumstances). In this sense, I would argue that even some of the more outrageous forms of make-believe play may have an adaptive role in clarifying for child players some of the necessary distinctions they must make in confronting the genuine difficulties of daily living. (See also Harris and Kavanaugh [1993] for a discussion of how children "flag" episodes as pretend sequences).

A SPECIAL ROLE OF PRETENDING IN EARLY CHILDHOOD GAMES

The classification of early childhood play into games of sensory-motor pleasure, games of mastery and physical skill, games with rules, and the symbolic play about which we have spoken primarily up to now can be dated to Piaget (1962) but is already anticipated in the earlier writings of Groos (1901). The joy of essentially unmotivated sensuality, feeling soft cloths or manipulating colored beads or waling on crinkly grass are delights that the baby, toddler, and young child repeat. Such sensuality never leaves us as a source of pleasure, and the positive hedonic quality of sensory experience may be reflected in more differentiated ways by adults, whether in the various sensory or motor delights obtained from listening to music, dancing, or smoking, or even in the simple repetitive acts of carrying "worry beads," which are so characteristic of men in the Eastern Mediterranean and Asia Minor areas.

Repetitive mastery efforts such as the child's repeatedly trying to manipulate blocks into some simple form, or the toddler's efforts to stay on its feet and walk different distances or to climb onto couches or chairs, eventually emerges in increased efforts at demonstrating motoric skills or, depending on the culture and family structure, mastering musical instruments, drawing, singing, and, of course, athletic types of play such as gymnastics. In games with rules, from the more primitive "hide and seek" through the board games of middle childhood, we can also sense the very beginnings of conceptions of social organization and, indeed, the primal basis for possession and for law. Other chapters in this volume address many of the theoretical issues concerning the possible adaptive role of these forms of play. Certainly, with the exception perhaps of games with rules and, of course, symbolic play, the first two types of play are evident even in the considerable range of other animals. In a remarkably thorough examination of the functional and evolutionary aspects of animal and human play, primarily of a rough-and-tumble nature, Peter K. Smith (1982) has indicated that there still remains a major question as to the ultimate adaptive nature of such play. At the same time, he has acknowledged that the pretend and make-believe games of early human childhood, associated as they are with language and almost certainly with private imagery, may have more long-term significance in development. This point is even further stressed by Brian Vandenberg (1986), who has impressively argued for the critical role of such fantasy play as a key feature of human use of private and cultural myth and of the nature of hope and aspiration. In the sections that follow, I should like to address a number of the specific possible "benefits" of imaginative play. While our conclusions, at this point, rest chiefly on correlational findings, it seems very likely from the training studies that have appeared over the years that imaginative play may lead to specific increases in language usage, imagery abilities, empathic potential, capacities for self-restraint and tolerance of delay, enhancement of the child's acquisition of the distinction between reality and fantasy, and a number of other specific features including the more conflict-resolving or identity-forming features that are so much a part of clinical applications of symbolic play (Singer, 1993a, 1993b; Singer and Singer, 1990).

Of course, make-believe play is consistently associated in preschoolers with just plain *fun*, as we found in our observations of two large samples of children who were followed over a full year's time (Singer and Singer, 1981; Singer and Singer, 1980). In our studies, observers specially trained to careful definitions of what would constitute make-believe play independently record ten-minute samples of children's spontaneous activities in nursery schools on a number of occasions over a year's time. We consistently found that those children who played more imaginatively were also much more likely to be scored as showing more smiling and laughing, more cooperation with teachers, and in general less evidence of the more negative affects such as anger, distress, or fatigue and sluggishness.

Make-Believe Play and the Theory of Mind

An intriguing area of theoretical speculation and research which emerged in the late 1980s and early 1990s has dealt with the question of the child's "theory of mind" (Flavell, 1988; Harris, 1991; Leslie, 1987; Lillard, 1993a,

1993b; Perner, 1991; and Wellman, 1990). These studies ask the question as to how early, and under what circumstances, children can begin to identify the fact that we generate private thoughts and images and, indeed, that such mental representations are different between individuals. In a seminal paper, Leslie (1987) proposed that a critical feature in the development of the child's notion of the existence of mental representation came through the activities of pretend play. Leslie could not provide actual systematic data that such play in an experimental format led to an increase in awareness of others' mental representations. He did, however, provide considerable ancillary evidence for the notion that, in the course of make-believe play, children are, on the one hand, becoming aware of their own representational processes and, on the other hand, gradually enhancing the likelihood that they could expect to identify others as having different mental processes than their own. Leslie's own work has strongly indicated that a major problem for autistic children in their inability to develop any evidence of self-awareness and their consistent failure on tests of theory of mind, such as the "false belief" tests, reflects the fact that they, for whatever reason, do not engage in imaginative play, in contrast not only to normal children but even to retarded children who are inferior to them in general intellectual ability (Leslie, 1988; 1991). A recent review by Lillard (1993a) and some experiments she conducted (Lillard 1993b) have raised questions about the extent to which pretend play in young children below five or six really reflects an awareness on their part of mental representation in its fullest sense. She proposes, instead, that there may be other explanations, including simply a linking of overt action in a pretend format to its presumed representation without being able to express the notion that such pretense is literally "in the head."

For our purposes here, it does not seem necessary to go into all the details of the controversies that swirl around the issue of theory of mind as reflected in the work of some of the authors cited above. What seems clear, however, is that engaging in make-believe play seems to be systematically associated also with a gradual incorporation for the child of what Leslie has called a "metarepresentational" style, a general orientation that reflects an awareness of the special properties of play situations that are separate from real situations. This, whether or not it takes the form (difficult to establish) that the child clearly recognizes mental images or interior thought processes, seems ultimately a part of a general adaptive trend linked to pretend play. In a study carried out with me, David Schwebel had observers reporting on the spontaneous play of nursery-school children between the ages of three and five. These observers scored imaginative play along the lines developed in our earlier research, that is, carefully looking for evidence that the child introduces settings, transformations of shape, sound effects, voice changes, and references to invisible characters. Children were also administered two forms of theory-of-mind measures used in the literature. What seemed especially clear in the results was that the children who played more imaginatively in their spontaneous games were also more likely to show the kind of reality-fantasy distinction elicited by the Flavell, Flavell, and Green (1987) measures as well as in one of Wellman's (1990) measures. The results were, however, stronger for the Flavell measure than for the Wellman false-belief procedure, particularly for the younger children. The likelihood is that there are also intriguing individual differences in the rate of emergence of imaginative play and concurrently awareness of reality and fantasy distinctions or of the possibility that others may hold false beliefs, in effect manifesting an awareness of mental representation. I would propose that researchers in this field have not paid sufficient attention to parent or other adult influences on the child's emerging ability to grasp the concept of representation. Parental reading to children, telling them stories, mediating the physical and social environment, and actually explaining to children about pretense may be more influential than has as yet been recognized in formal research. In looking to the future of play theory, as is suggested by the thrust of the present volume, we need to do much more work on the specifics of both the emergence of pretending games in children and their explanations of pretending in themselves and in others. We should include the generally neglected area of television pretending, which is an omnipresent feature of modern children's world. We can also examine children's generalization of these play or television-viewing experiences to an awareness of the private nature of human thought.

Imaginative Play and Language Usage

I had long ago proposed the likelihood that make-believe play may enhance complexity and richness in language in children because in the act of verbalizing the details of their play (Piaget's Parallel Monologues) children are hearing themselves use these words and practicing them. They are also, in the course of such overt verbalization, subject to correction by other children or by teachers or parents (Singer, 1973). It is difficult to disentangle vocabulary development from the actual degree of imaginativeness of play shown by children because observers must rely on the verbalizations to score pretend elements in the play. There are some suggestions in the literature that the two processes, vocabulary development and play complexity, are mutually enhancing. A study by Lewis (1973) was able to show that children who were more inclined to make-believe play also excelled in comprehensiveness, clarity, and organization of words used in describing pictures. The children also showed richer ability to produce verbal free associations and to provide more references to objects or events remote from themselves or their home environment. While it could be argued that both the imaginative play and the more complex verbal skills of these children were simply a common function of general intelligence, Lewis sought to confront that situation by identifying children of comparable high intelligence who differed in the degree of imaginative play. Those children who showed both more imaginative play and a high IQ produced greater organizational ability in their language usage than did children who showed relatively little imaginative play but were of comparable high general intelligence.

In the study carried out by Dorothy Singer and myself, where we observed children's play during eight separate ten-minute free-play sessions spread across a year's time, pairs of observers regularly reported all words used by the children during these sessions. We found, for example that those children who were scored as playing more imaginatively also used more future verbs and, indeed, were more likely to be using words reflective of a subjunctive mood, such as "might" or "would" (Singer and Singer, 1981). For more extensive review of the links between language and symbolic play, the reader is referred to Singer and Singer (1990).

Play, Divergent Thought, Imagery, and Verbal Fluency

Beyond the likelihood that children engaging in make-believe play are practicing verbal skills, one can also speculate on the possibility that the making up of little plots, the transformation of blocks into spaceships or nondescript rag dolls into mothers or fathers, necessitates some effort on the child's part to generate images or to recombine earlier memories of individuals or scenes with new projected mental representations. There is some evidence from so-called training studies which suggests that the causal link between such functions does go from increased imaginative play to increased divergent production, verbal fluency, and forms of imagery. Lillard (1993b) has suggested that it could well be that children who acquire a greater richness of cognition outside of play would then carry this over into their play; the question remains as to whether such enriching experiences actually build up outside play for children who do not themselves engage in a great deal of make-believe play. To test such a hypothesis one would have to show that children who engage in varieties of non-play-like home chores or simple construction activities of one kind or another and who show great richness in their verbalization during such activities then carry this over to heightened imaginative play full of novel constructions. But the bulk of the current evidence goes the other way.

Early studies of training in Israel certainly seemed to suggest that formal play-training did indeed lead to a variety of more generally adaptive behaviors (Feitelson, 1972; Feitelson and Ross, 1973; Smilansky, 1968). In a carefully controlled study, Joan Freyberg (1973) carefully trained a group of inner-city educationally disadvantaged kindergarten children. Such training actually involved eight 20-minute sessions of exposure of the children to various play themes such as "the family sitting around the dinner table," "sailors during a storm at sea," and "a magician performing tricks." Subsequent observation of spontaneous schoolyard play indicated that the scores for the experimental group who had received the training doubled in evidence of pretend play, with almost no change for the control group. Not only did Freyberg demonstrate increases in imaginative play but she also found, using raters for observations, evidence of greater positive emotionality, greater evidence of persistence in play behavior, and in general more ability to sustain in any kind of ongoing game. The children exposed to the training also produced richer verbal communications according to ratings obtained while they were waiting around in the playground, and this included more complex sentences and more verbal labeling and greater discrimination in their language usage. Studies by Saltz and Brodie (1982) and Saltz, Dixon, and Johnson (1977), also working with poor inner-city children, showed that training in thematic play served as an effective stimulant for cognitive and emotional development. Saltz and his group have proposed that attempts to attribute the positive effects of fantasy-play training to prior verbal skills or simply to the rapport or verbal encouragement of the training efforts alone cannot explain the results. The Saltz group conducted studies that involved four to six months of training with groups as large as 150 participants. Their data yielded evidence of verbal skill enhancement comparable to that reported by Freyberg. Studies by Dansky and Silverman also yielded consistent evidence that play training with an imaginative focus enhanced preschool children's associative fluency and heightened evidence of greater divergent thought processes, a precursor of creativity (Dansky and Silverman, 1973; Dansky and Silverman, 1975; Dansky, 1980). These results were similar to those reported by Feitelson (1972). More recently, Russ and Grossman-McKee (1990) also provided evidence of a consistent link between children's fantasy play and more divergent thought processes or creativity on the Rorschach Ink Blots. Dansky and Silverman have proposed that, on the basis of their work, the ability of children to generate both common and unusual associations after playing imaginatively with objects cannot be attributable simply to their ability to manipulate these objects in their play. Rather, they propose, such play behavior establishes an attitude or orientation that generates further production of novel sets and responses even to materials unrelated to those originally employed. Indeed, these authors argue that this type of playful style once enhanced may actually prove more useful for the children in acquiring new information from formal instruction than ordinary cognitive training of children.

In a study carried out at Yale, Diana Franklin (1975) provided alternative modeling opportunities in block play with four-year-olds at a day-care center. One group of children received "objective" block-play modeling, simply observing adults and following them in building constructions without any indication of an imaginative or make-believe component. The second group modeled adults performing much the same tasks but introducing elements of pretending and fantasy. It could be argued that this study, carried out many years before the current interest in theory of mind, made the distinction between objects as concrete givens and objects as manipulable mental representations (Leslie's "metarepresentational mode"). Of particular relevance is that in subsequent periods of observation during spontaneous play children showed more traces of the fantasy use of play of these blocks than just concrete structuring of them. The exposure to fantasy play yielded longer periods of play in general, more persistence, and positive emotionality. Interestingly, those children whose scores on the Rorschach Ink Blots indicated greater imaginativeness also showed more imaginative play both during the initial modeling opportunities and in later spontaneous floor-play sessions. The more imaginative players also showed a greater tendency to be reflective and to attribute positive events to their own actions while assuming that negative events were externally caused, a result generally found for normals rather than depressed persons in studies of attribution, as is well known.

In still another study, with somewhat older children (five- and six-year-olds), those who showed more predisposition to imaginative play based on their reports of home play activities as well as their scores on Rorschach Ink Blots were much more likely to show imaginative play with unstructured blocks. These children also indicated an ability to shift their point of view more frequently when asked to play with a given object in a different way than they had done so before. For example, they were presented with the figure of a cowboy, and having first played with it in that format were then asked to transform this game into a story about an airplane pilot. Those children who had been shown to be more imaginative on the basis of their Rorschach tests and home reports of play actually responded easily to this shift into the metarepresentational mode by transforming the cowboy into a pilot (Pulaski, 1973). Working with even older children, Litt (1973) interviewed ten-year-olds and identified those who reported more current evidence of persisting imaginative play. Those children also proved to score more highly on measures of their use of private imagery. They were particularly likely to produce vivid images. He also found evidence that (as has been reported in other studies) they scored higher on indications of creative fluency or divergent production.

Reality-Fantasy Distinctions and Self-Restraint

Almost forty years ago, working in a somewhat more psychoanalytic context, I had proposed, based on theoretical analyses and my own early children's research, that one feature of imaginative thought or of make-believe play was the way in which it linked the fantasy-reality distinction to various kinds of delayed gratification or self-restraint (Singer, 1955, 1961). It could well be that children's ability to produce transformations, whether in the shapes of objects or in the settings or through imagery, may help them to recognize not only the sequences they produce by themselves but may also gradually help them identify the markers and conditions that separate fantasy situations from reality. Such distinctions may also help them identify the differences between wishes and playful intentions and the actual overt implementation of impulsive desires. The fact that children can use various markers to help them in establishing pretense has recently been demonstrated in a series of research studies by Harris and Kavanaugh (1993). In addition, the work of Claire Golomb and her group have identified rather clearly the ways in which children seem to be learning to move in and out of pretend situations without confusing the two but without losing the imaginative richness of the play setting. As Golomb and Kuersten (1992) have indicated, it is very likely that between three and four years of age children do indeed develop some kind of functional notion of a boundary and this has important adaptive consequences. They suggest that for children the boundary permits the child to monitor events concurring both in reality and in pretense and to sustain a kind of "duality" between these two forms of thought. Such a conception is also compatible with the reversal theory of Michael Apter (1989) which distinguishes between telic and paratelic modes of pleasure. In the telic mode the pleasure stems chiefly from the actual feeling of progress towards a reasonably well-defined goal in addition to the actual attainment of the goal. In the paratelic mode the enjoyment comes from the very nature of the activity itself, including both sensual pleasure and competence awareness. The ability to reverse directions, as I am suggesting, and as the work of Golomb and her group also points to, may actually have a longer-term adaptive value even though the child's engagement in play may have no overt motive other than the sheer enjoyment of manipulating situations and ideas.

It may well be that the experience of playing at make-believe may help the child delineate an entire dimension of possible human experience in which one can, in a playful manner and with enjoyment, miniaturize the world's complexities. In this sense the play world may be seen as a prototype for our adult capacity for fantasy and daydreaming. In this mode we take our unfulfilled intentions or goals or confront the vicissitudes of our daily life and reduce them mentally to forms we can manipulate. If one has a background of experience in playfulness and fantasy one may be well aware of the distinction between such thought manipulation and the actual execution of certain functions, many of which might be unable to be retrieved once taken. In this sense, thought is in Freud's (1911 [1962]) "experimental action." In the sheer pleasure of the make-believe game for the child or the "idle" daydream of the adult there may be an underlying practice of alternative possibilities that, at the very least, may simply give pleasure. In many cases these processes may also be associated with a longer-term adaptive skill of distinguishing both a reality and fantasy dimension of human experience, as well as enhancing one's capacity for self-restraint in the face of adversity and for drawing on this miniaturizing capacity for making better adaptive plans in the future.

It is important to make a clear distinction between the notion of catharsis, which was an important feature of the earlier psychoanalytic drive-theory explanation of fantasy as a form of vicarious satisfaction, and the much better established current evidence that in the advantages for the child or the adult of using fantasy may not be because it reduces original intensity of wishes or goal direction but rather because it provides alternative possibilities that enhance a realistic and temporally graded approach to one's goals. An extensive discussion of the evidence against the catharsis phenomena need not be reviewed here (Singer and Singer, 1990). What is clear is that vicarious exposure to, for example, aggressive material has more of a cuing rather than a cathartic consequence for children. In an impressive recent study by Watson and Peng (1992), these investigators were able to show that boys who played with toy guns were much more likely to engage in overt aggression rather than play at pretend aggression or engage in nonaggressive play. Pretend games, in general, were negatively related to aggressive toys. There seemed to be a clear indication that while, of course, parental aggression was the best single predictor of overt aggressive behavior in children, play with toy guns by the children was also a likely predictor both of overt aggressive behavior or rough-and-tumble play rather than pretend play in free-play situations. Could it be that something about the lethal and realistic quality of most toy guns breaks down for children the playful quality that is necessary to sustain activities in the paratelic mode?

While the general thrust of my position and the current research on play-reality boundaries or metarepresentational thought (Leslie, 1987) suggests the importance of make-believe play in helping children establish a reality-fantasy distinction, we would need more extensive individual different studies to fully establish this point for the period of early childhood. There is at least one intriguing study with older children that suggests that make-believe tendencies may presumably be internalized into other forms of fantasy activity, as measurable by, for example, associating humans in action responses (the M response) to Rorschach Ink Blots, a response that has been extensively shown to be linked, on the one hand, to imaginative play or thought in children and adults and, on the other, to overt self-restraint (Singer and Brown, 1977; Singer and Singer 1990). Jane Tucker (1975), who had the unique opportunity (?) of being a student of mine as well as later of Brian Sutton-

Smith's studied more than 130 children between the ages of nine and twelve who had been administered the Ink Blot measures of fantasy, as well as questioned about their continuing engagement at home in private of make-believe games, or who had had a history of having an imaginary companion. She asked these children to listen carefully to a story and to be prepared to write down its details from memory as accurately and completely as possible. High-fantasy children showed superior performances not only in the completeness of their ability to record the story they had heard but also in the accuracy of the response and in the sustaining of the embellishing details of the story. They showed fewer errors in continuity in their account of the stories they were told, fewer serious distortions, and less likelihood of introducing new information not actually in the story. Such results could not be attributed to general intelligence of the children in the high-and low-fantasy groups.

With respect of the issue of self-restraint or the ability to wait, the likelihood is that a background in imaginative play or a capacity for private fantasy has been consistently shown to be associated with waiting ability. Indeed, the experiments have also shown that "filled time," that is, time that might be filled through engaging in private fantasy, seems to pass more rapidly than time spent in simply brooding about when the time will be up or when one's goal will be attained. In other words, resort to an active paratelic mode may actually sustain one's capacity to tolerate the frustration of long waits for a bus or for one to be called in during a doctor's visit. A number of studies have shown that children of kindergarten age or in early school age who have more numerous human movement responses to the Ink Blots were more likely to remain quietly occupied during extended waiting periods or to be able to simulate spacemen or astronauts by sitting quietly in an imaginary capsule for as long as they possibly could. Those children who had reported more make-believe play as part of their regular home activities and who also reported more imaginary companions were also likely to be able to tolerate the long wait and to hold out longer during this simulated capsule situation (Riess, 1957; Singer, 1961). With even older children and early adolescents studies have shown that those individuals who indicated greater imaginative behavior were also less likely to engage in various kinds of antisocial or impulsive behaviors (Herskovitz, Levine, and Spivak, 1959). Further evidence supporting the linkage of imaginative play or behavior to self-restraint, delay of gratification, persistence in play, and control of impulsivity have been found in studies by Mischel and Baker (1975), Meichenbaum and Goodman (1971), and Franklin (1975).

To summarize, I've attempted to outline a number of different ways in which the make-believe play of children, an activity engaged in primarily for sheer pleasure, may in a way assist the growing child in carving out an entirely new dimension of experience that has a number of significant adaptive functions. The data on individual differences suggests that those children who for various reasons have been given the opportunity or encouraged to engage in make-believe games by parents or other caregivers and who have also had environmental situations that allow for more of such play seem to gain advantages in the attainment of these skills (Singer and Singer, 1990). All of the links between developing a concept or theory of mind and developing a capacity for adopting a metarepresentational mode of thought or for using imaginative play or its internalized form of fantasy for the purposes of reality testing and self restraint have not been forged by any means. They point the way, however, for a rich research future in the field of play theory.

TELEVISION VIEWING AND CHILDREN'S IMAGINATION

There is reasonably good evidence that children seem to benefit considerably in the development of their imaginative play from early exposure to parents or other caregivers who read stories to them, tell them stories, or actually get down on the floor and initiate make-believe play games (Singer and Singer, 1990). There is, however, a new member of the family or perhaps a new feature of the environment of children: the television set. I have elsewhere detailed the implications of this medium and it is probably unnecessary to repeat all of this in this chapter with its focus on imagination. The critical things to consider are perhaps the following:

1. By framing and miniaturizing novel and complex situations in a box, the television set reduces the range and intensity of emotional reactivity, in contrast to the very large screen one finds in movie theaters or, of course, in relation to actual staged drama.

2. The characteristic (especially of American television) of rapid shifts and sequences, sound effects and background music, and relatively loud noise levels (especially for commercials) maximizes our orienting reflexes and holds our attention. This especially impacts children. Sometimes, the sheer shift of orientation on the set, even when material is not entirely comprehensible or familiar, may lead to what looks to be a pattern of unresponsive watching. This may not be completely the case, for research has also shown that children will tend to drift away from the set if the material is utterly unfamiliar and only turn back when musical cues or familiar voices signal that material that is schematically related is coming on.

3. Because of the close tie I have already mentioned between emotion and the child's memory system, there must be special attention paid to child programming. Plots and dramatic effects that often seem obvious to adults

may be utterly confusing to children. Such an example may be found in instances where a character's eyes suddenly look off to the distance and he or she says "I remember when" and then the scene shifts to a child playing with a sled in the snow. For an adult used to dramatic effects and also capable of comprehending the language references, this shift simply indicates a memory on the part of the television protagonist. For a child below four or five years of age and sometimes even older, there is often confusion about what happened to the original speaker. Who is this new child with the sled who appears?

4.   Because television viewing is so much a part of everyone's daily life, the medium could, in theory, play an important role in education and in encouraging a readiness for school learning in preschool children. We know very well from our research that when parents do talk to children and explain things, label things, and describe how human relationships or natural forces operate, they are reducing the outside world to a manageable size. Children's own games of make-believe and their use of imagery can help assimilate such material into memory schemas. Suppose, however, that the parents are themselves too busy, too stressed, or unavailable to play the mediating role. Television with age-appropriate programming *could* be especially valuable in reducing this big outside world to manageable proportions and it could serve a role in stimulating the imagination and positive emotions. Alas, there has been very little thought give by television producers until quite recently to issues such as these.

One television program that is especially sensitive to helping the preschool child make sense out of a confusing world is *Mister Rogers' Neighborhood*. Here the host, Fred Rogers, acts as a surrogate parent or good uncle, explaining through verbal repetition, music, puppets, and special guests or trips to various locations some of the more confusing features of the child's environment. Mister Rogers in his own persona tends to deal with facts— how animals are fed, how musical instruments are played, how balloons float in the air, or how one can carve wood. When he turns to imaginative developments and seeks especially to deal with some of the more troublesome and negative human emotions, he relies upon a make-believe world of puppets ruled by King Friday. In this case, he makes a clear distinction between his regular neighborhood, with him as the spokesperson and various real life visitors, and the Neighborhood of Make-Believe, to which one goes with a special little trolley.

There is actually reasonable evidence, as Dorothy Singer and I ourselves found in two studies, that viewing *Mister Rogers' Neighborhood* not only can promote social skills such as sharing and cooperation but can actually increase the likelihood that children will play imaginatively. Mister Rogers makes a special point of talking about the value of making-believe and pretend games under certain circumstances, and he even has a song called "Pretending," which he sings from time to time.

Although many adults are inclined to be skeptical and indeed even caustically critical of the slow pace and almost saccharine "niceness" of Mister Rogers, his impact on child viewers seems a lasting one. I have had the opportunity a number of times of observing Fred Rogers at visits he made to Yale University. I must admit, to my surprise, the turnout of so-called "sophisticated" college students at his talks has been amazing in terms of numbers and in terms of the great outpouring of affection shown for him by some of these often very burly athletic types.

While our research has produced some evidence that heavy television viewing by children, particularly of the more adult-oriented action, adventure, and violent programs, predicts less imagination a few years later on (Singer, Singer, and Rapaczynski, 1984), it is also possible that programming could enhance imagination under appropriate circumstances, as the Mister Rogers show has demonstrated. Most recently, Dorothy Singer and I have had the opportunity to study a new, phenomenally successful children's series, *Barney and Friends*. This show, originated by two Texas housewives seeking to find entertainment that could stimulate their own children, was eventually produced on public television, where it became a wild success. It was a remarkable instance of a national movement started in effect by three- and four-year-old children, whose sheer delight at the show stimulated their mothers to write in to their local television stations and to contact the Barney Company and (fortunately for the licensees) to clamor for Barney products in the stores. In contrast with other adult-initiated, well-orchestrated merchandising schemes carried out through advertising agencies with tie-ins to television programming (such as the "He Man of the Universe" or "Ninja Turtles" toy phenomena), this was an instance in which the sheer delight children take in the program initiated the entire thrust.

Why do children like Barney? Our observations of the show and of children watching the show suggest that it is, first of all, full of teaching material which can stimulate children to acquire new vocabulary, knowledge of colors and shapes, or even an awareness of foreign languages. In addition, it is full of extremely warm sentiment, the holding of hands and singing of simple, loving songs that seem to fill a desperate void in preschoolers nowadays. Of special importance for my purposes in this article is the fact that the *Barney and Friends* series puts strong emphasis on children's imagination. There are constant references to the encouragement of using one's imagination and of pretending in a variety of settings. The live children on the show engage in considerable play-acting. Barney is represented as a stuffed animal who, through the wishing of the children, becomes a purple dinosaur and continues his make-believe role through most of the show. Indeed, he takes on something of the avuncular role that Mister Rogers plays so well. This series is too new for us to be in a position to evaluate whether indeed there is a stimulation of imaginative play in children who observe the show, but it is clear that a conscious effort is being made to accept children's imagination as an extremely valuable feature of their development and to foster and encourage children in using this capacity in gentle ways. It remains to be seen whether the Barney phenomenon survives over several years, as Mister Rogers has, and whether indeed it does produce a "kinder, gentler, or more imaginative" child. (For further discussion of television and imagination, see Singer and Singer, 1990.

THE FATE OF IMAGINATIVE PLAY THROUGH THE LIFE SPAN

Once away from the television set, children left to their own devices show the peak of make-believe play either alone or with others in the four- and five-year-old period. Then the outside observer notices that overt make-believe play with the child vocalizing should effects and verbalizing the speeches of the various characters seems to disappear to some extent. Indeed, Piaget (1962), probably because of his primary focus on the epistemology of logical and orderly thought processes, believed that such play essentially faded, its contribution to formal operations completed in the developmental cycle. To the contrary, current observations of children's play in this period of middle childhood suggest rather that, while make-believe play in its overt form is certainly suppressed by the requirements of attention and decorum in school, it persists either completely in private with the solitary child or can be found in evidence in small groups of children playing outside the general observation sphere of adults. One might, indeed, propose that the great stream of symbolic play and pretending bifurcates so that it emerges throughout the rest of the life span as twin streams. One branch flows largely "underground" or in private experience (internalized in the form of human daydreaming and fantasy processes), while the other is openly evident only by the persisting love of children for pretend games in somewhat more formal contexts or ultimately in the way many adults periodically engage in dressing up and establishing a variety of quasi-conventional make-believe rituals (Singer and Singer, 1990). In effect, we learn to carry on many of the adaptive properties of make-believe play that characterized early childhood through the private method of inner speech and imagery. We can miniaturize the complex adult world by telling ourselves private stories or engaging in a variety of fantasies which still have the property of taking the complexities of our physical and social milieu and miniaturizing them into manipulable forms subject to our own control. Yet this does not take away a continuing interest in a more overt form of pretending and make-believe which often, however, must be stifled in the formal settings of school and work. Most societies provide outlets for adult make-believe through rituals ranging from certain kinds of religious observances through less formal avenues such as Mardi Gras dress-ups, secret societies, or a continuing abundance of amateur theatricals and clubs involving identity changes and historical reenactments.

Fantasy and Make-Believe in Middle Childhood

The position I am taking is that middle childhood, far from being a so-called "latency" phase, as some psychoanalysts still attest, is a period of tremendous flowering both of the imaginative life and of continuing efforts to create miniaturized make-believe play worlds under somewhat more restricted conditions. I have elsewhere described ways in which make-believe can be seen in various forms of board-game play and even in sports activities that boys may play on the street where they extend the formal rules games by also loudly pretending to give "play-by-play" accounts of their humble efforts (Singer, 1975). Sutton-Smith has also at various points in his novels and in some of his observations and writings documented a variety of the ways in which pretend elements enter into street games or more formal structured play. For many children not tied to organized groups such as the Brownies or Cub Scouts, or sometimes over and above such activities, there may develop small peer-generated clubs and gangs. It is only in relatively recent decades that the availability of guns and the use of such children's street gangs by older criminals has yielded the terribly lethal quality to such pretend play. In the early 1930s, when I was growing up in New York City, boys between the ages of nine and twelve would often form street "gangs." These gangs would sometimes be armed with wooden guns which were capable of projecting small pieces of cardboard at one another during the very rare actual battles that took place. Sometimes gang members would be assigned fairly special roles from leadership positions to front-line foot soldiers, messengers, or spies. I myself, at about age seven or eight, having newly arrived in the neighborhood, was designated by my Fifth Street gang to be a scout and to spy on the doings of the Sixth Street gang. I still remember when a negotiated alliance between the Fifth Street and Seventh Street boys led to a plan for a joint attack on the Sixth Streeters. I went to sleep the night before this great projected event with tremendous anticipation. The excitement of being a secret scout led to a fantasy that I used to use during school hours in the third or fourth grades at my new school. I would imagine, as we marched along (in those much more formal days of school discipline) from place to place in the school, that I was actually a specially placed spy. This fantasy came back to me years later during my period of military training in World War II, when I again made use of it to pass the time during long boring marches. To my great surprise, I actually was assigned to become a special agent in military intelligence following my basic training! One might even wonder if it was subsequently not a very large change to move from this background into a career in the new field of Clinical Psychology and Psychoanalysis.

One of the defining characteristics of middle childhood is that it exposes the child to a much broader world: the greater mixture of children who are together in the school situation; the tremendous influx of information about history and geography, science, and social science that begins to be presented in the school setting; the exposure to a more extended group of adults outside the family in the form of teachers, scout leaders, athletic leaders; and, in our media-rich world, exposure through television-viewing and reading to a huge range of interesting characters.

The critical role of one's own imagery capacities was certainly emphasized by Piaget and Inhelder in their important study *Mental Imagery in the Child* (Piaget & Inhelder, 1971). Yet again, in keeping with Piaget's emphasis on the sources of logical thought, this book with its ingenious studies continues to place its emphasis on images of physical objects, geometric shapes, rotation of shapes, and anticipatory images of such changed spacial relationships. All of this seems to be in the service of the proposition that images, however helpful as memory cues, are ultimately dependent on logical operations if they are to be useful for human knowledge. There is no reference in this volume to human representations, to memories of one's relationships or anticipations of future relationships or adventures, those images that are increasingly central to children's thinking as a variety of studies demonstrate and which become the sources for the tremendous richness of later biographical memories (Dias and Harris, 1988; Gottlieb, 1973; Harris and Beggan, 1993; Silvern, Williamson, and Countermine, 1986).

We see that, on the one hand, storytelling and pretending for children of this age group, carried out through reading and private fantasy, are not only sources of pure pleasure but also turn out to be useful communication tools for engaging the interests of peers and of teachers. And again, the gradual miniaturization and internalization of events in the manipulable form of fantasies increases a sense of control. Sometimes, without completely recognizing it, children may actually find that their taste for pretending helps to master school content, to confront the novelty of the school setting, and to remember better and to think more clearly than peers who have already "put aside such childish things" (Singer and Singer, 1990). Far from being the period of latency, it is during this age that children begin to establish a sense of identity and uniqueness, some of this through identification with pop music or television figures, some through recognition of salient components of their appearance or background which stand out from other classmates, as McGuire (1984) has shown.

As we have indicated, some overt floor play may actually persist during this period. Imaginative play also finds its outlet in board games, computer games, video games, theatricals that some children engage in, or the enjoyment of school plays or special uses of drama in the classroom by gifted teachers. It is also during this period that children begin to speculate internally about dozens of alternative lives, about adventure and romance, sometimes the former being more characteristic of boys and the latter of girls, as Gottlieb (1973) and Harris and Beggan (1993) found. There are more fantasies about heroism and (particularly now with the greatly increased sexual openness that characterizes comic books, novels, films, and television) there are increasing fantasies about sexual encounters. This is especially likely to emerge more strongly with the beginnings of physiological sexual changes and the emergence of masturbation, which often is linked to vivid fantasies that may have lifetime implications in terms of sexual appetite.

Sutton-Smith has often pointed to the contrariness, absurdity, and, of course, the frequent maliciousness of play in middle childhood and adolescence. I would like to propose that this is almost an inevitable feature of the child's increased awareness in this age period of the limitations and flaws, first of all, of one's own parents or older siblings and then increasingly of the society more generally. One begins to try out in overt play and in fantasy turning the simple beliefs and hopes of childhood on their heads. The attraction of obstreperous, wrong-headed, or rebellious characters such as the recent television figures like Bart Simpson or Beavis and Butthead, exemplify this new stage of development in which the child tries out absurdities and explores new contrary roles. The recent amazing phenomenon I have observed, the sheer love and devotion and obvious need of two-, three- and four-year-old children for the pure love provided by Barney and exemplified in the song that ends the show, "I Love You/You Love Me/We're A Happy Family," is turned by seven- and eight-year-olds into "I Hate You/You Hate Me/ Let's Get A Gun/And Shoot Barney." This great human capacity for tolerating ambiguities and playing and manipulating them in the miniaturized private world of thought allows us to sustain the inevitable disappointments and tragedies of growing up. But what of the child who has not sufficiently developed either the imaginative play capacity or the capacity for internalization? There is considerable evidence that such children are more at risk when they do not have the skills of private manipulation of possibilities. Such children are more likely to act directly on impulses of anger or distress rather than shape and reshape them privately and take into account the consequences (Singer and Singer, 1990).

In summary, while imaginative play in its overt form continues in middle childhood, it is increasingly less obvious and takes on somewhat different forms. Yet children yearn for it and teachers in the schools who use make-believe formats for teaching often final tremendous responsiveness from children who otherwise have not shown much exposure to storytelling and reading. With respect to more private fantasy, the period of middle childhood and adolescence is of course the great flowering field for this human capacity. I would, myself, propose that many of the most creative features of human development are already being foreshadowed by elaborate middle childhood fantasies and that the period is also characterized by increasing awareness of personal identity and anticipation of a range of possible selves which become crystallized by the academic, social, athletic, or artistic success and failure exposures of adolescence. I would carry this further and propose that some of the more unusual human appetites, whether along sexual or aggressive lines, are formed through the repetitive fantasies of this period. The psychoanalytic linking of neurosis to the very earliest phases of childhood seriously neglects the tremendous importance of the kinds of fantasies that are being internalized in middle childhood.

Daydreaming and Overt Pretend Play in Adult Life

I have elsewhere written very extensively on the nature of human daydreaming and private fantasy and do not wish to extend this chapter by elaborating on these themes (Singer and Bonanno, 1990; Singer, 1975). Not as widely recognized is the extent to which make-believe play continues to be a source of enjoyment to large numbers of adults. Indeed, there are a number of groups of adults who reenact historic battles using toy soldiers. One group in New York City endlessly refights Napoleon's campaigns, using large boards on which there are figures representing the different armies of the French, Austrians, British, Prussians, or Russians. Such mock wars usually attempt very precise reenactments by individuals who have taken the trouble of investigating the actual history or who at least are instructed in their moves by actual historians.

But moving beyond toy soldiers there are numerous examples of active dressing-up by adults and elaborate engagements in make-believe activities. Some of these include individuals who wear costumes of a particular historical period; these include the American Revolutionary and Civil Wars, with attempted reenactments of the encampments and battles of the periods. Another national organization in the United States is called the Society for Creative Anachronism, which is dedicated, in effect, to reliving the experiences of knights and ladies generally from the Middle Ages with some overlap to the Renaissance or to the so-called Dark Ages. The members of these groups actually assume names relating to the period they represent during the meetings or in their society correspondence and newsletters. They hold ranks within the organization and even have periodic coronations or ceremonies ennobling members. These individuals wear costumes that are rather carefully worked out and they try to repeat the games that were played in the period and to prepare food of those times. I actually have had a number of opportunities to visit festivals of this organization and it was impressive to see the large octagonal tents erected with pennants flying, pigs roasting on open spits, knights taking part in mock battles on the greens of college campuses or in a city like Norwich, Connecticut. At the banquets, one suddenly imagines that one has been transported back to Camelot.

There are, of course, other groups of an even more intellectual type, such as the Baker Street Irregulars, where the members often dress up in late Victorian or early Edwardian costumes and endlessly discuss nuances of the cases of Sherlock Holmes.

Of course, there continue to be organizations that date back hundreds of years and are linked to religious festivals such as the Mardi Gras or other carnivals, once representative of clear religious goals but now assuming primarily an opportunity for make-believe and dressing-up. Even fraternal organizations such as the Knights of Columbus, the Knights of Pythias, and various groups of Free Masons, provide a certain element of secret rituals, symbols, and allegories. The fact that these organizations no longer have craft or guild functions is irrelevant. They do adopt special signs and rings, secret handclasps, or passwords that are in many ways continuations of those manifested in children's secret clubs.

The Morris Dancing Groups of England involve assorted and bizarre costumes and extended periods of dancing with occasionally additional boisterous escapades. In Italy, during the months of July and August in the city of Siena, one observes in the Palio horse races a further extensive reenactment of the medieval or early Renaissance life of this town, replete with elaborate costumes and competitions between the town districts.

In conclusion, if we look toward the future of play research, many questions persist. We must ask, first of all, how the overt make-believe play of the preschool years becomes so richly incorporated (if indeed it does) into the private experiences of fantasy and mental extrapolation of subjunctive thought that characterize the adult stream of consciousness. Are these representations already being formed in the pretending of the two-, three- and four-year-olds, as Leslie (1987) would seem to be suggesting, or does it take some special feature of the restrictions of the school-age period to force the internalization process? Indeed, if I had the opportunity, I would put a much greater emphasis on research on the development of the great range of fantasies of the middle childhood period, so far relatively unstudied. There should be ways by which we can follow this process of private make-believe during the so-called bubble-gum years. Make-believe games transformed into private fantasy? What brain processes are involved? Can we program computers to simulate such a transformation? At the risk of losing myself completely in fantasy, let me conclude by asserting that there is indeed a rich future for theory and experiment in the study of children's symbolic play.

REFERENCES

Adler, A. (1968). *The practice theory of individual psychology*. New York: Humanities Press.

Angyal, A. (1965). *Neurosis and treatment: A holistic theory*. New York: Wiley.

Apter, M. J. (1989). *Reversal theory*. London: Routledge.

Bakan, D. (1966). *The duality of human existence*. Chicago: Rand McNally.

Blatt, S. J. (1990). Interpersonal relatedness and self-definition: Two personality configurations and their implications for psychopathology and psychotherapy. In J. L. Singer (Ed.), *Repression and dissociation*. Chicago: University of Chicago Press, 299–336.

Bower, G. (1972). The architecture of cognition, mental imagery and associative learning. In W. L. Gregg (Ed.), *Cognition in learning and memory*, 17–43. New York: Wiley.

Dansky, J. L. (1980). Make believe: A mediator between free play and associative fluency. *Child Development, 51*, 576–79.

Dansky, J. L., & Silverman, I. W. (1973). Effects of play on associative fluency in preschool-aged children. *Developmental Psychology, 9*, 38–43.

———. (1975). Play: A general facilitator of associative fluency. *Developmental Psychology*, 11, 104.

Dias, M. G., & Harris, P. L. (1988). The effect of make-believe play on deductive reasoning. *British Journal of Developmental Psychology, 6*, 207–21.

Ekman, P., Friesen, W., & Ellsworth, P. (1982). *Emotion in the human face* (rev. ed.). Cambridge: Cambridge University Press.

Erikson, E. H. (1962). *Childhood and society*. New York: Norton.

Fein, G. (1980). Pretend play in childhood: An integrative review. *Child Development, 52*, 1095–1118.

Feitelson, D. (1972). Developing imaginative play in pre-school children as a possible approach to fostering creativity. *Early Child Development and Care, 1*, 181–95.

Feitelson, D., & Ross, G. S. (1973). The neglected play factor. *Human Development, 16*, 202–23.

Flavell, J. H. (1988). The development of children's knowledge about the mind: From cognitive connections to mental representations. In W. Astington, P. L. Harris, & D. R. Olson (Eds.), *Developing theories of mind* (pp. 244–71). Cambridge: Cambridge University Press.

Flavell, J. H., Flavell, E., & Green F. L. (1987). Young children's knowledge about the apparent-real and pretend-real distinctions. *Developmental Psychology, 23*, 816–22.

Franklin, D. (1975). Block play modeling and its relationship to imaginativeness, impulsivity-reflection and internal-external control. Predissertation master's research, Yale University.

Franz, E., & White, K. (1985). Individuation and attachment in personality development: Extending Erikson's theory. *Journal of Personality, 53*, 224–56.

Freyberg, J. T. (1973). Increasing the imaginative play of urban disadvantaged children through systematic training. In J. L. Singer (Ed.) *The child's world of make-believe* (pp. 129–54). New York: Academic Press.

Freud, S. (1911 [1962]) Formulations regarding the two principles of mental functioning. In J. S. Strachey (Ed.) *The complete psychological works of Sigmund Freud*. Vol. 12. London: Hogarth.

Golomb, C., & Kuersten, R. (1992). The transition from pretense play to reality. Paper presented at American Psychological Association Annual Convention, Washington, D.C., August, 1992.

Gottlieb, S. (1973). Modeling effects upon fantasy. In J. L. Singer (Ed.), *The child's world of make-believe* (pp. 155–82). New York: Academic Press.

Groos, K. (1901). *The play of man*. New York: Appleton.

Gould, R. (1972). *Child studies through fantasy*. New York: Quadrangle.

Harris, M. J., & Beggan, J. K. (1993). Make-believe: A descriptive study of fantasies in middle childhood. *Imagination, Cognition and Personality, 13*, 125–45.

Harris, P. L. (1991). The work of the imagination. In A. Whiten (Ed.), *Natural theories of mind* (pp. 283–304). Oxford: Blackwell.

Harris, P. L., & Kavanaugh, R. D. (1993). *Young children's understanding of pretense*. Monograph of the Society for Child Development. Chicago: University of Chicago Press.

Herskovitz, H., Levine, M. & Spivack, G. (1959). Anti-social behavior of adolescents from higher socioeconomic groups. *Journal of Nervous and Mental Diseases, 125*, 467–76.

Izard, C. (1991). *The psychology of emotions*. New York: Plenum.

Jung, C. (1971). *Psychological types*. New York: Pantheon.

Kreitler, H., & Kreitler, S. (1976). *Cognitive orientation and behavior*. New York: Springer.

Leslie, A. M. (1987). Pretense and representation: The origins of "theory of mind." *Psychological Review, 94*, 412–26.

Leslie, A. (1991). The theory of mind impairment in autism: Evidence for a modular mechanism of development? In A. Whiten (Ed.), *Natural theories of mind* (pp. 63–78). Oxford: Basil Blackwell.

Lewin, K. (1935). *A dynamic theory of personality.* New York: McGraw Hill.

Lewis, P. H. (1973). The relationship of sociodramatic play to various cognitive abilities in kindergarten. Doctoral dissertation, Ohio State University.

Lillard, A. (1993a). Pretend play and the child's theory of mind. *Child Development, 64,* 348–71.

————. (1993b). Young children's conceptualization of pretense: Action or mental representation state? *Child Development, 64,* 372–86.

Litt, H. (1973). Imagery in children's thinking. Doctoral dissertation, Liverpool University.

Mandler, G. (1984). *Mind and body.* New York: Norton.

Markus, H., & Nurius, P. (1986). Possible selves. *American Psychologist, 41,* 964–69.

Meichenbaum, D., & Goodman, J. (1971). Training impulsive children to talk to themselves. *Journal of Abnormal Psychology, 77,* 115–21.

Miller, G., Galanter, E., & Pribram, K. (1960). *Plans and the structure of behavior.* New York: Holt, Rinehart & Winston.

Mischel, W., & Baker, N. (1975). Cognitive appraisals and transformations in delay behavior. *Journal of Personality and Social Psychology, 31,* 254–61.

Papousek, M., Papousek, H., & Harris, B. (1987). The emergence of play in parent-infant interrelations. In D. Gorlitz & J. Wohlwill (Eds.), *Curiosity imagination and play.* (pp. 214–46). Hillsdale, NJ: Erlbaum.

Perner, J. (1991). *Understanding the representational mind.* Cambridge: MIT Press.

Piaget, J. (1962). *Play, dreams and imitation in childhood.* New York: Norton.

Piaget, J., & Inhelder, B. (1971). *Mental imagery in the child.* New York: Basic.

Pulaski, M. (1973). Toys and imaginative play. In J. L. Singer (Ed.), *The child's world of make-believe.* (pp. 74–103). New York: Academic Press.

Rank, O. (1945). *Will therapy and truth and reality.* New York: Knopf.

Riess, A. (1957). A study of some genetic behavioral correlates of human movement responses in children's Rorschach protocols. Unpublished doctoral dissertation, New York University.

Russ, S., & Grossman-McKee, A. (1990). Affective expression in children's fantasy play, primary process thinking on the Rorschach and Divergent Thinking. *Journal of Personality Assessment, 54* (3–4) 756–71.

Saltz, E., & Brodie, J. (1982). Pretend play in childhood: A review and critique. *Contributions to Human Development, 6,* 97–113.

Saltz, E., Dixon, D., & Johnson, J. (1977). Training disadvantaged preschoolers on various fantasy activities: Effects on cognitive functioning and impulse control. *Child Development, 48*, 367–80.

Schank, R. C., & Abelson, R. P. (1977). *Scripts, plans, goals and understanding.* Hillsdale, NJ: Erlbaum.

Silvern, S. B., Williamson, P. A., & Countermine, T. A. (1986). Young children's story recall as a product of play, story familiarity and adult intervention. *Merrill-Palmer Quarterly, 32*, 73–86.

Singer, D. G. (1993a). *Playing for their lives.* New York: Free Press.

―――. (1993b). Fantasy and visualization. In C. E. Schaefer (Ed.), *The therapeutic powers of play* (pp. 189–221). Northvale, NJ: Jason Aronson.

Singer, D. G., & Singer, J. L. (1980). Television-viewing and aggressive behavior in preschool children: A field study. *Forensic Psychology and Psychiatry, Annals of the New York Academy of Science, 347*, 289–303.

―――. *The house of make-believe: Children's play and the developing imagination.* Cambridge: Harvard University Press.

Singer, J. L. (1955). Delayed gratification and ego-development: Implications for clinical and experimental research. *Journal of Consulting Psychology, 19*, 259–66.

―――. (1961). Imagination and waiting ability in young children. *Journal of Personality, 29*, 396–413.

―――. (1973). *The child's world of make-believe: Experimental studies of imaginative play.* New York: Academic Press.

―――. (1975). *The inner world of daydreaming.* New York: Harper & Row.

―――. (1984). *The human personality.* San Diego: Harcourt Brace Jovanovich.

―――. (1988). Psychoanalytic theory in the context of contemporary psychology. *Psychoanalytic Psychology, 5*, 95–125.

Singer, J. L. & Bonanno, G. & (1990). Personality and private experience: Individual variations in consciousness and in attention to subjective phenomena. In L. Pervin (Ed.), *Handbook of personality* (pp. 419–44). New York: Guilford.

Singer, J. L., & Singer, D. G. (1981). *Television, imagination and aggression: A study of preschoolers.* Hillsdale, NJ: Erlbaum.

Singer, J. L., & Brown, S-L. (1977). The experience type: Some behavioral correlates and theoretical implications. In M. C. Rickers-Ovsiankina (Ed.), *Rorschach Psychology.* (pp. 325–72). Huntington, New York: Krieger.

Singer, J. L., Singer, D. G., & Rapaczynski, W. (1984). Children's imagination as predicted by family patterns and television-viewing: A longitudinal study. *Genetic Psychology Monographs, 110*, 43–69.

Smilansky, S. (1968). *The effects of sociodramatic play on disadvantaged preschool children.* New York: Wiley.

Smith, P. K. (1982). Does play matter? Functional and evolutionary aspects of animal and human play. *Behavioral and Brain Sciences, 5*, 139–84.

Sutton-Smith, B. (1961). *Smitty does a bunk.* Wellington, New Zealand: Price Milburn.

————. (1986). The metaphor of games. In R. van der Kooij & J. Hellendoorn (Eds.), *Play, play therapy, play research.* Lisse, The Netherlands: Swets & Zeitlinger.

————. (1993). A memory of games and some games of memory. In J. Lee (Ed.), *Life before story.* New York: Praeger.

Sutton-Smith, B., & Kelly-Byrne, D. (1984). *The masks of play.* New York: Leisure Press.

Sutton-Smith, B., & Sutton-Smith, S. (1974). *How to play with your children.* New York: Hawthorn.

Tomkins, S. S. (1962). *Affect, imagery, consciousness.* New York: Springer.

Tomkins, S. S. (1970). A theory of memory. In J. S. Antrobus (Ed.) *Cognition and affect* (pp. 59–130). Boston: Little, Brown.

Tucker, J. (1975). *The role of fantasy in cognitive affective functioning: Does reality make a difference in remembering?* Unpublished doctoral dissertation. Teachers College, Columbia University.

Vandenberg, B. (1986). Play, Myth and Hope. In R. van der Kooij and J. Hellendoorn (Eds.), *Play, Play Therapy, Play Research.* Lisse, The Netherlands: Swets & Zeitlinger.

Vygotsky, L. S. (1966). Play and its role in the mental development of the child. *Soviet Psychology, 12*, 62–67.

Watson, M., & Peng, Y. (1992). The relation between toy gun play and children's aggressive behavior. Early Education.

Wellman, H. M. (1990). *The child's theory of mind.* Cambridge: MIT Press.

Zajonc, R. (1980). Feeling and thinking—Preferences need no inferences. *American Psychologist, 35*, 151–75.

10

LISE M. YOUNGBLADE AND JUDY DUNN _____

Social Pretend with Mother and Sibling: Individual Differences and Social Understanding

Eric, 11½ months, lies on a table during a routine diaper change. He picks up a cup that is part of a nesting cup set and puts it to his lips. He makes slurping sounds and looks at his mother. She continues to diaper him, so he repeats the action. Following the slurping he hands the cup to his mother and looks at her expectantly. She, not having picked up the clue, hands the cup back to the baby, who repeats the drinking action, with sound effects. He hands the cup back to his mother who finally mimics the drinking sequence. Eric squeals with delight, and the pretend drinking game begins again. (personal anecdote, Lise Youngblade)

Eric in this incident is not yet a year old, yet he is already able to pretend to drink with a toy and to share this pretend transformation with his mother—reaching a peak of pleasure when she, too, pretends to drink from the "inappropriate" plastic toy. It is a considerable intellectual achievement for an 11-month-old—and note the social situation in which it happens. The significance of such social exchanges for the development of pretend is one of the many issues highlighted by Brian Sutton-Smith in his work on children's play. He has urged us to incorporate the importance of social interaction into our theoretical approaches to the developmental significance of play:

> With respect to play interaction . . . it is my view that we more often deal with such things empirically than embed them theoretically in our conceptualizations of play as, say, we would if we looked for theory to Mead or Vygotsky rather than to Piaget. This lack of a social interactive epistemology is, I think, our most critical theoretical handicap. . . . (Sutton-Smith, 1985, p. 63)

Portions of this paper were presented at the Biennial Meeting of the Society for Research in Child Development, New Orleans, March 1993. The research reported herein was supported by an NIH grant (HD 23158) to Judy Dunn. We wish to thank Jane Brown, Cheryl Slomkowski, Caroline Tesla, Susan Evans, Stephanie McGhee, and Clare Stocker for their contributions to the project.

221

Throughout his career, Brian Sutton-Smith has been an ardent advocate of the needs and rights of children to play. Nearly two decades ago, he described (Sutton-Smith, 1976) certain basic characteristics of play (Caldwell, 1986): Children's play, he argued, is spontaneous and self-generated—in effect, intrinsically motivated. It is not too serious nor does it have set rules—that is, it is flexible. In other words, play is fun. And, particularly for young children, play is often nonliteral and involves fantasy or imagination.

This chapter will consider in some detail Sutton-Smith's third characteristic of play: pretend. In particular, we will focus on social pretense. The emergence of social pretense is a fascinating development in young children. The increasing frequency and sophistication with which youngsters take on roles, negotiate scripts, and direct such flights of fancy is truly remarkable; no less remarkable is the affective intensity, or *fun*, that accompanies such play. But even the earliest forays into pretend frequently—and possibly always (Dunn and Wooding, 1977)—take place, as did Eric's pretend drinking, in social situations.

What developmental significance might such exuberant, enjoyable activity hold? And if there is developmental significance to early social pretend play, what part do mothers and siblings play in the growth of children's exploration and enjoyment of the world of fantasy? In this chapter, we consider the developmental significance of pretend play in terms of its potential links to the development of social understanding. In doing so, we will consider individual differences in social experience in our analyses of both the production of social pretend and in terms of its correlation with sociocognitive development. Specifically, we will address three issues:

1. How are different close relationships linked to the production of social pretense? That is, are there differences in the amount and sophistication of a child's pretense based on who she or he plays with (i.e., mother or sibling)? Are there differences in the thematic content of this play?

2. How are individual differences within these relationships associated with the production of social pretense? Do individual differences in children's verbal ability, participation in discussions of other people's feelings, and the quality of their family relationships more broadly contribute to the amount and sophistication of pretense exhibited?

3. How does the production of pretense within and across these relationships relate to the child's developing understanding of other people's feelings and beliefs?

These issues will be discussed in the context of findings from a study of fifty second-born children from lower- and middle-class families in central

Pennsylvania, playing at home with their mothers and siblings. Unstructured home observations were conducted when the children were thirty-three months old. Transcripts of family conversation during the observation were made, including all family talk, details of context, and the nonverbal record. Measures of discourse and social pretend were garnered from these transcripts. Following the observation, the observer rated each family member's behavior toward each other family member in a series of rating scales (see Stocker, Dunn, and Plomin, 1989). At forty months, two sociocognitive assessments were given: (1) Bartsch and Wellman's (1989) false-beliefs task, which yielded a summary score of *offering explanation of action in terms of false belief*; and (2) Denham's (1986) affective pespective-taking task, which yielded an aggregate score of *affective labeling and pespective taking*. In this chapter, we summarize some of the findings relevant to the questions at issue. The detailed reports of the methodology and findings of the study can be found in Youngblade and Dunn (in press) and Dunn, Brown, Slomkowski, Tesla, and Youngblade (1991).

INDIVIDUAL DIFFERENCES IN SOCIAL PRETEND

Extant research on individual differences in pretend play highlights two important points. First, differences in a child's ability to pretend may be related to differences *across* types of relationships, that is, differences in the way children play with their siblings versus the way they play with a caregiver. Second, differences *within* these particular types of relationships may have implications for pretend play.

Based on the Vygotskian argument that play that is either guided or modeled by a more advanced partner may be more complex than solitary play (Bretherton, O'Connell, Shore, and Bates, 1984; Fenson, 1984; O'Connell and Bretherton, 1984), research on individual differences has most productively focused on social pretense. More sophisticated forms of pretend play are often collaborative: instead of simply producing a pretend action, children adopt a pretend role that calls for a partner to take on a complementary role (Dunn and Dale, 1984; Howes, Unger, and Seidner, 1989; Miller and Garvey, 1984).

Evidence on caregivers' engagement in pretend with young children suggests that such interactions facilitate the emergence and early elaboration of pretend play (e.g., Dunn, 1986; Dunn and Dale, 1984; Garvey, 1990). Mothers are not only responsive to young children's pretending but the form of their responses changes as children become more proficient players (Kavanaugh, Whittington, and Cerbone, 1983; Miller and Garvey, 1984; Sachs, 1980). Toddlers' pretend play with caregivers is more sustained (Dunn and Wooding, 1977; Slade, 1987a, 1987b), complex (Fiese, 1990; Slade, 1987a, 1987b) and diverse (O'Connell and Bretherton, 1984) than their solo pretending.

Joint play with a sibling appears to function differently than joint play with the mother. Mothers often participate through verbal commentary alone, supplemented by reference to a toy or prop. By contrast, siblings participate more as actors than as commentators, and they often call for a change of role, psychological state, or location, with less reliance on props (Dale, 1989; Dunn and Dale, 1984). Thus, social play with these different partners might have differential outcomes for the child in terms of the child's developing social cognition.

It is also the case that play experiences within relationship types vary. For example, it is not just the presence of a play patner but the caretaker's active interventions and suggestions that augment pretend play by one- and two-year-olds (DeLoache and Plaetzer, 1985; Fiese, 1990; O'Connell and Bretherton, 1984; Slade, 1987a). Although mothers' involvement usually facilitates pretend play, it can sometimes be disruptive if mothers intrude with questions or new activities (Fiese, 1990; Howes, 1992). Moreover, mothers (and siblings) vary in the way that they make themselves available to the child as play partners (see Slade, 1987a, 1987b) and in the way that they impart social meaning to a toddler's beginning attempts at pretense (Beizer and Howes, 1992; Hazen et al., 1991; Ramanan, Vandell, and Lederberg, 1992).

In the current study, we examined the extent to which children played with their mothers, with their siblings, and with all three together. To do so, we developed a coding system to assess bouts of naturally occurring social pretend play. Each pretend bout was coded along the following dimensions. First, the *theme* of the pretend bout was coded (a summary of the theme codes is presented in the Appendix). As an index of variety and richness of pretend play, a variable was created representing the *diversity of unique themes* in which the players participated. The diversity of pretend themes was calculated for all bouts the child participated in, all bouts in which only the sibling and child participated, all bouts in which only the mother and child participated, and all bouts in which all three participated.

Next, the number of *participatory* turns in which the speaker was actively involved in the pretend bout, either by contributing to the script negotiation (e.g., "I'll be the mommy, and you can be the baby"), playing a role (e.g., "I'm going to the mall; you be good, baby"), or actively manipulating a pretend prop as per the theme of the episode, was coded. Thus, this measure reflects active participation in—not just commentary about—the pretend bout. Summary variables were created to reflect total child participation (i.e., sum of all child-to-mother and child-to-sibling pretend turns), child-sibling total participation (i.e., the sum of all child-to-sibling and sibling-to-child pretend turns that occurred in bouts of child-sibling dyadic pretend play), child-mother total participation (i.e., the sum of all child-to-mother and mother-to-child pretend turns that occurred during bouts of child-mother dyadic pretend play), and child-mother-sibling total participation (i.e., the sum of all child, mother, and sibling pretend turns that occurred during bouts of triadic pretense).

For each bout the child was also rated as to whether she or he exhibited any evidence of playing a particular role, that is, *role enactment* (Huttenlocher and Higgins, 1978; Miller and Garvey, 1984). For this code, the child did not need to verbally define the role, merely to act it out (e.g., speaking in a character's voice or exhibiting behavior characteristic of a certain role, such as a daddy preparing to go to work, flying as superman, etc.). The child's verbal definition of the paticular role she or he was enacting (e.g., "I'm the doctor") was coded as participating in *role play* (Huttenlocher and Higgins, 1978; Miller and Garvey, 1984). Thus, role enactment involves mental representation by exemplifying a category of action. Role play, in contrast, is genuinely symbolic; the child's behavior designates the behavior of another person or character (Miller and Garvey, 1984). It should be noted that role play and role enactment were coded only for the child. Variables were created to reflect the proportion of bouts containing child role play and role enactment.

Differences Across Relationships

In this study, the majority of the child's pretend play involved the sibling. On average, children paticipated in about 8.5 bouts of pretend per hour, most of which occurred with their sibling. The majority of the child's participation turns in pretend occurred in play with the sibling, although more than half of the turns also occurred in the context of triadic play involving both mother and sibling. Pretense with the sibling was also more diverse than play with the mother or when all three were together. Children engaged in role enactment in about 11 percent of their pretend play bouts; they engaged in role play in about 3 percent of their pretend bouts.

When we examined the correlations between the various aspects of pretend, a striking finding emerged: the virtual independence of child-sibling and child-mother play. That is, child-mother and child-sibling participation and child-mother and child-sibling diversity of themes were not significantly correlated. Furthermore, examination of the part-whole correlations between the child-total and child-sibling, child-mother, or child-mother-sibling variables revealed that the child-total scores were more highly correlated with the child-sibling variables than the child-mother or child-mother-sibling variables. This suggests, again, that the majority of child pretense occurred within the context of the sibling relationship. Finally, the child's engagement in role enactment or role play was correlated with pretense with sibling, not with mother.

The fact that child-sibling and child-mother fantasy play were independent of each other, and the fact that children engaged in much more pretend with their sibling than they did with their mother is perhaps related to differences in how siblings and mothers act as playmates. Dunn and Dale (1984) suggest that mothers often act as observers in pretend play by offering guiding comments, rather than joining in as equal patners the way that siblings do. Similarly, Pellegrini (1984) found that adult (teacher) participation in preschool children's interactive dramatic play inhibited play, while peer participation encouraged this advanced play. It also may be that the thematic content of pretend play with sibling is different from—and more exciting than—fantasy play with mother.

What did these children pretend about? Table 10.1 outlines the themes in which the children were engaged. In general, the children in our study spent most of their time in "caregiver" pretend, that is, pretend involving "mommy/baby" and typically female household-chore themes. Miller and Garvey (1984) have traced the important part mothers play in the development of one particular role game—that of mother in "nurturing a baby." Here, it was also a prominent role game between siblings, somewhat more so, in fact, than with mothers. And, while many sibling pairs followed normative "scripts" in their "caregiver" pretend (e.g., feeding the baby, putting the baby to bed, etc.), there was considerable variation around this particular role game. One pair of sisters, for example, spent nearly an hour in sociodramatic play about the birth and care of a newborn baby—from preparing the mother (i.e., stuffing her shirt with the "baby"), to taking care of the mother during her bedridden pregnancy, to going to the hospital, to "unzipping the baby" (i.e., a Caesarean birth that was so much fun that it was repeated several times), and finally to feeding and caring for the newborn.

While the majority of pretend bouts in our sample involved a "caregiver" theme, children were also involved in a wide range of other themes. In play with siblings, children were involved in themes regarding adult occupations, animals, daily routines, and pretend with objects (e.g., building a city out of building blocks); themes about transportation, fantasy figures, adventure, and violence were also evident. Again, there was wide variety surrounding these theme categories. Themes regarding fantasy figures and adventure were particularly colorful, including sociodramatic play about Snow White, Ninja Turtles, alien space invaders, daring rescue attempts off a high mountain, camping trips disrupted by fierce acts of nature, and so on. Even such commonplace events as daily routines and adult occupations became exciting; for example, one sibling pair very boisterously made "egg soup," and another pair trudged off as archaeologists on an important dig. Play with mother was somewhat less vibrant, and prominent themes when mother and child played together included transportation (usually involving a plane, car, train, or bus ride somewhere), animals (usually involving farms or zoos), and pretense with objects. When all three played together, pretend typically revolved around

Table 10.1   Percentage of Bouts Spent in Each Theme

Theme	Child Total	Child-Sibling	Child-Mother	Child-Sibling-Mother
Caregiving/				
Female Tasks	24	23	17	25
Male Tasks	1	2	0	0
Adult Occupations	7	8	6	3
Violence	5	6	5	3
Being Animals	10	10	15	9
Daily Activities	8	10	3	9
Transportation	12	8	21	17
Fantasy Figures	6	8	2	4
Adventure	8	7	5	10
Music	1	2	2	0
Smoking, Drinking	1	1	0	2
Object Substitution/				
Building Blocks	13	13	18	15
Neighbors	3	0	3	2
Parties	1	2	3	1

transportation, adventure, animals, daily routines, and object substitution. Undoubtedly, such rich joint pretend play with different partners offers the child an opportunity for a wide variety of social learning experiences.

Individual Difference Correlates of Social Pretend

Children differ very much in the frequency and sophistication with which they engage in pretend. What accounts for such differences? We will examine three possibilities. The first has to do with structural characteristics of the family environment, such as socio-economic status (SES), child and sibling gender, and age of the children. The second consideration is that perhaps the way in which families discuss feeling states might promote the exploration of the causes and consequences of such states in the context of pretend. Third, aspects of the children's relationships with other family members, more broadly considered, may influence the production of pretense.

Sibling characteristics and family SES   The first set of analyses examined effects of structural characteristics of the sibling dyad and of family SES. We found no associations between pretend play and the gender composition of the sibling dyad; similarly, there were no significant correlations between pretend play and the child's nor the sibling's gender. In terms of age difference between the child, however, we found that the older the sibling, the more likely it was that the child would engage in role enactment. This finding is compatible with Vygotsky's (1965) argument that cognitive development is a process of internalizing the knowledge incorporated in social interactions with a more advanced partner. In addition, it is very likely the case that the younger child learns not only from interacting with but from watching the more sophisticated interactions of the older sibling with others (Dunn, Brown, Slomkowski, et al., 1991; Perner, Ruffman, and Leekam, 1994).

Considering the SES characteristics of the family, maternal and paternal education were positively correlated with child role-enactment. Although the literature on the relation of SES to pretend play is, in general, inconclusive about whether—and why—SES correlates with pretend play (McLoyd, 1986), the correlation between role enactment and parent education is congruent with other studies documenting less sociodramatic play among lower-class preschoolers than among middle-class preschoolers (Fein and Stork, 1981; Griffin, 1980; Rosen, 1974; Udwin and Shmukler, 1981).

Discourse   The next set of analyses considered the role of language and family conversation in the production of pretense. One possibility is that, simply, more verbally fluent children engage in more pretense. Our data, however, provide no support for the notion that social pretense is related to the child's verbal fluency, as measured by mean length of utterance (MLU; see Shatz and Gelman, 1973). We also employed a measure of the mother's verbal fluency—mother's MLU—as an index of "linguistic input" to the child. Mother's MLU was likewise unrelated to pretense.

A second possibility is that differences in participation in family conversation about emotion might be related to differences in pretend play. Göncü (1993) has argued that the origin of intersubjectivity in pretend play appears to be affective. Thus, it would not be unreasonable to suppose that children who engage in discussions about feeling states with their siblings and mothers might also be more disposed to engage in pretend than those who were not privy to such discussions. To examine this proposition, variables were created to reflect the total frequency of feeling-state talk that occurred *outside* the context of pretend play. Thus, feeling-state talk is independent from discourse in pretend. Summary variables were created as an index of total child feeling-state talk and total feeling-state discourse that occurred between child and sibling and between chld and mother.

The only significant associations with pretend play were in terms of conversation about feelings that occurred in the sibling relationship. Child-sibling feeling-state talk was positively related to child-total pretend participation, child-sibling pretend participation, and child-total and child-sibling diversity of themes.

Thus, in summary, differences in children's verbal fluency, as reflected in MLU, were not related to their social pretend play. However, children who participated relatively frequently in conversations about inner states were also likely to engage in frequent pretend play and their play was likely to include a diverse range of themes. This pattern of results raises two points. First, the findings argue against interpreting the findings solely in terms of continuity in *individual child* characteristics, and suggest, rather, that we should consider seriously the developmental importance of the child's social experiences. Second, it should be recalled that the correlations do not reflect discussion of inner states within joint pretend with the sibling. The measure of feeling-state talk specifically excluded talk about inner states within the context of pretend play. It appears that dialogue about inner states—one's own and those of others—that takes place outside the context of pretend play is related to (and may facilitate) the enactment of social pretense by providing affective-cognitive representations that are useful in enacting and negotiating pretend.

As to the question of why child-sibling rather than child-mother feeling-state conversation should show these associations, a relevant consideration could well be the differences in the context and nature of such conversations. When children talk about inner states with their mothers, the focus is less often the inner states of someone other than the child than it is in conversations with the sibling. The emotional and pragmatic natures of such conversations also differ (Brown and Dunn, 1992).

Family relationships   Our last foray into the correlates of individual differences in pretend play was a consideration of the quality of mother-child and sibling-child relationships as they related to engagement in joint pretense. Exploratory factor analysis of the observational rating scales of family relationships (Stocker, Dunn, and Plomin, 1989) yielded composite variables that characterized mother-child and sibling-child relations (see Youngblade and Dunn, in press, for description).

We examined the relations between the quality of the mother-child and the sibling-child relationship and the various measures of pretend. As in other studies (e.g., Dunn and Dale, 1984; Slade, 1987a, 1987b), we found that affection and involvement in the mother-child relationship was linked to participation and diversity in child-mother and triadic pretend.

In general, however, there were more associations between the child-sibling relationship and pretend than there were between the child-mother relationship and pretend. Our data indicated that positive sibling relationships and more sophisticated pretense covary—either because positive relationships foster social pretense or because children who can engage in sustained pretense are more enjoyable companions. It was also the case that sibling-to-child negativity was positively correlated with the child's participation in pretend and the diversity of themes when with mother and sibling. This correlation may reflect the fact that in famlies in which the siblings interact intensely and frequently the children can be both more positive and more negative towards each other than the siblings in families who are not interested in interacting: As with the interaction of preschool-aged peers, conflict and friendliness are not simply the opposite ends of a continuum, but can reflect the frequency and intensity with which children interact.

Siblings, Mothers and Pretend Play

What, then, can we say about thirty-three-month-olds' pretend play with different partners? The first issue concerns the frequency and sophistication with which these children pretend. Given the finesse with which these preschoolers engaged in sociodramatic play with their siblings and mothers, our data would seem to refute the claim that children of these young ages may simply not have grasped the notion that pretend play can be a social endeavor with shared rules about the production and communication of symbolic representations (see Rubin, Fein, and Vandenberg, 1983, p. 725).

In terms of pretense with different partners, the children in this study participated more in pretend with their siblings than with their mothers or with both family members together. In addition, child-sibling discourse and relationship measures were more strongly related to the pretend measures than were the equivalent mother-child measures. And, it was also the case that differences *within* relationships were associated with differences in children's participation in social pretend. Differences in child-sibling discourse concerning feelings, quality of parent-child and sibling relationships, age gap between siblings, and parent education were specifically related to the frequency and sophistication of social pretense.

Thus, our data underscore the point that children's experiences with different family partners differ widely. In particular, the data highlight the significance of the sibling relationship as a "pretend playground" for the child—perhaps due to the familiarity of the social world of child and sibling, the affection and support of the older sibling, and the older child's proficiency in the world of pretend, as well as his or her saliency as a model for the child (Dunn, 1986; Dunn and Dale, 1984).

We now turn our attention to the topic of social understanding and its links to early pretend.

PRETEND PLAY AND SOCIAL UNDERSTANDING

There is a long history of considering pretend play as an important window into the development of the child's growing cognitive and social competence (Bretherton, 1984; Piaget, 1962). Investigators have studied, for example, the relation of pretense to language development (Bates, et al., 1979; Corrigan, 1979; McCune-Nicolich, 1981), perspective taking (Connolly and Doyle, 1984; Rubin, 1976), individual differences in family interactions that facilitate the emergence and early elaboration of pretend play (Dunn, 1988; Dunn and

Dale, 1984) and friendship formation during preschool and the early elementary years (Gottman and Parker, 1986).

Recently, this cadre of research has grown to include theoretical interest in the links between pretense and the child's developing "theory of mind" (e.g., Harris and Kavanaugh, 1993; Leslie, 1987, 1988; Lillard, 1993a, 1993b). It has been argued that pretend actions have certain parallels with actions based on mistaken belief: both may be directed at situations that do not actually obtain (Harris and Kavanaugh, 1993). In fact, pretense seems to require many of the same skills as mental understanding (Leslie, 1987, 1988; Lillard, 1993a). Take the example of collaborative social pretend. If the other person is to be a genuine partner in joint pretend play, the child must decode the other's nonliteral actions and remarks since their underlying meaning will not fully coincide with their surface features (Harris and Kavanaugh, 1993). Such skills are relevant for the ability to understand another person's feelings or beliefs.

Interestingly, however, the skills required to engage in pretend play appear to emerge earlier than the child's understanding of false belief (Harris and Kavanaugh, 1993; Leslie, 1987, 1988; Lillard, 1993a). Thus, a reasonable hypothesis is that chldren who are adept at fantasy play have experiences that help them master the relationship between mental life and the real world (Taylor, Cartwright and Carlson, 1993).

Flavell and his colleagues (Flavell, Flavell, and Green, 1987) suggest that pretending might facilitate a child's understanding of the distinction between internal mental representations of external stimuli and the stimuli themselves. Once this distinction is practiced and mastered in pretend play, children might be better equipped to think about similar distinctions in other situations or contexts (Taylor et al., 1993). And, in fact, some data support this contention. Chandler, Fritz, and Hala (1991) found, for example, that the report of an imaginary playmate was a predictor of an early mastery of false belief. Other studies have demonstrated that, upon request, children can imagine or pretend that a given entity is in a given place, and they can then talk about the products of those pretend or imagined representations (Harris, et al., 1991; Harris and Kavanaugh, 1993; Wellman and Estes, 1986). Conversely, however, Lillard's (1993b) experimental data suggest that children under the age of six may not understand that pretending requires mental representation and that the mental representational skills needed for pretense might actually emerge later than those needed to represent false belief.

While acknowledging the interest of these studies, one could argue that current empirical assessments of the links between pretend play and children's developing social understanding do not address three important points. First, inferences are generally based on analyses of pretend exhibited in experimental conditions, rather than on analyses of pretend as it unfolds in natural settings. Second, the type of pretense analyzed is typically not social pretend. It is possible that children are motivated to think about pretend at a higher level in the context of maintaining a playful relationship with another person. Thus, the adoption of roles and the negotiation of what those roles signify, as well as the actions they produce, may be particularly salient to the child when the continuation of this social ineraction is dependent upon the child's understanding of the playmate. In fact, Göncü (1993) argues that children engage in play to share emotionally significant experiences with their playmates. At the same time, they metacommuniate to create a joint understanding that identifies the nature of the enterprise as pretense, and use language and actions as communicative devices to construct jointly the playful representation of experience. Thus, the highly charged social and emotional aspects of play, coupled with the cognitive aspects of play, may be important to developing social understanding.

Third, little attention has been paid to factors associated with individual differences in the links between pretend and sociocognitive assessments of theory of mind. Earlier we discussed individual differences in the production of social pretend play. Some evidence also exists to suggest that there are marked individual differences in young children's ability to understand other people's feelings and beliefs. In investigating these differences, we found that differences in family discourse about feelings and causality, verbal fluency of the mother and child, and quality of the mother-sibling and child-sibling relationships were all important predictors (Dunn, Brown, Slomkowski, et al., 1991). A second study also found that family conversations about feelings related to later affective pespective-taking assessments (Dunn, Brown, and Beardsall, 1991). And Perner, Ruffman, and Leekam (1994) provided data that children from larger families were better able than children from smaller families to perform on a false-beliefs task, suggesting that siblings provide an important context for developing social understanding. Interestingly, Perner (1993) also reported that children do better on false-belief tasks if they had a sibling who was close in age rather than distant. In the current study, we sought to examine whether individual differences in social pretend were systematically associated with children's ability to undersand other people's feelings and beliefs.

Relations Between Pretend Play and Children's Social Understanding

We looked at the correlations between the pretend-play measures and scores on the false-beliefs task and the measure of affective understanding. Children's scores on the false-beliefs task were positively correlated with role enactment that had been exhibited during pretend play seven months earlier. Specifically, children who engaged in more role enactment scored higher on the false-beliefs task than did those children who engaged in less role enactment. In terms of children's understanding of the situational causes of another's emotions, scores on the affective understanding task were positively related to child-total pretend participation and to child-sibling participation in pretend.

The results from the analysis of pretend play and performance on the social cognition tasks raise several issues. Clearly we cannot draw any strong conclusions about causality, since the associations between pretense and the social cognition tasks might reflect some common underlying ability rather than any direct causal link. Nevertheless, it does appear that children who engage in more social pretend early perform better on tasks of false belief and affective understanding. In particular, the child's propensity to role enact predicted success on the false beliefs task seven months later. These results correspond with data reported by Taylor, Gerow, and Carlson (1993) showing that four-year-olds who were paticularly inclined to engage in pretense appeared to be accelerated in their development of knowledge about the mind. They fit, too, with the proposition that children come to understand other people's and their own past mental states by simulation or role taking (Harris, 1991; Perner, 1991; Wimmer and Hartl, 1991) and its corrollary that more role-taking practice might help elevate performance levels earlier in life than would occur without such practice (Perner et al., 1994).

Second, it also appears that participation in pretend, particularly with an older sibling, is related to later understanding of the situational determinants of others' feelings. The extent to which children pretend with their sibling thus appears to be related to the development of the understanding of emotion (see also Dunn, 1988). The intense nature of the sibling relationship, combined with the inherent emotionality in pretense (e.g., Fein, 1989; Göncü, 1993), may provide a fertile ground for the development of social understanding, paticularly in terms of affective understanding.

CONCLUSION

The purpose of this chapter was to examine individual differences in the social pretend play of young children, examine correlates of these differences, and investigate the relationship of individual differences in young children's social fantasy to their developing understanding of other people's thoughts and feelings. Three main conclusions can be drawn from these findings:

First, there are indeed individual differences in the amount and sophistication of social pretend play engaged in by young children. These individual differences may be based, in part, on experiences in the relationships young children have with their mothers and siblings. In particular, the sibling relationship seems to be comparatively more strongly linked to the quality of children's pretend. However, the question of whether joint pretend play with sibling or mother is causally important remains untested. It could well be that mothers or siblings who participate with enthusiasm in social pretend play differ in other critical ways from mothers or siblings who are uninterested in such play.

Second, the data concerning individual difference correlates of joint participation in pretend highlight the variety of developmental paths by which children may achive the social understanding and communication skills on which joint pretend play depends. The quality of particular family relationships, with mother or with sibling, is likely to influence the particular pattern of development. As Brian Sutton-Smith (1985) has noted:

> If we study children continuously . . . in order to discover *processes* of individual *change* in the social or individual structurings that we temporarily describe, we are much more likely to discover the course of development, with all its individual variety, multilinearity, and mobility of operations. (p. 66)

Third, early experience in social pretend play may have important sociocognitive implications for children's developing understanding of other people's feelings and actions. However, while our study adds to the corpus of data regarding individual differences in young chldren's social pretend play and its links to the development of social understanding, our analysis does not permit inferences of cause and effect. And, because of the large number of correlations run, we should be cautious about generalizing from the results. What this chapter does underscore, however, is the importance of considering the context of social experience in our analyses of the child's developing knowledge about others, an issue strongly emphasized by Brian Sutton-Smith (1985), which deserves our continuing attention.

REFERENCES

Bartsch, K., & Wellman, H. (1989). Young children's attribution of action to beliefs and desires. *Child Development, 60,* 946–64.

Bates, E., Benigni, L., Bretherton, I., Camaioni, L., & Volterra, V. (1979). *The emergence of symbols: Cognition and communication in infancy.* New York: Academic Press.

Beizer, L., & Howes, C. (1992). Mothers and toddlers: Partners in early pretend play. In C. Howes (Ed.), *The collaborative construction of pretend: Social pretend functions* (pp. 25–44). Albany: State University of New York Press.

Borke, H. (1971). Interpersonal perception of young children: Egocentrism or empathy? *Developmental Psychology, 5,* 263–69.

Brennen, R. L., & Prediger, D. J. (1981). Coefficient kappa: Some uses, misuses and alternatives. *Educational and Psychological Measurement, 41,* 687–99.

Bretherton, I. (1984). Representing the social world in symbolic play: Reality and fantasy. In I. Bretherton (Ed.), *Symbolic play: The development of social understanding* (pp. 1–41). Orlando: Academic Press.

Bretherton, I., O'Connell, B., Shore, C., & Bates, E. (1984). The effect of contextual variation on symbolic play: Development from 20 to 28 months. In I. Bretherton (Ed.), *Symbolic play: The development of social understanding* (pp. 271–298). Orlando: Academic Press.

Brown, J. R., & Dunn, J. (1992). Talk with your mother or your sibling? Developmental changes in early family conversations about feelings. *Child Development, 63,* 336–49.

Caldwell, B. (1986). The significance of parent-child interaction in children's development. In A. W. Gottfried & C. C. Brown (Eds.), *Play interactions* (pp. 305–10). Lexington, MA: Lexington Books.

Chandler, M. J., Fritz, A. S., & Hala, S. (1991, April). *Children's theories of mental life and social practices.* Paper presented at the Biennial Meeting of the Society for Research in Child Development, Seattle, Washington.

Connolly, J. A., & Doyle, A. B. (1984). Relation of social fantasy play to social competence in preschoolers. *Developmental Psychology, 20,* 797–806.

Corrigan, R. (1979). Cognitive correlates of language: Differential criteria yield differential results. *Child Development, 50,* 617–31.

Denham, S. A. (1986). Social cognition, prosocial behavior, and emotion in preschoolers: Contextual validation. *Child Development, 57,* 194–201.

Dale, N. (1989). Pretend play with mothers and siblings: Relations between early performance and partners. *Journal of Child Psychology and Psychiatry, 30,* 751–59.

DeLoache, J., & Plaetzer, B. (1985, April). *Tea for two: Joint mother-child symbolic play.* Paper presented at the meeting of the Society for Research in Child Development, Toronto.

Dunn, J. (1986). Pretend play in the family. In A. W. Gottfried & C. C. Brown (Eds.), *Play interactions: The contribution of play materials and aprental involvement to children's development* (pp. 149–62). Lexington, MA: Lexington Books.

———. (1988). *The beginnings of social understanding.* Oxford: Basil Blackwell.

Dunn, J., Brown, J., & Beardsall, L. (1991). Family talk about emotions, and children's later understanding of other's emotions. *Developmental Psychology, 27,* 448–55.

Dunn, J., Brown, J., Slomkowski, C., Tesla, C., & Youngblade, L. M. (1991). Young children's understanding of other people's feelings and beliefs: Individual differences and their antecedents. *Child Development, 62,* 1352–66.

Dunn, J., & Dale, N. (1984). I a daddy: 2-year-olds' collaboration in joint pretend with sibling and with mother. In I. Bretherton (Ed.), *Symbolic play: The development of social understanding* (pp. 131–58). New York: Academic Press.

Dunn, J., & Wooding, C. (1977). Play in the home and its implications for learning. In B. Tizard & D. Harvey (Eds.), *Biology of play* (pp. 45-58). London: Heinemann.

Fein, G. G. (1989). Mind, meaning, and affect: Proposals for a theory of pretense. *Developmental Review, 9*, 345–63.

Fein, G. G., & Stork, L. (1981). Sociodramatic play in a socially integrated setting. *Journal of Applied Developmental Psychology, 2*, 267–79.

Fenson, L. (1984). Developmental trends for action and speech in pretend play. In I. Bretherton (Ed.), *Symbolic play: The development of social understanding*. Orlando: Academic Press.

Fiese, B. H. (1990). Playful relationships: A contextual analysis of mother-toddler interaction and symbolic play. *Child Development, 61*, 1648–56.

Finn, R. H. (1970). A note on estimating the reliability of categorical data. *Educational and Psychological Measurement, 30*, 71–76.

———. (1972). Effects of some variations in rating scale characteristics on the means and reliabilities of ratings. *Educational and Psychological Measurement, 35*, 255–65.

Flavell, J. H., Flavell, E. R., & Green, F. L. (1987). Young children's knowledge about the apparent-real and pretend-real distinctions. *Developmental Psychology, 23*, 816–22.

Garvey, C. (1990). *Play*. Cambridge: Harvard University Press.

Göncü, A. (1993). Development of intersubjectivity in social pretend play. *Human Development, 36*, 185–98.

Gottman, J., & Parker, J. (1986). *Conversations of friends: Speculations on affective development*. Cambridge: Cambridge University Press.

Griffing, P. (1980). The relationship between socioeconomic status and sociodramatic play among black kindergarten children. *Genetic Psychology Monographs, 101*, 3–34.

Haight, W., & Miller, P. (1993). *Pretending at home: Early development in a sociocultural context*. Albany: State University of New York Press.

Harris, P. L. (1991). The work of the imagination. In A. Whiten (Ed.), *Natural theories of mind: The evolution, development and simulation of everyday mindreading* (pp. 283–304). Oxford: Basil Blackwell.

Harris, P. L., Brown, E., Marriott, C., Whittall, S., & Harmer, S. (1991). Monsters, ghosts, and witches: Testing the limits of the fantasy-reality distinction. *British Journal of Developmental Psychology, 9*, 105–23.

Harris, P. L., & Kavanaugh, R. D. (1993). Young children's understanding of pretense. *Monographs of the Society for Research in Child Development, 58* (1, Serial No. 231).

Hauser, R. M., & Featherman, D. L. (1977). *The process of stratification: Trends and analysis.* New York: Academic Press.

Hazen, N. L., Bohman, T., Burton, H., DeSantis, R., Kemple, K., & Matula, K. (1991, April). *Parent-child interaction and toddlers' peer competence.* Paper presented at the Biennial Meeting of the Society for Research in Child Development, Seattle.

Howes, C. (1992). *The collaborative construction of pretend: Social pretend functions.* Albany: State University of New York Press.

Howes, C., Unger, O., & Seidner, L. B. (1989). Social pretend play in toddlers: Parallels with social play and with solitary pretend. *Child Development, 60,* 77–84.

Huttenlocher, J., & Higgins, E. T. (1978). Issues in the study of symbolic development. In W. A. Collins (Ed.), *Minnesota Symposia on Child Psychology* (vol. 12, pp. 29–55). Hillsdale, NJ: Lawrence Erlbaum.

Kavanaugh, R. D., Whittington, S., & Cerbone, M. J. (1983). Mother's use of fantasy in speech to young children. *Journal of Child Language, 10,* 45–55.

Leslie, A. M. (1987). Pretense and representation: The origins of "Theory of Mind." *Psychological Review, 94,* 412–26.

———. (1988). Some implications of pretense for mechanisms underlying the child's theory of mind. In J. W. Astington, P. L. Harris, & D. R. Olson (Eds.), *Developing theories of mind* (pp. 19–46). New York: Cambridge University Press.

Lillard, A. S. (1993a). Pretend play skills and the child's theory of mind. *Child Development, 64,* 348–71.

———. (1993b). Young children's conceptualization of pretense: Action or mental representational state? *Child Development, 64,* 372–86.

McCune-Nicolich, L. (1981). Toward symbolic functioning: Structure of early pretend games and potential parallels with language. *Child Development, 52,* 785–97.

McLoyd, V. C. (1986). Social class and pretend play. In A. W. Gottfried & C. C. Brown (Eds.), *Play interactions: The contribution of play materials and parental involvement to children's development* (pp. 175–96). Lexington, MA: Lexington Books.

Miller, P., & Garvey, C. (1984). Mother-baby role play: Its origins in social support. In I. Bretherton (Ed.), *Symbolic play: The development of social understanding* (pp. 101–31). Orlando: Academic Press.

O'Connell, B., & Bretherton, I. (1984). Toddler's play, alone and with mother: The role of maternal guidance. In I. Bretherton (Ed.), *Symbolic play: The development of social understanding* (pp. 337–68). Orlando: Academic Press.

Pellegrini, A. D. (1984). The social cognitive ecology of preschool classrooms: Contextual relations revisited. *International Journal of Behavioral Development, 7,* 321–32.

Perner, J. (1991). *Understanding the representational mind.* Cambridge: MIT Press.

————. (1993, March). *Theory of mind is contagious: You catch it from your sibs.* Paper presented at the Biennial Meeting of the Society for Research in Child Development, New Orleans.

Perner, J., Ruffman, T., & Leekam, S. R. (1994). Theory of mind is contagious: You catch it from your sibs. *Child Development, 65*(4), 1228–38.

Piaget, J. (1962). *Play, dreams and imitation in childhood.* New York: Norton.

Ramanan, J., Vandell, D. L., & Lederberg, A. (1991, April). *Mother-child pretend play and later social competence with peers.* Paper presented at the Biennial Meeting of the Society for Research in Child Development, Seattle.

Rosen, C. E. (1974). The effects of sociodramatic play on problem-solving behavior among culturally disadvantaged preschool children. *Child Development, 45,* 920–27.

Rubin, K. H. (1976). The relationship of social play preference to role taking skills in preschool children. *Psychological Reports, 39,* 823–26.

Rubin, K. H., Fein, G. G., & Vandenberg, B. (1983). Play. In P. M. Mussen (Ed.), *Manual of child psychology* (vol. 4, pp. 693–774). New York: Wiley.

Sachs, J. (1980). The role of adult-child play in language development. *New Directions for Child Development, 9,* 33–48.

Shatz, M., & Gelman, R. (1973). The development of communication skills: Modification in the speech of young children as a function of listener. *Monographs of the Society for Research in Child Development, 35* (5, Serial No. 152).

Slade, A. (1987a). A longitudinal study of maternal involvement and symbolic play during the toddler period. *Child Development, 58,* 367–75.

————. (1987b). Quality of attachment and early symbolic play. *Developmental Psychology, 23,* 78–85.

Stocker, C., Dunn, J., & Plomin, R. (1989). Sibling relationships: Links with child temperament, maternal behavior, and family structure. *Child Development, 60*, 715–27.

Sutton-Smith, B. (1976). *Play and learning.* New York: Gardner Press.

———. (1985). Origins and developmental processes of play. In C. Caldwell-Brown & A. W. Gottfried (Eds.), *Play interactions* (pp. 61–66). Skillman, NJ: Johnson & Johnson.

Taylor, M., Cartwright, B. S., & Carlson, S. M. (1993). A developmental investigation of children's imaginary companions. *Developmental Psychology, 29*(2), 276–85.

Taylor, M., Gerow, L. E., & Carlson, S. M. (1993, March). *The relation between individual differences in fantasy and theory of mind.* Paper presented at the biennial meeting of the Society for Research in Child Development, New Orleans.

Udwin, O., & Shmukler, D. (1981). The influence of sociocultural, economic and home background factors on children's ability to engage in imaginative play. *Developmental Psychology, 17*, 66–72.

Vygotsky, L. S. (1965). *Thought and language.* Cambridge: MIT Press.

Wellman, H. M., & Estes, D. (1986). Early understanding of mental entities: A reexamination of childhood realism. *Child Development, 57*, 910–23.

Wimmer, H., & Hartl, M. (1991). The Cartesian view and theory view of mind: Developmental evidence from understanding false belief in self and other. *British Journal of Developmental Psychology, 9*, 125–38.

Youngblade, L. M., & Dunn, J. (In Press). Individual differences in young children's pretend play with mother and sibling: Links to relationships and understanding of other people's feelings and beliefs. *Child Development.*

Appendix A Pretend Theme Codes

Female Activities:	Playing house—cooking, caretaking, typically "female" chores; mommy-baby, family-related themes; doll play—e.g., Barbies, babydolls, puppets (with a domestic theme).
Male Activities:	Fixing things; mowing lawn; working on car; tools; "male" chores; fishing; hunting.
Adult Occupations:	Nurse, doctor, hospital, teacher, waitress, salesperson, firefighter, police, community workers, musician, postal clerk, archaeologists, artists, etc., beauty parlor; Also, pretend involving "going to work."
Violence/Aggression:	Army, killing, cops-n-robbers, blood & guts, soldiers, guns, shooting, killing enemy invaders, bows & arrows, pretend fighting.
Animals:	Being animals or dinosaurs; farms, zoos.
Daily Activities:	Sleeping, eating, going to the bathroom; going shopping; telephoning.
Transportation:	Driving a car, boat, plane, etc.; travel, going on a trip.
Fantasy Figures:	Monsters, ghosts, superman, batman, Disney characters, king/queen.
Adventure:	Cowboys, old west; help-rescue; action figures—GI Joe, Star Trek; adventures in nature (snow storm, hurricane, etc.); mountaineering.
Music:	Marching band, parade, cheerleader; pretending to be in a band.
Adult "Deviant" Activities:	Smoking, drinking, kissing, sex.
Non-Literal Objects:	Building things with blocks, objects become non-literal; building forts, tents.
Neighbors/Friends/ Social Relationships:	Friends, neighbors.
Holidays/Parties/ Special Events:	Holidays, special rituals, birthday parties, weddings, etc.

Part IV

PLAY AS SELF

11

HELEN B. SCHWARTZMAN ⎯⎯⎯⎯⎯⎯⎯⎯⎯⎯⎯⎯⎯⎯⎯⎯⎯⎯⎯⎯⎯⎯⎯⎯⎯⎯

Representing Children:
Anthropologists at Work, Children at Play

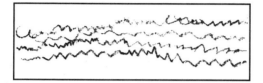

Linda's fieldnotes

I want to begin this chapter with a selection from fieldnotes that I wrote in 1972 when I was studying children's play in a day-care center in Chicago:

> March 17,1972—I'm sitting near the block corner watching Linda, Thomas, Paul, Sonia, and Karen pretend that they are on a "boat." I'm writing fieldnotes as fast as I can. Suddenly, I looked up and Linda had moved a chair into the middle of the "boat" and she was sitting in the chair scribbling on a piece of paper and looking at me. I asked her what she was doing and she said she was writing notes about me.

I begin with this brief example of reflexivity in the field because it seems to capture and express some of the newly problematized relationships among researcher/informant, writer/reader, and subject matter that a number of social scientists—especially anthropoligists writing under the rubric of interpretive, post-modern, or post-structuralist critiques of the discipline—have raised for investigators (see Marcus and Cushman, 1982; Marcus and Fischer, 1986; Clifford, 1988; Clifford and Marcus, 1989; Van Mannen, 1988).[1] James Clifford (1988) illustrates these concerns by posing a series of questions for researchers:

> If ethnography produces cultural interpretation through intense research experience, how is such unruly experience transformed into an authoritative written account? How, precisely, is a garrulous, overdetermined, cross-cultural encounter, shot through with power relations and personal cross-purposes circumsribed as an adequate version of a more-or-less discrete "otherworld," composed by an individual author? (p. 25).

One of the overriding questions from this perspective is: How do ethnographers represent in narrative (or other) forms the experiences and lives of the individuals and groups that they study? Researchers are concerned with several issues here, including: (1) how social realties are constituted and constructed

243

in everyday language and interaction; (2) how the authority of researchers as well as informants is established when we "write culture," and especially how the ethnographer is presented in his/her ethnography; (3) the political implications of researcher representations and ways to link micro- and local-level studies to global systems of control and domination; and (4) the possibility of developing alternative formats (like fiction, films, drama, diaries) for the presentation of multiple and conflicting realities and interpretations in ethnographies.

Brian Sutton-Smith is no stranger to these issues, as he has been concerned with the question of how researchers represent children, and especially how researchers' representations contribute to the "domestication" of children and their play, for quite some time (see Sutton-Smith and Kelly-Byrne, 1984). Sutton-Smith has also been concerned with examining how the investigator's life and experiences intersect with and influence research orientations, and he presents a biographical analysis of his own scholarly record in "A Memory of Games and Some Games of Memory" (1994). An interest in experimenting with different theoretical paradigms as well as representational formats is also evident in a great deal of Sutton-Smith's work (see 1981).

Sutton-Smith's work influenced my own analysis of how researchers' concepts of children affect their own descriptions, interpretations, and representations of children's behavior and actions in fieldwork situations. In *Transformations* (1978) I identified several metaphors that have guided researchers' studies of child socialization and I suggest that it is "important to explore not only the different types of cultures in which children grow up but also the variety of cultural schools in which anthropologists have been socialized. For just as these various theories of culture affect interpretations of play, they also influence interpretations of children" (p. 21).

The view of "children as primitive" influenced several studies of children (especially Western children) conducted in the nineteenth and early twentieth century. The impact of evolutionary theory on child-development research is evident in many studies. For example, G. Stanley Hall believed that "the best index and guide to the stated activities of adults in past ages is found in the instinctive, untaught and non-imitative plays of children" (1904, p. 202) He assumed that the play "stages" of children recapitulated the entire biocultural history of mankind. The "staging" of children's lives and children's play, which is now almost a taken-for-granted fact of life, is a direct outgrowth of this approach. Other metaphors that I identify and describe include the view of "children as copycats" and the representation of children, especially in their play, as passive imitators of adult life. The conception of "children as personality trainees" has also been influential in studies by early and more recent psychological anthropologists, who are concerned with examining relationships between personality and culture. In contrast, child ethologists assume that the behavior of children can be studied in the same way as the behavior of nonhuman primates. Representing "children as monkeys" reveals some features of children that allow for interspecies comparisons, but it conceals other important features of children's lives (especially the role of language play). Finally, I discussed studies that view "children as critics" and especially the ways that "children act as interpreters, commentators, and even critics of their own as well as adults' activities" (1978, p. 25). These metaphors were related to the theoretical orientation of the ethnographer, and I believe that they exert a powerful influence on how the researcher "sees" and portrays children in the field.

I would like to examine a series of recent ethnographies in light of the newly problematized relations among researcher/informant, writer/reader, and subject matter that I have described here. A number of studies of children's play have been conducted since the publication of *Transformations* in 1978 and many of them have been identified and briefly discussed in Salamone (1989). In this chapter I will limit my analysis to a small number of recent ethnographies that illustrate various solutions to the general issue of how researchers "represent children."

CONSTITUTING SOCIAL WORLDS

Early culture and personality studies, such as the configurationist studies of Margaret Mead and the child training and personality studies of Abram Kardiner and Ralph Linton and John and Beatrice Whiting, took the child's, and for that matter the adult's, social world for granted. How individuals produce and reproduce their social organization in their day-to-day interactions and cultural beliefs was not a problem for these researchers, who were focused on relating, for example, "basic personality structure" to "primary" and "secondary" institutions. Recent ethnographies of children in the United States as well as abroad have stepped away from this tradition and begun to examine how children "constitute their social world in the midst of moment-to-moment talk" (Goodwin, 1990, p. 1), and how "speech enables children to develop social relationships and participate in the give and take of everyday life" (Schieffelin, 1990, p. 1). Instead of taking (social) meaning for granted, these studies problematize meaning and make the process of understanding "how meaning is produced" a central goal of the research (ibid.).

He-Said-She-Said (1990) by Marjorie Harness Goodwin illustrates this turn toward meaning and the analysis of talk and social interaction in local contexts. In this ethnography Goodwin examines the social world of a group of urban African American children living on "Maple Street," a working-class neighborhood in southwest Philadelphia. Because she wants to understand how the children produce and reproduce their social world, the play activities of her informants are a central feature of her ethnography. In fact, this is one of the most extensively documented studies of African American children's play lives in the literature. It is particularly noteworthy because it is not a collection of texts but an examination of how specific types of play activities (especially verbal play activities) are situated within the context of a particular social setting—the peer group in the neighborhood. This shift from the school to the neighborhood peer group is another important feature of this study and in keeping with other more recent studies of children's play activities outside the school context (e.g., Haight and Miller, 1993). This shift also allowed Goodwin to examine play activities of same-age, same-sex groups as well as cross-sex, cross-age interactions.

The Maple Street children divide themselves into four different age/sex clusters: younger girls (4–10), younger boys (5–6), older girls (10–13), older boys (9–14). Some interesting age and gender contrasts are reported. For example, older girls participate in a wider variety of activities than boys, such as jump rope (especially "double dutch"), "house" and "school" dramatic play, and planning club meetings and club activities as well as making up dance steps and making things (like scarfs and hats) and food (pizza, cake, water ice) (pp. 36–37). Girls, however, play fewer games and team sports. Older boys spend less time engaged in different types of play activities but they have a larger reportoire of pastimes and games (yoyos, walking on hands, coolies or dead blocks, pitching pennies, flying kites, go-carts, marbles) and were more involved in team sports (especially football and basketball, which they played year round) (p. 37). Younger girls played similar, although less complicated, versions of the older girls play activities (p. 38). There was a greater difference between younger and older boys activities. Younger boys preferred dramatic play—such as playing soldiers, milkmen, doctors, sales-men, monsters, Batman, cowboys, et cetera—over games (p. 38). There was also much more age-heterogeneity in the older-girls group then the older-boys group because older girls had child-care responsibilities, and Goodwin suggests that this exposed the younger children in their care to a broad range of social experiences (p. 39).

Goodwin also presents interesting information on girls' and boys' styles of alliance formation and exclusion. In general, the Maple Street girls were more egalitarian, as contrasted with the more hierarchical boys, but Goodwin qualifies these differences in several ways. Noting for example that while boys' actions produce a more visible hierarchy and girls' actions emphasize similarity between members, Goodwin observes that there are also important "dynamics of coalition formation and shifting alliances that can provide con-siderable conflict" (p. 47) and produce elaborate, intricate, and changing so-cial relations (such as the he-said-she-said routines from which the book acquired its name). These routines are specific forms of gossip dispute that Maple Street girls used in which "one girl accuses another of a particular breach: having talked about her behind her back. The offended party con-

fronts an alleged offending party because she wants to 'get something straight' "
(p. 190). Some "he-said-she-said" disputes were brief and fairly inconsequen-
tial, but Goodwin illustrates how in some instances accusations could lead to
extended disputes with high drama and with great consequence for the social
organization of the girls' peer group (p. 190).

Girls and boys on Maple Street alternately joined and separated in their
play activities, or they might serve as direct or indirect audiences for each
others activities. Goodwin documented the variety of ways that boys and girls
engaged in talking and playing with each other, such as teasing, storytelling,
arguing, playing house, and exchanging ritual insults (p. 52), and she also
discusses how the "ecology of the street" facilitates a number of cross-sex
interactions which are more relaxed and of longer duration than those reported
in other studies (p. 49).

This study challenges many assumptions that have influenced child-
development researchers, such as the idea of separate gender worlds, which
may be apparent in school contexts but not in neighborhood contexts and
which also varies by social class and culture. The idea that female speech and
overall relationship style are different than male speech and style is also
questioned in this study. Contrary to Gilligan (1992), Goodwin's data suggest
that speaking styles must be related to *activities* as well as *gender* and that it
is very problematic to develop unidimensional views of girls' and boys'
orientations (p. 289). She illustrates these points while making some important contrasts in the literature:

> Thus the type of social structure as well as the moral themes expressed in
> speech actions varies from activity to activity and argues for a situated
> rather than a unidimensional view of girls' concerns. Cooperation and
> competition are not mutually exclusive agendas and often coexist within
> the same speech activities. In both pretend play and he-said-she-said con-
> frontations, participants work together to sustain a coherent activity with a
> well-defined structure. However, the specific type of joint action which is
> exhibited does not resemble "supportive" forms of collaboration described
> elsewhere as characteristic of female speech (see Maltz and Borker, 1983,
> p. 211). Moreover, the talk of the argumentative sequences examined in
> this book displays anything but "a tone of relaxed sweetness, sometimes
> bordering on the saccharin," which Hannerz (1969, p. 96) finds typical of
> black female adult speech, in contrast to black males' argumentative style.
> In Abrahams's view, female values of respectability and the home are
> contrasted with male values of reputation and the public world (Abrahams,
> 1976, p. 64); however, displaying one's character in a public arena is
> precisely what is at issue in a he-said-she-said, and girls can hold their
> own in arguments with boys. (p. 284)

Most importantly, Goodwin argues for a view of language (including language play) as constitutive of social worlds and social realities. In her terms,

speech does not just express or comment on social relationships. Instead, "language constitutes a powerful tool for organizing social groups" because talk creates "participation frameworks" (p. 286). Speakers/players can reformulate groups and interactions by switching from one speech event to another:

> For example . . . by switching from a contest of verbal contention to a story, a participant may dramatically reshape a dyadic form of interaction into a multiparty one; this may permit an opponent to recruit others to visibly confirm his/her position. Similarly, within the he-said-she-said confrontation, a field of negotiated action, complete with its own relevant history, is invoked through the structure of an opening accusation statement; a single utterance creates a complex past history of events, providing operative identity relationships for participants. Through careful framings of experience and "tactical uses of passion" (Bailey, 1983) in instigating stories, girls can call forth feelings of righteous indignation that are relevant to the shaping of a dispute which can last for over a month. (p. 286)

This study is most interesting because of its focus on the way children constitute social worlds and realities for themselves while speaking and playing. The one paradox of this research is that, while focusing on how children constitute their social worlds, the author chooses to place her own "constituting" activity as a researcher in the background. She deliberately chooses the role of observer and recorder of speech and behavior in order to be as unobtrusive as possible: "In order to disturb as little as possible the activities I was studying, I attempted to minimize my interaction with the children while I was observing them. In this respect my role was quite different from that of other ethnographers of children (see, for example, Corsaro 1981, 1985, p. 1–50), and indeed most anthropologists, in that I was more as observer of their activities than a participant observer" (1990, p. 23). Her research role influenced the way that she "wrote" the culture of the children because while presenting a rich and detailed analysis of their social, and especially their play, worlds her role in the construction of this world in both her actual fieldwork and especially in the written ethnography is minimized. This follows the tradition of "realist" ethnographic writing, where the author writes him/herself out of the monograph (see Marcus and Cushman, 1982). Her desire to not intrude on the lives of the children she was studying is understandable, but she was *there*, and I would like to have seen her presence marked more clearly in the ethnography.

RESEARCHER AS PLAYER

In Goodwin's study the researcher positions herself clearly in the background both in the research and in the writing of the ethnography. In contrast to the approach, Diana Kelly-Byrne's study entitled *A Child's Play Life* (1989) focuses specifically on what can be learned about play when the researcher becomes a player and a major participant in the child's play world. Kelly-Byrne was a student of Brian Sutton-Smith, and he encouraged her to conduct this unique study, which is the only study in the literature "based on . . . actually playing with a child over an extended peroid of time" (p. 1). Kelly-Byrne chose this approach for several reasons, feeling that "if play emerged as property of a relationship between participants, then it would be fruitful to observe the kind of relationship that emerged between playmates when they related to each other in a familiar environment and on a established and ongoing basis" (p. 1).

In her ethnography as in her fieldwork, Kelly-Byrne is a primary participant (she says "coparticipant") who never recedes into the background. The narrative form played an important role in the way that her play with Helen was structured and so she chooses to present her ethnography as a narrative of the phases in her play life with Helen. She sees her data and the product of her research—her ethnography—as "a series of texts and their interpretations" (p. 18). In this way we see her first meeting Helen (the seven-year-old child who becomes the subject of her research) as a baby-sitter:

> It was 5:00 of a summer's evening which I first met Helen. After she opened the front door to me, she rushed behind her mother, a tall, dark, attractive woman who smiled as she gestured for me to come in. Being intensely aware of Helen, who was, in contrast to her mother, blue-eyed, pale, and wan looking, I managed in the midst of these initial moments to greet the child, saying, "Hi! I'm Diana." What I heard in response from Helen was a comment that struck me as somewhat uncharacteristic of children one does not know. Under her breath, she said, "Um! Another Wonder Woman." (p. 37).

She is there forming and negotiating her role with Helen in the beginning of her research:

> I . . . said to her, "What have you been up to since I was last here?" She replied, "Waiting for you," quickly adding, "I've missed you. Where have you been?" "I've had lots of work to do," I said, "What work?" she inquired. "Oh, just work for the university." . . . Helen then got up from her bed where we had both been seated and walked about her room in contemplation. She began asking me what I wanted to do next. Being careful not to initiate the next activity, I kept saying that I did not much mind and turned the same question to her. After several unsuccessful attempts to elicit an answer from me, Helen went to the shelf on which her miniature animals sat. She threw a few onto the floor, saying they were mine, and then collected another handful, which she also scattered on the floor but with no comment. These were the same animals she had introduced into our play toward the end of the first meeting. On finally settling herself on the floor beside me she said, "Let's play that game." (p. 48)

She is there playing with Helen.

C: [Helen]: Woof! Woof!
A: [Kelly-Byrne]: (*Whistling*) Hi, doggie.
C: Woof! (*whispered cue about my next line*)
A: Come on dog. Come on for a walk.
C: (*Whispers for me to call her Sandy.*)
A: Come on, Sandy.
C: (*Quick barking*) Woof! Woof! Woof!
A: Be a good boy. What's the matter?
C: (*Much quicker barking continued*) (p. 83)

And she is there leaving Helen at the end of one year:

> I was ready to leave and told Helen so. She arose from the floor and walked downstairs with me. It was close to 4 P.M. As I called out to her father to let him know that I was leaving, he came out of the kitchen and instructed Helen to say goodbye to me. Rolling her eyes and muttering at her father, she walked quietly with me toward the door. I put my arm around her shoulder and said, "You know, I'm looking forward to seeing you and going to the movies. I'll call you okay? Perhaps tomorrow." But Helen's response revealed no enthusiasm at that moment: "I don't care. It's up to you," she said, with an air of detachment.
>
> With this heavy feeling between us. I finally said goodbye and walked quickly to my car, wishing only to get away. As I left I caught sight of Helen walking over to the fence and calling out to a child next door to come play with her. (pp. 201–2)

Not only is this book the only study based on the researcher's extended play with a child, but because of this quality it is the most experimental of all ethnographies of children's play. It is experimental because the researcher is paramount throughout the ethnography, as she was when the research was being conducted. The inclusion of a section on the researcher and her background, expectations, reactions, confusions, and frustrations is rare and refreshing. The format and grounding of the play in the everyday life of the child and her home is interesting and informative. The inclusion of lengthy transcripts which reveal the ways that play weaves together what seems like trivial details and dramatic happenings provides useful (and for the most part novel) information, in relation to other studies. These transcripts also illustrate the various ways that Helen attempted to control the relationship that she had established with Kelly-Byrne and the ongoing themes that organized the players activities. In Kelly-Byrne's terms these themes were "scripts" about the child's origin and identity; the battle between good and evil; the testing of her powers and weaknesses; her relationships with parents, peers, males, and females; strong women rescuing men who were weak and abandoned; the upgrading of her own supposedly inferior status as a girl by

performing super feats; understanding the polarities of smartness and dumb-
ness; sorting out the differences between good and bad mothering; making
sense of her own sexuality; and exploring the power of language to posit
worlds and transform situations (pp. 210–11).

Given the focus of the study, it would have been interesting to have
Helen comment on Kelly-Byrne's analyses or commentaries which follow
after each "session." (I also question the use of the term *session* because it
sounds too therapeutic.) With a study like this why should the researcher
always have the last word? What is most inventive and experimental about
this study is that it retains, in part, the playfulness of play. One of the ongoing
dilemmas of play research is that at the moment that we seek to understand
and investigate this phenomenon it evaporates before us. This happens at
times in this ethnography, but Kelly-Byrne is skilled as a researcher, as a
player, and as a writer, and she is able to let this be both a study of play and,
as she puts it, "a hymn to the play of childhood" (p. 253). She is able to do
this by assuming and maintaining the stance of play in both her research and
her writing.

CHILDREN, ECONOMIES, AND WORLD SYSTEMS

The child-development literature in many ways continues to operate with
romanticized images of children, as Sutton-Smith has repeatedly suggested
(see Sutton-Smith, 1983). Fortunately this is changing in several ways, and
anthropologists, sociologists, historians, and psychologists have contributed
to this refashioning of images. The recent work of Nancy Scheper-Hughes,
Death Without Weeping: The Violence of Everyday life in Brazil (1992), illustrates some ethnographers' concern with linking studies that deal with psychological issues (e.g., maternal behavior and child development) with research
on national and global systems of control and domination. This is a book
about "mother love and child death" on the Alto do Cruzeiro, a shantytown
annexed to the town of Bom Jesus da Mata located in northeast Brazil. The
residents of "O Cruzeiro" are, for the most part, plantation workers and
sugar-cane cutters in this area where "sugar is king" and has been since
Portuguese colonists arrived in the sixteenth century (p. 32). The sugar industry is examined in detail by Scheper-Hughes because it dominates life in this
area. This is a book that recognizes the critique of anthropology and the
writing of ethnography initiated by Marcus, Clifford, and others. In this case
Scheper-Hughes is "writing against terror" (see Taussig, 1987) as she uses
her experience as a Peace Corps worker in the 1960s and as an ethnographer
in the 1980s to challenge assumptions about cultural relativity and the separation of ethnography from political activism. It is a book that attempts to be
both "active and committed" and a book where the author does not hide
behind "the role of an invisible and omniscient third-person narrator. Rather, I

enter freely into dialogues and sometimes into conflicts and disagreements with the people of the Alto, challenging them just as they challenge me on my definitions of the reality in which I live" (p. 25). She is very concerned about using ethnography "as a tool for critical reflection" and as a "tool for human liberation," and she believes that one of the most important things about ethnography is to "give voice" to those "who have been silenced, as have the people of the Alto by political and economic oppression and illiteracy and as have their children by hunger and premature death" (p. 28). In this way Scheper-Hughes uses the voices of Lordes, Biu, Antonieta, and the other Alto women who are the primary focus on her study "to illustrate in a graphic way the consequences of hunger, death, and abandonment and loss on ways of thinking, feeling, acting, and being in the world" (p. 25).

This is not an easy book to read, but it is hard to put down because of Scheper-Hughes's narrative abilities. She presents compelling personal portraits of the lives of people who "are always sick and always hungry" and how they survive (those that do) and how they die (especially the children). We hear the voices and the weeping of the women as they try to cope with thirst, hunger, sickness, and death, and we hear Scheper-Hughes's reaction to the oppression, injustice, and violence which are a part of the everyday life of her informants, but we do not hear much from the children (except the crying). In fact, the title of the book is related to crying and the reaction of mothers to a life where child survival is not expected and where maternal thinking and practices (i.e., "that infants and babies are easily replacable or that some infants are born wanting to die" [p. 20]) are related to this expectation. The children who do survive are, in Scheper-Hughes's terms, "lively observers of human life and activity, full of sharp wit, and playful with words" (p. 156), but children's play is not a focus of this book. Play, however, does appear as an important way for individuals to "get by" and "make do" in this context, and the celebration of Carnaval as well as religious rituals and dramas of resistance are portrayed as important activities that "enhance the lives of the *moradores* and that hint at the possibilities of a new world, one free of hunger, social injustice, and violence" (p. 21).

A number of researchers (e.g., Garbarino, Dubrow, Kostelny, and Pardo, 1992; Garbarino, Kostelny, and Dubrow, 1991) have begun to examine the impact of everyday violence and trauma on children in various areas of the world (e.g., Mozambique, Cambodia, Israel, and Chicago). In these studies researchers have found that children are able to play even in the most distressing and deprived of circumstances. In some instances children use play and fantasy to create pockets of perceived safety in a world of danger. For example, Fish-Murray (as quoted in Garbarino et al., 1992) spoke to "one boy living in a dangerous neighborhood in Boston [who] took solace from an empty deodorant bottle that he kept by the side of his bed, a bottle that was labeled 'guaranteed 100 percent safe' " (p. 5). Children will also frequently reenact traumatic events in their play in an attempt to make sense of and try to "master" the experience.

> Sheila was almost five years old when she was shot in the hand. The circumstances of the shooting remain unclear to the staff of her local preschool program. She was with family members when it happened, and they were preparing lunch at the time she was shot. In the months following the incident, Sheila's teachers have observed her playing "shooting" during lunchtime. She "shoots" at the other children, saying "pow, pow, pow!" When asked, Sheila acknowledges, "Yeah, we're playing shoot guns." (p. 77)

Scheper-Hughes presents a compelling account of life on the Alto do Cruzeiro, but she missed an opportunity to present a detailed account of how the children of the Alto "make out" and "make do." Recent research by Garbarino et al. (1992) and others suggests that play may be an important way of "making do" in contexts like the Alto. Scheper-Hughes presents a strong case for examining how "mother love and attachment" are shaped by powerful "economic and social constraints" (p. 341). In this context we see the mother's struggle to survive and to help her children survive, but as an anthropologist concerned with the study of children's play I missed her observations on what happens to play in this environment. In a study which she describes as a "political economy of emotions," the phenomenon of children's play deserves some attention, as it is clearly influenced by the experience of scarcity, loss, and deprivation.

CONCLUSION

Anthropologists have begun to raise questions about how the lives of their informants are represented in their own writings and texts. James Clifford (1988) asks how it is that the "unruly" experience of fieldwork "is transformed into an authoritative written account" (p. 25). As anthropologists struggle to examine how they "write culture" and to what ends, their struggles suggest issues for other researchers to consider. In this paper I have discussed three recent ethnographies which illustrate three different attempts to represent children: (1) how children construct social worlds and realities in their everyday activities and especially in their play, (2) what can be learned when researchers become players, and (3) the value of studies that link psychological studies to political economy. Each of these ethnographies tells us something important about the process of representing children's lives and the significance of recognizing that these representations are always the result of a complicated interaction between anthropologists at work and children at play.

NOTES

1. The "postmodern critique" of researcher representations has itself become the subject of critique, especially for encouraging "navel-grazing" and "hyper self-consciousness" or "self-absorption" (Clifford, 1986, p. 15). Scheper-Hughes (1992) argues against an approach that makes ethnographers, and not the other, the subject of anthropological interest (p. 28).

REFERENCES

Abrahams, R. (1976). *Talking black*. Rowley, MA: Newbury House.

Bailey, F. G. (1983). *The tactical uses of passion: An essay on power, reason, and reality*. Ithaca: Cornell University Press.

Clifford, J. (1988). *The predicament of culture*. Cambridge: Harvard University Press.

Clifford, J., & Marcus, G. (1986). *Writing culture*. Berkeley: University of California Press.

Corsaro, W. A. (1981). Friendship in the nursery school: Social organization in a peer environment. In S. R. Asher and J. M. Gottman (Ed.), *The development of children's friendships*. (pp. 207–41) Cambridge: Cambridge University Press.

Corsaro, E. A. (1985). *Friendship and peer culture in the early years*. Norwood, NJ: Ablex.

Fish-Murray, C. (1990). Memories of trauma: Place and path. Keynote Presentation, NAIM Foundation Conference on Children and Trauma. Washington, D.C., October 10.

Garbarino, J., Dubrow, B., Kostelny, K. & Pardo, C. (1992). *Children in danger*. San Francisco: Jossey-Bass.

Garbarino, J., Kostelny, K., & Dubrow, B. (1991). *No place to be a child: Growing up in a war zone*. Lexington, MA: Lexington Books.

Gilligan, C. (1982). *In a different voice*. Cambridge: Harvard University Press.

Goodwin, M. H. (1990). *He-said-she-said: Talk as social organization among black children*. Bloomington: Indiana University Press.

Haight, W. L., & Miller, P. J. (1993). *Pretending at home*. Albany: State University of New York Press.

Hall, G. S. (1904). *Adolescence* (vol. 1). New York: Appleton.

Hannerz, U. (1969). *Soulside: Inquiries into ghetto culture and community*. New York: Columbia University Press.

Kelly-Byrne, D. (1989). *A child's play life: An ethnographic study*. New York: Teacher's College Press.

Maltz, D. N., & Borker, R. A. (1983). A cultural approach to male-female miscommunication. In J. J. Gumpez (Ed.), *Communication, Language, and Social Identity* (pp. 196–216). Cambridge: Cambridge University Press.

Marcus, G., & Cushman, D. (1982). Ethnographies as texts. *Annual Review of Anthropology, 11*, 25–69.

Marcus, G., & Fischer, M. (1989). *Anthropology as cultural critique*. Chicago: University of Chicago Press.

Salamone, F. A. (1989). Anthropology and play: A bibliography. *Play and Culture, 2*, 158–81.

Scheper-Hughes, N. (1992). *Death without weeping: The violence of everyday life in Brazil*. Berkeley: University of California Press.

Schieffelin, B. B. (1990). *The give and take of everyday life*, New York: Cambridge University Press.

Schwartzman, H. B. (1978). *Transformations: The anthropology of children's play*. New York: Plenum Press.

Sutton-Smith, B. (1981). *The folkstories of children*. Philadelphia: University of Pennsylvania Press.

———. (1983). Play theory and cruel play of the nineteenth century. In F. E. Manning (Ed.), *The world of play*, (pp. 103–10). West Point, NY: Leisure Press.

———. (1994). A memory of games and some games of memory. In J. Lee (Ed.), *Life before story: The autobiographies of psychologists from a narrative perspective*. (pp. 125–142) New York: Praeger.

Sutton-Smith, B., & Kelly-Byrne, D. (1984). The idealization of play. In P. K. Smith (Ed.), *Play in animals and humans*, (pp. 305–21) New York: Basil Blackwell.

Taussig, M. (1987). *Shamanism, colonialism and the wild man: A study in terror and healing*. Chicago: University of Chicago Press.

Van Maanen, J. (1988). *Tales of the field: On writing ethnography*. Chicago: University of Chicago Press.

12

BERNARD MERGEN _____

Past Play: Relics, Memory, and History

INTRODUCTION

Children's play, as Brian Sutton-Smith has argued, is often defined by the rhetoric of progress, the idea that play prepares the child for adulthood. Conceived in this way, children's play is held to be irrelevant to an understanding of adult play, which is defined by the rhetorics of conflict and community, the game itself and the freedom of the player (Sutton-Smith, 1993). Sutton-Smith rejects the dichotomy between child and adult play by suggesting that children too may play for both extrinsic and intrinsic motives. In support of his hypothesis, I offer three episodes of play (in the sense of incidents within the larger historical narrative): sledding, make-believe play (especially imaginary others), and street and neighborhood play observed in 1913 and in the 1980s. Each episode demonstrates, I think, the multiple meanings of play to children and their adult observers and suggests that children's play is more than a rehearsal for the drama of adult play, that it may also involve the resolution of conflicts, the building of community, and pure creativity.

RELICS OF PLAY

"Rosebud." The word, whispered by Orson Wells playing the dying publisher Charles Foster Kane in the 1941 motion picture "Citizen Kane," is the name of a child's sled, glimpsed in a scene of young Kane playing in the snow, and revealed at the end of the movie to be a symbol of lost opportunities and happiness. Aside from its name, a private joke between the film's writers, the sled was an excellent choice to evoke nineteenth-century childhood and to explore the meanings of play.[1]

In the scene in which Rosebud is glimpsed initially, young Charlie is heard shouting "Up and at 'em! The Union forever!" obviously playing Civil War, even though his only companion is a snowman. His snowball war is interrupted when his mother calls him to meet the banker who will become his guardian, whereupon Charlie pushes the man down into the snow with the sled. Snowball fighting, with and without sleds, plays a prominent role in a wide range of American literature (Aldrich, 1990; Beard,

257

1880; Adams, 1918), but it is difficult to know how children themselves regarded these activities.

Because children, even when literate, leave few written records of their activities, except at the request of adults, one of the basic sources for historical research—written documents—does not exist. Generalizations about the history of childhood and children's play must, therefore, be based on a combination of surviving artifacts such as pictures and playthings, recollections, and adult observations. The past is, as David Lowenthal (1985) observes, a foreign country, known only by memory, history, and relics (pp. 185–259). Let Rosebud represent sleds, one type of relic of past play.[2]

Sleds, and other material artifacts of the past, become relics in Lowenthal's sense when memory and history declare them important. They are said to be valuable for the information they provide about bygone technologies and social activities. They symbolize beliefs, attitudes, and behaviors. Yet their meanings can be reinterpreted for different purposes and in different historical contexts. The ambiguity of objects, illustrations, and other nonverbal material, as the archaeologist Ian Hodder (1983) has argued, means that they should be considered "more like a performance or play than an abstract code or language" (p. 214). Toys play with memories. Historians must gather "Rosebuds" with the less exotic specimens of sleds to create a satisfying history of play.

Early-nineteenth-century illustrations of children sledding depict a variety of sleds that are little more than boards with runners nailed to each side. The runners were often barrel staves; homemade sleds were patched together from scraps of lumber. They had names such as "Ranger," "Rover," "Racer," and, after 1865, "General Grant." Until the 1870s, most children expected to make their own playthings. The implications of this for an understanding of the meanings of children's play are profound. Children remained producers of their culture while the industrial revolution was turning their parents into consumers. In many ways, becoming a consumer is a passage to adulthood. Contemporary advertising seeks to make children part of the community of consumers, erasing the distinction between them and adults, by displaying scaled-down versions of the clothing, cars, and electronics available to their parents (Seiter, 1993). The replacement of handmade playthings by manufactured toys as early as the 1880s was noted by William Allen White, editor of the *Emporia Gazette*: "In the boy's world, it meant that homemade sleds and little homemade wagons would pass; that the bows and arrows which boys made by seasoning the hickory behind the stove and scraping and polishing them with glass, would as an art disappear forever out of the life of American boys" (White, 1946, p. 44).

Thus, the relics of children's play preserved in lithographs and in museum collections suggest that an activity such as sledding may have involved both more manual skill and more individual effort than it does at present.[3] The illustrations also suggest that sledding was seen by adults to involve gender and age distinctions: girls and young boys are shown seated on their sleds, feet forward; older boys are depicted belly down and face forward. Patent applications in 1859 and 1862 for manufactured sleds confirm that the sledding hill was literally contested terrain: " . . . the medical board have remonstrated against the practice of lying upon the stomach and chest while the sleigh is in motion," argued B. P. Crandall, "and as young America still persists in this practice, I offer the above as an improvement in the construction of children's sleds, that will prevent in a measure, the many fatal accidents" (Crandall, 1859). Crandall's design included a carved horse's head at the front of the sled that made it difficult for a child to lie face forward.

The other patent application involved a pivoted runner attached to a tiller for steering: "Boy's sleds of the ordinary construction—such as are generally used for 'coasting' or going down over the slope of the hill—are guided by pushing the heel or foot down on the side to which it is desired to head the sled. This operation causes considerable wear and tear of the boots, particularly with boys having little practice in coasting, and if the motion of the sled is rapid and the snow which is scraped off by pushing the heel down flies up on the inside and outside of the pantaloons and causes a disagreeable feeling to the operator" (Brown, 1862). While the inventor here assumes that boys are seated with legs forward, not "belly bumping," and the concern seems to be more with "wear and tear on the boots" than with safety, the purpose is similar—the enforcement of parentally approved sledding form.

No self-respecting young man or woman accepted these prescriptions on sledding technique. Mary Ellen Chase, who grew up in Maine in the 1890s, recalled coasting "down the slopes for hours with a wonderful sense of freedom. When the road outside the gate had been broken after a storm and pounded smooth by sledges and sleighs, we coasted down our long hill, going 'belly-bump' on our sleds, a quarter-mile slide nearly to the village" (1954, p. 45). Freedom and speed remain the twin goals of children's sled play, while better steering and safety continue to occupy adult designers and play supervisors. Municipal recreation departments attempt to restrict sledding to parks and traffic-free streets, but children still find pleasure in careening past pedestrians and risking the hazards of traffic. Little wonder that most nineteenth century sleds have been destroyed and survive only in the written descriptions of keen observers like Emily Dickinson:

> Glass was in the street—in tinsel Peril
> Tree and Traveller stood—
> Filled was the Air with merry venture
> Hearty with Boys the Road—

Shot the lithe Sleds like shod vibrations
Emphasized and gone
It is the Past's supreme italic
Makes this Present mean—
(Johnson, 1970, 630)

The most successful of all adult inventors of sleds, Samuel L. Allen, patented what soon became the "Flexible Flyer" in 1889, providing some control with no sacrifice of speed. He also showed a genius for promotion by adopting a logo with an American eagle holding arrows in both talons, thereby appropriating the combative spirit of earlier sledding. The sled was flexible in more than its steering. Company lore claims that Allen built his first sled for his daughter, yet he successfully marketed his product for both boys and girls at a time when other companies were still manufacturing "gooseneck" sleds and toboggans for girls (Blazon-Flexible Flyer brochure, 1988; Sears Roebuck, 1919).

What "Rosebud" the fictional sled and "Flexible Flyer" the generic sled have in common is what Sutton-Smith (1992) has called the play of "multiple selves . . . and their collective fantasies" (p. 100). Relic sleds lie mute in attics, in museums, and in picture books, but they spring to life in the fantasies of adults who mentally "belly-bump" to a place they can play. Nor am I surprised, thanks to what Sutton-Smith and others have observed about gender and play, that women write passionately about sledding. From the "long delirious descent" that Edith Wharton gave Ethan Frome and Mattie Silver, to the sledding that "tapped some madness in us" described in a poem by Florence Grossman, women have shown that children's play provides opportunities to avoid, challenge, and subvert the established order (Wharton, 1911, p. 124; Grossman, 1989, p. 464).

The prominence of the sled in depictions of children's play in the 1850s; its frequent mention by both boys and girls in Worcester, Massachusetts, in 1896; and the dozens of models available in stores in the 1990s suggests that sledding holds an important place in the history of children's play, regardless of its low ranking in Sutton-Smith and Rosenberg's survey of game preferences of children in northwestern Ohio in 1959 (Croswell, 1898, p. 326; Rosenberg and Sutton-Smith, 1961, pp. 17–46). Despite being limited to a single season in the northern regions of the United States, the sled is an important tool for both adults and children in the construction of an identity. Boys aggressively threatening pedestrians, girls experiencing forbidden madness, and filmmakers dramatizing the corruption of innocence all contribute to a history of sled play. That history shows a remarkable persistence over time. Urbanization has limited the opportunities for sledding, but technology offers more types of sleds. Adults continue to search for the safest sled, children continue to prefer the most dangerous (Ridenour, 1989).

MEMORIES OF IMAGINED PLAY

Una Mary is not as renowned as Rosebud, but she should be. The imaginary companion of Una Clarke, who was born in Cincinnati in 1876, Una Mary was vividly recalled in 1914 by her creator, Una Atherton (Clarke) Hunt. *Una Mary: The Inner Life of a Child* is an example of history through memory. Hunt's autobiography of childhood focuses on play, especially fantasy play. This in itself is unusual in the literature of childhood, but what sets the book apart and makes it particularly useful is the author's skill in recreating convincing childhood experiences while offering her own analysis of her childhood fantasies. *Una Mary* makes a good case for Sutton-Smith's proposition that play in childhood is a dialectic and that solitary play and fantasy provide more than simple escape.

Una Clarke created Una Mary when she was about three and a half years old to differentiate herself "from the Una who was just a member of a family, so different from the me our friends saw and talked to, who played with toys, sat on people's laps, and 'took walks,' dragged about the streets by the nurse who wheeled my sister's carriage; and, above all, who wore the clothes I hated, of dark blue or brown, because they 'did not show the soot like white' " (Hunt, 1914, p. 6). Una Clarke's litany of a child's complaints against adults is interesting. She was the first child of parents whom she describes as Bostonians and Unitarians who believed in "plain living and high thinking" (p. 26). Her father was a professor of chemistry at the University of Cincinnati, who moved when Una was nine to Washington, D.C., where he worked for the Smithsonian Institution. Una's response to what seems a typical upper-middle-class childhood of the 1880s was a rejection of plain living, but an elaboration of high thinking.

Although the imaginary Una Mary wore rings, bracelets, and colorful clothes, she was concerned with the mysteries of birth and death. A trip to the woods with her father inspired Una to create an imaginary place, "My Country," and another companion, Edward, who later became "Edward Christ," a young man of about nineteen, a prince of "My Country," which shared space on the Persian rug with "the holey land" and was populated by chessmen. Summers in the country, where she read *Ivanhoe* and *The Last of the Mohicans*, led Una to create more imaginary lands and people. "It was Una who played the Mythology games," the author writes, "but Una Mary to whom parts of Mythology became religion" (p. 89). Una Clarke's voracious reading, which included *Pilgrim's Progress*, Kate Greenaway, Washington Irving, and Cervantes, as well as Greek mythology, was clearly an inspiration for many of her fantasies; others sprang from the ghost stories she heard from the African American, Chinese, and Irish servants of her own and her friends' families.

While Una is depicted as living largely in a world of make-believe, she is also shown playing with friends and relatives. The play occurs outdoors as well as indoors, is active as well as quiet. The author's treatment of Una's play makes little distinction between games and fantasy play; they are almost continuous. Her school friends joined in her fantasy world, helping her create a magazine they called *The Ghost's Companion* and a dictionary of words they made up to express feelings unique to childhood, such as "pliditrants" (children left alone in the night) and "mingy" (the "half-exhilarated, half-giddy feeling while swinging to the top of a beam" [pp. 237–38]). She and her friends identify themselves by colors and things. Una was a sailboat, a pair of forceps, and a picture book, Una Mary a crystal ball and a gold ring. Her fantasy world and the book end at age thirteen with a reconciliation of the two personalities and her acceptance of Una as real.

I have been unable to find additional biographical information on Una Atherton Clarke Hunt, except that she wrote another volume of autobiography, but it is clear that Una Mary remained vividly in her mind until she was in her thirties. Is her autobiography a valid source for the history of children's play? My recent survey of seventy-eight autobiographies of childhood found that only 10 percent of the women authors and only 2 percent of the male autobiographers mention imaginary others, while 71 and 48 percent respectively mention make-believe play. Make-believe or "pretend" play was by far the most frequently mentioned kind of play by women autobiographers and was a close third, after games of skill and violent (rough-and-tumble) play, among the male writers (Mergen, 1992, p. 163). An earlier study of imaginary playmates concluded that 25 percent of Americans have an imaginary other at some time in their lives (Thompson and Johnson, 1977).

Imaginary companions are a variation on make-believe play and probably should not be treated separately, nor are they necessarily the products of solitary children in isolated surroundings. Imaginary playmates may, as Hunt shows, be shared with others, or, as in another case, be created by siblings (Gillespie, 1976, pp. 7, 42). Like other episodes of pretend play, they involve the invention of characters who can do things better than their creators. They are wishes that, within the "virtual reality" of play, can be fulfilled. Nor does the fact that the wish is not recognized by others completely destroy its usefulness. As long as the fantasy satisfies its creator, it will survive as an alternative reality.

I became convinced of this when reading the reminiscences of ex-slaves as recorded by interviewers from the Federal Writer's Project in the 1930s. More than 300 of the approximately 3,000 interviews mention some form of play. Albeit data from these life histories are limited by the shortcomings of the interviewers and the fading memories of ex-slaves, who were all well past seventy years of age, but the value of their testimony lies in its uniqueness. No comparable data exists for other populations in this period. The former slaves provide a voice for children of the 1850s. By my count, doll play was the most popular kind of play among girls, marble games among boys (Mergen, 1982, pp. 45, 53). Playing house and other forms of make-believe play were also mentioned frequently by both sexes.

Not surprisingly, the children of slave owners initiated the fantasies, which tended to confirm racial inequalities. One woman remembered that "Miss Lee have a china doll with a wreath of roses round its head. We take turns playn' with it. I had a rag doll, and it jes' a bundle of rags with strings tied round it to give it shape" (Rawick, 1972, ser. 1, vol. 5, p. 147). A man's recollections cast light on the complex mix of racial and gender roles when playing with his master's daughter: "I help her to make mud pies many a day and put them on the chicken coop, in de sun to dry. Her had two dolls; deir names was Dorcas and Priscilla. When de pies got dry, she's take them under de big oak tree, fetch out de dolls and talk whole lot of child-mother talk 'bout de pies, to de Dorcas and Priscilla rag dolls" (Rawick, ser. 1, vol. 3, p. 39).

Making mud pies was appropriate male play, "child-mother talk" was not. Playing house was recalled by women, as were playing church and pretend funerals. Zillah Cross Peel told the interviewer about an incident that reveals both the dimensions of play and adult attitudes toward it in the ante-bellum south:

> One of Mr. Parks' daughters was about one and a half years older than I was. We had a play house back of the fire place chimney. We didn't have many toys; maybe a doll made of a corn cob, with a dress made from scraps and a head made from a roll of scraps. We were playing church. Miss Fannie was the preacher and I was the audience. We were singing "Jesus all to Heaven is gone." When we were half way through with our song we discovered that the passengers from the stage coach had stopped to listen. We were so frightened at our audience that we both ran. But we were coaxed to come back for a dime and sing our song over. I remember that Miss Fannie us a big leaf for a book. (Rawick, ser. 1, vol. 8, pp. 11–12)

The travelers appear to have treated slave and mistress as equals in childhood and their play as amusement worthy of purchase. Such play must have been common in the religious communities of the south. An ex-slave from Mississippi remembered playing by the cabins, making rows of graves and decorating them with weeds and wild flowers (Rawick, 1977, ser. 2, vol. 8, p. 892). More than fifty years later in Burnside, Kentucky, Harriet Arnow played a game in which a child pretended to be dead and others buried her in leaves and preached a sermon. The "dead man" could become a ghost and take a more active role in the game (Arnow, 1977, p. 55).

Boys played war. "When de war came, we'd play Yankee an' 'Federates, 'course de whites was always de 'Federates. Take us black boys prisoners an' make b'lieve dey was gonna cut our necks off. Guess dey got dat idea from dere fathers," said a former slave from Virginia, and a man who went to school during Reconstruction recalled that, "Jes' for fun us call ourselves big names to de teacher, some be named General Lee and Stonewall Jackson. We be one name one day, 'nother name next day" (Perdue et al., p. 109; Rawick, ser. 1, vol. 5, p. 184). Although details are lacking, it is plausible to imagine that the war games of slave children were played as intensely and violently as were the mock World War I battles played by Woody Guthrie in Oklahoma in the 1920s, which employed barrels as tanks and fire-heated rocks as ammunition (Guthrie, 1943, p. 103).

As Sutton-Smith's collection of children's folkstories (1981) shows, children still possess fervid imaginations, although their opportunities to act on them may be more limited. The assumption by many play researchers that children need to develop their imaginations in order to develop social competence in adulthood cannot be supported by historical evidence. What is also unclear are the long-term effects of television viewing on children's fantasies.

There is no question that children in the 1990s watch a lot of television. Criticism of excessive watching has been strong since the 1970s, when a major study concluded that children as young as five were watching as much as thirty hours a week (Comstock et al., 1978, p. 177). More recent surveys estimate less than half that amount, but all studies report that younger children watch more than older children and boys watch more than girls (Carpenter, Huston, and Spera, 1989, p. 177). In Washington, D.C., watching television, including videos, and playing video games are the preferred indoor fun of boys aged fourteen to sixteen, both alone and with friends. Girls agree, except that they prefer talking on the telephone to watching television when playing with friends (Mergen, 1991, pp. 278–79).

What are children watching and what effect does it have on their make-believe play? In a year in which Barney the dinosaur is criticized for being too saccharine, while *Beavis and Butt-head* is condemned for nihilism, it is clear that adult critics focus chiefly on text rather than the context of viewing. Children are often aware of adult criticisms and show rather mature cynicism toward both programs and advertising (Buckingham, 1991). Dorothy Singer, who has studied the effects of television on children's imaginative play for more than twenty years, has concluded that children watch for at least four reasons: to escape from problems of everyday life, because they identify with a character, as a form of wish fulfillment, and for information (Singer, 1978, pp. 146–47). Other studies have shown that children "eat, drink, dress and undress, play, fight, and do other things while in front of the set" (Comstock, et al., 1978, pp. 146–47).

Clearly, television has been the single most important change in children's use of time and in their leisure behavior in the past half century. Equally clear in my view is the way in which it functions—as reading, radio, popular live entertainment, and events of daily life function—to stimulate children's imaginations. Television programs teach children the rudiments of narrative structure, commercials teach them to desire the status symbols of the adult world. When the messages of educational media and commercial entertainment conflict, children are left (occasionally with parental help) to resolve the contradictions. The Una Hunt of the television age may be Donald Bowie, who, in his youthful autobiography *Station Identification: Confessions of a Video Kid* (1980), declared that Howdy Doody taught him naughtiness and that Froggie the gremlin on the Buster Brown Show of the 1950s made him realize that there was a battle-line between "discipline and fun, restraint and the lack of it." Froggie's magic twanger and raucous laugh signaled chaos and escape from "the drab, workaday world where most people live, [where] being happy is in itself an act of rebellion" (pp. 27–33).

It is doubtful that Bowie had to learn from Howdy Doody how to be naughty, but his point about seeking happiness in everyday life is revealing. It is one of the paradoxes of everyday life that it is about everything and nothing, both a universal and a unique condition. The French historians and philosophers who have made the concepts of *quotidien* and *quotidiennete*— the everyday and everydayness—a touchstone of recent cultural analysis admit the banality of everydayness but argue that "the surreal, the extraordinary, the surprising, even the magical, [are] also part of the real" (Lefebvre, 1987, p. 9). To explain the effects of television on children's play, I submit, we need to see it as part of the child's everyday life, like school, work, encounters with grown-ups, and play.

William James, as Jay Mechling reminds us, proposed that we experience everyday life as a whole, not as discreet moments, and that we have only vague ideas about what is happening to us as it takes place (Mechling, 1985, p. 305). Therefore, we constantly seek to interpret what we experience. Most of this interpretation is done subconsciously, especially by children, who are still in the process of acquiring the verbal skills necessary to communicate their interpretations to others. They can, however, express their feelings and reactions in the running, shouting, hiding, seeking, building, destroying, mimicking, and pretending activities that are called "play." That television provides much of the form and content incorporated into play is less important than the fact that the form and content is transformed by a process that seems similar to pretelevision fantasy. An illustration of what I mean is provided by two stories written by six-year-old girls. The first is by Lesley Frost, daughter of the poet Robert Frost, who entered the following in her diary in 1905:

> my bow and arrow
>
> this spring we thought uf making a bow and arrow we have got the bow redy and the string redy but not the arrow and if i shoot it in the snow i will loos it this spring i will have to go out without carol [her brother] because i mit hurnt him and i will go ufu in the grov and play shoot woolfs and carol cood not go with me and snider [her dog] will come ufu with me and bark up trees. (Frost, 1969).

The second comes from a child in a day-care center in New York City in 1974, as reported by Sutton-Smith (1981):

> The mouse that came from outer space
>
> Hi! I am the mouse from the other world in Joopatre. [Teacher corrected spelling.] Jupiter is a fasanting world in Jupiter I go ear skating but there are dajrs [dangers] too. Like when you are skating you might slip and you could break a bone and I would think you would die. So in Jupiter be careful because you can hurt hoursalf. Also in Jupiter you can go slipiripring but I wood think that you wook hate yourself so be carflle thats the sakind time that I told you abot darnjer so stil be cafl in Jupiter. (pp. 162–63).

Although it is risky to generalize too much from these stories, it seems to me that the world has changed more than six-year-old girls. Both are preoccupied with danger and injury, both are developing a sense of themselves as individuals. The difference that I am emphasizing is that Frost's interpretation of her experience is based on the activity of making a toy, while the young New Yorker's story incorporates knowledge of the larger universe, knowledge of which may easily have come from television.

Children's make-believe play has a history, but a history so ephemeral that it is usually lost. All we can do as historians is look closely at the specifics of everydayness in the past. What daily events affected children and what did the experiences of everyday life provide them with? What banalities and what wonders did children need to escape from or to? A partial answer lies in adult descriptions of a child's day.

HISTORIES OF PLAY TIMES AND PLACES

Relics and memories need interpretation. History is interpretation. In this third episode of play, "Mostly Just Fooling" joins Rosebud and Una Mary. "Mostly Just Fooling" is the adult historians' verdict on most children's activities. Children's play began to have a history in the 1880s, when the folklorist William Wells Newell, the psychologist G. Stanley Hall, and the autobiographer Lucy Larcom published their books (Newell, 1883; Hall, 1883;

Larcom, 1889). Although Louisa May Alcott (1868), Thomas Bailey Aldrich (1869), and Mark Twain (Clements, 1876) had led the way with evocative accounts of children's lives in the 1840s, the dawning of the social sciences led to the study of children's play with a new self-consciousness and a reformist spirit. Children's play not only had a history, but that history was coming to an end: "The vine of oral tradition, of popular poetry, which for a thousand years has twined and bloomed on English soil, in other days enriching with color and fragrance equally the castle and the cottage, is perishing at the roots; its prouder branches have long since been blasted, and children's song, its humble but longest-flowering offshoot, will soon have shared their fate" (Newell, 1883, p. 1).

Newell collected rhymes and games, mostly from children on the streets of New York City, in the tradition of English and European folklorists. He was struck by the paradox that children were both very inventive in their fantasy play and very conservative in their repetition of rhyming and singing games. He found in this traditional play the history of European aristocratic society—"the country retained what the city forgot"—a history that was being overwhelmed by the tide of immigrants from southern and eastern Europe (p. 7). Newell, and later the leaders of the Playground Association of America, collected to conserve. Their conservation movement, like that of the Progressive movement in general, was based on efficient use, not pure nostalgia. Children's play could no be preserved or restored to some early-nineteenth-century ideal, but it could be managed, reshaped, and directed toward socially desirable goals.

Hall and Larcom inspired different approaches to children's play, one striving for objectivity through quantification, the other for emotion through personal memory, but both contextualized play in time. Larcom's immediate successors, William Dean Howells (1890) and Edward Everett Hale (1893) created detailed inventories of their boyhood play, presenting it as a product of almost rural and preindustrial conditions. Hall, on the other hand, trained graduate students to conduct surveys of children's play (Croswell, 1898), which in turn inspired other surveys (McGhee, 1900). By June 23, 1913, when the Chief Medical Inspector and Assistant Superintendent in Charge of Physical Education in Cleveland, Ohio, organized a census of children's activities, there was general agreement that play was important for education and human development and that play was defined as organized games (Johnson, 1916).

From a contemporary perspective these surveys are deeply flawed, and any attempt to use them to measure historical changes in children's play are doomed to failure. The early surveyors tell us little of their sampling methods. Nevertheless, the studies done in the 1890s and early twentieth century provide a rough baseline against which to compare more recent surveys. Let us contrast children's everyday activities on a June day in 1913 in Cleveland with a few days in April–May, September–October in Lawrence Kansas, in the late 1980s (Carpenter, Huston, and Spera, 1989).

The twelve Cleveland surveyors counted a total of 14,683 children: 7,799 on streets, 3,581 in yards, 833 in vacant lots, 1,869 in playgrounds, and 551 in alleys. There is a strong possibility that some of these children were counted more than once. There were 8,920 boys and 5,763 girls, suggesting that more girls than boys were inside during all or part of the census. The largest number, 58 percent of the boys and 44 percent of the girls, were on the streets. Slightly more girls were seen in yards, more boys in alleys and on vacant lots. Only 11 percent of the boys and 15 percent of the girls, a total of 1,869 children, were in playgrounds, a statistic similar to surveys in other cities (Johnson, 1916, p. 51; Norton, 1937, pp. 12–13; Children's Bureau, 1917, p. 14). Moreover, only half the children were categorized as playing: 10 percent were working and 40 percent were "doing nothing," while of those who were playing, 43 percent were "mostly just fooling" rather than playing approved games. The census takers found no differences between boys and girls in "doing nothing" and "just fooling." Although the surveyors included "fighting, teasing, pitching pennies, shooting craps, stealing apples, 'roughing a peddler,' chasing chickens, and tying can to dog" as play, they excluded such activities as "playing with fire," "breaking electric light bulbs," "chalking suggestive words on buildings," "shooting air guns," "bumming around aimlessly," "building dens," "fighting," "junk picking," and "telling bad stories" (Bellamy, 1916, pp. 31–32).

More than seventy years later, research was conducted with 117 boys and girls seven to eleven years old in "a small Midwestern city" to determine their use of out-of-school time and to correlate their activities with variables such as adult supervision, gender, social status, and intellectual development (Carpenter, Huston, and Spera, 1989, pp. 169–71). The method used to survey the children's activities was a week-long diary in which each child was asked to record his or her activities at fifteen-minute intervals from 3 P.M. to midnight on weekdays and from 6 A.M. to midnight on weekends. The diary entries were then coded in twenty categories, including "chores," "personal hygiene," "sleep," "transportation," "pet care," "interactions with people," "reading/homework," "listening to music," "lessons," "television," "video games," "shopping," "meals and snacks," "in-the-home organized activities," "in-the-home unorganized activities" (the distinction was based on whether the child generated his/her own rules for the activity!), "loafing," "out-of-the-home organized and unorganized activities" (organized trips to ball games as opposed to "roaming the neighborhood"), "sports," and "undetermined" (pp. 173–75).

A simple comparison of the categories of children's activities reveals the sweeping changes in adult attitudes toward children and children's play in little more than three generations. A simple tripart division of work, play, and doing nothing has been replaced by a classification that distinguishes between television viewing and video games, attending a ball game and participating in it. Even when the categories of sleeping, eating, homework, lessons, and other in-the-home activities are removed because they were beyond the scope of the Cleveland survey, the American child of the 1980s is seen to be engaged in many more identifiable activities, each measurable and related to other variables of socialization and development. More significant, I think, is the impact of the technology developed since 1913: the automobile, radio, television, tape recorder, and video games. Notable, too, is the obvious omission of playgrounds from the 1989 data. The focus of concern in 1913 was on where children's time was spent; today it is on how that time is spent.

Despite the vast differences in purpose and method of the two surveys, it is possible to make some comparisons and draw some conclusions about the history of children's play in the twentieth century. Work, for example, is far less important for children in 1989, filling a little over five of the eighty-one hours studied during the week. Organized sports occupy about the same amount of time, less than two hours a week of boys' time and less than an hour of girls', based on the assumption that the 16 percent of Cleveland boys seen playing baseball spent about three hours a game, while the other 84 percent were doing something else. Since I have already discussed television watching, it remains only to point out that "loafing," if it is roughly equivalent to "doing nothing," has almost disappeared as a children's activity. Neither boys nor girls have more than a few minutes a week to loaf (Carpenter, Huston, and Spera, 1989, p. 177).

Of course, some of the differences are the result of sampling. The Cleveland survey presumably included children younger than seven and older than eleven. Others are caused by the self-recording diary method. Changed definitions of play also present a problem for the historian. Unorganized activities in and out of the home probably included some examples of make-believe play, but neither set of researchers included this kind of play in their surveys, despite that fact that Peter K. Smith and Ralph Vollstedt (1985) found that observers in nursery schools consistently "recognize play as being enjoyable, flexible, and most typically characterized by pretend" (p. 1049). It is unfortunate if laboratory studies and ecological studies exclude each other's definitions of play and other children's activities.

Those concerned with where children play offer evidence that points to both continuity and change in children's play. Robin C. Moore (1986), tireless advocate for redesigning cities for children, not surprisingly finds that children prefer to play on lawns, in playgrounds, in school yards, and in parks, yet concedes that streets, pavements, footpaths, parking lots, vacant lots, and bus stops are also attractive places for many children (p. 41). Sanford Gaster's interesting study of children's use of the Inwood neighborhood at the northern tip of Manhattan from 1915 to 1976 concludes that children in the periods 1915–1940 and 1940–1960 were allowed to go away from home at a slightly earlier age than children of the mot recent generation and that they recalled visiting slightly more places in the neighborhood (Gaster, 1991, p. 79). In contrast, Amanda Dargan and Steven Zeitlin (1990) offer evidence that children's play in lower Manhattan is still varied and complex, although they, too, call for "a conscious effort" to preserve play spaces in cities (p. 173).

CONCLUSIONS

I have briefly described and discussed three episodes of play: sledding, make-believe, and frequently seen everyday activities. Perhaps what I have described is not play; perhaps it is a mask for something else. If play is a "devious kind of expression and communication" (Sutton-Smith and Kelly-Byrne, 1984, p. 197) that is sometimes labeled play by the players, sometimes by observers, sometimes by neither, and sometimes by both, then I think my selection of examples serves its purpose. Sledding is almost certainly defined as play by both participants and observers, make-believe is sometimes regarded as something less or more than play, while everyday activities run the gamut of play and not-play behaviors. All three of these episodes contain examples of historical continuity and of change. Forms change, functions remain the same (sleds). Functions change, forms remain (make-believe—shifting from active creation to passive escape). Functions and forms change (everyday activities—work, play, "mostly just fooling").

I think of the past as an abandoned playground. I walk through it measuring and photographing the rusting apparatus. I recall the things I used to do there. Panels of experts reconstruct it. A few children join us in play. On a distant hill a few others are sledding. Hidden in basements, yards, and alleys some children are pretending. More are loafing in front of television sets, watching others play. The invisible but real boundary the children create between play and not-play is perpetually shattered and rebuilt in the course of the day. The moments of play, however defined, are brief compared to the time spent anticipating and preparing for play, then remembering it. It is this everydayness of play that the historian must seek to recover and describe. The contribution of the historian to the study of play is to remind the psychologist, sociologist, and anthropologist that all play is *past play* in the double sense.

First, whether in the laboratory or in its natural environments, both the text and the context of whatever is defined as play is the product of earlier experiences of play. Second, play observed, recorded, analyzed, and classified is itself a kind of fantasy, one that satisfies the adult desire to explain and to pretend to know what play is.

NOTES

1. See Robin Bates (1987, p. 5) for a review of the sources for Orson Welles and Herman Mankiewicz's selection of "rosebud," a slang term for female genitalia.

2. In the spirit of Brian Sutton-Smith, I am indulging in a bit of word play, intending two meanings to the phrase "past play." In one sense I mean historical play, specifically children's play, but in another sense I mean an activity that is taken beyond the usual definition of play—a game that becomes a metaphor, a fantasy that inspires a creative act, a toy that becomes an icon. I hope this will became clear in the three episodes of play provided in this essay.

3. Perhaps the earliest depiction of sledding in America is an 1809 watercolor by Baroness Hyde de Neuville of a winter scene in Manhattan (Dargan and Zeitlin, 1990, p. 95). Lithographs made in the 1860s often show children sledding. My source for the names of sleds is titled "Winter," and was published by Haskell and Allen of Boston. It is reproduced in Mergen (1989, p. 178). Another good illustration is an engraving by Granville Perkins, "Winter Sports: Coasting in the Country," *Harper's Weekly*, February 17, 1877. I have also looked at sleds in the collections of The Margaret Woodbury Strong Museum in Rochester, New York, and other museums, and, with help from my graduate student, Peggy Hermann, I have examined more than forty patents for sleds registered between 1859 and 1975. I thank her for her assistance.

REFERENCES

Adams, H. (1918). *The education of Henry Adams*. Boston: Massachusetts Historical Society.

Alcott, L. M. (1868). *Little women*. Boston: Roberts Brothers.

Aldrich, T. B. (1990). *The Story of a Bad Boy*. Hanover & London: University Press of New England. [Originally published, 1869.]

Allen, S. L. (1889). Sled. Patent No. 408,681. United States Patent Office.

Arnow, H. S. (1977). *Old Burnside*. Lexington: University of Kentucky Press.

Bates, R. (1987). Fiery speech in a world of shadows: Rosebud's impact on early audiences. *Cinema Journal, 26*(2), 3–26.

Beard, D. C. (1880, January). Snow-ball warfare. *St. Nicholas Magazine*, 263–66.

Bellamy, G. A. (1916). City recreation. In *Play and Recreation*, 30–41. Bloomington: Bulletin of the Indiana Extension Division of Indiana University.

Blazon-Flexible Flyer (1988). Snow products [catalog]. New York.

Bowie, D. (1980). *Station identification: Confessions of a video kid.* New York: M. Evans.

Brown, J. N. (1862). Improvement in boys' sleds. Patent No. 34,874. United States Patent Office.

Buckingham, D. (1991). What are words worth? Interpreting children's talk about television. *Cultural Studies, 5*, 228–45.

Carpenter, C. J., Huston, A. C., & Spera, L. (1989). Children's use of time in their everyday activities during middle childhood. In M. N. Bloch & A. D. Pellegrini (Eds.), *The ecological context of children's play* (pp. 165–90). Norwood, NJ: Ablex Pub. Co.

Chase, M. E. (1954). *The white gate: Adventures in the imagination of a child.* New York: Norton.

Children's Bureau. (1917). *Facilities for children's play in the District of Columbia.* Washington, D.C.: U.S. Department of Labor, Miscellaneous Series No. 8, Bureau Publication No. 22.

Clemens, S. L. [Mark Twain]. (1987). *The adventures of Tom Sawyer.* Hartford, CT: American Publishing Co.

Comstock, G., (1978). *Television and human behavior.* New York: Columbia University Press.

Crandall, B. P. (1859). Childs sled. Patent No. 26,164. United States Patent Office.

Croswell, T. R. (1899). Amusements of Worcester school children. *The Pedagogical Seminary, 6*, 314–71.

Dargan, A., & Zeitlin, S. (1990). *City play.* New Brunswick, NJ: Rutgers University Press.

Frost, L. (1969). *New Hampshire's child: The Derry journals of Lesley Frost.* Albany: State University of New York Press.

Gaster, S. (1991). Urban children's access to their neighborhoods: Changes over three generations. *Environment and Behavior, 23*, 70–85.

Gillespie, J. (1976). *With a merry heart.* New York: Harper & Row.

Grossman, F. (1989, April 3). Sledding. *The Nation*, 464.

Guthrie, W. (1943). *Bound for glory.* New York: Dutton.

Hale, E. E. (1893). *A New England boyhood.* Boston: Cassell.

Hall, G. S. (1883). The contents of children's minds. *Princeton Review, 11*, 249–72.

Hodder, I. (1983). *The present past: An introduction to anthropology for archaeologists.* New York: Pica.

Howells, W. D. (1890). *A boy's town.* New York: Harper & Bros.

Hunt, U. A. (1914). *Una Mary: The inner life of a child.* New York: Scribner's.

Johnson, G. E. (1916). *Education through recreation.* Cleveland: Survey Committee of the Cleveland Foundation.

Johnson, T. H. (Ed.). (1970). *The complete poems of Emily Dickinson.* London: Faber and Faber.

Larcom, L. (1889). *A New England girlhood.* Boston: Houghton Mifflin.

Lefebvre, H. (1987). The everyday and everydayness. *Yale French Studies, 73*, 7–11.

Lowenthal, D. (1985). *The past as a foreign country.* New York: Cambridge University Press.

McGhee, Z. (1900). A study of the play life of some South Carolina children. *The Pedagogical Seminary, 7*, 459–78.

Mechling, J. (1985). Introduction: William James and the philosophical foundations for the study of everyday life. *Western Folklore, 44*, 301–10.

Mergen, B. (1982). *Play and playthings.* Westport, CT: Greenwood Press.

———. (1989) Winter landscape in the early republic. In M. Gidley and R. Lawson-Peebles (Eds.) *Views of American Landscapes. New York: Cambridge University Press, 167–182.*

———. (1991). Ninety-five Years of historical change in the game preferences of American children. *Play and Culture, 4*, 272–83.

———. (1992). Children's play in American autobiographies, 1820–1914. In K. Grover (Ed.), *Hard at play: Leisure in America, 1840–1940* 161–87. Amherst and Rochester: University of Massachusetts Press and the Strong Museum, 161–87.

Moore, R. C. (1986). *Childhood's domain: Play and place in child development.* London: Croom Helm.

Newell, W. W. (1883). *Games and songs of American children.* New York: Harper Brothers.

Norton, E. V. (1937). *Play streets.* New York: Barnes.

Perdue, C. L., T. E. Barden, and R. K. Phillips, Eds. (1976). *Weevils in the wheat: Interviews with Virginia ex-slaves.* Charlottesville: University of Virginia Press.

Rawick, G. P. (1972–1977). *The American slave: A composite autobiography* (series 1, 19 vols.; series 2, 12 vols.). Westport, CT: Greenwood.

Ridenour, M. V. (1989). Children's snow sleds: Age appropriateness and safety. *Perceptual and Motor Skills, 68*, 883–90.

Rosenberg, B. G., & Sutton-Smith, B. (1961). Sixty years of historical change in the game preferences of American children. *Journal of American Folklore, 74*, 17–46.

Sears Roebuck & Co. (1919). *General catalogue*. Chicago.

Seiter, E. (1993). *Sold separately: Parents and children in consumer culture*. New Brunswick, NJ: Rutgers University Press.

Singer, D. G. (1978). Television and imaginative play. *Journal of Mental Imagery, 2*, 145–64.

Smith, P. K., & Vollstedt, R. (1985). On defining play: An empirical study of the relationship between play and various play criteria. *Child Development, 56*, 1042–50.

Sutton-Smith, B. (1981). *The folk stories of children*. Philadelphia: University of Pennsylvania Press.

———. (1986). *Toys as culture*. New York: Gardner.

———. (1992). Notes towards a critique of twentieth-century psychological play theory. *Homo Ludens: Der spielende Mensch* Günter G. Bauer, Ed. (pp. 95–107). München and Salzburg: Verlag Emil Katzbichler.

———. (1993a). A memory of games and some games of memory. In *Life before story: The autobiographies of psychologists from a narrative perspective*, John Lee, Ed. New York: Praeger.

———. (1993b). Suggested rhetorics in adult play theories. *Journal of Play Theory and Research, 1*, 102–16.

Sutton-Smith, B., & Kelly-Byrne, D. (1984). The masks of play. In B. Sutton-Smith and D. Kelly-Byrne (Eds.), *The Masks of Play* (pp. 184–98). New York: Leisure Press.

Thompson, E. H., & Johnson, T. F. (1977). The imaginary playmate and other imaginary figures of childhood. In P. Stevens, Jr. (Ed.), *Studies in the Anthropology of Play* (pp. 210–22). West Point, NY: Leisure Press.

Wharton, E. (1911). *Ethan Frome*. New York: Scribner's.

White, W. A. (1946). *The autobiography of William Allen White*. New York: Century.

CONCLUSION: THE PERSUASIVE RHETORICS OF PLAY

IS THERE ANY FUTURE FOR PLAY THEORY?

A skeptic reading the chapters in this volume might easily come to the conclusion that the future of play theory is that play theory has no future. There seem to be so many difficulties in locating the appropriate phenomena as well as in locating a useful methodology to capture such phenomena. There is, of course, the reassurance that the ambiguity and paradoxical nature of play is already well known to these investigators in this field. And there is perhaps the intellectual lift of realizing that the heteroglossia and multiplicity announced as the heart of postmodernism's attempt to interpret the human sciences has always been taken for granted by outstanding play theorists like, for example, Bakhtin (1981), Spariosu (1989), and Derrida (1978). And there is the reassurance, too, that it is the point of this volume to bring together a variety of play researchers representing the diverse fields of biology, ethology, leisure science, education, psychology, sports sociology, anthropology, history, and communications, of which the very disciplinary diversity might itself suggest some way of grappling with the problem of play's own diversity.

Thus there are several kinds of promise for the future offered by the various disciplines. From Fagen there is the promise of understanding that not only do humans play in many different ways but that the lower species also are widely different in their kinds of play, from jerky solo movements to solo motion to social contact to games which appear to have "plots" and finally to intimacy. Most of this activity is highly repetitive, but some of it is improvisational and in general it is characterized by high involvement. The parallel to human caricature at one end and narrative and foreplay at the other, and the parallel to human play repetitiveness and improvisation, is intriguing. Again, it is perhaps not an accident, in this age of information and cybernetics, that so many of the researchers here have focussed on symbolic play or imagination, sometimes fearing the constricting consequences of modern media (television, video, etc.), as in historian Mergen, psychologist

275

Singer, and communication theorist Kline. At the same time they and others—Youngblade and Dunn, and Fein—are implying a brighter future if such imagination and narrative skill is properly stimulated. Perhaps the strongest note in this work is that the future is indeed brighter if there is more time for children's make-believe, even perhaps also for the make-believe of adults, as Singer's examples suggest. But we also have on the one hand Fagen the biologist saying that play is an accessory to well-being on the animal level, and on the other Singer saying it is a companion to humanizing subjunctivity. Both appear to make it worthwhile to continue scientifically with this subject matter. But then we have both Smith and Chick and Barnett suggesting that any hard-nosed view of the evidence is not really very supportive. So we are left with a certain contradictory feeling about what we know about the positive value of play.

In the chapters by Loy and Hesketh, Pellegrini, and Goldstein we are suddenly in that quite different play world of male contest and rough-and-tumble. This is a world that has, in general, been avoided within the discipline of child psychology, though it is very much a part of sports sociology. In fact most child psychologists and educators seem ready to argue that such competitive sport is not play at all but is rather some kind of work. Loy and Hesketh, as sports sociologists, show us some of the historical constituents of the warlike way of life and suggest some of the psychological correlates of the competitiveness and prestige-seeking amongst males that it involves. Pellegrini, by contrast, seeks in school playgrounds to track down whether being a play-fighter does anyone any good and concludes that its a useful talent in young boys but not so valuable in the adolescent. Goldstein examines whether the violence in television or play with war toys is doing anyone any harm and concludes that there doesn't seem to be much evidence for either. What is most interesting is the contrast implied between the revered historical contests of male life in Loy and Hesketh's chapter and the more skeptical questions about the value of these things to males and to society in general in the chapters of Pellegrini and Goldstein. Once again the mass media, seen earlier to intrude on the imagination, are now being queried for carrying the messages of a more war-like world in which most of us would rather not live. Judged by the attitudes of these researchers, the imagination is more imperiled by the mass media than is the play-fighting. And yet, paradoxically, both the mass media and the imagination are symbolic media whereas most play-fighting, particularly rough-and-tumble, is not. The mass media currently mediate the virtues of rough-and-tumble better than they apparently mediate the virtues of playful mediation, of which they are themselves paradoxically an exemplar.

So much then for the promises of a play future in part positive and in part negative. Wafting through some of the chapters, however, there are also strong sounds of skepticism about being able to technically predict anything about the future for children's play. Not only doesn't children's play predict very clearly their other cognitive competences (Smith), it doesn't even predict very well how children's child play effects their play as adults (Chick and Barnett). In part the problem lies in the lack of agreement between various scholarly disciplines as to the appropriate way to go about the science of play (Fagen), and in part it is due to the investigators' inability to agree on what they think the basic play category actually includes or whether there is any such thing (Chick and Barnett). But as so well said, by psychologist Smith, the investigators themselves have been at fault for experimenter effects in their research and, to the contrary by anthropologist Schwartzman, that investigators do not sufficiently reckon their own participation as a part of their own research. The psychologist Smith wants objective distance in his investigators from their data gathering and the anthropologist Schwartzman wants candid admission by her investigators of the effects of their own participation upon those they study. Here we go beyond differences in what are play data into differences in what can be known in the first place about the world we live in. It is doubtful if any world of the future is going to remove these epistemological differences in preference, although from the present author's point of view they are both capable of revealing interesting information about their players even though their approaches are quite diverse, as Schwartzman's own accounting of the differences between Goodwin and Kelly-Byrne make clear. These two students from the University of Pennsylvania, having taken much of their understanding from the same teachers— Birdwhistell, Goffman, Labov, and Hymes—neverthless end up with entirely different views of what it is worth to understand about play. Goodwin focuses on the discourse that surrounds the play, while Kelly-Byrne attempts to understand play as a relationship between herself and the child player.

PERSUASIVE DISCOURSES

As a potentially useful interdisciplinary step beyond the impass of different data, different methodology, and different epistemology, I wish to suggest that all play investigators tend to group themselves into a variety of persuasive discourses about the cultural value of their particular play science. It has long been argued that supposedly objective science is not a neutral and value-free phenomenon but exists within a complex value system whose partialities do not derive only from science itself but derive also from other values within the cultural system and the personality of the scholars. This is a point emphasized here in one way by Mergen, in his suggestion that there is always history or "past play" in the play before our eyes, and by Singer in another when he contrasts the potentially differential and clearly amusing effects of his and my own sibling diversities on our own work. What I would like to suggest here is that the different interests of the investigators are in part at least dictated by their implicit allegiance to a whole host of such values— large and small, historical and personal.

Furthermore, I will suggest that these congeries of value fall hypothetically into four comprehensive and persuasive cultural discourses about play and that the "science" of each of the above investigators takes its place within one or other of these discourses. These persuasive discourses are a part and parcel of our general cultural life and almost too obvious for us to even know we are influenced by them. The four discourses that seem most relevant at this time in our history are those that are occupied with play as *progress*, play as *power*, play as *fantasy*, and play as *self*.

Fagen's, Smith's and Chick and Barnett's work is here largely focussed within the progress discourse: Loy and Hesketh's, Pellegrini's, and Goldstein's within the power discourse; Youngblade and Dunn's, Fein's, Singer's, and Kline's within the fantasy discourse. There is no representative amongst these writers of the currently most prevalent kind of self discourse, a discourse typified by the well known writings of Mihaly Csikszentmihalyi (1975). Nevertheless, several of the authors deal with the self at a quite another level of explanation. Both Mergen and Schwartzman question the role of the reflexive self of the investigator and how that effects what they come to think play actually is.

My personal metaphor for these historically derived persuasive discourses is that they may be viewed like the factors in factor analysis. That is, each factor is composed of a congery of historically, sociologically, and psychologically derived variables which show some significant correlations amongst themselves but in general do not show significant associations with the variables in the other factor clusters, although there can be exceptions in which one variable will appear in several factors. Now obviously this metaphor is only a statistical fiction and what happens in life is even more complicated. Just why persons give their attention to one rather than another of these discourses depends at least upon factors alluded to by some of our contributors as cultural history (Mergen), disciplinary involvements (Fagen), methodological epistemologies (Schwartzman), and personality dynamics (Singer).

Each discourse is meant by me to be a particular "play history" in our culture at this time. My own selection of the four is based on a lifetime as an interdisciplinary person trying to deal with the quite different ways in which different disciplines contain their play ideas and methodologies often in complete isolation from equally interesting and potentially valid ideas in other disciplines. But as in factor analysis, the separations are not complete, and there are multiple other factors (other persuasive discourses) lurking below the threshold of the four I will present here, including the possibility that some of the major variables within each of these factors really deserve to be treated separately by themselves. As my prior articles on these issues indicate, my own attempts to formulate our interdisciplinary play problems in this manner have a most tentative status and would require a much larger historical and analytic effort than I have used here (Sutton-Smith, 1993a, 1993b).

PLAY AS PROGRESS

There has been an obsession in this century amongst life-science scholars with demonstrating that children learn something useful from their play, a latter-day outcome, apparently, of the eighteenth-century Enlightenment view of humanity as susceptible to scientific study and therefore as capable of progress. When this historicism (originally the view that progress is inevitable) became allied with the fate of children and their increasing separation from adults at about the same time, then in effect our own worth and our own future as a people became translated to the necessity for children to receive and find equal opportunity for progress through their schooling. Incessantly they were told that their future and the future of our civilization depended upon them. While simplistic historicism ultimately lost ground with most historians in this century (wars, nuclear bombs, holocausts, etc.), the widespread hope for future generations retained children as a residual legatee of these expectations for human progress. Adding the theory of evolution to this work, the psychologists of this century set out to persuade us that indeed play is the child's work and that children advance through it to predictable stages of ever greater maturity. It was said that the children are young in order to play so that adaptive skills can be acquired. In the earlier part of the century the emphasis was on motor and later on social skills, but more recently it has been on cognitive outcomes such as those documented in the paper by Singer in this volume, though questioned by Smith. This shift in psychology's focus has mirrored the shift from the manual to the nonmanual in the worlds of work. From Karl Groos (1901) to Piaget (1951) we have expected some payoff from play and have tried with great strenuousness to find it. Despite a fairly limited payoff after thousands of relevant studies, we apparently continue to need to believe that child play has some adaptive usefulness to children. Smith is most poignant, as well as lucid, in his account of his pursuit of this goal and in his reluctant acceptance of the lack of scientific support for it within the kinds of experiments that have prevailed in the last several decades.

Since the death of Puritanism it has not been easy to find a self-respecting scholar of childhood who would announce that play is of no damn use whatsoever. Strangely, it is quite easy to find educators and administrators and politicians who act in a practical way as if play is of no damn use whatsoever by closing playgrounds, by abolishing recess, and by organizing children's free time in every possible way. Even those who have announced recently that they are in favor of children's rights to play usually wish to organize it in some way and not leave it to "nature," and certainly they don't want to leave it to television. So in our times we still carry in different cultural groups the quite contrary attitudes that play is or is not of practical value.

What we need ask is what makes it so important to us as twentieth century adults to find such rational functionalism in play as a kind of progress. What frightens us about children's play? Were children increasingly rationalized in the eighteenth century in a Foucauldian (1973) kind of way (as were the insane, the criminal and the defective) by being institutionalized in schools; does schooling have as much to do with being a confinement as being an opportunity for learning? And was this ultimately meant to be a guarantee that we ourselves as adults could be free of our own madness, our own animal and especially sexual tendencies, because these were now harnessed in children, as some have written recently? I rather suspect that my own personal advocacy of children's play as at times an irrational and "dark" undertaking as well as a rational one, though perhaps motivated by my ordinal sibling struggles (*sic* Jerry Singer), actually has its source in this larger calculus of inhibitive adult self-respect in modern society. I see a hypocrisy in denying our own adult play irrationalities through constantly studying only the rationality of children's play. Having spent my several doctoral dissertation years observing in children's playgrounds, and having been a vigorous team player most of my own life, I was never under any illusion that play and sanity were the same thing. Any reading of the great school playground observers—the Opies (1968), Slukin (1981), and most recently Beresin (1993)—would give the same impression.

Put another way, the real negative upon which this progress discourse continues is the exaggerated dichotomy of children and adults. Children's play is said to be innocent and adaptive. Adult play is said not to exist. Adult pursuits are said to be things called leisure, recreation, and sports, but they are not said to be play, and they are said to have an entirely different significance from play. But as an interdisciplinary scholar looking at the writings of Fagen, Loy, Mergen, and Schwarzman, one is struck by the similarity between children and adults. The major characteristics of all forms of play are that they are highly stylized, highly repetitive and typically highly involving to the players themselves. In this respect there is little ludic difference between the arduous ritualistic hours playing make-believe house, playing tag, and being chased by monsters, and playing professional football. By ignoring these similarities we are enabled to put children on a pedestal (or our ambitions for them on a pedestal), thus neglecting the great importance of power-striving amongst children and neglecting their need for participation in the immortal (chase-escape, attack-defend, escape-capture) dramas of children's folk culture. In addition, it also allows us to neglect the hidden transcripts of the children's subcultural revolt against the powerful figures who dominate their own lives. To disclose this kind of heteronomy between child and adult is to question our own rights to control their world. The issue is perhaps not too different in kind to the difference between self-adulating autocracy and mutually disrespecting democracy.

But Surely Play Is Adaptive

Still, despite assertions of childhood play being encapsulated into such a persuasive discourse about progress, there is still the issue of whether children aren't at least making some kind of progress in their own play. Trying to abstract the reality of adaptation from the myth of progress, however, may be something of an illusion. The concept of adaptation is itself typically phrased in terms which echo the rational orientation of our own scientific culture. There may be no escape from rhetoric here. Nevertheless, let's try to see what can be said.

We cannot deny that players are usually getting more skilled at their play as they get older. So perhaps what one learns from play is how to play better. Apparently, as Chick argues, that may have little predictive value for what is played later. As he and Roberts have shown in earlier research, those who have mastered a particular kind of play generally have to move it on to a more complex, perhaps competitive or professional, status or move on to something else because they become bored with it (Roberts and Chick, 1976).

It follows that if playing at something repetitively makes you better at it, surely there ought to be some transfer of the skills involved. Those who play physical skill games should be likely to be physically superior in relevant skills to those who don't get involved in such skill games, although they also take the risks and dangers of injury, as Fagan has shown for animals. Those who play mental games surely ought to be more intellectually flexible and quicker in thought than those who don't, and those who engage in dramatic play likewise should be more expert in the management of emotion and of their fellows, as Youngblade and Dunn suggest. But the evidence suggests that we can make no such clear pronouncements. There are apparently too many other life-events intervening for such simple cause and effect relationships between play-skill and life-skill to be easily predictable.

We do, however, have a predictable curvilinear relationship between play participation and general adaptation. Those children who do not get to play with others because they are withdrawn or too aggressive are generally also doing badly at school. If they can't make it in play with their peers, life is going to be harder for them. That evidence seems fairly solid but of course whether the lack of play is merely an expression of other deficiencies or is itself the cause of the deficiencies is not self-evident. Our belief that play can at least be helpful in reducing those deficiencies comes from a hundred years of play therapy with children. Some children who are having emotional or behavioral difficulties, as well as children who are in hospitals, seem to benefit and gain more control over themselves and their lives after repeated play-therapy sessions. Play can be a bridge to normality in some cases. It is also established that those suffering from mental disorders, whether child or adult, have little success in any kinds of play, but then they have little success with anything else either.

At the other end of the normal curve there are some play fanatics, like gambling addicts or sporting fiends, who allow their play to totally ruin or make unbalanced the rest of their lives. Sports' widows or widowers have been complaining about that for years. Play as sports is sometimes a resort for addiction.

Between these extremes, moderate amounts of play usually seem to be connected with well-being, as Fagen suggests. Those who play moderately are generally physically, socially, mentally, and emotionally healthier individuals. The problem here is that there are all kinds of play and much of it is of the solitary and mental kind and therefore unobservable. As we grow out of childhood we can play in our heads incessantly and there has been little scientific reckoning of those kinds of mental phenomena, though Singer has pursued it more rigorously than anyone else. In sum, however, without giving up the notion of some adaptive value it is clear that the evidence is not overwhelming. Maybe the function of play is quite different from the kinds of things we have been looking at, or perhaps we have been looking at the wrong kinds of function. Perhaps we need another kind of rhetoric for human beings and their play than the one that focuses always on some kind of skill—physical, cognitive, or emotional.

The Problem of Embeddedness

One major problem with the discussion about adaptation lies in our assumption that play is a separate category of events. We have made it appear separable by having play places (like playgrounds, playrooms, and sports' arenas) and play times (like vacations, recess, game nights, etc.). And within our science we believe that phenomena which can't be defined separately can hardly be dealt with scientifically, as Chick and Barnett show so well. But what impresses one in the anthropological evidence is that play is typically connected with a variety of kinds of other political and religious matters. Play outcomes can be a means of determining boundaries, or of moving the dead onto the next kingdom (those who play on the dead's side must win the game so that the spirit will move onto another life and not haunt the village, or in other burial cases the extensiveness of the playful theatric improvisation is an indication of the prestige of the dead one and of his successors). If we focus upon childhood it is almost impossible by observation to sort out when the child is playing or when he or she is exploring and learning. The two interact constantly. So if we seek to ask what kind of learning is involved in play, do we mean learning as a result of the play itself, or learning about the objects or acts in the play, or only that learning which is not a part of the play.

But how can we distinguish these things? Is the learning which is involved in the development of a new fantasy any less of a learning than that required to put the ghostly robe together while getting ready? Perhaps there is some help from our knowledge that most of the time children say they are playing they are, from our point of view, only getting ready or rehearsing. They call this all play, but much of it is of a more realistic quality than the drama that ultimately emerges. Still, the point to be made is that when we ask what price the play we are usually artificially separating from a large and more complex behavior the end point. It is a little like in the arts or festivals or sports only paying attention to the final performance and ignoring the years of effort, practice, preparation, organization, and the multiplicity of learned moments that have gone into this production. Our modern orientation to play is to think of it as an outcome, a production or performance, when any full accounting must acknowledge that even in a play frame the playing person is most of the time treating his or her materials and actions or skills in a quite realistic way, getting them ready for the performance even if dreaming of the play while doing so. Another way to put this is to say that we treat play too often as a separable text, when in fact it always exists complexly interacting with the various contexts—human and symbolic—of which it is a part, as Greta Fein's analysis of storymaking shows so interestingly. Whatever the consequence, adaptive or otherwise, of such play, clearly the whole phenomenon—diversely rooted in a variety of kinds of relationships and activities, real or fantasied, rehearsive or performative—must be attended to.

All of these matters of play's relationship to adaptation are endlessly more complex than can be introduced by these few words. The major thesis being advanced, however, is that the simplistic discourse of play as progress is preventing us from a true accounting of the generality and complexity of play, its rationality and irrationality as it participates with everything else in the lives of both children and adults. Further, when we try to grasp what is adaptive about play, the subject matter is as extraordinary elusive as the phenomenon itself. We certainly must conclude at least that play is a most malleable cultural form, susceptible to being incorporated into multiple persuasive rhetorics and therefore making its peculiar contribution to their ideological health within the culture as a whole. That play is a medium for propaganda of one propaedeutic sort or another is undeniable.

PLAY AS POWER

The discourse of power is not typically found in child psychology and education, but is more often found in history, sociology, and anthropology. It involves an acceptance of the view that a major play preoccupation of adults is with competitive sports and with festivals. In general, a great deal of theoretical rationalization happens here in the attempts by sports' scholars to show how functional—individually or structurally—these practices are for the societies of which they are a part. In some cases, in these academic discourses, such mass plays are treated disrespectfully as manipulative epiphenomena of the governing classes meant to keep their subjects in check; and in other cases they are treated more respectfully as an essential part of the communal carthasis or as a representation of individual freedom of choice. Contrarily, there is recognition, especially in anthropology and folklore, of the irrationality of much of this mass play, as in Mardi Gras–type accounts of inversive festivals in which the life of the societies involved is caricatured and often mocked, as well as sometimes accompanied by orgy and rioting. There is also recognition in some quarters that the conflicts within societies among territories, ethnic groups, and nations can be mirrored, as well as sometimes exacerbated or assuaged, by the great athletic and competitive sports to which they give rise. As Hillary Clinton said while in Lillehammer in the winter of 1994, exemplifying the latter alternative in common parlance and referring to the Winter Olympics as she looked back at Sarajevo, "It so much better to show you are the best without having to kill each other."

This kind of large-scale play is of massive social impact, transcending temporarily the ordinary lives of all who follow it. At the same time this play occasionally leads to the kind of social breakdown that is not so different from the turmoil and war of which cultural category it is always a kind of schematic and, typically, a quasi-peaceful member. But the point to be made here is that this athletic rough-and-tumble of nations is not too amazingly different from the rough-and-tumble of children. Both Loy and Hesketh and Pellegrini are showing at the least that in many nations the male members, whether children or adult, are going about the same plays of being tough and tender, testing each other and forming hierarchies of physical skill. This is again at least another reminder that children and adult play is not fundamentally as different as most of those immured within the progress rhetoric would have us believe. After all, when one arrives home as an adult from a day of golf, there is seldom any discussion of what has been learned today. Adult play is certainly about something else. Perhaps children's play is also.

Although the term *power* is used as the key concept for this most persuasive traditional discourse, we could as well have keyed in on the concepts of *contest, conflict,* or *group identity and tradition,* which also have a major role in these kind of adult phenomena, as well as in the explanations of sport and festival by many theorists. Perhaps it is not surprising that two of the major leading theorists of adult mass play, Huizinga (1949) and Spariosu (1989), devote themselves almost entirely to the role of contest and of rational or irrational power in play. While Huizinga sees contests as a basically positive force in the growth of civilization, Spariosu shows how it has been increasingly difficult in modern rational scientific civilization for most scholars to acknowledge the sheer irrationality of much that passes for play. There is no way that a great deal of human mass play has anything at all to do with progress, at least as enunciated in the first rhetoric above and as especially evidenced in, for example, our adult passion for gambling, which accounts for more of the national budget than all other kinds of recreation together. One is struck with the endless repetition in mass sports and chance games which seems to have to do with warding off mere ordinariness or perhaps disempowerment or even mortality by investment in the legendary possibilities of star players or of serendipitous dice. These games and sports all appear to be exemplars of an endless Nietzschean kind of eternal return. One could argue indeed that these sports, festivals, and games can be as much an adult preoccupation with our powerlessness in immortal matters as the games of children are with their childish disempowerment within everyday life. Both children and adults on this kind of accounting would be playing or railing against their respective powerlessness with displays of fictional fortitude.

The association of the agonistic sports with war, war training and males documented here by Loy and Hesketh makes rather irrelevant the attempts of many leisure scholars to also find very modern individualistic justification for them in terms of that most modern of subject variables, "self-esteem," or in terms more commonly of such self-oriented variables as intrinsic motivation, autotelia, stimulus arousal, and free choice, which are variables central to the fourth discourse below. Sports scholars sometimes seek to attribute to sports the same twentieth-century subjective values, more typically and sentimentally used of children's play, in order to give persuasiveness to these power and leisure discourses. The data of Loy and Hesketh and others makes clear that there was seldom any free choice about these extrinsically dominated sporting requirements harnessed as much to national, parochial, or feudal survival needs in those days as professional sports are harnessed to commercial requirements in these.

It appears that "collective" explanations for these kinds of phenomena are more in order than their reduction to more hallowed contemporary explanations of an individualistic kind. For example, an earlier collective kind of explanation, which still prevails, is the nineteenth-century doctrine of Amateurism, in which it was maintained that games should be played for the sake of the game (paratelia) and not for monetary gain; which is now often argued in sociology to have been a way of protecting the wealthy from participation with the working classes. The rugby game for the game's sake, and the game as a moral tutor, was a collective explanation even if it was, as Susan Stewart might aver (1991), a crime of play morality in which an upper-class prejudice inflicted a depriviologing upon the play of many generations of lower-class players, making their play forever beyond the pale and, by participation, an indictment of the players' own basic social inferiority. It was thus with soccer as compared with rugby. Insofar as participation in certain national sports (particularly baseball and football) is still a hallowed undertaking—even if uneasily maintained, due to the errant behaviors of many individual participants—this older notion of sports play being a collective morality still prevails. Although now it is not the upper classes who are privileged by attendance on them, it is perhaps the males with a more red-blooded sense of their aspired identity who participate in one way or another.

While we have rejected the "reduction" of the importance of power rhetorics throughout the ages solely to modern notions like self-esteem, it would take a great deal of self-control not to consider the charge that academics who occupy themselves with these agonistic studies may have an investment in machismo values. Whether this charge is worth any merit when it comes, as it does, from others with an investment in antagonistic feminist values, it nevertheless helps us to see that such a debate is a powerful indication of the fact that this "science" of sports and festivals is likely to fall within the hegemony of one or the other of these gender rhetorics. Gender must be a strong part of the variance in this factor.

So, in sum, to this point we have progress play theory, which attempts to make children's play quite distinct from that of adults, a distinction we deny; and then we have adult power-oriented play theory attempting to rationalize itself by pretending to be explained by the play theories of modern subjectivity, which seem, however, to have very little relevance to the great historical parade of compulsory and collective agonistic excess.

PLAY AS FANTASY

Alternative key concepts for play as fantasy might well be 'the imagination,' 'genius,' 'creativity,' 'flexibility,' 'the play of signifiers,' or even 'postmodernism.' The papers by Youngblade and Dunn, Fein, Singer, and Kline all pursue the vicissitudes of the imagination in one way or another. The historical point of origin for this factor we take to be Romanticism and the writings of Schiller, Kant, Wordsworth, and others. In general, in this persuasive discourse protagonists share the distaste for industrialism, bureaucracy, mechanization, organized play, and (today) violent mass media and mass toys. What is being celebrated here is the creativity of the individual players and, not surprisingly therefore, this play discourse is more often to be found in literature, the arts, and the humanities.

The chapter by Jerome Singer is an excellent exemplification of this discourse, and he, in particular, has given his life to its diligent pursuit, writing at least two classic books with the term *make-believe* in their titles (1974, 1992). What is remarkable in the current cognitive era of play psychology is that so much attention has been paid to make-believe or pretense or symbolic play or fantasy or sociodrama, as if this kind of progress in play is really most worthy of our attention. This rhetoric is a subset of the first on progress and, like the first, is not particularly interested in or even sympathetic to the concerns with physical play of the second rhetoric. There is a gender connotation here also, with the second power rhetoric clearly identified with maledom, whereas this present third rhetoric, while not excluding maledom, shows an affinity for the play of girls, who have always been more touted for their imaginative play than have boys, a distinction replicated here in Fein's work on narrative. Some boys, of course, manage to escape the stereotype of organized sports, and are amongst those who are the most imaginative of all, reminding us of Schwartzman's warning about overgeneralizing gender differences, because there are always particular subsets when some part of any given gender behaves in a way antithetical to prevailing stereotypes.

Another point here is that "the imagination" has for a long time been a rallying point for play advocates often of an upper-class or academic kind against the banalities and normative practices of the schools or cultures in which they find themselves and their children entrapped. One would suppose, therefore, the imagination to be somewhat freer and more improvisational than the other kinds of play already mentioned. This is, however, an empirical question yet to be decided. There is much in the repetitiveness of personal fantasy, daydreams, and dreams, and in the cyclical nature of much soap opera, theatre, and the arts, to suggest that play in the mind may not be so vastly different from play in the body, either solitary or social. There are also innovative players of all kinds (physical, mental, solitary, social), though it is not surprising if, in this largely nonmanual twentieth-century world, we academics increasingly give greater value to improvisation of the imagination than to improvisation in sports. But choosing between Michael Chrichton and Michael Jordan indicates the fallacy of such exclusiveness.

The repetitive character of the imagination is more obvious when viewing group play than when viewing solitary play, as the example of the seemingly endless everyday recurrence of all forms of sports, baseball, basketball, et cetera seems to indicate. But it applies also to children, as has been found recently by Mechley (1994), whose research indicates that from the instant preschool children innovate a behavior and it is accepted by the others, it becomes a ritual for everyone to carry out that behavior in the same way.

That is, in play, as soon as the behavior has been created it is dealt with conservatively, as if was always a group tradition. Over a period of time a group of contingent players carry out the same games in the same way and in the same order, even if they are not themselves the initial creators. Once it occurs, play is thus transformed into the timelessness of being something that was always that way. In Mechley's data with twelve preschool children playing together over a year's time, play and ritual are, it seems, typically completely interlocked. What her children do with make-believe play is then not very different from the more obvious examples of the traditional games of older children or the sports of adults, where the game arrives already as a set of rituals for appropriate behavior, even though they are still constantly modified, and as still constantly ritualized, as the conventional way it is done in their group. We need, therefore, to be careful about overemphasizing the fluidity and creativity of imaginative social play. Typically, in a stable group, play's social constructions are likely to last and become group traditions.

Having made that point, however, a real boost to the speculation about solitary play as the fluent imagination has come recently from work in semiotics and poststructuralism. Here the mind is reconsidered not in terms of the earlier structural rigidities of everyone from Saussure to Piaget to Levi Strauss, but in terms of the free-ranging character of the individual's mental signifiers and the capacity for deconstructing all kinds of orthodoxies of opinion. In addition, the ways in which such freedom of the mind is accelerated by computer networks and even by the mass media's novelty-hungry commercialism are emphasized as moving us into a world of radical semiurgy, a world in which the multiplicities and heterglossias of the playful mind are at the center, not the periphery, of intellectual concern (Aycock, 1993). There are some grounds for thinking that if the first historical romanticism was characterized as the great aesthetic turn in Western culture, the present romanticism can be characterized as the "ludic turn" in Western culture. We might playfully suggest, for example to Schwartzman, that the metaphor of the five blind men and the elephant is no longer sufficient for the modern persuasion. There may or may not be an elephant there, and some of the men are blind and some are not, and of those, some who can see, see nothing, and some who can't see, see the elephant. Again, some of them see Schwartzman, and some of them see the readers of this work as well as the writer of this chapter, and some even think we are all elephants.

So we end this section with the paradox, once again, of both the lability and conservatism of play, even in the areas where its flexibility seems most obvious, that is, in fantasy.

THE PLAY OF THE SELF

The newest persuasive discourse about play is that it is best understood in terms of the quality of the individual subjective experience that it affords.

Play has been increasingly chosen as the location for the kind of optimal or peak experience it provides and that is said to make life worthwhile. There are various theories contingent on this kind of focus, the oldest philosophical roots probably being in phenomenology, with its emphasis on certain kinds of subjectivity as having an existential status.

Economically, the basis for the popularity of experiential play discourse has probably been the growth of consumer capitalism, within which the good way of life is defined as access to the choice of multiple material or symbolic goods, including personal experiences. Increasingly, play has also been exalted as the place where such voluntary choice is possible, where one can be motivated just by one's own interests (intrinsic motivation, autotelia) (Kerr and Apter, 1991) or can follow one's personal physiological inclinations (arousal needs) or one's engagement in states of high self-control, relative uncertainty, great awareness without self-consciousness, fun, et cetera (or "flow," as some such states have been termed by their successful formulator Mihaly Csikzsentmihalyi [1988]). This shift towards the secular experiential view of life's meaning—as compared, say, with an older religious view or a scientific view of life's ultimate meaning—is a feature of our times. It is not surprising, therefore, that it should filter down into play theories, nor that the traditional opposition between trivial play and serious work should have raised the former to a higher plane in a world where so much of what is called work is for masses of people a rather boring routine, and where self-chosen leisure has become in consequence the reward.

A major limitation of this emphasis on the subjective self as play's crucible is that it concentrates almost totally only on the voluntaristic aspects of selfhood. The only issue seems to be that the play is freely chosen and internally motivated. This orientation conflicts with much historical and anthropological work which indicates that play is obligatory, not optional. The individual plays what his class, gender, or age—or the seasonal or festival sequence—requires. Even today, when we place so much emphasis upon choice, mostly we still play what our friends, neighbors, peers, or family members expect of us. Certainly, children in a school playground are confronted with innumerable peer pressures which belie the notion that they have available there any smorgasbord of play choice. What this means is that valuing choice is largely a rhetoric about playing rather than a sufficient description of play's motivation.

In addition, there are other phenomenological traditions in which the self is characterized more in terms of desire than in terms of freedom, and those kinds of theories might be much more relevant to the case of play. Play theorist Brian Vandenberg makes an existential case for play as a projection of one's view of one's own future (1988). He says that whereas Freud argues that we are our past and that the play of children reflects this, philosopher

Heidegger asserts that we are our future and that the imaginative act of playing with some act or thought is the first step in the process of willing. In these terms, play is a primordial form of wishing.

An extended way of putting this, we might add, would be to see play as the conative (willing it to be) side of foresight. It is associated biologically with ever higher levels of intelligence, which means, amongst other things, the cognitive ability to consider possible alternatives, as in the subjunctive mood. In this mood one thinks about what might happen, or what could happen, as we do when pretending. But what is usually neglected, when this cognitive subjunctive statement is made about play, is that only the cognitive aspect of the subjunctive mood is considered and not the "mood" aspect itself. In contrast, we might contend that though play surely does envisage possibility, it does so primarily in terms of the conative *enactment* of a figment of what that possibility might be. In play, one is not like Hamlet, unsure whether to be or not to be; nor like Bateson in pronouncing play as both about being and not being (1972); but more like Henry V in saying "Once more unto the breach, dear friends." This echoes the centrality given to the affective components by Greta Fein.

What is really striking about make-believe is the way in which the participants act as if what they are doing has a stronger motivation than most other kinds of real belief. Yet the players typically know that it has not. To be or not to be is certainly at the edges of typical play, and it can flood out the play in untoward circumstances, as Goffman illustrates so well (1974). Typical players, however, commit themselves to play, acting as if they can truly act whatever they wish to act, indicating thus that although play is make believe, its purpose is to demonstrate belief in their own enactments. One's identification with the strong reality of the play phenomenon seems to guarantee a complete commitment to the action. One pretends to be brave, or to be a mother, or to be a football star. And at the adult levels, the audience yells and screams to maintain the illusions of such legendary and near immortal competence and victory.

Further, this notion of wilful subjunctivizing or, as we prefer, *meta-action* is a way of phrasing things that could be applied to animals as well as humans. The subjunctive is in all species a way of acting out the primordial envisagement of what might be the case even when at the lowest level it is just the anticipation of pretending to capture or escape from one's enemies. One of the problems of an information age like our own is that we tend not to see that throughout history the adaptive advantage has often gone to those who ventured upon their possibility with cries of exultant commitment. What is adaptive about play, therefore, may not be the skills that happen to be a part of it, but the willful belief in one's own capacity for a future. The opposite of play is not a present reality, it is vacillation, or worse it is depression. To play is to pretend life and to act as if one is gung-ho about one's prospects.

Self theory as a discourse on play can, therefore, derive from views that associate play with some kind of voluntary action; or, as we have just seen, it can derive from existential theories within which play is an acting out of various mortal or immortal desires. But there are other and recursive possibilities suggested for the self in this volume also. Mergen suggests that the study of play is "itself a kind of fantasy, one that satisfies the adult desire to explain and pretend to know what play is." Here he puts the scholar's self in the limelight and indicates cynically that the scholar may trespass on the phenomena itself, deriving its truths from his or her own intuitions. As one who has spent most of his life trying to be intuitive about play, I cannot deny the contention. The chapter by Schwarzman also exemplifies Mergen's contention. She lauds Kelly-Byrne for actually playing along with her subject in order to discover what the nature of play actually is, which is going at least one step further than merely projecting your own intuitions. At the same time Schwarzman herself, perhaps unwittingly, symptomizes how the theorist herself can become possessed by a postmodern "ludic" turn and perceive the world through those most variable eyes. Just as we have multiple selves when we are at play, so our study of play can reflect those multiplicitous other selves. She shows what is also clear in a number of the other chapters and a major point of this conclusion: that the persuasive discourse is usually a very personal way of looking at play, even though in each case it is situated within a complex historical as well as personal context.

CONCLUSION

So is there any play beyond these rhetorics? Can we find some residual meaning after all the argumentation has gone by? What the prior examples suggest is that if we add from the self theories the somewhat compulsive character of the desire that underlies play and that allies the wilful enactment of that desire to the demonstrations of instantiating collective rituals in festivals, and then keep in mind the material dealt with in the section on power, we may say that the self at play either individually or collectively aspires to a ritualistic and timeless involvement in mythic redress for the inadequacies of being unempowered but ultimately of being mortal. And if there is anything adaptive about this, then possibly it is in the increased assurance that life has a currency and future and can be lived.

In saying this, however, I attempt to reach beyond the rhetorics to some universal meanings, which after all is what everybody in this book is also trying to do. What I have called "rhetoric" they would call "theory." So there is a paradox here in trying now to state some essentialistic meanings which are just science and beyond rhetoric. It would take a lot of hubris for me to suppose that the words I have used above, such as "wilful desire," "subjunctivity," "timeless involvement," "instantiated ritual," "mythic redress," "meta-action" and "empowerment" are context-free. And yet it is such universality that we all strive for, despite the acceptance of the cultural relativity of all the theories presented within. The most influential of play theorists, Huizinga, opined that the forms of play are indeed universal and parallel those of human culture; Bateson argued cogently that play, whatever else it is, is metacommunication; animal theorists clearly suppose that the play-fighting phenomena they record give us a peek into the evolution of play. It is not difficult to ask, therefore, whether there are mental mechanisms that instigate play, just as there are supposedly such mechanisms instigating language. Is play, because it is *meta-action*, rather than instinctive action, the first appearance of "culture" in animals as well as in humans? Is it then succeeded by the Neanderthal culture of mimicry in ritual, dance and art; and is that then succeeded by the *Homo sapiens* culture of language? And do these mechanisms express themselves negatively as the negations of instinct (the bite) and positively as the formulations of alternatives of action and of plot (the nip), exemplified here on the animal level by Fagen and on the human narrative level by Fein? They all have in common that they are deferred reflex and instinct. Obviously the simplicity of this essentialism is outrageous, but I mean it to indicate that just as play has a dialectical relationship with its contexts (Sutton-Smith, 1978), so do rhetoric and theory have a dialectical relationship with each other, and up to this point in the twentieth century there has been too much emphasis on theory and insufficient emphasis on the context of rhetoric in which that theory was embedded.

The problem with rhetorical analysis, however, is that it inevitably turns upon itself so that the author is forced to declare what his or her own rhetoric is in making such a case. Have I made this case because it is true that all of our science is always so rhetorically contexted, or because I have been a professor in several disciplines (psychology, education and folklore) and have written in history and anthropology as well as in those other disciplines? Is eclecticism my problem? Or am I an unruly kind of person who likes to irritate authority of one kind or another and this is just my latest way of doing it? Or am I a player of considerable variety (in sports, as an actor, as jokester, as wit) so that I feel a certain intuitive base in challenging limited theories. Perhaps I am even a facetious person who enjoys the play of there being no elephant there in the first place. All of these possibilities may have some truth to them, but as well I do earnestly think that the matter of play is quite complex and that this rhetorical way of proceeding might actually help us unravel it in due course.

For the meantime, then, I think that playing progressively contributes to our mood of confidence about the matters that we play at, whether embodied in physical or fantasied terms; and that play is a meta-active power of body and mind; but that it is also a most labile behavior system, enhancing whatever persuasion the player most needs for such optimism, whether it be in matters of combat or fancy. Typically, it also arrives in already existing collective packages, where the passions and the procedures are well prescribed. Modern focus on solitary and mental play is quite obviously most modern.

A PERSONAL EPILOGUE

I wish to thank the authors of these chapters and especially the adventurous editor, Tony Pellegrini, for the gift of this volume and all that it means in terms of our mutual understanding of play. I have known some of the authors for over twenty years, in particular Jerome Singer and Greta Fein, who with Catherine Garvey and I held a series of seminars on play at various psychology meetings during the 1970s. I first met John Loy in 1969 while attending a sociology of sport meeting in Switzerland. Garry Chick and I were both collaborators of the outstandingly stimulating play anthropologist John M. Roberts, and along with Fagen, Loy, Mergen, and Schwarzman were also all members and presidents of the Association for the Study of Play, which came into existence in 1971. Pellegrini, Smith, Goldstein, and Kline have all been a part of a more recent mutual effort to establish an international association for toy research. Judy Dunn and I met in association with one of the play and toy seminars of Johnson & Johnson, and in addition we have both spent much of our lives on sibling research.

As well as these researchers I would also like to thank those other members of the Association for the Study of Play, who also honored me with an earlier festschrift in two issues of their journal *Play and Culture* (1992). They were Gary Chick, Gary Fine, Nancy King, Rimmert van der Kooij, David F. Lancy, Frank and Virginia Salamone, James F. Christie, Andrew W. Miracle, Robert H. Lavenda, Kendall Blanchard, Robert Horan, Peter Johnsen, Helen Schwarzman, George Eisen, Phillip Stevens, Jr., Jay Mechling, Bernard Mergen, Linda Hughes, and Lynn Barnett. This group, TASP, has nurtured and sustained my interest in play over the past twenty years by their own most diverse and intensive interest in the scholarship of all kinds of play, wherever they could find it. It takes considerable courage to continue to study a subject matter that most other scholars do not appreciate and which will often be, in consequence, of no help in their own personal academic advancement. Important also was their participation in TASP's own play forms, including amongst other festivals a most playful and concupiscent "roast" of which I was the recipient. I count it a singular honor to have been both festschrifted and roasted by the same association. I certainly deserved the latter and do indeed count it an honor to have been thought worthy of the former.

I would like to mention also the fourteen doctoral dissertations which focussed on play or narrative out of about the sixty I sponsored at Columbia University, Teachers College, New York, and the Graduate School of Education and Department of Folklore at the University of Pennsylvania. Their playful authors, beginning in the 1970s, were David Abrams, Gilbert Botvin; and in the 1980s Linda Hughes, Diana Kelly-Byrne, Robert Horan, and Mary Ann Magee; and in the 1990s John Gerstemyer, Linda Snow, Felicia McMahon, Anna Marjanovic-Shane, Ann Richman Beresin, Alice Mechley, Monica McCale-Small and Kevin Sheehan.

Indeed, I feel I have been very lucky to have spent a great deal of my research life in pursuit of the "ludic turn." It has never seemed like work and has contributed enormously to my own playfulness. I believe that, in the long run, all of our studies may add up to justifying a more vivid life for everyone.

REFERENCES

Aycock, A. (1993). Hearing voices: Bakhtin and the study of play. *Journal of Play Theory and Research, 1*, 76–86.

Bakhtin, M. M. (1981). *The dialogic imagination.* Austin: University of Texas Press.

Bateson, G. (1972). *Steps to an ecology of mind.* New York: Ballantine.

Beresin, A. R. (1993). The play of peer cultures in a city schoolyard. Doctoral dissertation, University of Pennsylvania.

Burke, K. (1951). *A rhetoric of motives.* New York: Prentice Hall.

Csikszentmihalyi, M. (1975). *Beyond boredom and anxiety.* San Francisco: Jossey-Bass.

Derrida, J. (1978) *Writing and difference.* Chicago: University of Chicago.

Foucault, M. (1973). *Madness and civilization.* New York: Vintage.

Goffman, E. (1974). *Frame Analysis.* Cambridge: Harvard University Press.

Groos, K. (1901). *The play of man.* New York: Appleton.

Huizinga, J. (1955). *Homo ludens: A study of the play element in culture.* Boston: Beacon.

Kerr, J. H. (1991). *Adult play.* Amsterdam: Swets & Zeidlinger.

Mechley, A. (1994). The social construction of young children's play. Doctoral dissertation, University of Pennsylvania.

Opie, I., & Opie, P. (1968). *The language and lore of schoolchildren.* New York: Oxford University Press.

Piaget, J. (1951). *Play dreams and imitation in childhood.* New York: Macmillan.

Roberts, J. M., & Chick, G. E. (1979). Butler country eight ball: A behavioral space analysis. In J. H. Goldstein (Ed.), *Sports, Games and Play: Social and Psychological Viewpoints* (pp. 65–99). Hillsdale, NJ: Lawrence Erlbaum.

Roberts, R. H., & Good, J. M. M. (1993). *The recovery of rhetoric*. Charlottesville: University Press of Virginia.

Singer, J. L. (1973). *The child's world of make believe*. New York: Academic Press.

Singer, J. L., & Singer, D. (1992). *The house of make believe*. Cambridge: Harvard University Press.

Slukin, A. (1981). *Growing up in the playground*. Ithaca, NY: Cornell University Press.

Spariosu, M. (1989). *Dionysus reborn*. Ithaca, NY: Cornell University Press.

Stewart, S. (1991). *Crimes of writing*. New York: Oxford University Press.

Sutton-Smith, B. (1978). *Die Dialektik des Spiel*. Schorndorff, Germany: Verlag Karl Hoffman.

———. (1993a). Suggested rhetorics in adult play theories. *Play Theory and Research, 1*, 102–16.

———. (1993b). Play rhetorics and toy rhetorics. *Play Theory and Research, 1*, 239–50.

Vandenburg, B. (1988). The realities of play. In D. C. Morrison (Ed.), *Organizing Early Experience* (pp. 198–208). Amityville, NY: Baywood.

APPENDIX: A LIST OF BRIAN SUTTON-SMITH'S PLAY-RELATED PUBLICATIONS

Abrams, D. M., & Sutton-Smith, B. (1977). The development of the trickster in children's narratives. *Journal of American Folklore, 90*, 29–47.

Avedon, E. M., & Sutton-Smith, B. (1971). *The study of games.* New York: Wiley.

Botvin, G. J., & Sutton-Smith, B. (1977). The development of structural complexity in children's fantasy narratives. *Developmental Psychology, 13*, 377-88.

Gump, P. V., & Sutton-Smith, B. (1955a). The "it" role in children's games. *The Group, 17*, 3–8.

———. (1955b). Activity setting and social interaction. *American Journal of Orthopsychiatry, 25*, 755–60.

Hellendoorn, J., VanDerKooij, R., & Sutton-Smith, B. (Eds.). (1994). *Play and intervention.* Albany: State University of New York Press.

Herron, R. E., & Sutton-Smith, B. (1971). *Child's play.* New York: Wiley.

Laurence, B., & Sutton-Smith, B. (1968). Novel responses to toys: a replication. *Merrill-Palmer Quarterly, 14*, 159–60.

McMahon, F., & Sutton-Smith, B. (1995). The past in the present: Theoretical directions for children's folklore. In B. Sutton-Smith, J. Mechling, T. Johnson, & F. McMahon. (Eds.), *Children's folklore: a sourcebook.* New York: Garland.

Redl, F., Grump, P., & Sutton-Smith, B. (1971). The dimensions of games. In E. Avedon & B. Sutton-Smith (Eds.), *The study of games.* New York: Wiley.

Roberts, J. M., Hoffman, H., & Sutton-Smith, B. (1965). Pattern and competence: A consideration of tick tack toe. *El Palacio, 72*, 17–30.

Roberts, J. M., & Sutton-Smith, B. (1962). Child training and game involvement. *Ethnology, 1*, 166–85.

———. (1966). Cross-cultural correlates of a game of chance. *Behavior Science Notes, 3*, 131–44.

Roberts, J. M., Sutton-Smith, B. & Kendon, A. (1963a). Strategy in folktales and games. *Journal of Social Psychology, 61*, 185–99.

Roberts, J. M., Thompson, W. E., & Sutton-Smith, B. (1966). Expressive self-testing and driving. *Human Organization, 25*, 54–55.

Rosenberg, B. G., & Sutton-Smith, B. (1959). The development of masculinity and femininity in children. *Child Development, 30*, 373–80.

———. (1960). A revised conception of masculine-feminine differences in play activities. *Journal of Genetic Psychology, 96*, 165–70.

———. (1964). The measurement of masculinity and femininity in children: An extension and revalidation. *Journal of Genetic Psychology, 104*, 259–64.

Savasta, M. L., and Sutton-Smith, B. (1979). Sex differences in play and power. In B. Sutton-Smith (Ed.), *Die dialektik des spiels*. Axhoensodd: Holtman.

Sutton-Smith, B. (1951). The meeting of Maori and European cultures and its effects upon the unorganized games of Maori children. *Journal of Polynesian Society, 60*, 93–107.

———. (1952). New Zealand variants of the game Buck. *Folklore, 63*, 329–33.

———. (1953). The traditional games of New Zealand children. *Folklore, 64*, 411–23.

———. (1959a). *Games of New Zealand children.* Berkeley: University of California Press.

———. (1959b). A formal analysis of game meaning. *Western Folklore, 18*, 13–24.

———. (1959c). The kissing games of adolescents in Ohio. *Midwestern Folklore, 9*, 189–211.

———. (1960a). The cruel joke series. *Midwestern Folklore, 10*, 11–12.

———. (1961). Cross-cultural study of children's games. *American Philosophical Society Yearbook*, 426–29 (Grant No. 2716, 1960).

———. (1964a). Why children play. *Education in New Zealand, 13*, 31–36.

———. (1964b). Review of *The encounter* by E. Goffman. *American Journal of Psychology, 106*, 13–37.

——— (1965). Play preferences and play behavior: A validity study. *Psychological Reports, 16*, 65–66.

———. (1966a). Piaget on play: A critique. *Psychological Review, 73*, 104–10.

———. (1966b). Role replication and reversal in play. *Merrill-Palmer Quarter, 12*, 285–98.

————. (1966c). Review of *Song games from Trinidad and Tabago* by J. D. Elder. *Western Folklore, 25*, 265–66.

————. (1967a). Games, play, daydreams. *Quest, 10*, 47–58.

————. (1967b). The role of play in cognitive development. *Young Children, 6*, 361–70.

————. (1968). Novel responses to toys. *Merrill-Palmer Quarterly, 14*, 151–58.

————. (1969a). Review of *the psychology of play* by S. Miller. *Child Development Abstracts, 43*, 146.

————. (1969b). The two cultures of games. In G. Kenyon (Ed.), *Aspects of contemporary sport sociology*. Chicago: Athletic Institute.

————. (1970a). The cross-cultural study of games. In G. Luschen (Ed.), *A cross-cultural analysis of sports and games*. Champaign, IL: Stipes.

————. (1970b). Review of *The effects of sociodramatic play on disadvantaged preschool children. The Record, 71*, 529–31.

————. (1970c). The psychology of childlore. *Western Folklore, 29*, 1–8.

————. (1970d). Review of "The effects of sociodramatic play on disadvantaged preschool children. "*The Record* 71:529–31.

————. (1971a). Children at play *Journal of The American Museum of Natural History, 80*, 54–59.

————. (1971b). Child's play. *Psychology Today, 5*, 55–59.

————. (1971c). The expressive profile. *Journal of American Folklore, 84*, 80–92.

————. (1971d). Play, games and controls. In J. P. Scott (Ed.), *Social control*. Chicago: University of Chicago Press.

————. (1971e). The playful modes of knowing. In *Play: The child strives towards self-realization*. Special Monograph of the National Association for the Education of Young Children.

————. (1971f). Review of *The question of play* by Joyce McCelland, *Young Children*, January, 191.

————. (1972a). *The Folkgames of Children*. Austin: University of Texas Press.

————. (1972b). The expressive profile. In A. Paredes (Ed.), *Towards new perspectives in folklore*. Austin: University of Texas Press.

————. (1973a). A developmental approach to play, games and sports. *Proceedings of the 2nd World Symposium on the History of Sport* (pp. 75–83). Banff: University of Alberta.

———. (1973b). Comment on play. *Forum for Contemporary History*, December 14, 23.

———. (1973c). Games: The socialization of conflict. *Sportswissenschaft, 3*, 41–46.

———. (1973d). Play as the mediation of novelty: Games as the socialization of conflict. In O. Grupe (Ed.), *Sport in the modern world: chances and problems.* Berlin: Springer Verlag.

———. (1973e). Review of *Step it down: Games, plays, songs. Journal of American Folklore, 86*, 307–08.

———. (1974a). The anthropology of play. *Association for the Anthropological Study of Play, 2*, 8–12.

———. (1974b). Developmental structural aspects of play and games. *Proceedings of the British Commonwealth and International Conference on Health, Physical Education and Recreation.* Christchurch, New Zealand.

———. (1974c). Play as novelty training. In *One child indivisible: Conference Proceedings NAEYC*, 227–58.

———. (1974d). Review of *Play and development* by E. Erickson et al. *Teachers College Record, 74*, 444.

———. (1974e). Review of *World play* by P. Farb. *Natural History, 84*, 81–83.

———. (1974f). Review of *Play as exploratory learning* by M. Reilly. *Opening Education, 2*, 25–26.

———. (1974g). The sporting balance. In R. Albonïco (Ed.), *The sociology of sport.* Magglingen Symposium, Switzerland.

———. (1975a). Play as adaptive potentiation. *Sportswissenschaft, 5*, 103–18.

———. (1975b). Play, the useless made useful. *School Review, 83*, 197–214.

———. (1976a). Current research in play, games and sports. In T. T. Craig (Ed.), *Human movement.* Schorndorf, Germany: Verlag Karl Hoffman.

———. (1976b). A developmental structural account of riddles. In B. Kirschblatt-Gimblett (Ed.), *Speech play.* Philadelphia: University of Pennsylvania Press.

(1976c). The psychology of childlore: A theory of ludic models. *Resources of Education.* ERIC (July).

———. (1976d). A structural grammar of games and sports. *International Journal of Sports Sociology, 2*(11), 117–38.

———. (1976e). *Studies in play and games (3 vols.).* New York: Arno.

———. (1977a). Games of order and disorder. *Newsletter of the Association for the Anthropological Study of Play, 4*, 119–26.

————. (1977b). Play and curiosity. *International encyclopedia of neurology, psychiatry, psychoanalysis and psychology* (vol. 8).

————. (1977c). A sociolinguistic approach to ludic action. In H. Lenk (Ed.), *Handlungen theories interdisziplinar (vol. 4)*. Munchen: Wilhem Fink Verlag.

————. (1977d). Structural approaches to play; Towards an anthropology of play; Play as adaptive potentiation: A footnote to the 1976 keynote address. In P. Stevens (Ed.), *Studies in the anthropology of play*. New York: Leisure Press.

————. (1977e). The world of play, sport and leisure. *Bulletin of the American Society for Information Science, 4*, 12–13.

————. (1978a). *Die dialektik des spiels*. Schorndorf, Germany: Verlag Karl Hoffman.

————. (1978b). The dialectics of play. In F. Landry and W. Oban (Eds.), *Physical activity and human well-being*. Miami: Symposia Specialists.

————. (1979a). The development of folklore and games in the Pacific. *Proceedings of the International Conference: History of Sport and Physical Education in the Pacific Region*. School of Physical Education, Otago, New Zealand.

————. (1979b). Folkgames. In H. Cohen (Ed.), *American Folklore Series*. Delanda, Florida: Cassette Curriculum.

————. (1979c). The meanings of play. *The Newsletter of the Association for the Anthropological Study of Play, 6*, 12–18.

————. (1979d). *Play and learning*. New York: Gardner.

————. (1979e). Play as innovation. In M. Wolman (Ed.), *Taking early childhood seriously*. The Evangeline Burgess Memorial Lectures. California: Pacific Oaks.

————. (1979f). The play of girls. In C. B. Kopp & M. Kirkpatrick (Ed.), *Becoming females: Perspectives on development*. New York: Plenum.

————. (1979g). Presentation and representation in fictional narrative. In E. Winner & H. Gardner (Eds.), *Fact, fiction and fantasy in childhood*. San Francisco: Jossey-Bass.

————. (1979h). Toys for object and role mastery. In K. Hewitt and L. Roomet (Eds.), *Educational toys in American: 1800 to the present*. Burlington, Vermont: Hull Fleming Museum.

————. (1980a). Children's play: Some sources of play theorizing. In K. Rubin (Ed.), *Children's play: new directions for child development* (vol. 9). San Francisco: Jossey-Bass.

————. (1980b). The social psychology and anthropology of play and games. In G. Sage (Ed.), *Sport and American society: Selected readings*. Reading, MA: Addison-Wesley.

————. (1980c). A sportive theory of play. In H. Schwartzman (Ed.), *Play and Culture*. New York: Leisure Press.

————. (1981a). *The folkstories of children*. Philadelphia: University of Pennsylvania Press.

————. (1981b). *A History of children's play*. Philadelphia: University of Pennsylvania Press.

————. (1981c). The new meanings of play. In J. Shallcrass (Ed.), *Recreation reconsidered into the eighties*. Auckland, New Zealand: New Zealand Council for Recreation and Sport.

————. (1982a). Review of *Children's riddling* by J. McDowell. *Language and Society, 11*, 150–51.

————. (1982b). Een prastatie—theories over relaties met leeftijdgenoen. In N. H. A. van Rossum (Ed.), *Motorisch gedrag en ontwikkeling*. Netherlands: Nijmegen, dekker and van de Vagt.

————. (1982c). Die idealisierung des spiels. In O. Grupe, H. Gabler, & U. Gohner (Eds.), *Spiel, spiele, spielen*. Schorndorf, Germany: Verlag Karl Hoffman.

————. (1982d). One hundred years of change in play research. *Newsletter of TAASP, 9*(2), 13–17.

————. (1982e). A performance theory of peer relationships. In K. M. Borman (Ed.), *The social life of children in a changing society*. Hillsdale, NJ: Lawrence Erlbaum.

————. (1982f). Piaget on play: Revisited. In W. F. Overton (Ed.), *The relationship between social and cognitive development*. Hillsdale, NJ: Lawrence Erlbaum.

————. (1982g). Review of *Growing up in the playground* by A. Slukin. *Contemporary Psychology, 27*, 729–30.

————. (1982h). Play theory and the cruel play of the nineteenth century. In F. Manning (Ed.), *The world of play*. New York: Leisure Press.

————. (1982i). Play theory of the rich and the poor. In P. Gilmore & A. Glathorn (Eds.), *Children in and out of school*. Washington, D.C.: Center for Applied Linguistics.

————. (1983a). Child's play: Idealizing the savage. *The Miquon Conference on Progressive Education.*, April 7–9, 98–111.

————. (1983b). Commentary on social class differences in sociodramatic play in historical context: A reply to McLoyd. *Developmental Review, 3*, 1–5.

————. (1984a). From narcissism to charisma: The vicissitudes of central person games. *Newsletter of TAASP, 10*(1), 10–19.

————. (1984b). Recreation as folly's parody. *Newsletter of TAASP, 9*(4), 4–13.

————. (1984c). Text and context in imaginative play. In F. Kessel and A. Göncü (Eds.), San Francisco: Jossey-Bass.

————. (1984d). A toy semiotics. *Children's Environmental Quarterly, 50*, 19–22.

————. (1985a). Introduction: The history and meaning of children's play; Projection: The future of play. In *Children's play, past, present and future.* Philadelphia: Please Touch Museum.

————. (1985b). Play research: State of the art. In J. Frost & S. Sunderlin (Eds.), *When children play.* Washington, D.C.: Association for Childhood International.

————. (1986a). *Toys as culture.* New York: Gardner.

————. (1986b). Review of *Symbolic play* by I. Bretherton, (Ed.), *American Journal of Education: 94*, 265–67.

————. (1987a). The game as a metaphor in social science research. In P. Engelen (Ed.), *Play—play therapy, play research.* Amsterdam: PAOS.

————. (1987b). In search of the imagination. In D. Nadaner & K. Egan (Eds.), *Education and the imagination.* New York: Teachers College Press.

————. (1984c). Introduction. In W. Stephenson (Ed.), *The play theory of mass communication.* New Brunswik, NJ: Transaction Books, Rutgers.

————. (1987d). Review of *The singing game* by I. Opie & P. Opie. *Journal of American Folklore, 99*, 239–40.

————. (1987e). School play: A commentary. In J. H. Bock & N. R. King (Eds.), *School play.* New York: Garland.

————. (1987f). The spirit of play. In G. Fein & M. Rivkin (Eds.), *The young child at play.* Washington, D. C.: NAEYC.

————. (1987g). The struggle between sacred play and festival play. In D. Berger (Ed.), *Play as a learning medium.* New York: Heineman.

————. (1988a). Children's play. In M. A. Johnson (Ed.), *Leaders in education.* New York: University Press of America.

————. (1988b). Creativity and vissitudes of play. *Annals of Adolescent Psychiatry, 15*, 307–18.

————. (1984c). Jouets et culture. *Proceedings de 16eme congress de l'ICCP*, Suhl, October 12–16.

————. (1988d). Les jouets comme fonction d'isolement dans la societie moderne. *L'education par le jeu et l'environment*, 4emetrimester, 3–8.

————. (1988e). Play and creativity. In P. J. Heseltine (Ed.), *Creativity through play.* Report of the 10th Conference of the International Association for the Child's Right to Play. Cambridge: University Printing Service.

————. (1988f). Republication of "Spiel und sport als potential der erneuerung." In A. Flitner (Ed.), *Das Kinderspiel.* Munich: Piper.

————. (1988g). War toys and childhood aggression. *Play and Culture, 1,* 57–69.

————. (1989a). Forward to *A child's play: An ethnographic study* by D. Kelly-Byrne. New York: Teachers College Press.

————. (1989b). Review of *Captain Cook chased a crook* by June Factor. *Children's Folklore Newsletter, 12,* 2.

————. (1989c). Childhood: The multi-vocal mind. In L. R. Williams & D. P. Fromberg (Eds.), *Proceedings of defining the field of early childhood education.* Charlottesville, Virginia: A. W. Alton Jones Foundation.

————. (1989d). Childrens' folkgames as customs. *Western Folklore, 47,* 33–42.

————. (1989e). Review of *Fun and games* by W. Andrei & L. Zoknay. *Journal of American Folklore, 102,* 503–05.

————. (1989f). Introduction to play as performance, rhetoric and metaphor. *Play and Culture, 2,* 189–92.

————. (1989g). Models of power. In R. Bolton (Ed.), *The Content of culture constants and variants: Studies in honor of John M. Roberts.* New Haven: HRAF Press.

————. (1990a). The future agenda of child study and the implications for the study of children's folklore. *Childrens' Folklore Review, 1,* 17–21.

————. (1990b). The school playground as festival. *Children's Environments Quarterly, 7*(2), 3–7.

————. (1991). Preface to *Play and Playscapes* by J. L. Frost. Albany, NY: Delmar.

————. (1992a). Commentary: At play in the public arena. *Early Education and Development, 3,* 390–400.

————. (1992b). Review of *Dionysus reborn* by M. Spariosu. *Play and Culture, 5,* 314–22.

————. (1984c). Les rhetoriques du jeu au 20eme siecle. *L'Education par le jeu.* Summer, *46,* 9–13.

————. (1992d). Notes towards a critique of twentieth century play theory. *Jahrging* (Austria), 95–107.

————. (1992e). Response to Handleman. *Play and Culture* 5:20–21.

————. (1992f). Tradition from the perspective of children's games. *Children's Folklore Quarterly, 14*(2), 3–16.

————. (1993a). Dilemmas in adult play with children. In K. McDonald (Ed.), *Parent-child play descriptions and implications.* New York: State University of New York Press.

————. (1993b). The elusive historical child: Ways of knowing the child of history and psychology. In G. H. Elder, J. Modell, & R. D. Parke (Eds.), *Children in time and place.* Cambridge: Cambridge University Press.

————. (1993c). Play rhetorics and toy rhetorics. *Play Theory and Research, 1,* 239–50.

————. (1993d). Suggested rhetorics in adult play theories. *Play Theory and Research, 1,* 102–16.

————. (1994a). The future of toys. In J. Goldstein (Ed.), *Toys and child development.* New York: Cambridge University Press.

————. (1994b). Memory of games and some games of memory. In D. J. Lee (Ed.), *Life and story: autobiographies for a narrative psychology.* Westport, CT: Praeger.

Sutton-Smith, B., & Abrams, D. (1978). Psychosexual material in the stories told by children. In R. Green (Ed.), *Sexology: Proceedings of the International Congress in Sexology,* Montreal, 1976.

Sutton-Smith, B., Gerstmyer, J., & Mechley, A. (1988). Playfighting as folkplay amongst preschool children. *Western Folklore, 47,* 161–76.

Sutton-Smith, B., & Kelly-Byrne, D. (1982). The phenomenon of bipolarity in play theories. In T. D. Yawkey & A. D. Pellegrini (Eds.), *Child's play: developmental and applied.* Hillsdale, NJ: Lawrence Erlbaum.

————. (1984). *The masks of play.* New York: Leisure Press.

Sutton-Smith, B., Mechling, J., Johnson, T., & McMahon, F. (1995). *Children's folklore: A sourcebook.* New York: Garland.

Sutton-Smith, B., & Roberts, J. M. (1963). Game involvement in adults. *Journal of Social Psychology, 60,* 15–30.

————. (1964). Rubrics of competitive behavior. *Journal of Genetic Psychology, 105,* 13–37.

————. (1979). Play, toys, games and sports. In A. Heron & E. Kroeger (Eds.), *Handbook of cross-cultural psychology: developmental psychology* (vol. 4). New York: Allyn and Bacon.

Sutton-Smith, B., Roberts, J. M., et al. (1967). Studies in an elementary game of strategy. *Genetic Psychology Monographs, 75,* 3–42.

Sutton-Smith, B., & Rosenberg, B. G. (1960). Manifest anxiety and game preference in child. *Child Development, 31*, 307–11.

————. (1961). Sixty years of historical change in the game preferences of American children. *Journal of American Folklore, 74*, 17–46.

————. (1965). Age changes in the effects of ordinal position on sex role identification. *Journal of Genetic Psychology, 107*, 61–73.

Sutton-Smith, B., Rosenberg, B. G., & Morgan, E. (1963). The development of sex differences in play choices during preadolescence. *Child Development, 34*, 119–26.

Sutton-Smith, B., & Sutton-Smith, S. (1974). *How to play with your children.* New York: Hawthrone.